Studies in Empirical Economics

Studies in Empirical Economics

Aman Ullah (Ed.)
Semiparametric and Nonparametric Econometrics
1989. ISBN 3-7908-0418-5

Walter Krämer (Ed.)
Econometrics of Structural Change
1989. ISBN 3-7908-0432-0

Wolfgang Franz (Ed.)
Hysteresis Effects in Economic Models
1990. ISBN 3-7908-0482-7

John Piggott and John Whalley (Eds.)
Applied General Equilibrium
1991. ISBN 3-7908-0530-0

Baldev Raj and Badi H. Baltagi (Eds.)
Panel Data Analysis
1992. ISBN 3-7908-0593-9

Josef Christl
The Unemployment/Vacancy Curve
1992. ISBN 3-7908-0625-0

Jürgen Kaehler and Peter Kugler (Eds.)
Econometric Analysis of Financial Markets
1994. ISBN 3-7908-0740-0

Klaus F. Zimmermann (Ed.)
Output and Employment Fluctuations
1994. ISBN 3-7908-0754-0

Jean-Marie Dufour and Baldev Raj (Eds.)
New Developments in Time Series Econometrics
1994. ISBN 3-7908-0766-4

John D. Hey (Ed.)
Experimental Economics
1994. ISBN 3-7908-0810-5

Arno Riedl, Georg Winckler and Andreas Wörgötter (Eds.)
Macroeconomic Policy Games
1995. ISBN 3-7908-0857-1

Thomas Url and Andreas Wörgötter (Eds.)
Econometrics of Short and Unreliable Time Series
1995. ISBN 3-7908-0879-2

Steven Durlauf, John F. Helliwell and Baldev Raj (Eds.)
Long-Run Economic Growth
1996. ISBN 3-7908-0959-4

Daniel J. Slottje and Baldev Raj (Eds.)
Income Inequality, Poverty, and Economic Welfare
1998. ISBN 3-7908-1136-X

Robin Boadway and Baldev Raj (Eds.)
Advances in Public Economics
2000. ISBN 3-7908-1283-8

Bernd Fitzenberger, Roger Koenker and José A. F. Machado (Eds.)
Economic Applications of Quantile Regression
2002. ISBN 3-7908-1448-2

James D. Hamilton
Baldev Raj
Editors

Advances in Markov-Switching Models

Applications in Business Cycle Research and Finance

With 58 Figures
and 56 Tables

Springer-Verlag Berlin Heidelberg GmbH

Editors

Prof. James D. Hamilton
University of California, San Diego, Department of Economics
9500 Gilman Drive, La Jolla, CA 92093-0508, USA

Prof. Baldev Raj
Wilfrid Laurier University, School of Business and Economics
75 University Avenue
Waterloo, Ontario, Canada N2L 3C5

First published in "Empirical Economics", Volume 27, Issue 2, 2002

ISBN 978-3-642-51184-4 ISBN 978-3-642-51182-0 (eBook)
DOI 10.1007/978-3-642-51182-0

Library of Congress Cataloging-in-Publication Data applied for
Die Deutsche Bibliothek – CIP-Einheitsaufnahme
Advances in Markov Switching Models:
Applications in Business Cycle Research and Finance /
James D. Hamilton; Baldev Raj (Eds.). –
Heidelberg; New York: Physica-Verl., 2002
(Studies in Empirical Economics)

http://www.springer.de

Cover design: Erich Kirchner, Heidelberg

SPIN 10885541 88/2202-5 4 3 2 1 0 – Printed on acid-free papaer

Preface

This book is a collection of state-of-the-art papers on the properties of business cycles and financial analysis. The individual contributions cover new advances in Markov-switching models with applications to business cycle research and finance. The introduction surveys the existing methods and new results of the last decade. Individual chapters study features of the U.S. and European business cycles with particular focus on the role of monetary policy, oil shocks and co-movements among key variables. The short-run versus long-run consequences of an economic recession are also discussed. Another area that is featured is an extensive analysis of currency crises and the possibility of bubbles or fads in stock prices. A concluding chapter offers useful new results on testing for this kind of regime-switching behaviour. Overall, the book provides a state-of-the-art overview of new directions in methods and results for estimation and inference based on the use of Markov-switching time-series analysis.

A special feature of the book is that it includes an illustration of a wide range of applications based on a common methodology. It is expected that the theme of the book will be of particular interest to the macroeconomics readers as well as econometrics professionals, scholars and graduate students.

We wish to express our gratitude to the authors for their strong contributions and the reviewers for their assistance and careful attention to detail in their reports. We also wish to thank Ms Carolyn Holden for her organisational effort, both in co-ordinating this project and her help in completing the project on time. Special thanks to Dr. Werner Müller, Economics Editor, and his editorial staff namely Ms Renate Münzenmayer and Ms Katharina Wetzel for their support throughout this endeavour. None of these people are responsible for any residual shortcomings. Finally, we thank our respective universities for providing a supportive research environment that contributed to the completion of this research project.

James D. Hamilton
Baldev Raj

Contents

I Introduction and Overview

New directions in business cycle research and financial analysis

James D. Hamilton[1], **Baldev Raj**[2]

[1] Department of Economics, 0508, University of California, San Diego, La Jolla, CA 92093-0508 (e-mail: jhamilton@ucsd.edu)
[2] School of Business and Economics, Wilfrid Laurier University, 75 University Aveneu, Waterloo, Ontario, Canada N2L 3C5 (e-mail: braj@wlu.ca)

First Version Received: August 2001/Final Version Received: October 2001

Abstract. This chapter serves as a partial introduction to and survey of the literature on Markov-switching models. We review the history of this class of models, describe their mathematical structure, and exposit the basic ideas behind estimation and inference. The chapter also describes how the approach can be extended in a variety of directions, such as non-Gaussian distributions, time-varying transition probabilities, vector processes, state-space and GARCH models, and surveys recent methodological advances. The contributions of the other chapters in this book are reviewed. A final section offers conclusions and implications for policy.

Key words: Markov-switching, regime-switching, business cycles

JEL classification: C32, E32

1. Introduction: The basic Markov-switching framework

The normal behavior of economies is occasionally disrupted by dramatic events that seem to produce quite different dynamics for the variables that economists study. Chief among these is the business cycle, in which capitalist economies depart from their normal growth behavior and a variety of indicators go into decline. Other examples include currency crises, stock market bubbles, and sharp changes in the volatility of asset prices or exchange rates.

One natural way to describe such features is with an autoregressive process. Suppose that y_t represents the growth rate of real GDP in quarter t. In normal times, its dynamic behavior might be well characterized with a first-order autoregression,

$$y_t = c_1 + \phi_1 y_{t-1} + \varepsilon_t,$$

where $\varepsilon_t \sim N(0, \sigma^2)$. In such times, one would forecast the growth of GDP for quarter $t+1$ according to

$$\hat{y}_{t+1|t} = c_1 + \phi_1 y_t.$$

During a recession, however, an alternative forecasting rule might be better, perhaps using different values for the coefficients c and ϕ:

$$y_t = c_2 + \phi_2 y_{t-1} + \varepsilon_t.$$

One can write the above two expressions compactly by letting the regime indicator $s_t = 2$ if the economy is in a recession in quarter t and $s_t = 1$ otherwise:

$$y_t = c_{s_t} + \phi_{s_t} y_{t-1} + \varepsilon_t. \tag{1}$$

A full description of the dynamics of y_t could be obtained if we had a probabilistic description of how the economy changes from one regime to another. The simplest such model would be a Markov chain:

$$\Pr(s_t = j \mid s_{t-1} = i, s_{t-2} = k, \ldots, y_{t-1}, y_{t-2}, \ldots) = \Pr(s_t = j \mid s_{t-1} = i) = p_{ij}. \tag{2}$$

Suppose that the econometrician observes y_t directly but can only make an inference about the value of s_t based on what we see happening with y_t. Then equations (1) and (2) constitute an example of a simple regime-switching process, more elaborate versions of which underlie all the chapters of this book. Theoretical descriptions of why the economy might behave in such a way have been proposed by Cooper and John (1988), Diamond and Fudenberg (1989), Howitt and McAfee (1992), Cooper (1994), Acemoglu and Scott (1997), Startz (1998), Chamley (1999), and Jeanne and Mason (2000). See Raj (2002) and the concluding section of this chapter for a review of this and other related research.

Such a description is sometimes called a "hidden Markov model," since the realizations of the Markov chain s_t are not observed directly by the econometrician. The first treatments of such processes appear to have been by Lindgren (1978) and Baum, et. al. (1980). Hidden Markov models were an important tool in speech recognition algorithms developed in the 1980's; see Rabiner (1989) for a survey. In such applications, the "signal" y_t is often discrete-valued, so that in place of an autoregression such as (1) we would have

$$\Pr(y_t = k \mid s_t = j) = w_{jk}. \tag{3}$$

These early applications did not include the time-series components ϕ_1 or ϕ_2. Instead, the assumption was that, if one could condition on the regime $\{s_1, s_2, \ldots, s_T\}$, the sequence of observations $\{y_1, y_2, \ldots, y_T\}$ would be i.i.d. (independent and identically distributed).

The suggestion of using a switching autoregressive model such as (1) and (2) to describe the business cycle was made independently by Neftci (1982) and Sclove (1983), though neither proposed methods for calculating the likelihood function of y_t or trying to forecast such a process. The solutions were developed by Hamilton (1989), and turn out to be closely related to the algorithms for estimating Markov-switching regression functions discovered by Lindgren (1978) and Cosslett and Lee (1985). The key component in Hamilton's solution is an iterative algorithm analogous to the Kalman filter. The Kalman filter can be described as an algorithm for forming an estimate of an unobserved state variable x_t based on observations of y through date t:

$$\hat{x}_{t|t} = E(x_t \mid y_t, y_{t-1}, \ldots, y_1).$$

In the usual formulation of the Kalman filter, the unobserved state variable x_t itself follows a Gaussian autoregression and y_t is a linear function of x_t plus Gaussian measurement error, in which case the optimal inference $\hat{x}_{t|t}$ turns out to be a linear function of $(y_t, y_{t-1}, \ldots, y_1)$; see for example Hamilton (1994b). The Kalman filter is an iterative algorithm, whose input for step t is the value of $\hat{x}_{t-1|t-1}$ and y_t, and whose output is $\hat{x}_{t|t}$.

In a model such as (1) and (2), the unobserved state variable s_t follows a discrete-valued Markov chain, in contrast to the continuous-valued Gaussian autoregression usually assumed for x_t in the Kalman filter. The optimal inference about such a variable would take the form of a probability. Conditional on observing $(y_t, y_{t-1}, \ldots, y_1)$, for example, the observer might conclude that there is a probability 0.8 that the economy has entered a recession and a probability of 0.2 that the expansion is continuing.

The variable that takes the place of $\hat{x}_{t|t}$ is thus $\hat{\xi}_{t|t}$ which represents a vector of probabilities. The first element of $\hat{\xi}_{t|t}$ is $\Pr(s_t = 1 \mid y_t, y_{t-1}, \ldots, y_1)$, and the second element is $\Pr(s_t = 2 \mid y_t, y_{t-1}, \ldots, y_1)$. If there are K different possible regimes, $\hat{\xi}_{t|t}$ would be a $(K \times 1)$ vector, each of whose elements is between zero and unity. If one knew the value $\hat{\xi}_{t-1|t-1}$, it would be a simple matter to form a forecast of the regime for period t given what is known at time $t-1$. For example,

$$\Pr(s_t = 1 \mid y_{t-1}, y_{t-2}, \ldots, y_1) = \sum_{i=1}^{K} p_{i1} \Pr(s_{t-1} = i \mid y_{t-1}, y_{t-2}, \ldots, y_1). \tag{4}$$

A vector that collected the corresponding terms for the probabilities of $s_t = 2, 3, \ldots, K$ would naturally be denoted $\hat{\xi}_{t|t-1}$.

A model such as (1) or (3) can be interpreted as specifying the probability law of the observed variable y_t conditional on s_t and its own past values, $f(y_t|s_t, y_{t-1}, y_{t-2}, \ldots, y_1)$. For example, for (1) we see

$$f(y_t \mid s_t = 1, y_{t-1}, y_{t-2}, \ldots, y_1) = \frac{1}{\sqrt{2\pi}\sigma} \exp\left[-\frac{(y_t - c_1 - \phi_1 y_{t-1})^2}{2\sigma^2} \right]. \tag{5}$$

This could be collected along with the corresponding expressions for $s_t = 2, \ldots, K$ in a $(K \times 1)$ vector $\boldsymbol{\eta}_t$. The joint probability of y_t and s_t is then given by the product

$$\begin{aligned} &f(y_t, s_t = 1 \mid y_{t-1}, y_{t-2}, \ldots, y_1) \\ &\quad = f(y_t \mid s_t = 1, y_{t-1}, y_{t-2}, \ldots, y_1) \Pr(s_t = 1 \mid y_{t-1}, y_{t-2}, \ldots, y_1). \end{aligned}$$

The conditional density of the tth observation is the sum of these terms over the different possible values for s_t, which will be recognized as simply the inner product of $\boldsymbol{\eta}_t$ with $\hat{\boldsymbol{\xi}}_{t|t-1}$:

$$f(y_t \mid y_{t-1}, y_{t-2}, \ldots, y_1) = \sum_{j=1}^{K} f(y_t, s_t = j \mid y_{t-1}, y_{t-2}, \ldots, y_1) = \boldsymbol{\eta}_t' \hat{\boldsymbol{\xi}}_{t|t-1}. \tag{6}$$

The ith element of $\hat{\boldsymbol{\xi}}_{t|t}$ is then given by

$$\frac{f(y_t, s_t = i \mid y_{t-1}, y_{t-2}, \ldots, y_1)}{f(y_t \mid y_{t-1}, y_{t-2}, \ldots, y_1)}.$$

Hence with these simple calculations one can go from the input $\hat{\boldsymbol{\xi}}_{t-1|t-1}$ to the output $\hat{\boldsymbol{\xi}}_{t|t}$, calculating the conditional density of the tth observation (6) as a by-product. The same principles can be used to form an inference about the regime the economy was in at date t, where the inference is based on information observed through the end of the sample,

$$\Pr(s_t = j \mid y_T, y_{T-1}, \ldots, y_1),$$

which, following the parallel with calculations for the Kalman filter, are called the "smoothed" probabilities. See Hamilton (1994a, Chapter 22) for further details.

2. Extensions of the basic framework

Although the above approach was described in terms of the particular examples (1) of a Gaussian autoregression or (3) a discrete observed scalar, the procedure works exactly the same way for an arbitrary collection of different densities $\boldsymbol{\eta}_t$. For example, instead of Gaussian innovations, we could have assumed a Student t distribution with ν degrees of freedom:

$$f(y_t \mid s_t = 1, y_{t-1}, y_{t-2}, \ldots, y_1)$$
$$= \frac{\Gamma[(\nu+1)/2]}{(\pi\nu)^{1/2}\Gamma(\nu/2)\sigma}\left[1 + \frac{(y_t - c_1 - \phi_1 y_{t-1})^2}{\sigma\nu}\right]^{-(\nu+1)/2}. \tag{7}$$

The variance could be time-varying with an ARCH process whose parameters themselves are subject to change (e.g., Hamilton and Susmel, 1994), the degrees of freedom parameter ν could itself change (e.g., Dueker, 1997), or the elements of $\boldsymbol{\eta}_t$ could even come from different families of densities. Whatever the form of the elements of $\boldsymbol{\eta}_t$, they are used in the recursion in the same way through equation (6).

The above example also assumed that changes in regime follow a Markov chain. However, the calculations go through in exactly the same way if $\Pr(s_t = j \mid s_{t-1} = i)$ is replaced with $\Pr(s_t = j \mid s_{t-1} = i, y_{t-1}, y_{t-2}, \ldots, y_1)$, allowing time-varying transition probabilities. For example, suppose for $k = 2$ states that the probability of a change in regime is modeled as

$$\Pr(s_t = j \mid s_{t-1} \neq j, y_{t-1}, y_{t-2}, \ldots, y_1) = \frac{\exp(\beta y_{t-1})}{1 + \exp(\beta y_{t-1})},$$

then (4) generalizes to

$$\begin{aligned}
&\Pr(s_t = 1 \mid y_{t-1}, y_{t-2}, \ldots, y_1) \\
&\quad = \frac{1}{1 + \exp(\beta y_{t-1})} \Pr(s_{t-1} = 1 \mid y_{t-1}, y_{t-2}, \ldots, y_1) \\
&\quad + \frac{\exp(\beta y_{t-1})}{1 + \exp(\beta y_{t-1})} \Pr(s_{t-1} = 2 \mid y_{t-1}, y_{t-2}, \ldots, y_1),
\end{aligned}$$

See Diebold, Lee, and Weinbach (1994), Filardo (1994) and the papers by Peria and by Schaller and van Norden in this volume for illustrations of regime-switching models with time-varying transition probabilities.

Furthermore, no modification of the above discussion is necessary when $\mathbf{y}_t$ is a vector of observations on n different variables. In this case, expressions such as (5) or (7) might be replaced by a scalar such as

$$\begin{aligned}
&f(\mathbf{y}_t \mid s_t = 1, \mathbf{y}_{t-1}, \mathbf{y}_{t-2}, \ldots, \mathbf{y}_1) \\
&\quad = \frac{1}{(2\pi)^{n/2}} |\boldsymbol{\Omega}|^{-1/2} \\
&\quad \times \exp[-(\mathbf{y}_t - \mathbf{c}_1 - \Phi_1 \mathbf{y}_{t-1})' \boldsymbol{\Omega}^{-1} (\mathbf{y}_t - \mathbf{c}_1 - \Phi_1 \mathbf{y}_{t-1})/2].
\end{aligned}$$

One could also allow different elements of $\mathbf{y}_t$ to be governed by different regimes, or some coefficients to depend on the current regime and some on the lagged regime, with a simple redefinition of variables. For example, suppose that s_{1t} determines the coefficients of the first row of Φ and s_{2t} determines the coefficients of the second row, with s_{1t} and s_{2t} each taking on one of two possible values. One can define a summary regime s_t according to

$$s_t = \begin{cases} 1 & \text{if } s_{1t} = 1 \text{ and } s_{2t} = 1 \\ 2 & \text{if } s_{1t} = 1 \text{ and } s_{2t} = 2 \\ 3 & \text{if } s_{1t} = 2 \text{ and } s_{2t} = 1 \\ 4 & \text{if } s_{1t} = 2 \text{ and } s_{2t} = 2 \end{cases}$$

and s_t follows a 4-state Markov chain. Illustrations are provided by Hamilton and Lin (1996) and Hamilton and Perez-Quiros (1996). For a survey of these and other extensions and applications of the Markov-switching framework, see Raj (2002).

3. State-space and GARCH models

One important dimension in which a generalization is less obvious is when the dynamic behavior depends not just on a finite collection of regimes (such as $s_t, s_{t-1}, \ldots, s_{t-p}$) but instead depends on the infinite past $(s_t, s_{t-1}, s_{t-2}, \ldots)$. An example is when one wishes to apply the regime-switching approach to a GARCH as opposed to an ARCH model, such as

$$y_t = \sigma_t v_t,$$

with $v_t \sim$ i.i.d. $N(0, 1)$ and

$$\sigma_t^2 = \zeta_{s_t} + \alpha_{s_t} y_{t-1}^2 + \delta_{s_t} \sigma_{t-1}^2. \tag{8}$$

By recursive substitution in (8), we see

$$\sigma_t^2 = \zeta_{s_t} + \alpha_{s_t} y_{t-1}^2 + \delta_{s_t}(\zeta_{s_t-1} + \alpha_{s_{t-1}} y_{t-2}^2) + \delta_{s_t}\delta_{s_{t-1}}(\zeta_{s_t-2} + \alpha_{s_{t-2}} y_{t-2}^2) + \cdots.$$

The whole history of regimes is necessary to calculate the density of the tth observation. A related problem arises in a regime-switching state-space model, with state equation

$$\mathbf{x}_t = \mathbf{F}_{s_t}\mathbf{x}_{t-1} + \mathbf{v}_t \tag{9}$$

and observation equation

$$\mathbf{y}_t = \mathbf{H}'\mathbf{x}_t + \mathbf{w}_t \tag{10}$$

implying

$$\mathbf{y}_t = \mathbf{w}_t + \mathbf{H}'\mathbf{v}_t + \mathbf{H}'\mathbf{F}_{s_t}\mathbf{v}_{t-1} + \mathbf{H}'\mathbf{F}_{s_t}\mathbf{F}_{s_{t-1}}\mathbf{v}_{t-2} + \mathbf{H}'\mathbf{F}_{s_t}\mathbf{F}_{s_{t-1}}\mathbf{F}_{s_{t-2}}\mathbf{v}_{t-2} + \cdots.$$

Such regime-switching state-space models are extremely important for studying the business cycle, in which we anticipate that a large number of observed series may be influenced by common unobserved components.

One solution to this problem was proposed by Gray (1996), who suggested that we consider an alternative data-generating process for which the problem does not appear, replacing (8) with

$$h_{it} = \zeta_i + \alpha_i y_{t-1}^2 + \delta_i h_{t-1}^2$$

$$\begin{aligned} h_{t-1} = {} & \Pr(s_{t-1} = 1 \mid y_{t-2}, y_{t-3}, \ldots, y_1) h_{1,t-1} \\ & + \Pr(s_{t-1} = 2 \mid y_{t-2}, y_{t-3}, \ldots, y_1) h_{2,t-1} \end{aligned} \tag{11}$$

and $\sigma_t^2 = h_{1t}$ when $s_t = 1$ and h_{2t} when $s_t = 2$. Thus, instead of the lagged magnitude σ_{t-1}^2, which depends on the infinite history of past regimes, the value of σ_t^2 depends only on the current regime s_t and the previous period's *inference* about s_{t-1}. The inference itself depends only on observed data through date $t-1$, so there is no multiplication of states as t increases. In this book, Klaassen proposes that instead of (11) we use

$$h_{t-1} = \Pr(s_{t-1} = 1 \mid y_{t-1}, y_{t-2}, \ldots, y_1) h_{1,t-1} + \Pr(s_{t-1} = 2 \mid y_{t-1}, y_{t-2}, \ldots, y_1) h_{2,t-1}$$

which turns out to be a substantially more convenient formulation for purposes of calculating multi-period-ahead forecasts.

A closely related method of collapsing the history using the current filtered probabilities was developed for regime-switching state-space models by Kim (1994), albeit with a slightly different motivation. Kim proposed a state-space analog of (11) (using the smoothed probabilities) not as a data-generating process but as a tool for approximating the likelihood function of data that were truly generated by a process such as (9); See Kim and Nelson (1999b) for details. This approach is adopted in the chapters by Kim and Murray and Mills and Wang in this book.

An alternative solution uses recent advances in numerical Bayesian methods to solve this problem, as developed by Albert and Chib (1993) and Shephard (1994). In the Bayesian formulation, rather than estimating parameters such as ϕ_1 and ϕ_2 by maximum likelihood, the goal is to characterize one's subjective probability distribution of these parameters, given the observed data $(\mathbf{y}_T, \mathbf{y}_{T-1}, \ldots, \mathbf{y}_1)$. The mean of the subjective distribution of ϕ_1 is often close to the maximum likelihood estimate $\hat{\phi}_1$, and if the former is much easier to calculate, even classical econometricians can be drawn to the Bayesian approach. The basic idea behind numerical Bayesian methods is that, even though one may not be able to characterize analytically the Bayesian posterior distribution, one can generate draws from it. Specifically, in a state-space model such as (9) and (10) it turns out to be straightforward to generate a draw from the distribution of $(\mathbf{x}_1, \mathbf{x}_2, \ldots, \mathbf{x}_T)$ conditional on $(\mathbf{y}_1, \mathbf{y}_2, \ldots, \mathbf{y}_T)$, $(s_1, s_2, \ldots, s_T)$, and the conventional parameters $\boldsymbol{\theta}$ which includes $(\mathbf{F}_1, \mathbf{F}_2, \ldots, \mathbf{F}_K)$, $\mathbf{H}$, the variances of $\mathbf{v}_t$ and $\mathbf{w}_t$, and the p_{ij} parameters. When $(s_1, s_2, \ldots, s_T)$ is regarded as a known set of numbers, this distribution of $(\mathbf{x}_1, \mathbf{x}_2, \ldots, \mathbf{x}_T)$ is known analytically from the standard Kalman filtering and smoothing recursions. Likewise one can characterize the distribution of $(s_1, s_2, \ldots, s_T)$ conditional on $(\mathbf{y}_1, \mathbf{y}_2, \ldots, \mathbf{y}_T)$, $(\mathbf{x}_1, \mathbf{x}_2, \ldots, \mathbf{x}_T)$, and $\boldsymbol{\theta}$ – if one could observe $(\mathbf{x}_1, \mathbf{x}_2, \ldots, \mathbf{x}_T)$, none of the problems of infinite expansion of states would arise in calculating the likelihood function, so the methods described in Section 1 above could be applied directly. Finally, if one could observe $(\mathbf{y}_1, \mathbf{y}_2, \ldots, \mathbf{y}_T)$, $(\mathbf{x}_1, \mathbf{x}_2, \ldots, \mathbf{x}_T)$, and $(s_1, s_2, \ldots, s_T)$, none of the problems associated with either state-space models of regime-switching would be present, and the posterior distribution of $\boldsymbol{\theta}$ given these other magnitudes is readily obtained from known results about Bayesian GLS.

One can thus construct a chain of simulations, first generating $(\mathbf{x}_1, \mathbf{x}_2, \ldots, \mathbf{x}_T)$, then taking these simulated values as if observed data to simulate $(s_1, s_2, \ldots, s_T)$, taking these as data in turn to generate $\boldsymbol{\theta}$, and then generating a new set $(\mathbf{x}_1, \mathbf{x}_2, \ldots, \mathbf{x}_T)$. This sequence constitutes a Markov chain, and the average value of $\boldsymbol{\theta}$ across the chain should converge to the ergodic distribution of the chain, which is the unconditional distribution of $\boldsymbol{\theta}$ given the data, the object of interest. An excellent introduction to and survey of this approach are provided by Kim and Nelson (1999b). Numerical Bayesian methods are also extremely convenient for estimating regime-switching models with time-varying transition probabilities, as shown by Filardo and Gordon (1998). Papers in this book that apply these advances in numerical Bayesian methods include Kaufmann and Chauvet, Juhn, and Potter.

This book collects some of the most exciting and promising new applications of these methods to understanding economic phenomena. The current book features state-of-the-art applications and development of some innovative approaches to regime-switching models, with substantive contributions in new descriptions of the business cycle, both in the U.S. and elsewhere, new descriptions of financial markets, and methodological contributions. The following sections briefly summarize these respective contributions.

4. The business cycle in the US

Three chapters contribute new discoveries about the nature of the U.S. business cycle. Kim and Murray, in their chapter "Permanent and Transitory Components of Recessions," propose a model that allows them to measure the permanent and transitory consequences of recessions separately. They study a monthly vector system including industrial production, personal income, sales, and employment in which there is a common permanent and common transitory component, both of which undergo potential changes in regime. They find that the transitory component of recessions accounts for more than three-fourths of the variance of the individual series, and suggest that the U.S. business cycle exhibits three separate phases: recession, rapid growth as the economy initially pulls out of the recession, followed by a normal growth phase.

Clements and Krolzig, in "Can Oil Shocks Explain Asymmetries in the US Business Cycle," study the role of oil price shocks in the business cycle. They investigate a cointegrated quarterly vector system including employment and output subject to shifts in regime, and look at measures of business cycle asymmetry in such a system based on the steepness and deepness of contractions. They find business cycle asymmetry regardless of whether one conditions on oil prices, and conclude that U.S. business cycle asymmetry can not be attributed to the role of oil shocks in propagating recessions. They also find evidence in support of a three-regime description of the business cycle: recessions are typically followed by a rapid-growth recovery phase, moving from there into either a slower growth phase or perhaps back into recession.

"Markov Switching in Disaggregate Unemployment Rates" by Chauvet, Juhn, and Potter, studies quarterly U.S. unemployment rates disaggregated by age. The disaggregation helps separate the role of secular demographic changes from business cycle effects. In contrast to the other two papers on the U.S. business cycle, this paper uses a two-state model, one state corresponding to a high degree of labor market mismatch (whose inferred probabilities adhere remarkably to conventional NBER recession dates) and the second a more normal state. The paper finds that demographic changes are very important in explaining the secular trends in unemployment, while business cycles dominate the short run movements.

5. The business cycle in other countries

Three other chapters study business cycles in other countries. "A Markov-Switching Vector Equilibrium Correction Model of the UK Labour Market," by Krolzig, Marcellino, and Mizon, studies quarterly data on UK output, employment, labor force, and real wage. The system is cointegrated with the vector of constant terms in the VAR subject to shifts in regime. The chapter provides abundant evidence that the data are well described by a three-regime model. In regime 1, output, employment, and the labor supply all fall, while in regime 3, they all rise. In regime 2, output grows even as employment is stagnant. The chapter finds that allowing for the changes in regime can significantly change the inferences one would draw from linear impulse-response functions.

"Plucking Models of Business Cycle Fluctuations: Evidence from the G-7 Countries," by Mills and Wang, studies quarterly real GDP for each of the G-7 countries. They use Kim and Nelson's (1999a) model in which recessions bring output temporarily below trend growth, with recovery then allowing reversion back to trend. They find that this offers a good description of the business cycle for the U.S., U.K., France, and Italy, with somewhat weaker performance for Canada, Germany, and Japan.

6. Financial applications

Sylvia Kaufmann's "Is There an Asymmetric Effect of Monetary Policy over Time?" studies the relation between monetary policy and the business cycle for Austria. Her model relates quarterly GDP to its own lags and lagged changes in the 3-month interest rate, with the constant term, coefficients on the interest rates, and standard error of this relation allowed to change between two regimes. The results suggest that monetary policy (as measured by the interest rate) makes a difference for the Austrian economy primarily when the economy is in a downturn.

Three other chapters contribute to our understanding of regimes in asset prices. "A Regime-Switching Approach to the Study of Speculative Attacks: A Focus on EMS Crises" by Peria studies monthly data on exchange rates, central bank reserves, and interest rate differentials. She estimates trivariate vector systems separately for 7 different European countries (Belgium, Denmark, France, Ireland, Italy, Spain, and UK). Speculative currency attacks show up as sharp movements in one or more of these indicators for any country. By describing a speculative attack as a shift in the coefficients of a VAR, the chapter gives new insights into the causes of speculative attacks, concluding that budget deficits are a key factor.

Schaller and van Norden, in their chapter "Fads or Bubbles," investigate dramatic changes in the joint behavior of an index of monthly U.S. stock prices and dividends over 1926–1989. They allow the coefficients in a regression of stock returns on alternative measures of the deviation between the lagged stock price and the "fundamentals" value to change with different regimes. Such a structure could be consistent either with investors following fads or bubbles. The chapter shows how to distinguish between these two, and reports evidence of regime-switching in stock returns that could be interpreted as reflecting investing fads.

"Improving GARCH Volatility Forecasts with Regime-Switching GARCH" by Klaassen studies the volatility of daily dollar-pound, dollar-mark, or dollar-yen exchange rates. He uses a GARCH representation for expected squared exchange rate changes, allowing the coefficients to change with different regimes. This model yields substantially improved forecasts of exchange rate volatility.

7. Methodological contributions

Although all of these chapters produce new empirical results of substantive economic interest, they are also methodologically innovative and up-to-date, representing current best known methods for estimating regime-switching processes. These include how to handle vector autoregressions with changes in regime, both with cointegration (Krolzig-Marcellino-Mizon and Clements-Krolzig) and without (Peria). Several chapters illustrate the approach to systems in which there is a latent unobserved variable besides the regime indicator itself. In dynamic factor models, this unobserved variable is the state of the economy or business cycle, while in GARCH models, this unobserved variable is the lagged conditional variance. In dynamic factor models, the technical problems this introduces can be solved either with Kim's (1994) approximate maximum likelihood algorithm for collapsing the infinite past into approximate indexes, as in Kim-Murray and Mills-Wang, or with numerical Bayesian methods, as in Chauvet-Juhn-Potter. In the GARCH context, Klaassen proposes an improvement on Gray's (1996) earlier idea in which the collapsing approximation is in fact regarded as the data-generating process. Numerical Bayesian methods and Frühwirth-Schnatter's (2001) permutation approach are also featured in Kaufmann's chapter. Markov-switching models in which the regimes follow more complicated dynamics than a simple Markov chain are illustrated by the chapters by Peria and Schaller and van Norden.

Finally, the book includes a pure methodological contribution by Patrick Coe entitled "Power Issues when Testing the Markov Switching Model with the Sup Likelihood Ratio Test Using U.S. Output." A common problem in these applications is testing the null hypothesis that there are no changes in regime. One popular approach is a test suggested by Garcia (1998). Coe's chapter uses Monte Carlo experiments to study the power properties (the probability of correctly concluding that there is regime-switching) of Garcia's test, and finds the test does reasonably well. This result may be quite useful in future applications of these methods.

8. Policy implications and concluding remarks

In earlier sections we provided the motivation for regime-switching models and gave an account of advances in this area as related to business cycle analysis, financial applications and methodological developments. Ten chapters in the book give a representative picture of the scope and breadth of the regime-switching framework in these areas. These chapters plus this introduction and overview chapter can serve as a window to the regime-switching literature for not only experienced readers but also new readers. Specifically, five chapters are on business cycle analysis, four on financial applications and one on methodology, although several other chapters made contributions to this dimension. These provide a good account of the background and new advances on the topic. Below we provide some additional remarks plus give a brief account of some policy implications of regime switching models, especially in the context of business cycle research, for completeness.

Regime-switching models are designed to capture the asymmetry observed in the business cycle, along with some of its other known stylized features. The interest in this feature of the business cycle has a long history in economics that dates back to Keynes (1936). It is concerned with one of the key stylized facts of business cycles – expansions and contractions are quite different from each other, with the former typically long-lived and the latter more violent. Specifically, when output expands towards a peak, the economy is said to be in boom or an expansion. Conversely, when output falls towards a low point or trough, the economy is in recession. This period is characterized by negative rates of growth.

One of the main goals of theoretical macroeconomics is to understand the reasons for the asymmetry and other features of the business cycle. The applied or empirical analysis, on the other hand, is concerned with testing alternative theories and description of how well one or more theoretical models of the business cycle fit the observed features of business fluctuations found in the data. It can also be concerned with establishing stylized facts of the business cycle.

A good way to assess the business cycle is by examining the departure of the economic variable from its trend line that depicts the long-term growth or economic development of the economy. The tendency over the business cycle of variables such as labor productivity to move in the same directions as the gross domestic output in a procyclical way is often also of interest. Similarly the tendency of other economic variables to move in the opposite direction or countercyclically, such as the unemployment rate, is also part of business cycle research. The tendency of business cycles of various industrialized countries to be related to each other can also be of interest. Finally, the tendency of economic variables to depict stochastic equilibrium (or form a cointegration relation) among several variables being jointly studied for the business cycle analysis can also be of interest.

A theoretical description of why the economy might exhibit regime-switching behavior is that there can be multiple equilibria in aggregate activity, as developed by Cooper and John (1988). This theory uses a representative agent framework where the agent chooses the value of some variable, which one could call output for specificity, by taking other agents' choices as given, and is concerned about his position relative to others. Moreover, if his reaction function is nonlinear, and is bounded between zero and some positive value, then multiple equilibria are possible. In this set up, more than one equilibrium occurs since the reaction function crosses with the equilibrium line of the representative agent in relation to the output level of others an odd number of times. Moreover, since the reaction function must begin above the equlibria line and end up below it, some equilibria will be unstable while others stable under plausible assumptions about dynamics. A model with multiple equilibria, when outputs are Pareto-ranked, is sometimes also known as a coordination-failure model.

One of the implications of these models is that fundamentals do not fully determine outcomes since economic activity can also be influenced by other factors such as animal spirits, self-fulfilling prophecies, and sunspots. This occurs because agents' believe such nonfundamentals affect aggregate economic activity. Furthermore, the possibility of coordination failures suggests that the economy can get stuck in unemployment equilibrium where the output is low in relation to what it could be since everyone believes that it will be. Moreover, there would be absence of an inherent force to restore the aggregate output to a normal level. Thus, there is scope for government policies that coordinate expectations of agents to a high-output equilibrium such as a temporary fiscal and monetary stimulus that might move the economy to a better equilibrium state. However, in this framework there can be a potential for a strategic interplay between private economic agents and government or institutions or policy makers. Accordingly, the role of the reputation or commitment and time consistency becomes important for the success of the policy. These implications are obtained by applying game theory tools to macroeconomic policy analysis. Furthermore, the possibility of low level of output equilibrium underscores the importance of information and media management in regard to communicating policy tools to the citizens to remedy business cycle problems at the hands of political leaders and public officials by enlisting the cooperation of most economic agents. Also, the role of coalition building becomes important for the success of policy to avoid coordination failures. Finally, it suggests the role of leadership and governance can prove to be quite important to take the economy out of the low-output state and move towards a high-output state.

While business cycles occur in the coordination-failure models from movements among multiple equilibria, business cycles in the traditional Keynesian and real-business cycle models can arise from some type of market imperfection and/or real shocks. Business cycles can occur in a Keynesian model where markets fail to clear due to presence of imperfection in one or more markets of the nominal rigidity variety. Conversely, fluctuations where markets clear arise in the real-business models due to technology and other real shocks, and incomplete information. Finally, in new Keynesian business cycle models, the primary focus is on the presence of real rigidities or imperfections in one or more markets of the economy. In these models, the concern is about one or more factors that can produce real rigidity to nominal adjustments. The consequence of such rigidity can be that the firm's profit function becomes less sensitive to the price of its product. On the cost front, the firm's incentive to cut its price could become smaller, the smaller the fall in the marginal cost. For instance, thick-market externalities may make it more likely that a smaller downward shift in the profit function will occur when there is fall in aggregate demand. Within this type of setup, the purchase of inputs and the sale of final products by firms becomes easier when there is a high level of economic activity, reducing the incentive for a firm to lower its price relative to other firms. Similarly, agglomeration economies may lower the relative cost of some firms, another form of imperfection that can produce second-best type equilibria in the economy. Imperfections in the labor market are another important source of cost swings that could almost swamp the effect of other real rigidities. Imperfections in the labor market such as search and contracting models (e.g. see Diamond, 1982, and Howitt, 1988) and efficiency wage models (see Shapiro and Stiglitz, 1985) are two prime examples of such real rigidities. Such imperfections are important since firms' incentive to vary prices in situations of downward shifts of demand is reduced.

On the revenue side, a real rigidity can arise from imperfect information that makes existing customers more responsive to price increases than decreases relative to prospective new customers (see Stigitz, 1979). Another source of imperfection is related to capital-market imperfection that induces firms to raise prices during recessions if they are facing liquidity constraints (see Greenwald et al., 1984, and Chevalier and Schafstein, 1996).

It is important to note that there is a close link between real rigidity models and the coordination failure model of Cooper and John. One implication of this link is that as there are many potential sources of real rigidity, there are many potential sources of coordination failure, and hence many more models. Another implication is that real rigidities and/or coordination failure can make the equilibrium quite sensitive to technology and other real shocks, credit market imperfections or other nominal shocks, and uncertainty about future government policies. A complete discussion of the strengths and limitations of various approaches to business cycle theory along with applied examples is provided by Romer (1996).

In summary, there is a growing consensus among economists that regime changes might be more appropriately modeled as arising from a probability process such as the Markov process instead of deterministic structural changes. Moreover, the regime-switching framework can capture regime changes in diverse set of macroeconomics and financial time series. Also, this framework is well suited to modeling asymmetry of business cycles analysis. In addition, the framework is flexible to allow regime changes in the trend component as in Hamilton (1989) and extensions, and regime switching in the transitory component as in Kim and Nelson (1999). Another model of regime switching allows for the autoregressive coefficients to change as in Ang and Bekaert (2001), which is suitable for modeling the Fed asymmetric policy response to alternate inflationary regimes. The regime-switching framework is easily extended to deal with a variety of situations encountered in economics, as demonstrated by various chapters in this book. Other applications are covered in the recent survey of the regime-switching models by Raj (2002). Finally, the regime-switching framework is well suited to modeling volatility in financial time series, including fads and bubbles.

References

Acemoglu D, Scott A (1997) Asymmetric business cycles: Theory and time-series evidence. Journal of Monetary Economics 40:501–33

Albert J, Chib S (1993) Bayes inference via Gibbs sampling of autoregressive time series subject to Markov mean and variance shifts. Journal of Business and Economic Statistics 11:1–15

Ang A, Bekaert G (2001) Regime switches in interest rates. Journal of Business and Economic Statistics, forthcoming

Baum LE, Ted P, George S, Weiss N (1980) A maximization technique occurring in the statistical analysis of probabilistic functions of Markov chains. Annals of Mathematical Statistics 41:164–171

Chamley C (1999) Coordinating regime switches. Quarterly Journal of Economics 114:869–905

Chevalier JA, Scharfstein DS (1996) Capital market imperfections and countercyclical markups: Theory and evidence. American Economic Review 86:703–725

Cooper R (1994) Equilibrium selection in imperfectly competitive economics with multiple equilibria. Economic Journal 104:1106–1122

Cooper R, John A (1988) Coordinating coordination failures in keynesian models. Quarterly Journal of Economics 103:441–463

Cosslett SR, Lee L-F (1985) Serial correlation in discrete variable models. Journal of Econometrics 27:79–97

Diamond PA (1982) Aggregate demand management in search equilibrium. Journal of Political Economy, 90 (October): 881–894. Reprinted in Mankiw and Romer (1991) Eds. New Keynesian Economics 2 Volumes. Cambridge: MIT Press

Diamond PA, Fudenberg D (1989) Rational expectations business cycles in search equilibrium. Journal of Political Economy 97:606–19

Diebold FX, Lee J-H, Weinbach GC (1994) Regime switching with time-varying transition probabilities. In: Hargreaves C (ed) Nonstationary Time Series Analysis and Cointegration, Oxford: Oxford University Press

Dueker M (1997) Markov switching in GARCH processes and mean-reverting stock-market volatility. Journal of Business and Economic Statistics 15:26–34

Filardo AJ (1994) Business cycle phases and their transitional dynamics. Journal of Business and Economic Statistics 12:299–308

Filardo AJ, Gordon SF (1998) Business cycle durations. Journal of Econometrics 85:99–123

Frühwirth-Schnatter S (2001) Markov chain Monte Carlo estimation of classical and dynamic switching and mixture models. Journal of the American Statistical Association 96:194–209

Garcia R (1998) Asymptotic null distribution of the likelihood ratio test in Markov switching models. International Economic Review 39:763–788

Gray SF (1996) Modeling the conditional distribution of interest rates as a regime-switching process. Journal of Financial Economics 42:27–62

Greenwald BC, Stiglitz JE, Andrew W (1994) Informational imperfections in capital markets and macroeconomic fluctuations. American Economics Review 74 (May): 194–199

Hamilton JD (1989) A new approach to the economic analysis of nonstationary time series and the business cycle. Econometrica 57:357–384

Hamilton JD (1994a) Time series analysis. Princeton, NJ: Princeton University Press

Hamilton JD (1994b) State-space models. In: Engle R, McFadden D (eds) Handbook of Econometrics, Volume 4, pp. 3039–3080, Amsterdam: North Holland

Hamilton JD, Lin G (1996) Stock market volatility and the business cycle. Journal of Applied Econometrics 11:573–593

Hamilton JD, Perez-Quiros G (1996) What do the leading indicators lead? Journal of Business 69:27–49

Hamilton JD, Susmel R (1994) Autoregressive conditional heteroskedasticity and changes in regime. Journal of Econometrics 64:307–333

Howitt P (1988) Business cycles with costly search and recruiting. Quarterly Journal of Economics 103 (February): 147–165

Howitt P, McAfee P (1992) Animal spirits. American Economic Review 82:493–507

Jeanne O, Masson P (2000) Currency crises, sunspots, and Markov-switching regimes. Journal of International Economics 50:327–350

Keynes JM (1936) The general theory of employment, interest and money. London: Macmillan

Kim CJ (1994) Dynamic linear models with Markov-switching. Journal of Econometrics 60:1–22

Kim CJ, Nelson CR (1999a) Friedman's plucking model of business fluctuations: Tests and estimation of permanent and transitory components. Journal of Money, Credit, and Banking 31:317–334

Kim CJ, Nelson CR (1999b) State-space models with regime switching. Cambridge, Massachusetts: MIT Press

Lindgren G (1978) Markov regime models for mixed distributions and switching regressions. Scandinavian Journal of Statistics 5:81–91

Neftci SN (1982) Optimal prediction of cyclical downturns. Journal of Economic Dynamics and Control 4:225–241

Rabiner LR (1989) A tutorial on hidden Markov models and selected applications in speech recognition. Proceedings of the IEEE 77:257–286

Raj B (2002) Asymmetries of business cycle: The Markov-switching approach. In: Ullah A, Wan A, Chaturvedi A (eds) Handbook of Applied Econometrics and Statistical Inference, Marcel Dekker, Chapter 31, pp 687–710

Romer D (1996) Advanced macroeconomics. NY: McGraw-Hill Companies, Inc

Sclove SL (1983) Time-series segmentation: A model and a method. Information Sciences 29:7–25

Shaprio C, Stiglitz JE (1984) Equilibrium unemployment as a worker discipline device. American Economic Review 74 (June): 433–444. Reprinted in Mankiw and Romer (1991) Eds. New Keynesian Economics 2 Volumes. Cambridge: MIT Press

Shephard N (1994) Partial non-gaussian state space. Biometrika 81:115–131

Startz R (1998) Growth states and shocks. Journal of Economic Growth 3:203–15

Stiglitz JE (1979) Equilibrium in product markets with imperfect information. American Economic Review 69 (May): 339–345

II The Business Cycle in the U.S.

Permanent and transitory components of recessions

Chang-Jin Kim[1], **Christian J. Murray**[2]

[1] Department of Economics, Korea University, Seoul, 136-701, Korea
(e-mail: cjkim@korea.ac.kr)
[2] Department of Economics, University of Houston, Houston, TX 77204-5019
(e-mail: cmurray@mail.uh.edu)

Final version April 5, 2001

Abstract. We propose a generalization of existing empirical business cycle models that allows us to decompose recessions into permanent and transitory components. We find that the transitory component of recessions accounts for between 77% and 96% of the observed variance of monthly indicator series. Our results suggest the following three-phase characterization of the business cycle: recession, high-growth recovery during which output *partially* reverts to its previous peak, and normal growth following the recovery. In addition, we find significant timing differences between the permanent and transitory components of recessions; most notably the lack of the usual high-growth recovery phase following the 1990–91 recession.

Key words: Business cycle asymmetry, comovement, partial peak-reversion

JEL Codes: C32, E32

1. Introduction

Early scholars of the business cycle recognized the importance of the comovement of economic time series and business cycle asymmetry. In their landmark study, Burns and Mitchell (1946) highlighted comovement as one of the two empirical regularities of the business cycle:

> "... a cycle consists of expansions occurring at about the same time in many economic activities, followed by similarly general recessions, contractions, and revivals which merge into the expansion phase of the next cycle."

We thank James Hamilton, Charles Nelson, and two anonymous referees for helpful comments and discussions.

The other regularity of the business cycle, asymmetry, is the idea that expansions are fundamentally different from recessions. This goes back at least as far as Mitchell (1927):

> ".... the most violent declines exceed the most considerable advances. The abrupt declines usually occur in crises; the greatest gains occur in periods of revival,... Business contraction seems to be a briefer and more violent process than business expansion."

Recently, researchers have used the tools of modern time series analysis to model comovement and asymmetry explicitly. Stock and Watson (1989, 1991, 1993) estimate a linear dynamic factor model that captures the comovement across economic time series through an unobserved permanent component common to each series. Hamilton (1989) incorporates business cycle asymmetry in a univariate nonlinear model that allows the growth rate of output to be dependent on the 'state' of the economy. The results from his regime-switching model suggest that the business cycle is characterized by two states: positive growth (expansion) or negative growth (recession).

While comovement and asymmetry have traditionally been analyzed in isolation, in a recent paper, Diebold and Rudebusch (1996) provide empirical and theoretical support for comovement and asymmetry as important features of the business cycle and suggest that they should be analyzed simultaneously. Accordingly, M.-J. Kim and Yoo (1995), Chauvet (1998), and Kim and Nelson (1998) estimate a unified model in which the common growth component in Stock and Watson's (1989, 1991, 1993) dynamic factor model is subject to the type of regime switching advocated by Hamilton (1989).

Meanwhile, recent literature has provided ample evidence supporting the notion that recessions are transitory in nature, *i.e.* they only temporarily lower the level of output. Within a univariate framework, Beaudry and Koop (1993), Sichel (1994), and Kim and Nelson (1999a) provide evidence of 'peak-reverting' behavior in real output; a tendency for output to revert to its previous peak following a recession. A direct implication of 'peak-reversion' is that shocks during recessions are transitory. In light of this finding, Sichel (1994) proposes a three-phase characterization of the business cycle: recession, high-growth recovery during which output reverts to its previous peak, and moderate growth following the recovery.

The literature also provides evidence that all recessions are not alike. Sichel (1994) and Boldin (1994) are among those who suggest that the 1990–91 recession was unique. In particular, Sichel notes the lack of a high-growth recovery phase following the 1990–91 recession.

The regime-switching dynamic factor models estimated by M.-J. Kim and Yoo (1995), Chauvet (1998), and Kim and Nelson (1998) are unable to capture peak-reversion in output, since they restrict attention to a two phase business cycle, as in Hamilton's (1989) univariate model. In addition, recessions only arise from one source, a switch in the common growth component.

In this paper, we present a more general regime-switching dynamic factor model of the business cycle that allows for peak-reversion, as well as the possibility that recessions arise from more than one source. Our results suggest that peak-reversion is important in explaining business cycle dynamics within a multivariate framework. Specifically, the transitory component of recessions accounts for between 77% and 96% of the observed variance of monthly indicator series. This suggests that following a recession, there is a high-growth recovery phase during which monthly indicator series *partially* revert to their previous peaks. In addition, we find significant timing differences between the permanent and transitory components of recessions; most notably the lack of the usual high-growth recovery phase following the 1990–91 recession.

This paper is organized as follows. Section 2 provides a review of comovement and asymmetry in the empirical business cycle literature. Section 3 presents a generalization of previous regime-switching dynamic factor models, which allows for a common peak-reverting component that switches independently of the common growth component. Section 4 presents our empirical results and Section 5 discusses alternative explanations for the slow recovery beginning in 1991. Finally, Section 6 summarizes and offers concluding remarks.

2. Business cycle asymmetry and comovement in the empirical literature

2.1. Asymmetry within a univariate framework: Asymmetry in growth rates vs. peak-reversion in levels

Since the seminal paper by Neftçi (1984) on the first formal statistical test of asymmetry in economic time series, the literature has modeled business cycle asymmetry in at least two ways: asymmetry in the growth of real output, and asymmetry in the transitory component of real output. Hamilton (1989) is an example of the former while Beaudry and Koop (1993), Sichel (1994), and Kim and Nelson (1999a) are examples of the latter.

Hamilton (1989) models business cycle asymmetry by allowing the growth rate of real output to be governed by an unobserved Markov switching state variable. His results characterize the economy as being in one of two states: positive growth (expansion) or negative growth (recession).

While the two-state model of Hamilton (1989) has been successful at identifying the NBER business cycle dates, it is unable to capture the peak-reverting behavior of real output following a recession, or asymmetry in the persistence of shocks, as reported in the more recent literature. For example, Beaudry and Koop (1993) and Sichel (1994), using data on postwar U.S. real GDP, show that a variable measuring the current depth of a recession contains information useful for predicting the subsequent growth of real GDP. This suggests the existence of a third, high-growth recovery phase. Furthermore, Beaudry and Koop (1993) report that innovations during recessions are much less persistent than those during booms, suggesting asymmetry in the persistence of shocks between booms and recessions. A direct implication of this peak-reverting behavior is that declines in economic activity contain an important transitory component.[1] At first glance, extending Hamilton's (1989) two-state model of the business cycle into a three-state Markov-switching model may seem fruitful in capturing a third, high-growth recovery phase. However, Sichel (1994) reports that the three-phase Markov model is not especially informative about the particular pattern of the three phases in his sample.

[1] This is consistent with Friedman's (1964, 1993) 'plucking' model of the business cycle, in which output cannot exceed a ceiling level, but will sometimes be plucked downward by a recession. DeLong and Summer's (1988) 'output-gaps' view of the business cycle would also predict such behavior.

In an effort to capture peak-reverting behavior and asymmetry in the persistence of shocks, Kim and Nelson (1999a) propose a model of the business cycle in which they allow for asymmetric behavior in the transitory component of real output. They allow the transitory component of output to be 'plucked' down during a recession. Their results suggest that during expansions output fluctuations are mainly permanent, and that during recessions they are mainly transitory. This is in line with Friedman's (1964, 1993) 'plucking' model of economic fluctuations. Evidence in favor of Friedman's plucking model, or asymmetry in the transitory component of output, has also been reported by Wynne and Balke (1992), and Goodwin and Sweeney (1993).

2.2. Comovement within a linear multivariate framework

The comovement of economic time series over the business cycle has been extensively exploited in the construction of composite indexes of coincident and leading economic indicators. These indexes, initially developed by Mitchell and Burns (1938), have played an important role in summarizing and forecasting aggregate macroeconomic performance. However, only recently has the comovement of economic time series been investigated, by Stock and Watson (1989, 1991, 1993), within the context of explicit probability models.

The essence of the linear dynamic factor model proposed by Stock and Watson is that the comovement across economic time series can be captured by a single unobserved factor common to all the series. Utilizing the Kalman filter, Stock and Watson extract an estimate of the common component, which is then interpreted as a new experimental composite index of economic activity. By employing the four monthly coincident indicator series used to construct the Department of Commerce (DOC) composite index, they show that the new experimental index implied by the model corresponds closely to the DOC index.

Indeed, Stock and Watson's probability model has provided a unified statistical framework for analyzing comovement across economic time series. Gregory et al.'s (1997) measure of the world business cycle, for example, is one of the interesting recent applications of Stock and Watson's linear dynamic factor model.

2.3. A synthesis: Asymmetry in the common growth component within a multivariate framework

Filardo (1994) and Diebold and Rudebusch (1996) note that when Hamilton's (1989) Markov-switching model is applied to monthly coincident variables, the correlation between inferences on the state of the business cycle and the NBER reference cycle is much weaker than originally documented by Hamilton (1989) for quarterly real GNP. One potential reason for this failure is that monthly data are noisier than quarterly data, as outliers in monthly data are averaged out in quarterly data. Making inferences on the state of the economy from noisier monthly data would be more difficult. However, employing additional information has helped alleviate this problem. Filardo (1994), for example, exploits the time varying nature of the transition probabilities as functions of leading indicators within a univariate framework. Alternatively, Diebold and Rudebusch (1996) suggest taking advantage of the 'comovement' feature of economic time series over the business cycle, and thus, propose a regime-switching dynamic factor model that embodies the two defining features of the business cycle established by Burns and Mitchell (1946): business cycle asymmetry and comovement.

In order to combine these two features of the business cycle, Diebold and Rudebusch (1996) propose a dynamic factor model in which the common growth component of Stock and Watson (1989, 1991, 1993) is subject to a regime switching Markov state variable as in Hamilton (1989). Accordingly, M.-J. Kim and Yoo (1995), Chauvet (1998), and Kim and Nelson (1998) estimate a dynamic factor model with regime switching. All three papers construct experimental indexes of coincident indicators that encompass both comovement across economic time series and asymmetry. Much sharper inferences on the state of the economy are obtained by analyzing the coincident indicators simultaneously rather than individually.[2]

3. A generalization: Asymmetry in the common growth component and peak-reversion with a multivariate framework

3.1. Model specification

A potential drawback to the regime-switching dynamic factor model proposed by Diebold and Rudebusch (1996) and estimated by M.-J. Kim and Yoo (1995), Chauvet (1998), and Kim and Nelson (1998), is that it is unable to capture the potential transitory nature of recessions discussed in Section 2.1. As in Hamilton's (1989) univariate model, since the growth rate of the common component is assumed to be regime-switching, their model lacks a mechanism through which peak-reverting behavior may be incorporated. In addition, they only allow recessions to arise from one source, a switch in the common growth component.

Even though the literature discussed in Section 2.1, such as Wynne and Balke (1992), Beaudry and Koop (1993), Sichel (1994), and Kim and Nelson (1999a) provides copious evidence of the transitory nature of recessions, their results are entirely univariate. The purpose of this section is to provide a model with which one can analyze the potential transitory nature of recessions within a multivariate framework, and assess the relative importance of permanent and transitory shocks during recessions. This is done by generalizing previous regime-switching dynamic factor models to include a regime-switching common transitory (or peak-reverting) component, as well as a regime-switching common permanent component.

Each individual time series Y_{it} (in logs), for $i = 1, \ldots, N$ consists of a deterministic time trend DT_{it}, a stochastic permanent component with a unit root P_{it}, and a transitory component T_{it}. We write each series as:

$$Y_{it} = DT_{it} + P_{it} + T_{it} \tag{3.1}$$

[2] Kim and Nelson (2001), in their Bayesian tests of Markov switching in the business cycle, also argue that the evidence of Markov-switching, or asymmetry, is much more compelling within a multivariate framework.

$$DT_{it} = a_i + D_i t \tag{3.2}$$

$$P_{it} = \gamma_i C_t + \zeta_{it} \tag{3.3}$$

$$T_{it} = \lambda_i x_t + \omega_{it} \tag{3.4}$$

where C_t and x_t are the common permanent and common transitory components, respectively; ζ_{it} and ω_{it} are the idiosyncratic permanent and transitory components, respectively. The γ_i terms are permanent factor loadings, and indicate the extent to which each series is affected by the common permanent component, C_t. Similarly, the transitory factor loadings, λ_i, indicate the extent to which each series is affected by the common transitory component, x_t.

To anticipate our empirical results, our data appear to be integrated, but not cointegrated. Thus, if we take first differences[3] we have:

$$\Delta Y_{it} = D_i + \gamma_i \Delta C_t + \lambda_i \Delta x_t + z_{it} \tag{3.5}$$

where $z_{it} = \Delta\zeta_{it} + \Delta\omega_{it}$.

The common permanent component is subject to the type of regime-switching proposed by Hamilton (1989):

$$\phi(L)\Delta C_t = \delta + \mu_{S_{1t}} + v_t, \quad v_t \sim iid\, N(0,1) \tag{3.6}$$

$$\mu_{S_{1t}} = \mu_0 + \mu_1 S_{1t}, \quad S_{1t} = \{0,1\} \tag{3.7}$$

$$\Pr[S_{1t} = 0 \mid S_{1,t-1} = 0] = q_1, \quad \Pr[S_{1t} = 1 \mid S_{1,t-1} = 1] = p_1. \tag{3.8}$$

S_{1t} is a latent Markov-switching state variable that switches between 0 and 1 with transition probabilities given by equation (3.8).

Given ΔY_{it}, δ and D_i are not separately identified. We concentrate these parameters out of the likelihood function by writing the model in deviations from means:

$$\Delta y_{it} = \gamma_i \Delta c_t + \lambda_i \Delta x_t + z_{it} \tag{3.9}$$

where $\Delta y_{it} = \Delta Y_{it} - \Delta \overline{Y}_i$ and

$$\phi(L)\Delta c_t = \mu_{S_{1t}} + v_t \tag{3.10}$$

The (demeaned) common permanent component, c_t, grows at rate $\phi(1)^{-1}(\mu_0)$ when $S_{1t} = 0$, and at rate $\phi(1)^{-1}(\mu_0 + \mu_1)$ when $S_{1t} = 1$.

In order to capture peak-reversion, the common transitory component is subject to the type of regime switching advocated by Kim and Nelson (1999a):

$$\phi^*(L)x_t = \tau_{S_{2t}} + u_t, \quad u_t \sim iid\, N(0,1) \tag{3.11}$$

$$\tau_{S_{2t}} = \tau S_{2t}, \quad S_{2t} = \{0,1\} \tag{3.12}$$

[3] Writing the model in first differences insures stationarity, and allows us to use the unconditional mean of the unobserved state variable as a starting value for the Kalman Filter; see Hamilton (1994).

$$\Pr[S_{2t} = 0 \mid S_{2,t-1} = 0] = q_2, \quad \Pr[S_{2t} = 1 \mid S_{2,t-1} = 1] = p_2. \tag{3.13}$$

S_{2t} is a latent Markov-switching state variable, independent of S_{1t}, whose transitions are governed by the probabilities in equation (3.11). The term, τ, is the size of the 'pluck'. If $\tau < 0$, then the transitory component is plucked down during a recession. Following the pluck then there is a tendency for output to revert to its previous peak.

We assume that the idiosyncratic components have the following autoregressive structure:

$$\psi_i(L)z_{it} = e_{it}, \quad e_{it} \sim iid\, N(0, \sigma_i^2). \tag{3.14}$$

The innovation variances of the common components have been normalized to unity to identify the model; all innovations are assumed to be mutually and serially uncorrelated at all leads and lags; and the roots of $\phi(L) = 0$, $\phi^*(L) = 0$, and $\psi_i(L) = 0$ lie outside the unit circle.

Our model reduces to models previously estimated in the literature with the appropriate restrictions. With only one series ($N = 1$), $\tau = 0$, and one root of $\phi^*(L) = 0$ on the unit circle, we have Hamilton's (1989) univariate model. With $N = 1$, and $\mu_1 = 0$ we have Kim and Nelson's (1999a) univariate model. In the multivariate framework, when $\lambda_i = 0$ and $\mu_1 = 0$, the linear dynamic factor model of Stock and Watson (1989, 1991, 1993) emerges. When $\lambda_i = 0$, we have Diebold and Rudebusch's (1996) nonlinear dynamic factor model estimated by M.-J. Kim and Yoo (1995), Chauvet (1998), and Kim and Nelson (1998).

Note that in our model, the common growth component, Δc_t, and the common transitory component, x_t, are governed by two different state variables, S_{1t} and S_{2t}. This allows a recession to arise from one of two sources: a switch in the common growth component, or a 'pluck' in the common cycle. In addition, the timing and duration of S_{1t} and S_{2t} are allowed to vary across recessions.

3.2. Estimation of the model

Since the state variables, S_{1t} and S_{2t}, are unobserved, our model is nonlinear, and calculation of the exact Gaussian likelihood function is not possible. To estimate the parameters, as well as the unobserved components, we cast our model into its state space representation and use Kim's (1994) approximate maximum likelihood estimation algorithm. Section 1 of the Appendix presents the state space representation of our model. Section 2 presents a detailed description of the estimation algorithm. Section 3 demonstrates how we construct C_t from Δc_t.

4. Permanent and transitory components of recessions: Empirical results

4.1. Data

Our data consist of four monthly series on the index of industrial production (IP), personal income less transfer payments (GMYXPQ), manufacturing and trade sales (MTQ), and civilian labor force employed in nonagricultural industries (LHNAG).[4] The first three series are from the Department of Commerce (DOC) list of coincident indicators. Even though the DOC lists employees on nonagricultural payrolls (LPNAG) as a coincident indicator, Stock and Watson (1989, 1991, 1993) report the variable as somewhat lagging. In order to avoid the additional complexity that arises from including a lagging variable, we follow Chauvet (1998) in considering LHNAG as a replacement for LPNAG. Chauvet (1998) has shown that the LHNAG series is a coincident variable, unlike the LPNAG series. The four series are available monthly from 1959.01 through 1998.10. Personal income less transfer payments and manufacturing and trade sales are expressed in chained 1992 dollars, and the index of industrial production is equal to 100 between 1992.06 and 1992.07.

All four series appear to be individually integrated, but not cointegrated. Using Augmented Dickey-Fuller tests, we fail to reject the unit root null at the 10% level for any of the series.[5] Using Johansen's (1991) tests for cointegration, we fail to reject the null hypothesis that there are no cointegrating vectors at the 10% level.

4.2. Empirical results

Concerning the dynamic specification of the common and idiosyncratic components in equations (3.10), (3.11), and (3.14) we considered 1st and 2nd order autoregressions to describe their dynamics. We considered four cases in which both of the common components are either an AR(1) or an AR(2), and all idiosyncratic components are either an AR(1) or an AR(2). Based on various diagnostic checks we settled on a parsimonious AR(1) specification for all components, as in Chauvet (1998). Empirical results are robust to alternative specifications. For all autoregressive structures considered, the implied factors, as well as filtered and smoothed probabilities, are virtually indistinguishable. The parameter estimates of the model and their standard errors are reported in Table 1.

If the factor loadings for the transitory component, λ_i, $i = 1, 2, 3, 4$ are all zero, our model collapses to a dynamic factor model with a regime-switching common growth component. As we cannot test the joint hypothesis that these transitory factor loadings are all zero due to the non-standard nature of the problem,[6] we test whether the factor loadings for the transitory component are individually significant. The asymptotic t-ratios for these parameters indicate that they are all individually significant at the 1% level. This suggests that the common transitory factor may not be ignored in explaining the data.

---

[4] DRI codes are in parentheses.

[5] We use the general to specific lag selection procedure studied by Hall (1994) and Ng and Perron (1995). Results are invariant to a maximum lag of 12 and 24.

[6] Under the null hypothesis that $\lambda_i = 0$ for all i, the parameters associated with common transitory component, x_t, in equation (3.9) are not identified. While such problem has received attention from Hansen (1992, 1996) and Garcia (1998), the distribution of the test statistic in the presence of nuisance parameters that exist only under the alternative hypothesis is unknown for the state space model we are dealing with. However, the individual hypothesis that $\lambda_i = 0$ for *one* i does not render any parameters unidentified under the null hypothesis, and standard distribution theory is valid.

Table 1. Maximum likelihood estimates, monthly data, 1959.01–1998.10 (i = IP, GMYXPQ, MTQ, LHNAG)

Transition Probabilities			
q_1	0.977 (0.012)	p_1	0.846 (0.074)
q_2	0.984 (0.006)	p_2	0.837 (0.053)
Regime Dependent Parameters			
μ_0	0.248 (0.083)	μ_1	−2.136 (0.434)
τ	−6.361 (0.935)		
Permanent Factor Loadings			
γ_1	0.243 (0.065)	γ_2	0.272 (0.075)
γ_3	0.164 (0.048)	γ_4	0.196 (0.050)
Transitory Factor Loadings			
λ_1	0.435 (0.054)	λ_2	0.197 (0.040)
λ_3	0.279 (0.038)	λ_4	0.127 (0.031)
Autogressive Parameters for the Common Components			
ϕ	0.663 (0.114)	ϕ^*	0.693 (0.046)
Autoregressive Parameters for the Idiosyncratic Components			
ψ_1	0.124 (0.115)	ψ_2	−0.081 (0.054)
ψ_3	−0.340 (0.046)	ψ_4	−0.242 (0.048)
Idiosyncratic Innovation Standard Deviations			
σ_1	0.466 (0.046)	σ_2	0.754 (0.031)
σ_3	0.762 (0.028)	σ_4	0.861 (0.030)
$\ln L = -1056.583$			

Standard errors are in parentheses.

We are now in a position to calculate the relative importance of permanent and transitory shocks during recessions. In order to do this, we set the symmetric innovation variances of the idiosyncratic components to zero. We view this restriction is harmless, since the explicit idea in the work of Burns and Mitchell (1946) was that a recession only occurred when a number of eco-

Table 2. The relative importance of the transitory component during recessions

Series	$S_{1t} \neq S_{2t}$	$S_{1t} = S_{2t}$
Industrial Production	96.29%	98.20%
Personal Income	80.83%	98.04%
Manufacturing and Trade Sales	95.94%	98.83%
Employment	77.21%	93.17%

nomic variables simultaneously contracted. Thus, if there is a negative idiosyncratic shock to the transitory component of industrial production, *i.e.* $\omega_{1t} < 0$, this will not lead to a decline in the other three series, and is therefore not a recessionary shock. We also eliminate the common symmetric shocks since the ability of these models to predict recessions has been judged entirely on the estimated behavior of the unobserved Markov-switching variables. We then write the variance of each observed series, due to asymmetric shocks, as:

$$\mathrm{var}(\Delta y_{it}) = \gamma_i^2 \,\mathrm{var}(\Delta c_t) + \lambda_i^2 \,\mathrm{var}(\Delta x_t). \tag{4.1}$$

This calculation requires the variance of the unobserved state variables. Hamilton (1989) demonstrates that the variance of S_{it} is calculated by:[7]

$$\mathrm{var}(S_{it}) = p_i(1 - p_i)p_{i0} + q_i(1 - q_i)(1 - p_{i0}) \tag{4.2}$$

where $p_{i0} = (1 - q_i)/(2 - q_i - p_i)$ is the steady state probability that $S_{it} = 1$.

We decompose the variance of each individual series into that due to the common permanent component and that due to the common transitory component. The second column of Table 2 reports the fraction of the observed variance that can be attributed to the common transitory component, x_t. Our parameter estimates indicate that between 77% and 96% of the observed variance of monthly indicator series during recessionary periods is temporary. This suggests that the high-growth recovery phase exhibits 'partial peak-reversion.' Accordingly, we would characterize the business cycle as having the following three phases: recession, high-growth recovery during which output *partially* reverts to its previous peak, and normal growth following the recovery.

We now focus on the timing and duration of the two common components. The smoothed probabilities of contraction for the common permanent component and the common transitory component are depicted in Figures 1 and 2 respectively. The probability that the common permanent component is contracting accords quite well with the shaded NBER recessionary dates, as in M.-J. Kim and Yoo (1995), Chauvet (1998), and Kim and Nelson (1998). However, the probability that x_t is contracting is in general different from that of C_t. Table 3 reports the contractionary periods for C_t and x_t, as well as the NBER reference cycle dates. Both common components contract during the first five recessions in the sample, although their timing and duration are somewhat different. With the exception of the 1960–61 recession, x_t has a shorter contractionary duration than C_t. This is consistent with an expected

[7] See Hamilton (1989, p. 362).

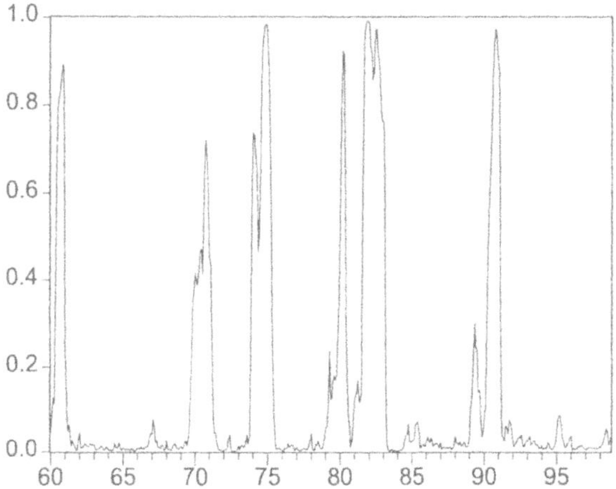

Fig. 1. Smoothed Probability that C_t is Contracting

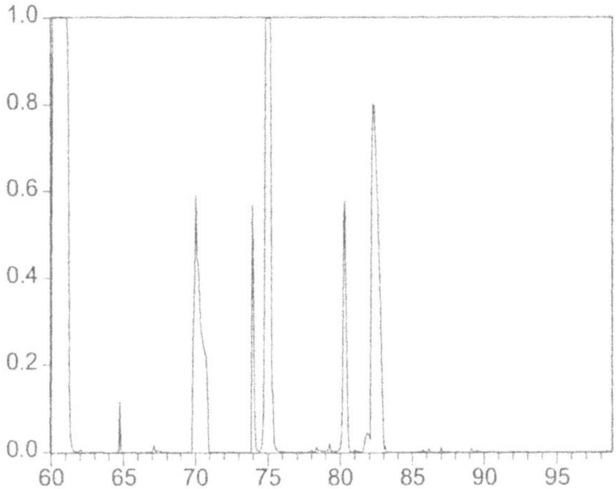

Fig. 2. Smoothed Probability that x_t is Contracting

contractionary duration of 6.49 months and 6.13 months for C_t and x_t respectively.[8]

The most notable difference however between the two components is that the common transitory component completely misses the 1990–91 recession. Comparing the estimates of the common permanent and transitory factors in Figures 3 and 4 also confirms this. This corroborates Sichel's (1994) finding that there was no high-growth recovery phase following the 1990–91 recession.

[8] With constant transition probabilities, the expected duration of a contraction is $(1 - p_i)^{-1}$ for $i = 1, 2$.

Table 3. Contractionary periods for both common components

C_t	x_t	NBER Chronology
1960.06–1960.12 (07)	1960.02–1961.03 (14)	1960.04–1961.02 (11)
1970.08–1970.12 (05)	1970.09–1970.11 (03)	1969.12–1970.11 (12)
1973.12–1975.04 (17)	1973.12–1975.03 (04)	1973.11–1975.03 (17)
1980.01–1980.05 (05)	1980.03–1980.06 (04)	1980.01–1980.07 (07)
1981.08–1983.02 (19)	1981.10–1982.01 (04)	1981.07–1982.11 (17)
1990.05–1991.02 (10)		1990.07–1991.03 (09)

Note: C_t is said to contract when $\Pr[S_{1t} = 1 \mid \psi_T] > 0.5$ and x_t is said to contract when $\Pr[S_{2t} = 1 \mid \psi_T] > 0.5$, where ψ_T denotes information available at time T. Durations of the contractionary periods are in parentheses. Ommited from the table is a one period contraction that occurred for x_t during 1970.01.

Our results thus suggest that each recession differs in terms of the contribution of the common permanent and common transitory factors. While the first five recessions contain both permanent and transitory variation, the timing and duration of the common components is different. In addition, the 1990–91 recession does not contain a transitory component.

The fact that the common components switch at different times may cast doubt on our calculations of the relative importance of transitory shocks reported in Table 2. For instance, since there was no common transitory shock during the 1990–91 recession, it is obviously not true that 96% of the variance of industrial production during this recession was transitory. As a diagnostic check, and to assess the robustness of our results in Table 2, we estimated our model with the restriction that $S_{1t} = S_{2t}$, *i.e.* both common components switch together. For this restricted model, the fraction of the variance of the indicator series that is due to the common transitory component is reported in the third column of Table 2. The results now range from 93% to 98%, bolstering our earlier finding that the transitory component accounts for most of the observed recessionary variance. We should note that this restricted model completely misses the 1990–91 recession. Therefore, the permanent/transitory decomposition in the third column of Table 2 only applies to the first five recessions in the sample.

We should note two features of the business cycle that we do not consider in this paper. The first is duration dependence. Diebold and Rudebusch (1990), Diebold, Rudebusch, and Sichel (1993), Durland and McCurdy (1994), and Kim and Nelson (1998) discuss asymmetry in the duration dependence of booms and recessions. They find that postwar recessions exhibit positive duration dependence whereas postwar expansions are not duration dependent. The Kim and Nelson (1998) paper is most closely related to our work. Even though they find positive duration dependence in recessions, their estimated common factor, factor loadings, and recessionary probabilities do not change. For this reason we do not explicitly consider duration dependence.

Recent work by Kim and Nelson (1999c) and McConnell and Perez-Quiros (2000) highlights the possibility that the economy has recently become more stable. Analyzing postwar quarterly real GDP, they find that the difference between expansionary and recessionary growth rates has narrowed since the first quarter of 1984. When we augmented our model to account for this possibility, our results were essentially unchanged.

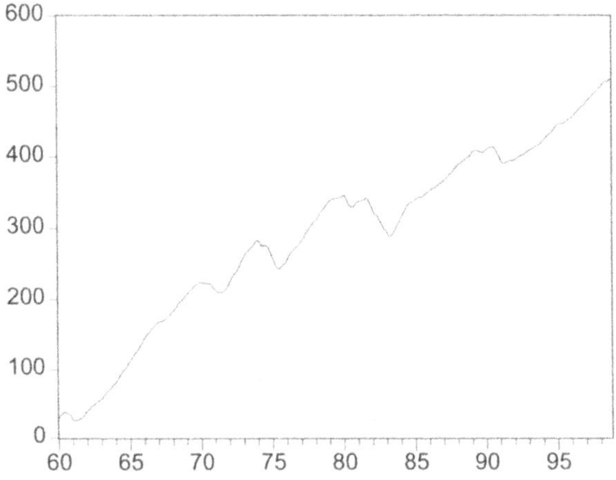

Fig. 3. Common Permanent Component

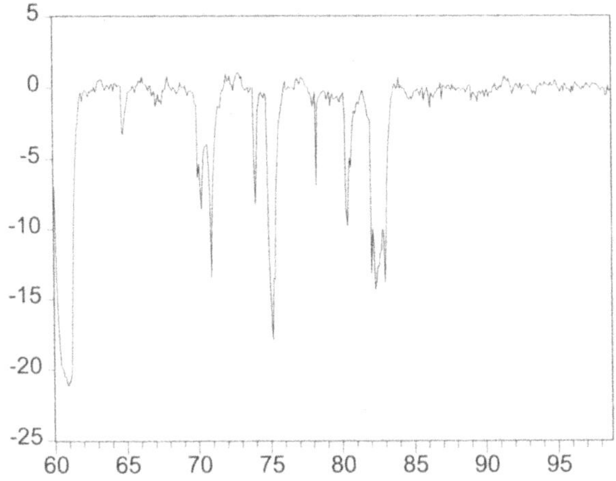

Fig. 4. Common Transitory Component

5. Why was there no high-growth recovery following the 1990–91 recession?

There are several potential explanations for what did and did not cause the slow recovery following the 1990–91 recession. Sichel (1994) argues that changes in real inventory investment are the source of the three-phase business cycle. Specifically, real final sales (real GDP less inventories) do not display above average growth following a recession, but inventory investment does display above average growth. Sichel notes that on average, inventory investment contributes 2.4% to real output growth during the first two quarters following a recession. However, during the first two quarters following the

1990–91 recession, inventory investment only contributed 0.7% to real output growth.

Blanchard (1993) argues that a negative consumption shock was responsible for the slow recovery. He finds that consumption on nondurables and services played a larger than average role (relative to other recessions) in causing the recession. Furthermore, his estimates suggest that the effect on output of this consumption shock was long lasting, which is consistent with the slow recovery.

Blinder (1991) points out that a high-growth recovery is the result of a deep recession. Since the 1990–91 recession was not severe, it should be expected that lackluster growth would follow. Also, real output growth has slowed since the early 1970s. Thus, a 1% drop in GDP today (assuming it is transitory) implies a smaller deviation from trend than it used to. Therefore, a smaller recovery is required for output to revert to its previous peak.

Romer and Romer (1994) document a moderate tendency for the Federal Funds Rate (FFR), both real and nominal, to increase during a recovery. Specifically, during the first five quarters following the eight postwar recessions, the FFR increased two thirds of the time. It was only after the 1990–91 recession that the FFR fell for five consecutive quarters. This suggests that monetary policy was responding to the slow recovery, not causing it.

Finally, Hansen and Prescott (1993) argue that technology shocks did not cause the slow recovery. A model economy with technology shocks matches the timing and duration of the 1990–91 recession, but the recovery in the model economy is much faster than what is observed in the data.

6. Summary and conclusions

While existing business cycle models that incorporate both comovement and asymmetry have been successful at identifying recessionary periods and constructing indexes of economic activity, they have two possible shortcomings. First, since they only model asymmetry in the common growth component of economic time series, they are unable to capture potential peak-reverting behavior. Second, they only allow recessions to arise from one source. This prevents certain qualitative differences to exist between recessions, such as the absence of a high-growth recovery phase following the 1990–91 recession.

We propose a generalization of existing business cycle models that allows us to decompose recessions into permanent and transitory components. Specifically, we extend the regime-switching dynamic factor model proposed by Diebold and Rudebusch (1996) to allow for a common transitory, as well as a common permanent, component. Our results indicate that between 77% and 96% of the observed recessionary variance of monthly indicator series is due to the common transitory component. This suggests that most negative shocks over the business cycle are temporary. We call this 'partial peak-reversion.' Accordingly, we view the business cycle as having three phases: recession, partial recovery, and normal growth.

In addition, we find that each recession differs in terms of the contribution of the common permanent and common transitory factors. Five of the six recessions from 1959–1998 contain both a permanent and transitory component, although they vary both in timing and duration. The most notable recessionary difference is the absence of the usual high-growth recovery phase following the 1990–91 recession.

References

Beaudry P, Koop G (1993) Do recessions permanently change output?. Journal of Monetary Economics 31:149–163

Blanchard OJ (1993) Consumption and the recession of 1990–1991. American Economic Review, Papers and Proceedings of the Hundred and Fifth Annual Meeting of the American Economic Association 83:270–274

Blinder A (1991) What's so bad about a nice little recovery?. Business Week, June 24:22

Boldin MD (1994) Dating turning points in the business cycle. Journal of Business 67:93–131

Burns AF, Mitchell WA (1946) Measuring business cycles. National Bureau of Economic Research, New York

Chauvet M (1998) An econometric characterization of business cycle dynamics with factor structure and regime switching. International Economic Review 39:969–996

DeLong JB, Summers LH (1988) How does macroeconomic policy affect output?. In: Brainard WC, Perry GL (eds.) Brookings papers on economic activity. The Brookings Institution, Washington, DC, pp. 433–494

Diebold FX, Rudebusch GD (1990) A nonparametric investigation of duration dependence in the American business cycle. Journal of Political Economy 98:596–616

Diebold FX, Rudebusch GD (1996) Measuring business cycles: A modern perspective. The Review of Economics and Statistics 78:67–77

Diebold FX, Rudebusch GD, Sichel DE (1993) Further evidence on business cycle duration dependence. In: Stock JH, Watson MW (eds.) Business cycles, indicators, and forecasting. University of Chicago Press, Chicago, pp. 255–280

Durland JM, McCurdy TH (1994) Duration-dependent transitions in a Markov model of U.S. GNP growth. Journal of Business and Economic Statistics 12:279–288

Filardo AJ (1994) Business cycle phases and their transitional dynamics. Journal of Business and Economic Statistics 12:299–308

Friedman M (1964) Monetary studies of the national bureau, the national bureau enters its 45th year. 44th annual report 7-25; reprinted in Friedman M (1969) The optimum quantity of money and other essays. Aldine, Chicago

Friedman M (1993) The 'plucking model' of business fluctuations revisited. Economic Inquiry 31:171–177

Garcia R (1998) Asymptotic null distribution of the likelihood ratio test in Markov switching models. International Economic Review 39:763–788

Goodwin TH, Sweeney RJ, International evidence on Friedman's theory of the business cycle. Economic Inquiry 31:178–193

Gordon K, Smith AFM (1988) Modeling and monitoring discontinuous changes in time series. In: Spall JC (ed.) Bayesian analysis of time series and dynamic linear models. Marcel Dekker, New York, pp. 359–392

Gregory AW, Head AC, Raynauld J (1997) Measuring world business cycles. International Economic Review 38:677–701

Hall AR (1994) Testing for a unit root in time series with pretest data-based model selection. Journal of Business and Economic Statistics 12:461–70

Hamilton JD (1989) A new approach to the economic analysis of nonstationary time series and the business cycle. Econometrica 57:357–384

Hamilton JD (1994) Time series analysis. Princeton University Press, Princeton

Hansen BE (1992) The likelihood ratio test under non-standard conditions: Testing the Markov switching model of GNP. Journal of Applied Econometrics 7:S61–S82

Hansen BE (1996) Inference when a nuisance parameter is not identified under the null hypothesis. Econometrica 64:413–430

Hansen GD, Prescott EC (1993) Did technology shocks cause the 1990–1991 recession?. American Economic Review, Papers and Proceedings of the Hundred and Fifth Annual Meeting of the American Economic Association 83:280–286

Harrison PJ, Stevens CF (1976) Bayesian forecasting. Journal of the Royal Statistical Society, Series B 38:205–247

Johansen S (1991) Estimation and hypothesis testing of cointegration vectors in gaussian vector autoregressive models. Econometrica 59:1551–1580

Kim C-J (1993) Unobserved-component time series models with Markov-switching hetero-

skedasticity: Changes in regime and the link between inflation rates and inflation uncertainty. Journal of Business and Economic Statistics 11:341–349
Kim C-J (1994) Dynamic linear models with Markov switching. Journal of Econometrics 60:1–22
Kim C-J, Nelson CR (1998) Business cycle turning points, a new coincident index, and tests for duration dependence based on a dynamic factor model with regime switching. The Review of Economics and Statistics 80:188–201
Kim C-J, Nelson CR (1999a) Friedman's plucking model of business fluctuations: Tests and estimates of permanent and transitory components. Journal of Money, Credit, and Banking 31:317–334
Kim C-J, Nelson CR (1999b) State-space models with regime switching: Classical and Gibbs-sampling approaches with applications. MIT Press, Cambridge
Kim C-J, Nelson CR (1999c) Has the U.S. economy become more stable? A Bayesian approach based on a Markov-switching model of the business cycle. The Review of Economics and Statistics 81:608–616
Kim C-J, Nelson CR (2001) A Bayesian approach to testing for Markov switching in univariate and dynamic factor models. International Economic Review 42 (4) 989–1013
Kim M-J, Yoo J-S (1995) New index of coincident indicators: a multivariate Markov switching factor model approach. Journal of Monetary Economics 36:607–630
McConnell MM, Perez-Quiros G (2000) Output fluctuations in the United States: What has changed since the early 1980's?. American Economic Review 90:1464–1476
Mitchell WA (1927) Business cycles: The problem and its setting. NBER, New York
Mitchel WA, Burns AF (1938) Statistical indicators of cyclical revivals. NBER Bulletin 69, New York
Neftçi SN (1984) Are economic time series asymmetric over the business cycle?. Journal of Political Economy 92:307–328
Ng S, Perron P (1995) Unit root tests in ARMA models with data dependent methods for the selection of the truncation lag. Journal of the American Statistical Association 90:268–281
Romer CD, Romer DH (1994) What ends recessions?. In: Fischer S, Rotemberg J (eds.) NBER macroeconomics annual. MIT Press, Cambridge, pp. 13–57
Sichel DE (1989) Are business cycles asymmetric? A correction. Journal of Political Economy 97:1055–1060
Sichel DE (1991) Business cycle duration dependence: A parametric approach. The Review of Economics and Statistics 73:254–260
Sichel DE (1994) Inventories and the three phases of the business cycle. Journal of Business and Economic Statistics 12:269–277
Stock JH, Watson MW (1989) New indexes of coincident and leading indicators. In: Blanchard OJ, Fischer S (eds.) NBER macroeconomics annual. MIT Press, Cambridge, pp. 351–393
Stock JH, Watson MW (1991) A probability model of the coincident economic Indicators. In: Lahiri K, Moore GH (eds.) Leading economic indicators: New approaches and forecasting records. Cambridge University Press, New York, pp. 63–85
Stock JH, Watson MW (1993) A procedure for predicting recessions with leading indicators: Econometric issues and recent experiences. In: Stock JH, Watson MW (eds.) Business cycles, indicators, and forecasting. University of Chicago Press, Chicago, pp. 95–156
Wynne MA, Balke NS (1992) Are deep recessions followed by strong recoveries?. Economics Letters 39:183–189

Appendix

1. Representation

In this section, we discuss representation of the model presented in Section 3. We employ the following state space representation for equations (3.5)–(3.14) assuming AR(1) dynamics for the common growth, common transitory, and idiosyncratic components. Even though our model involves two unobserved Markov-switching variables, S_{1t} and S_{2t}, the dynamics can be represented by a single Markov-switching variable, S_t, in the following manner:

$$S_t = 1 \quad \text{if } S_{1t} = 0 \text{ and } S_{2t} = 0$$

$$S_t = 2 \quad \text{if } S_{1t} = 0 \text{ and } S_{2t} = 1$$

$$S_t = 3 \quad \text{if } S_{1t} = 1 \text{ and } S_{2t} = 0$$

$$S_t = 4 \quad \text{if } S_{1t} = 1 \text{ and } S_{2t} = 1$$

with

$$\Pr[S_t = j \mid S_{t-1} = i] = p_{ij}$$

and

$$\sum_{j=1}^{4} p_{ij} = 1.$$

Independence between S_{1t} and S_{2t} amounts to restrictions on the transition probabilities which describe the dynamics of the newly defined S_t. In our case, p_{ij} are functions of q_1, p_1, q_2, and p_2. For example,

$$\begin{aligned} p_{11} &= \Pr[S_t = 1 \mid S_{t-1} = 1] = \Pr[S_{1t} = 0 \mid S_{1,t-1} = 0] \Pr[S_{2t} = 0 \mid S_{2,t-1} = 0] \\ &= q_1 q_2. \end{aligned}$$

We employ the following state space representation:

Measurement Equation: $\Delta y_t = H\xi_t$

Transition Equation: $\xi_t = \alpha_{S_t} + F\xi_{t-1} + V_t$

$$E(V_t V_t') = Q,$$

where

$$H = \begin{bmatrix} \gamma_1 & \lambda_1 & -\lambda_1 & 1 & 0 & 0 & 0 \\ \gamma_2 & \lambda_2 & -\lambda_2 & 0 & 1 & 0 & 0 \\ \gamma_3 & \lambda_3 & -\lambda_3 & 0 & 0 & 1 & 0 \\ \gamma_4 & \lambda_4 & -\lambda_4 & 0 & 0 & 0 & 1 \end{bmatrix},$$

$$\xi_t = \begin{bmatrix} \Delta c_t \\ x_t \\ x_{t-1} \\ z_{1t} \\ z_{2t} \\ z_{3t} \\ z_{4t} \end{bmatrix}, \quad \alpha_{S_t} = \alpha_{S_{1t}, S_{2t}} = \begin{bmatrix} \mu_{S_{1t}} \\ \tau_{S_{2t}} \\ 0 \\ 0 \\ 0 \\ 0 \\ 0 \end{bmatrix}, \quad V_t = \begin{bmatrix} v_t \\ u_t \\ 0 \\ e_{1t} \\ e_{2t} \\ e_{3t} \\ e_{4t} \end{bmatrix},$$

$$F = \begin{bmatrix} \phi & 0 & 0 & 0 & 0 & 0 & 0 \\ 0 & \phi^* & 0 & 0 & 0 & 0 & 0 \\ 0 & 1 & 0 & 0 & 0 & 0 & 0 \\ 0 & 0 & 0 & \psi_1 & 0 & 0 & 0 \\ 0 & 0 & 0 & 0 & \psi_2 & 0 & 0 \\ 0 & 0 & 0 & 0 & 0 & \psi_3 & 0 \\ 0 & 0 & 0 & 0 & 0 & 0 & \psi_4 \end{bmatrix}$$

and

$$Q = \begin{bmatrix} 1 & 0 & 0 & 0 & 0 & 0 & 0 \\ 0 & 1 & 0 & 0 & 0 & 0 & 0 \\ 0 & 0 & 0 & 0 & 0 & 0 & 0 \\ 0 & 0 & 0 & \sigma_1^2 & 0 & 0 & 0 \\ 0 & 0 & 0 & 0 & \sigma_2^2 & 0 & 0 \\ 0 & 0 & 0 & 0 & 0 & \sigma_3^2 & 0 \\ 0 & 0 & 0 & 0 & 0 & 0 & \sigma_4^2 \end{bmatrix}.$$

2. Estimation

Defining S_t and its transitional dynamics as in equations (3.6)–(3.13), the above state-space model is a special case of that considered by Kim (1994). The following describes Kim's approximate maximum likelihood estimation algorithm. For details of the nature of the approximation and the Bayesian alternative to the estimation procedure, readers are referred to Kim and Nelson (1999b).

If the Markov-switching state variables were observed, the state space model presented in Section 3 would be linear and Gaussian, and calculation of the exact likelihood function with the Kalman filter would be possible. The unobservability of the state variables, however, induces nonlinearity in the transition equation of the state space representation, and calculation of the exact likelihood function via the Kalman filter is computationally intractable. As noted by Harrison and Stevens (1976) and Gordon and Smith (1988), if there are M possible states at each time period (4 in our case), each iteration of the filter produces an M-fold increase in the number of states to consider. With a sample size of T, there would be us 4^T cases to consider; an impractical computational burden. Kim (1994) proposes a method to approximate the likelihood function for state space models with Markov switching in both the measurement and transition equations. The algorithm is computationally efficient, and experience suggests that the degree of approximation is small; see Kim (1994) and Kim and Nelson (1999b).

Conditional on $S_t = j$ and $S_{t-1} = i$, the Kalman filter equations can be written as:

$$\xi_{t|t-1}^{(i,j)} = \alpha_{S_j} + F\xi_{t-1|t-1}^{i}$$

$$P_{t|t-1}^{(i,j)} = FP_{t-1|t-1}^{i}F' + Q$$

$$\eta_{t|t-1}^{(i,j)} = \Delta y_t - H\xi_{t|t-1}^{(i,j)}$$

$$f_{t|t-1}^{(i,j)} = HP_{t|t-1}^{(i,j)}H'$$

$$\xi_{t|t}^{(i,j)} = \xi_{t|t-1}^{(i,j)} + P_{t|t-1}^{(i,j)}H'[f_{t|t-1}^{(i,j)}]^{-1}\eta_{t|t-1}^{(i,j)}$$

$$P_{t|t}^{(i,j)} = (I - P_{t|t-1}^{(i,j)}H'[f_{t|t-1}^{(i,j)}]^{-1})HP_{t|t-1}^{(i,j)}$$

where $\xi_{t|t-1}^{(i,j)}$ is an inference on ξ_t based on information up to time $t-1$, conditional on $S_t = j$ and $S_{t-1} = i$; $\xi_{t|t}^{(i,j)}$ is an inference on ξ_t based on information up to time t, conditional on $S_t = j$ and $S_{t-1} = i$; $P_{t|t-1}^{(i,j)}$ and $P_{t|t}^{(i,j)}$ are the MSE matrices of $\xi_{t|t-1}^{(i,j)}$ and $\xi_{t|t}^{(i,j)}$ respectively; $\eta_{t|t-1}^{(i,j)}$ is the conditional forecast error of Δy_t based on information up to time $t-1$; $f_{t|t-1}^{(i,j)}$ is the conditional variance of $\eta_{t|t-1}^{(i,j)}$.

As noted by Harrison and Stevens (1976) and Gordon and Smith (1988) each iteration of the Kalman filter produces a 4-fold increase in the number of cases to consider. To render the Kalman filter operational, we need to collapse the 4^2 posteriors ($\xi_{t|t}^{(i,j)}$ and $P_{t|t}^{(i,j)}$) into 4 at each iteration. Collapsing requires the following approximations suggested by Harrison and Stevens (1976):

$$\xi_{t|t}^{j} = \frac{\sum_{i=1}^{4} \Pr[S_{t-1} = i, S_t = j \mid \Omega_t]\xi_{t|t}^{(i,j)}}{\Pr[S_t = j \mid \Omega_t]},$$

and

$$P_{t|t}^{j} = \frac{\sum_{i=1}^{4} \Pr[S_{t-1} = i, S_t = j \mid \Omega_t]\{P_{t|t}^{(i,j)} + (\xi_{t|t}^{j} - \xi_{t|t}^{(i,j)})(\xi_{t|t}^{j} - \xi_{t|t}^{(i,j)})'\}}{\Pr[S_t = j \mid \Omega_t]},$$

where Ω_t refers to information available at time t.

In order to obtain the probability terms necessary for collapsing, we perform the following procedure due to Hamilton (1989):

Step 1:

At the beginning of the tth iteration, given $\Pr[S_{t-1} = i \mid \Omega_{t-1}]$, we calculate

$$\Pr[S_t = j, S_{t-1} = i \mid \Omega_{t-1}] = \Pr[S_t = j \mid S_{t-1} = i] \Pr[S_{t-1} = i \mid \Omega_t],$$

Step 2:

Consider the joint density of Δy_t, S_t, and S_{t-1}:

$$f(\Delta y_t, S_t = j, S_{t-1} = i \mid \Omega_{t-1})$$
$$= f(\Delta y_t \mid S_t = j, S_{t-1} = i, \Omega_{t-1}) \Pr[S_t = j, S_{t-1} = i \mid \Omega_{t-1}]$$

from which the marginal density of Δy_t is obtained by:

$$f(\Delta y_t|\Omega_{t-1}) = \sum_{i=1}^{4}\sum_{j=1}^{4} f(\Delta y_t, S_t = j, S_{t-1} = i \,|\, \Omega_{t-1})$$

$$= \sum_{i=1}^{4}\sum_{j=1}^{4} f(\Delta y_t \,|\, S_t = j, S_{t-1} = i, \Omega_{t-1})$$

$$\times \Pr[S_t = j, S_{t-1} = i \,|\, \Omega_{t-1}]$$

where the conditional density $f(\Delta y_t \,|\, S_t = j, S_{t-1} = i, \Omega_{t-1})$ is obtained via the prediction-error decomposition:

$$f(\Delta y_t \,|\, S_t = j, S_{t-1} = i, \Omega_{t-1})$$

$$= (2\pi)^{-T/2} |f_{t|t-1}^{(i,j)}|^{-1/2} \exp\left\{ -\frac{1}{2} \eta_{t|t-1}^{(i,j)'} f_{t|t-1}^{(i,j)^{-1}} \eta_{t|t-1}^{(i,j)} \right\}.$$

Step 3:
Once Δy_t is observed at the end of time t, we update the probability terms:

$$\Pr[S_t = j, S_{t-1} = i \,|\, \Omega_t]$$

$$= \Pr[S_t = j, S_{t-1} = i \,|\, \Omega_{t-1}, \Delta y_t]$$

$$= \frac{f(S_t = j, S_{t-1} = i, \Delta y_t \,|\, \Omega_{t-1})}{f(\Delta y_t|\Omega_{t-1})}$$

$$= \frac{f(\Delta y_t \,|\, S_t = j, S_{t-1} = i, \Omega_{t-1}) \Pr[S_t = j, S_{t-1} = i \,|\, \Omega_{t-1}]}{f(\Delta y_t|\Omega_{t-1})}$$

with

$$\Pr[S_t = j \,|\, \Omega_t] \sum_{i=1}^{4} \Pr[S_t = j, S_{t-1} = i \,|\, \Omega_t].$$

To initialize the above filter, we use the steady-state probabilities.

As a byproduct of the above filter in Step 2, we obtain the log likelihood function:

$$\ln L = \sum_{t=1}^{T} \ln(f(\Delta y_t \,|\, \psi_{t-1}))$$

which can be maximized with respect to the parameters of the model.

3. Constructing C_t from Δc_t

Since the data are in deviations from their means, δ and $D = [D_1 \;\; D_2 \;\; D_3 \;\; D_4]'$ are concentrated out of the likelihood function. As in

Stock and Watson (1991), we can use the steady state Kalman gain retrieve these terms in the following manner:

$$\delta = E'(I_r - (I_r - K^*H)F)^{-1}K^*\Delta\bar{y},$$

$$\tilde{D} = \begin{bmatrix} D_1 \\ D_2 \\ D_3 \\ D_4 \end{bmatrix} = \Delta\bar{y} - \begin{bmatrix} \gamma_1 \\ \gamma_2 \\ \gamma_3 \\ \gamma_4 \end{bmatrix} \delta,$$

where K^* is the steady state Kalman gain, $E_1' = [1\ 0\ 0 \cdots 0]'$, and r is the dimension of the state vector. Once δ is retrieved, given $\Delta\tilde{c}_T = [\Delta c_1\ \Delta c_2 \cdots \Delta c_T]'$, and arbitrary initial value C_0, we obtain $C_t = \delta + \Delta c_t + C_{t-1},\ t = 1, 2, \ldots, T$.

Can oil shocks explain asymmetries in the US Business Cycle?

Michael P. Clements[1], **Hans-Martin Krolzig**[2]

[1] University of Warwick, Dept. of Economics, CV4 7AL Coventry, U.K. (e-mail: m.p.clements@warwick.ac.uk)
[2] Oxford University, Department of Economics, Manor Road Building, Oxford, OX1 3UQ and Nuffield College (e-mail: hans-martin.krolzig@nuf.ox.ac.uk)

First Version Received: December 2000/Final Version Received: September 2001

Abstract. We consider whether oil prices can account for business cycle asymmetries. We test for asymmetries based on the Markov switching autoregressive model popularized by Hamilton (1989), using the tests devised by Clements and Krolzig (2000). We find evidence against the conventional wisdom that recessions are more violent than expansions: while some part of the downturn in economic activity that characterises recessionary periods can be attributed to dramatic changes in the price of oil, post-War US economic growth is characterized by the steepness of expansions.

Key words: Oil prices, Business cycle asymmetries, Markov-switching models

JEL classification: E32, C32, E24

1. Introduction

A number of recent papers have explored the relationship between oil prices and the macroeconomy. Hooker (1996) shows that the linear relationship between oil prices and output proposed by Hamilton (1983) does not appear to hold from 1973 onwards. He also casts doubt on the asymmetric relationship proposed by Mork (1989): that output responds negatively to oil price increases but is unaffected by oil price declines. Hamilton (1996) suggests that output should be related to the *net increase* in oil prices over the previous year, and constructs a variable that is the maximum of the percentage change in the oil price in the current quarter over the previous year's high, and zero. According to this approach, increases in the price of oil which simply reverse previous (within the preceding year) declines do not depress output growth.

Raymond and Rich (1997) have investigated the relationship between oil prices and the macroeconomy by including the net increase in the oil price

(NOPI) in the two-regime Markov-Switching (MS) model of US output growth of Hamilton (1989) for the period 1951–1995. Hamilton's model generated shifts between negative and positive growth states such that the former corresponded closely with the NBER recessions. The key insight of Raymond and Rich (1997) is that if oil prices are an important determinant of the periods of negative output growth, then a MS model – which includes oil prices as an explanatory variable of the conditional mean – may either no longer generate shifts that match the NBER chronology or estimate a negative growth mean. Thus of interest is whether the recurrent shifts between expansion (high growth) and contraction (low growth, or declines in output) suggested by the Markov-switching model remain a feature of post War US output once an allowance has been made for the effects of oil price increases. A plausible hypothesis is that increases in the oil price may explain (at least part of) the low trend growth states, so that the model with oil prices no longer generates recessions that match the NBER dating. Raymond and Rich (1997) conclude that '*while the behavior of oil prices has been a contributing factor to the mean of low growth phases of output, movements in oil prices generally have not been a principal determinant in the historical incidence of these phases* ...' (p. 196). They also allow the oil price to affect the transition probabilities of the states directly, following the approach of Diebold, Rudebusch and Sichel (1993), Filardo (1994) and Filardo and Gordon (1998), but find little support for this channel of influence.

Our approach follows that of Raymond and Rich (1997) in that we are concerned with the impact of oil prices on the regime-switching features of the data. But we ask a different question: are oil prices responsible for business cycle *asymmetries*? That is, assuming that our findings match those of Raymond and Rich (1997)[1], in that oil prices do not appear to account for the low growth output phases, is it nevertheless the case that oil prices account for asymmetries between the expansion and contraction phases? Of course, this question is only of interest if there are asymmetries to be accounted for. The finding that a nonlinear model (as opposed to a linear model) characterizes the data may of itself suggest asymmetry: see e.g., Luukkonen and Teräsvirta (1991). The argument is that models such as self-exciting threshold autoregressive models (see, e.g., Tong and Lim, 1980, Tong, 1995), and smooth transition autoregressive model (see, e.g., Luukkonen, Saikkonen and Teräsvirta, 1988, Teräsvirta and Anderson, 1992) have different dynamic structures across regimes so that the probability of remaining in a regime, once entered, may not be equal across regimes. Different 'exit' probabilities suggest different durations, and therefore asymmetry on the definition due to Sichel (1993, p. 224), that an asymmetric cycle is '*one in which some phase of the cycle is different from the mirror image of the opposite phase*'.

Clements and Krolzig (2000) show Markov-Switching autoregressive (MS-AR) models are able to generate symmetric cycles, or cycles that exhibit one (or more) of the different types of steepness, deepness, and sharpness asymmetries discussed in the literature. These asymmetries are typically tested for using separate non-parametric tests, but restrictions on the parameters of the MS-AR model can be derived, which, if they hold, would rule out a particular

[1] This need not be the case because we use a bivariate MS model of output and employment changes to infer the contribution of the regime-switching component, in preference to Raymond and Rich's univariate model of output growth.

type of asymmetry. Wald tests of these restrictions are then formulated. The tests of Clements and Krolzig (2000) are able to detect asymmetries in the propagation mechanisms of shocks, or first-moment asymmetries, while the usual non-parametric tests based on the coefficient of skewness of the (first-differenced) detrended series are unable to discriminate between first-moment asymmetries and asymmetries in the shocks. The parametric tests are applied to the bivariate model of output and employment, and asymmetries are detected. The tests can also be applied to MS-AR models with exogenous variables, to see whether such variables account for asymmetries in the observed output growth series.

We use the data set in Hamilton (2000)[2]. In addition to NOPI (and a variant that calculates the maximum relative to the previous *three* years, N3OPI), Hamilton also makes available three other oil price series that have recently been used to explain US output growth. One is the growth rate of the oil price (Doil), so that linear models employing this variable will not allow for asymmetric responses to increases and decreases. The other two are a time series of exogenous supply shocks (Quant: see Hamilton, 2000, for details), and a variable used by Lee, Ni and Ratti (1995) (LNR), that is, the real increase in the oil price adjusted for the variability in the real oil price. We briefly consider which transformation of the oil price variable gives the best explanation of output changes in a linear setting, using David F. Hendry and Hans-Martin Krolzig's PcGets program (section 3). On the basis of this, we focus on the LNR variable in the analysis of the impact of oil prices on business cycle asymmetries, though we report results of the key tests for all the oil price measures.

The plan of the paper is as follows. Section 2 briefly reviews notions of business cycle asymmetries, non-parametric tests of these features, and the parametric tests proposed by Clements and Krolzig (2000): the latter paper gives a complete discussion of the material in this section. Section 3 discusses the selection of the oil price variable, the selection of the MS model, describes the bivariate model to which the tests are applied, and the results of testing for asymmetries. Section 4 concludes.

2. Testing for business cycle asymmetries

2.1. Steepness, deepness and sharpness (SDS)

There has been much interest in whether macroeconomic variables behave differently over the phases of the business cycle. The conventional wisdom as

---

[2] Freely available from http://weber.ucsd.edu/~jhamilto
All the data are quarterly, and are in terms of quarterly percentage changes, calculated by taking the first difference of the natural logarithm of the series, and multiplying by one hundred. The basic oil price variable is the producer price index for crude petroleum, seasonally adjusted, and constructed from the monthly series by selecting the last month in quarter values. The *net increase* variables are calculated directly from this series. The calculation of the Lee, Ni and Ratti variable is detailed by Hamilton. The variable is based on the real oil price variable, where the deflator is the implicit GDP deflator. The real quarterly change is divided by the conditional standard deviation derived from a GARCH model. The GDP series is real, chain-weighted in 1996 dollars, and seasonally adjusted. The employment series used in the bivariate model is calculated from seasonally adjusted, monthly figures of total nonfarm payroll employment. We follow the literature in using GDP as the output measure in preference to narrower measures such as industrial production.

expressed by Mitchell (1927, p. 290) is that '*the most violent declines exceed the most considerable advances [...] Business contractions appear to be a briefer and more violent process than business expansions*'.

Sichel (1993) distinguishes two types of business cycle asymmetry: '*steepness*' and '*deepness*'. The former relates to whether contractions are steeper (or less steep) than expansions, the latter to whether the amplitude of troughs differs from that of peaks. He suggests a test of deepness based on the coefficient of skewness calculated for the detrended series. Deepness of contractions will show up as negative skewness, since it implies that the average deviation of observations below the mean will exceed that of observations above the mean. Steepness implies skewness in the first difference of the detrended series. Positive skewness suggests steepness of expansions: increases should be larger, though less frequent, than decreases. On the basis of these tests, deepness is found to characterize quarterly post-War US unemployment and industrial production, with weaker evidence for GNP, while only unemployment (of the three) appears to exhibit steepness.

Because the observations on the detrended series typically exhibit some dependence, Sichel (1993, p. 227–8) calculates an asymptotically heteroscedastic and serial correlation consistent standard error for the coefficient of skewness using the Newey and West (1987) procedure.

Sharpness or *turning point asymmetry* (see McQueen and Thorley, 1993), results if, e.g., troughs are 'sharp' and peaks more rounded. In the literature, sharpness has been tested by considering the magnitude of growth rate changes around NBER-dated peaks and troughs. The mean absolute changes are calculated for peaks and troughs separately, and the test for asymmetry is based on rejecting the null of the population mean changes in the variable at peaks and troughs being equal. Alternatively, a testing procedure could be based on the transition probabilities of a, e.g., second-order three-state Markov chain.

Formally, steepness, deepness and sharpness (SDS) can be defined as follows, letting $\{x_t\}$ denote the detrended series:

Definition 1. *Deepness. Sichel (1993). The process $\{x_t\}$ is said to be* ***non-deep (non-tall)*** *iff x_t is not skewed:*

$$\mathsf{E}[(x_t - \mu_x)^3] = 0.$$

Analogously we can define steepness as skewness of the differences:

Definition 2. *Steepness. Sichel (1993). The process $\{x_t\}$ is said to be* ***non-steep*** *iff Δx_t is not skewed:*

$$\mathsf{E}[(\Delta x_t)^3] = 0.$$

Negative skewness of x_t and Δx_t indicates deep and steep contractions. The opposite case are tall ($\mathsf{E}[(x_t - \mu_x)^3] > 0$) and steep ($\Delta x_t$ positively skewed) expansions, although all combinations are possible.

Definition 3. *Sharpness. McQueen and Thorley (1993). The process $\{x_t\}$ is said to be* ***non-sharp*** *iff the transition probabilities to and from the two outer regimes are identical:*

$$p_{m1} = p_{mM}, \quad p_{1m} = p_{Mm},$$

for all $m \neq 1, M$, where M denotes the number of regimes, and:

$$p_{1M} = p_{M1}.$$

Note that for $M = 2$ only the second part of the definition is operative.

In a two-regime model, for example, non-sharpness implies that $p_{12} = p_{21}$. In a three-regime model, it requires $p_{13} = p_{31}$ and in addition $p_{12} = p_{32}$ and $p_{21} = p_{23}$.

2.2. Asymmetries in MS-AR processes

We can write the MS-AR model as:

$$x_t - \mu(s_t) = \sum_{k=1}^{p} \alpha_k (x_{t-k} - \mu(s_{t-k})) + u_t, \quad u_t | s_t \sim \mathsf{NID}(0, \sigma^2). \tag{1}$$

This formulation exhibits Markov-switching in the *M*ean of the process (and which we label as MSM(M)-AR(p)), so that $\mu(s_t)$ takes on one of the values $\mu_1 < \cdots < \mu_M$, depending on which of the M regimes the process is in. The Markov chain is ergodic, irreducible, and there does not exist an absorbing state, i.e., $\bar{\xi}_m \in (0,1)$ for all $m = 1, \ldots, M$, where $\bar{\xi}_m$ is the ergodic or unconditional probability of regime m. The findings of Raymond and Rich (1997) support the assumption of time-invariant transition probabilities:

$$p_{ij} = prob(s_{t+1} = j \,|\, s_t = i), \quad \sum_{j=1}^{M} p_{ij} = 1 \quad \forall i, j \in \{1, \ldots, M\}. \tag{2}$$

Clements and Krolzig (2000) establish the following propositions concerning the restrictions on the parameter space of the MSM-AR model that correspond to the concepts of steepness and deepness (the restrictions implied by sharpness follow immediately):

Proposition 1. *An MSM(M)-AR(p) process is* ***non-deep*** *iff*

$$\sum_{m=1}^{M} \bar{\xi}_m (\mu_m - \mu_x)^3 = 0 \tag{3}$$

where $\bar{\xi}_m$ is the unconditional probability of regime m, and $\mu_x = \sum_i \mu_i \bar{\xi}_i$ is the unconditional mean of x_t.

Example 1. Consider the case of two regimes. The MSM(2)-AR(p) process can be written as the sum of two independent processes: $x_t - \mu_x = \mu_t + z_t$, where $\mathsf{E}[\mu_t] = \mathsf{E}[z_t] = 0$. While the process $z_t = \sum_{j=1}^{p} \alpha_j z_{t-j} + u_t$ is Gaussian, μ_t represents the contribution of the Markov chain, $\mu_t = (\mu_1 - \mu_2)\zeta_t$, with

$\zeta_t = \xi_{1t} - \bar{\xi}_1$, which equals $1 - \bar{\xi}_1$ if the regime is 1 and $-\bar{\xi}_1$ otherwise. Invoking proposition 1, the skewness of the Markov chain is given by:

$$\mathsf{E}[(\mu_t - \mu_x)^3] = \sum_{m=1}^{2} \bar{\xi}_m(\mu_m - \mu_x)^3 = \bar{\xi}_1(\mu_1 - \mu_x)^3 + (1 - \bar{\xi}_1)(\mu_2 - \mu_x)^3$$

where $\mu_x = \bar{\xi}_1\mu_1 + (1 - \bar{\xi}_1)\mu_2$ and $\bar{\xi}_1 = p_{21}/(p_{12} + p_{21})$ is the unconditional probability of regime one. Thus:

$$\mathsf{E}[(\mu_t - \mu_x)^3] = \bar{\xi}_1(1 - \bar{\xi}_1)[1 - 2\bar{\xi}_1](\mu_1 - \mu_2)^3.$$

As the Markov-switching model implies that $\mu_1 \neq \mu_2$ and $\bar{\xi}_1 \in (0, 1)$, non-deepness, $\mathsf{E}[(\mu_t - \mu_x)^3] = 0$, requires that $\bar{\xi}_1 = 0.5$. Hence the matrix of transition probabilities must be symmetric, $p_{12} = p_{21}$. This also implies that the regime-conditional means μ_1 and μ_2 are equidistant to the unconditional mean μ_y.

Hence, in the case of two regimes we can test for non-deepness by testing the hypothesis $p_{12} = p_{21}$. This is equivalent to the test of non-sharpness. For processes with $M > 2$ we propose to test for non-deepness conditional on μ_x and the $\bar{\xi}_m$.

Proposition 2. *An MSM(M)-AR(p) process is* ***non-steep*** *if the size of the jumps, $\mu_j - \mu_i$, satisfies the following condition:*

$$\sum_{i=1}^{M-1} \sum_{j=i+1}^{M} (\bar{\xi}_i p_{ij} - \bar{\xi}_j p_{ji})[\mu_j - \mu_i]^3 = 0. \tag{4}$$

Symmetry of the matrix of transition parameters (which is stronger than the definition of sharpness) is sufficient but not necessary for non-steepness.

In contrast to deepness, the condition for steepness depends not only on the ergodic probabilities, $\bar{\xi}_j$, but also directly on the transition parameters.

Example 2. In an MSM(2)-AR(p) process, condition (4) gives:

$$\mathsf{E}[\Delta\mu_t^3] = (\bar{\xi}_1 p_{12} - \bar{\xi}_2 p_{21})[\mu_2 - \mu_1]^3.$$

This is necessarily equal to zero, so a two-regime Markov-switching model is always non-steep. Since $\bar{\xi}_1/\bar{\xi}_2 = p_{21}/p_{12}$, we have that $\bar{\xi}_1 p_{12} - \bar{\xi}_2 p_{21} = 0$ and hence $\mathsf{E}[\Delta\mu_t^3] = 0$.

Clements and Krolzig (2000) derive Wald test of the restrictions that imply the absence of steepness, deepness and sharpness asymmetries. These tests have standard asymptotic chi-squared distributions because they condition upon the number of regimes. Being Wald tests, the MS model only needs to be estimated unrestrictedly, and not under the restrictions outlined above, which would be more difficult. The finite-sample performance of the tests can be evaluated in Monte Carlo experiments which reveal good size and power properties. While non-parametric tests are adversely affected by regime-dependent heteroscedasticity, the parametric SDS tests work reasonably well even if the data are generated from other types of regime-switching models.

3. Oil prices and the US Business Cycle

3.1. Oil price transforms

The discussion in the introduction suggests that the relevance of oil price changes, as an explanation of output changes, may depend on the transformation of the oil price variable employed. Consequently, whether oil prices are able to account for asymmetries in the Business Cycle may depend upon the oil price transform. For this reason, we present results for each of the oil price measures. It transpires that some of the main results do not depend on the oil price transform. However, for the purpose of presenting graphical displays of regime probabilities and model fits when we condition on the oil price, it is convenient to focus on a single measure. This measure could be selected in a number of ways – we choose the transformation of the oil price that gives the best fit in an autoregressive-distributed lag (ADL) model with the change in output as the dependent variable. Specifically, we begin with a general unrestricted model containing four lags of the dependent variable, and lags from one to four on each of the five oil price variables. We then test down, with the aim of arriving at a simple model, which might indicate that a particular oil price variable is 'best'. However, because the oil price variables are highly collinear, as is apparent from figure 1, the final model may depend on the precise way in which the successive rounds of simplifications are carried out, and on

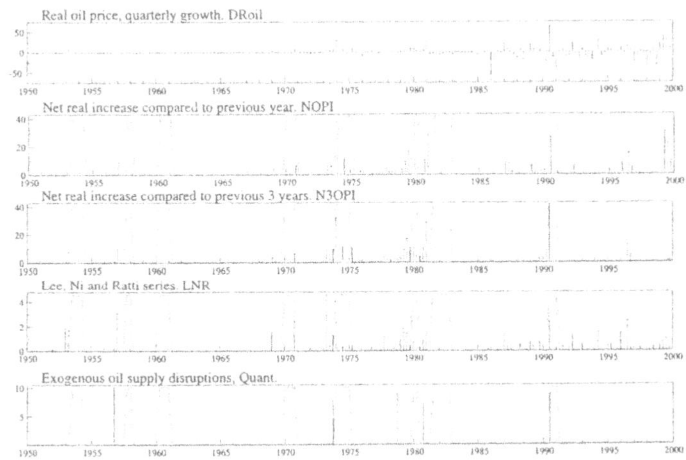

Fig. 1. Oil price transforms. The panels show (i) the quarterly growth rate in the oil price (Doil), (ii) Hamilton's net oil price variable (NOPI), (iii) Hamilton's net oil price variable relative to the previous three years (N3OPI), (iv) the Lee, Ni and Ratti (LNR) variable, and (v) a time series of exogenous supply disruptions (Quant). Also shown are the NBER-dated recessions.

the order in which 'insignificant' variables (or groups of variables) are deleted. We use David F. Hendry and Hans-Martin Krolzig's PcGets to automate the simplification procedure. By searching all the possible paths, and then comparing all the candidate models so obtained, the problem of path-dependence is solved: see Krolzig and Hendry (2001) for details of the algorithms.

The PcGets program can be used in several modes. Initially, we employed the 'outlier correction' facility, which automatically adds impulse dummies to the general model to correct for outliers, before simplifying. Four dummy variables were selected for an estimation period of 1952:1 to 1999:4. The final model retained all the dummy variables, and included lags 1 and 3 of the dependent variable, and lags 1, 3 and 4 of LNR. The significance of the dummies in the general model and the final specification could be interpreted as suggesting the linear relationship is inadequate, possibly pointing toward a non-linear model, although other explanations, such as omitted variables, are at least as plausible. Omitting the outlier dummies from the general model resulted in a similar, though simpler final model, in which the third lag of the dependent variable, and the first lag of LNR, dropped out:

$$\Delta y_t = \underset{(8.88)}{0.88} + \underset{(3.22)}{0.22}\ \Delta y_{t-1} - \underset{(3.79)}{0.39}\ LNR_{t-3} - \underset{(4.05)}{0.43}\ LNR_{t-4},$$

where Δy_t is output growth (the difference of the natural logarithm of the GNP series, multiplied by one hundred), which is similar to equation (3.6) in Hamilton (2000).

Because the MS model in which we test for asymmetries is a joint model of output and employment growth (see section 3.2) we repeat the above exercise with the change in employment as the dependent variable. The final model included all four lags of the dependent variable, the third and fourth lags of LNR, and the first lag of Quant (which bordered on significance at the 5% level).[3] The outcome of this exercise suggests the LNR transformation of the oil price provides the best *linear* fit. This suggests using LNR in the MS model, but because the ADL model findings are only indicative – we cannot show that the transformation that offers the best linear fit is the most appropriate in the MS model framework – we also check the asymmetry results for other oil price variables.

3.2. Markov-switching models of the US Business Cycle

Within the class of Markov-Switching autoregressive (MS-AR) models, there are a large variety of models that could be used to investigate the role of oil prices. The seminal article of Hamilton (1989) modelled the quarterly percentage change in US real GNP for the period 1953 to 1984 using a two-regime model with switching in mean and four autoregressive lags, which we write following equation (1) as MSM(2)-AR(4). A number of authors have used

[3] We also experimented with more general models of output and employment growth that included four lags of the other variable in addition to the five oil price transforms. For employment growth, none of the output terms were retained in the final model, and the model was as described in the text. For output, the final model included the four lags of employment but once again the third and fourth lags of LNR were retained.

shorter autoregressive lag orders, for example, Clements and Krolzig (1998) and Anderson and Vahid (2001) set $p = 2$, and Raymond and Rich (1997) do not have any autoregressive lags. More importantly, a number of authors have found that a three-state model offers a better description of post War US output growth: see Hess and Iwata (1995), Boldin (1996) and Clements and Krolzig (1998). For example, Clements and Krolzig (1998) found that the two-regime model under-estimated the durations of recessions for sample periods of 1947–90 and 1959–96, suggesting that the business-cycle interpretation of the model becomes rather laboured when the estimation period includes the end of World War II and the Korean War, or the nineties data. However, adding a third regime re-instated the close match to the NBER dates observed by Hamilton. Sichel (1994) has argued convincingly that post-War business cycles typically consist of three phases: contraction, followed by high-growth recovery, and then a period of moderate growth. Clements and Krolzig (1998) capture this in a parametric model via a three-state heteroscedastic model with a switching *I*ntercept (labelled MS*I*(3)-AR(4)):

$$\Delta y_t = \mu(s_t) + \sum_{k=1}^{4} \alpha_k \Delta y_{t-k} + u_t, \tag{5}$$

which also allows the variability of the disturbances to depend on the regime. Thus, $u_t|s_t \sim \mathsf{NID}(0, \sigma^2(s_t))$ where $s_t \in \{1, 2, 3\}$ is generated by a Markov chain. The '*H*eteroscedasticity' is flagged by writing the model as MSI*H*(3)-AR(4). The hypothesis of homoscedastic errors is clearly rejected in the three-state model using a standard likelihood ratio test (which is asymptotically χ^2 with $M - 1$ degrees of freedom). The three-state model also obtains theoretical support from the 'plucking model' of Friedman (1969, ch. 12; 1993), as noted by Sichel (1994, p. 269).

Formal tests between the two and three-state models are made difficult and unreliable by the well-documented problems that affect inference. Conventional testing approaches are not applicable due to the presence of unidentified nuisance parameters under the null of linearity (that is, the transition probabilities) and because the scores associated with parameters of interest under the alternative may be identically zero under the null. As an example, we note that Hansen (1992, 1996) is unable to reject a linear AR(4) in favour of Hamilton's model (on the Hamilton data) using a standardized LR test designed to deliver (asymptotically) valid inference, i.e., one regime cannot be rejected against two But Hansen's approach delivers only a bound on the asymptotic distribution of the standardized LR test, and the test may be conservative, tending to be undersized in practice and of low power. Similar problems are likely to arise in testing two against three regimes. For these reasons, model selection is based on the relative abilities of the models to characterise the post War business cycle, rather than on formal tests.

Table 1 offers one measure of the match between the MS models' inferred probabilities of expansions and contractions and the NBER chronology. The 'Univariate, 2-state' model in the table is the MSM(M)-AR(p) defined in (1) with two regimes ($M = 2$) and $p = 2$. The 'Univariate, 3-state' model is the MSIH(3)-AR(4) model of equation (5). The remaining 'Bivariate, 3-state' model will be discussed in section 3.3. 'Synchronization' reports the frequency with which the NBER-dated cycle and the Markov chain are in the same state

Table 1. Synchronization of MS-AR models' states and the NBER-dated expansions and contractions

	Univariate 2-state	Univariate 3-state	Bivariate 3-state
Synchronization	0.898	0.874	0.9513
$\Pr(s_1 = 1 \mid \text{recession})$	0.842	0.898	0.9186
$\Pr(s_1 = 1 \mid \text{expansion})$	0.091	0.131	0.0429

The models are: the MSM(2)-AR(0) model, the MSIH(3)-AR(4) model, and a bivariate MS-VECM model of output and employment growth.
'Synchronization' is the sum of the MS model smoothed probabilities of a recession for NBER-dated recessionary periods and the smoothed probabilities of expansions for NBER dated expansions divided by the total number of observations. '$\Pr(s_1 = 1 \mid \text{NBER recession})$' is measured as the average of the MS model smoothed probabilities of being in regime 1 for those observations for which the US economy is in a recession according to the NBER. Similarly, '$\Pr(s_1 = 1 \mid \text{NBER expansion})$' reports the probability of a recession from the MS model when the US economy is in the state of an expansion according to the NBER.

of recession or expansion, based on the MS model smoothed probabilities (see table legend for details). The table also focuses on the synchronization of MS model and NBER recessions ('$\Pr(s_1 = 1 \mid \text{NBER recession})$') and records the probability of a recession from the MS model when the US economy is in the state of an expansion according to the NBER ('$\Pr(s_1 = 1 \mid \text{NBER expansion})$'). From the table it is apparent that the three-regime model is superior at signalling recessions, but that there are more false signals of recession when the economy is actually in expansion.

Finally, we note that the MS-AR framework can be readily extended to multivariate settings (see e.g., Ravn and Sola, 1995, Diebold and Rudebusch, 1996, Hamilton and Lin, 1996, Krolzig, 1997, Krolzig and Sensier, 2000, and Krolzig and Toro, 1998), which is a distinct advantage given that business cycles were originally viewed as consisting of co-movements in many economic variables (see, e.g., Burns and Mitchell, 1946). If the business cycle is a common feature of a number of macroeconomic time series, modeling the system should improve statistical inference aimed at extracting the common 'business cycle' component from the group of economic time series. Thus we suspect that multivariate models may be superior to univariate Markov-switching models in terms of capturing the features of the business cycle. In the next section we describe how we generalize the MS-AR models considered so far to a cointegrated Markov-switching vector equilibrium correction model (MS-VECM) of US output and employment. Hopefully this will sharpen our judgment on the asymmetry of the business cycle, and on the effects of oil price shocks. The final column of table 1 records the same synchronization measures for the MS-VECM as for the univariate models, and suggests that a closer match has in fact been achieved.

3.3. MS model of output and employment

The bivariate model we adopt is the Krolzig and Toro (1998) model of post-war US employment and output. It is a cointegrated vector autoregressive

Markov-switching process, which models employment and output as having a common cyclical component, and satisfying a proportional cointegrating relationship, with a trend (t) included as a proxy for technological progress and capital accumulation. More formally, the long-run relationship between (the logs of) output, y_t, and employment, n_t, is given by the cointegration vector $\beta' = (1 : -1)$ and the regime-dependent deviation from the trend in per-capita output $\mu(s_t) = \mathsf{E}[y_{t-1} - n_{t-1} - \gamma(t-1)]$. Then each regime m is associated with a particular attractor (μ_m, δ^*_m) given by the equilibrium growth rate δ^*_m and the equilibrium mean μ_m:

$$\begin{bmatrix} a_{11}(\mathsf{L}) & a_{12}(\mathsf{L}) \\ a_{21}(\mathsf{L}) & a_{22}(\mathsf{L}) \end{bmatrix} \begin{bmatrix} \Delta y_t - \delta^*(s_t) \\ \Delta n_t - \delta^*(s_t) \end{bmatrix}$$

$$= \begin{bmatrix} \alpha_1 \\ \alpha_2 \end{bmatrix} (y_{t-1} - n_{t-1} - \gamma(t-1) - \mu(s_t)) + \begin{bmatrix} u_{1t} \\ u_{2t} \end{bmatrix}, \tag{6}$$

where $u_t|s_t \sim \mathsf{NID}(0, \Sigma(s_t))$. Thus the regime-dependent drift term $\delta^*(s_t)$ is the equilibrium growth rate, and shifts in the $\delta^*(s_t)$ map out changes in the business cycle state (e.g., expansion, contraction). The equilibrium mean $\mu(s_t)$ gives the state-dependent equilibrium level of labour productivity: shifts in $\mu(s_t)$ reflect changes in equilibrium per-capita output. As in the univariate MS models, the unobservable regime variable s_t is governed by a Markov chain with a finite number of states defined by the transition probabilities p_{ij}.

Following Krolzig (2001) who shows that US data from 1960 to 1997 strongly support the cointegration hypothesis underlying (6), we use data from 1960:1 to 1999:4. The maximum likelihood (ML) estimation of the model is based on a version of the Expectation-Maximization (EM) algorithm discussed in Hamilton (1990) and Krolzig (1997), and follows the two-stage procedure suggested by Krolzig (1996). The cointegration properties of the system are analyzed within a linear VAR(4) representation using the ML method of Johansen (1995). The trace test indicates a single cointegrating vector, which is identified as trend-adjusted productivity:

$$yn_t = y_t - n_t - 0.244t. \tag{7}$$

Equation (7) defines yn_t as the (stationary) deviation of labour productivity from its trend with productivity growing at an average rate of about 2.4% per year. Krolzig and Toro (1998) interpret yn_t a labour-based measure of capacity utilization with $n_t + 0.244t$ as the potential output.

Short-run and long-run dynamics are jointly estimated in a Markov-switching vector-equilibrium-correction (MS-VECM) model, with the three regimes representing recession, growth and high growth. The ML estimation results for a first-order model estimated are presented in table 2, for the model parameterized as:

$$\begin{bmatrix} \Delta y_t \\ \Delta n_t \end{bmatrix} = \begin{bmatrix} \nu_1(s_t) \\ \nu_2(s_2) \end{bmatrix} + \begin{bmatrix} a_{11} & a_{12} \\ a_{21} & a_{22} \end{bmatrix} \begin{bmatrix} \Delta y_{t-1} \\ \Delta n_{t-1} \end{bmatrix} + \begin{bmatrix} \alpha_1 \\ \alpha_2 \end{bmatrix} yn_{t-1} + \begin{bmatrix} u_{1t} \\ u_{2t} \end{bmatrix}, \tag{8}$$

with $\nu(s_t) = \delta(s_t) - \alpha\mu(s_t)$.

Table 2. ML estimation results for the MS-VECM, 1960:1–1999:4

	Δy_t		Δn_t	
Regime-dependent intercepts				
ν_1	−0.4297	(0.2025)	−0.2244	(0.0906)
ν_2	0.7692	(0.1139)	0.2473	(0.0436)
ν_3	1.3161	(0.1946)	0.4348	(0.0718)
Short-run dynamics				
Δy_{t-1}	−0.0512	(0.0924)	0.0030	(0.0327)
Δn_{t-1}	0.2279	(0.1636)	0.5679	(0.0584)
Equilibrium correction				
yn_{t-1}	−2.5337	(4.1919)	3.0889	(1.4884)
Standard Errors				
Regime 1	0.7834		0.3408	
Regime 2	0.4592		0.1362	
Regime 3	0.7855		0.3086	
Correlation				
Regime 1	0.6165			
Regime 2	0.3572			
Regime 3	0.6128			

Fitting	MS-VECM	linear VECM
log Lik	−141.5922	−183.2934
AIC	2.1207	2.4439
HQ	2.3323	2.5302
SC	2.6418	2.6563

p_{ij}	$s_{t-1}=1$	$s_{t-1}=2$	$s_{t-1}=3$	Duration
$s_t=1$	0.7713	0.0449	0.0412	4.37
$s_t=2$	0.0256	0.9551	0.0608	22.27
$s_t=3$	0.2030	.000003	0.8981	9.81

Notes: The numbers in brackets represent the standard errors of the estimated coefficients.

Figure 2 gives a graphical display of the fit of the model and the estimated regime probabilities for each observation. The smoothed probabilities assign each observation to a particular state using all the sample information; the filtered use information available only up to that observation. We have overimposed the NBER Business Cycle on the inferred probabilities of recession. The findings confirm the view that the business cycle consists of three phases: recession, growth, and high growth. Regime 1 depicts very precisely the NBER recessions of 1970, 1973/74, 1979/80 and 1990. Regime 2 represents normal growth episodes; while regime 3 characterizes high-growth 'recovery'[4] episodes mainly occurring after recessions, and is not realized after 1985. After 1985 expansions are characterized by the lower mean growth rate, and the reduced

[4] The duration of the 'recovery phase' is estimated at around two and a half years (see table 2) which perhaps strains this interpretation. However, the average duration is exaggerated by the high growth of the first half of the 1960's. Moreover, the estimated transition probability of entering this state from recession is around 20% – from the 'normal growth' state it is virtually nil.

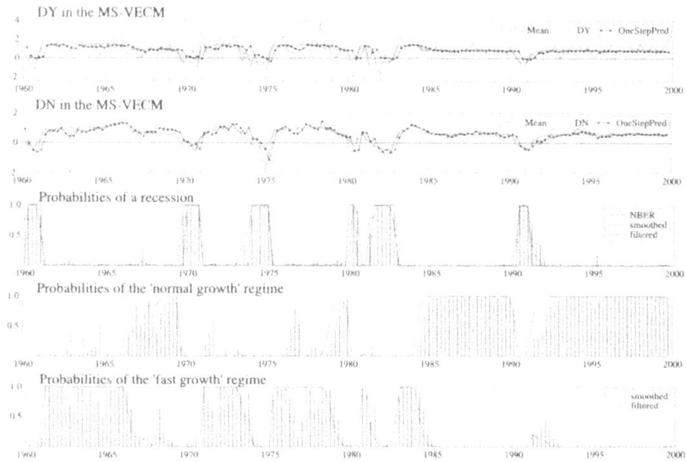

Fig. 2. The US Business Cycle in output and employment The top two panels display the actual series and fitted values (the dashed lines) for output growth and employment growth. The lower three panels record the filtered probabilities (the bars) and the smoothed probabilities for the contraction, 'normal growth' and 'fast growth' regimes respectively

volatility of macroeconomic fluctuations, of regime 2 (compared to a mix of regimes 2 and 3). McConnell and Perez-Quiros (2000) present evidence of a structural break in the volatility of US output growth occurring at the same time. They report a substantial reduction in the volatility of durable goods production from 1984 Q1 onwards, which appears to be correlated with a decline in the share of durable goods accounted for by inventories.

Figure 3 shows the results when the MS-VECM of output and employment (8) is conditioned on the first four lags of LNR. Compared to the bivariate MS-VECM, the reconstructed recessions are shorter. The 1973/74 recession is explained by peaks in the LNR regressor at the time of the first OPEC oil-price shock, and thus is not marked by a switch to the recession regime.

3.4. Testing for asymmetries

The results of calculating the non-parametric (NP) tests discussed in section 2.1 are recorded in table 3 for the 1952–99 sample period used for the univariate models and for the 1960–1999 period for which the MS-VECM is estimated. Reported are the sign of the sample skewness, the value of the test statistic, and the p-value for the null of a zero third moment. The interpretation of the table in terms of tests of deepness and steepness is seen to depend upon (i) the method of detrending and (ii) whether a correction is made for serial correlation in the data. We address each of these in turn.

There are any number of detrending methods that could be employed (see, e.g., Canova, 1998). Because the MS model is typically applied to the first differences of variables such as output and employment, which might reasonably be assumed to possess a unit root, it seems sensible to consider first dif-

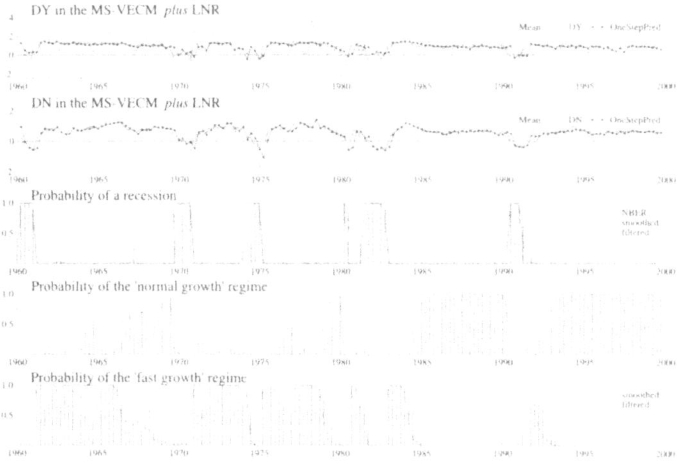

Fig. 3. The US Business Cycle in output and employment when conditioned on LNR The top two panels display the actual series and fitted values (the dashed lines) for output growth and employment growth. The lower three panels record the filtered probabilities (the bars) and the smoothed probabilities for the contraction, 'normal growth' and 'fast growth' regimes respectively

ferencing as a method of detrending. So a test of the skewness of the first-order difference (FoD) is a test for deepness,[5] and a test of skewness in the difference of the difference (second-order difference – SoD) is a test of steepness. However, the Hodrick-Prescott (HP) filter (with a smoothing parameter of 1600) typically extracts cycles of 4–6 years duration, matching the NBER determined cycles, and has become a popular method of detrending amongst macroeconomists. Thus we also calculate the test of skewness for the estimate of the cyclical component from the HP filter.

Canova (1998) suggests 'prewhitening' the data to take account of serial correlation before testing for skew. That is, each series is regressed on six of its own lags and the tests are applied to the residual.[6]

When the data are not prewhitened, both the FoD and HP series suggest negative skew in the output series over the whole sample (1952–99) (i.e., deepness of recessions) but this is less evident when the sample is truncated. For the employment series there is clear evidence of skew on both samples, with for example the FoD and SoD series suggesting deepness of recessions and steepness of expansions.

When the data are prewhitened, there is no evidence of asymmetries for the 1952–99 period, except for positive skew in the SoD of employment, indicating steepness of expansions. If the period is truncated to 1960–99, the tests on the FoD and SoD of output suggest 'tallness' of peaks, and steepness of expansions

[5] However Sichel (1993) argues that FoD delivers the change in the cyclical or detrended component, so that a test for skewness of the FoD is in fact a test for steepness. This issue turns on the underlying model assumed for the generation of the series and its trend and cyclical components, and is beyond the scope of our paper.

[6] Alternatively, one could use a Newey and West (1987) standard error as in Sichel (1993).

Table 3. Non-parametric evidence for asymmetries in US output and employment

asymmetry	skewness (ψ)	no pre-whitening						pre-whitening with 6 lags					
		1952:1–1999:4			1960:1–1999:4			1952:1–1999:4			1960:1–1999:4		
		sign	statistic	*p*-value	sign	statistic	*p*-value	sign	statistic	*p*-value	sign	statistic	*p*-value
Output													
NonDeepness	Δy_t	–	4.064	[0.044]*	–	1.951	[0.163]	+	0.179	[0.672]	+	3.127	[0.077]+
NonDeepness	$y_t - \bar{y}_t$	–	5.285	[0.022]*	–	2.810	[0.094]+	–	0.526	[0.469]	+	1.105	[0.293]
NonSteepness	$\Delta^2 y_t$	+	1.281	[0.258]	+	0.493	[0.483]	+	0.528	[0.468]	+	4.384	[0.036]*
NonSteepness	$\Delta(y_t - \bar{y}_t)$	–	1.436	[0.231]	–	0.145	[0.704]	–	1.166	[0.280]	+	0.264	[0.608]
Employment													
NonDeepness	Δn_t	–	30.490	[0.000]**	–	30.060	[0.000]**	+	1.713	[0.191]	–	0.215	[0.643]
NonDeepness	$n_t - \bar{n}_t$	–	3.015	[0.083]*	–	4.197	[0.040]**	+	0.803	[0.370]	–	7.138	[0.008]**
NonSteepness	$\Delta^2 n_t$	+	4.113	[0.043]*	+	15.730	[0.000]**	+	6.545	[0.011]**	+	0.072	[0.789]
NonSteepness	$\Delta(n_t - \bar{n}_t)$	–	38.030	[0.000]**	–	16.270	[0.000]**	+	0.243	[0.622]	–	8.635	[0.003]**

The table records (i) the sign of the sample skewness $\hat{\psi} = \frac{m_3}{m_2^{3/2}}$, where $m_i = \sum_{t=1}^{T}(x_t - \bar{x})^i$ and $\bar{x}$ is the the sample mean of the series $\{x_t\}$, (ii) the value of the test statistic, $\frac{T}{6}\hat{\psi}^2$, and (iii) the *p*-value for the null that $\psi = 0$ using a χ^2-distribution with one degree of freedom.

** indicates significance at the 1% level;
* indicates significance at the 5% level;
+ indicates significance at the 10% level.

Pre-whitening corresponds to taking the residual from a regression of the series on six of its own lagged values. $\bar{x}_t$ is trend of x_t as obtained by applying the Hodrick-Prescott filter with a smoothing parameter of 1600. Thus $x_t - \bar{x}_t$ denotes the estimate of the cyclical component of the level (of the log) of the series.

Table 4. Tests for asymmetries in MS-VECMs of US output and employment growth, 1960:1–1999:4

	MS-VECM			MS-VECM *plus* DRoil			MS-VECM *plus* LNR			MS-VECM *plus* N1DRoil			MS-VECM *plus* N3DRoil			MS-VECM *plus* Quant		
Test	sign	statistic	*p*-value	sign	statistic	*p*-value	sign	statistic	*p*-value	sign	statistic	*p*-value	sign	statistic	*p*-value	sign	statistic	*p*-value
NonSharpness		3.4984	[0.3210]		2.3609	[0.5010]		6.1185	[0.1060]		2.5155	[0.4725]		3.1720	[0.3659]		0.3340	[0.9535]
$p_{12} = p_{32}$		0.2471	[0.6191]		0.0710	[0.7899]		0.0033	[0.9539]		0.1563	[0.6926]		0.0993	[0.7527]		0.3195	[0.5719]
$p_{13} = p_{31}$		3.4747	[0.0623]$^{+}$		2.1939	[0.1386]		6.1078	[0.0135]*		2.3434	[0.1258]		3.0620	[0.0801]$^{+}$		0.0135	[0.9077]
$p_{21} = p_{23}$		0.0100	[0.9203]		0.0026	[0.9592]		0.0085	[0.9266]		0.0007	[0.9789]		0.0133	[0.9082]		0.0005	[0.9813]
NonDeepness (Δy_t)	−	1.5833	[0.2083]	−	2.0707	[0.1502]	−	3.4789	[0.0622]$^{+}$	−	2.4720	[0.1159]	−	2.1612	[0.1415]	−	3.2081	[0.0733]$^{+}$
NonSteepness (Δy_t)	+	5.4891	[0.0191]*	+	4.7949	[0.0285]*	+	4.3867	[0.0362]*	+	6.0498	[0.0139]*	+	5.4029	[0.0201]*	+	6.4975	[0.0108]*
NonDeepness (Δn_t)	−	1.5652	[0.2109]	−	1.2038	[0.2726]	−	4.2876	[0.0384]*	−	1.3800	[0.2401]	−	2.5327	[0.1115]	−	3.1078	[0.0779]$^{+}$
NonSteepness (Δn_t)	+	4.3341	[0.0374]*	+	3.1728	[0.0749]$^{+}$	+	4.1180	[0.0424]*	+	4.0938	[0.0430]*	+	4.6269	[0.0315]*	+	5.8674	[0.0154]*
Ergodic prob.																		
$\Pr(s_1 = 1)$		0.1598			0.1609			0.1329			0.1586			0.1304			0.1231	
$\Pr(s_1 = 2)$		0.5219			0.5010			0.4966			0.5162			0.5217			0.5087	
$\Pr(s_1 = 3)$		0.3183			0.3380			0.3704			0.3252			0.3478			0.3681	

Table 4. Continued

	MS-VECM	MS-VECM *plus* DRoil	MS-VECM *plus* LNR	MS-VECM *plus* N1DRoil	MS-VECM *plus* N3DRoil	MS-VECM *plus* Quant
Synchronization						
NBER	0.9513	0.9420	0.9536	0.9435	0.9588	0.9419
$\Pr(s_1 = 1 \mid \text{rec.})$	0.9186	0.9627	0.8249	0.9793	0.8317	0.7337
$\Pr(s_1 = 1 \mid \text{exp.})$	0.0429	0.0617	0.0235	0.0628	0.0186	0.0211
AIC	2.1207	2.1782	2.1589	2.1746	2.1539	2.1166

Under the null of symmetry, the SDS test statistics are χ^2 with one degree of freedom; the NonSharpness has three degrees of freedom.
** indicates significance at the 1% level;
* indicates significance at the 5% level;
+ indicates significance at the 10% level.
A '+' ('−') in the columns headed 'Sign' indicates positive (negative) skewness.
'Synchronization' reports the frequency that the NBER dated cycle and the Markov chain are in the same state of recession or expansion. '$\Pr(s_1 = 1 \mid$ NBER recession)' denotes the synchronization of MS and NBER recessions. It is measured as the average smoothed probability of beeing in regime 1 of the estimated MS-model when the US economy is in a recession according to the NBER. Similarily '$\Pr(s_1 = 1 \mid$ NBER expansion)' reports the probability of a recession infered from the MS-VAR when the US economy is in state of an expansion according to the NBER.
The NBER turning points over this period are 54:2(T), 57:3(P), 58:2(T), 60:2(P), 61:1(T), 69:4(P), 70:4(T), 73:4(P), 75:1(T), 80:1(P), 80:3(T), 81:3(P), 82:4(T), 90:3(P), 91:1(T), where T & P denote trough and peak, respectively.

at the 4 and 8% levels, respectively.[7] The tests on the HP series have the same signs for output, but are not significant. For the employment series for 1960–99 the HP series indicate deepness and steepness of recessions, though there is no skew in either the FoD or SoD, making the overall picture difficult to interpret.

As mentioned in the introduction, the MS model-based tests have power to detect asymmetries that arise from a non-linear propagation mechanism (of, say, Gaussian shocks), as distinct from asymmetries resulting from the linear propagation of asymmetric shocks. As such, they might give a clearer picture. They will be especially useful if, as is often the case in business cycle analysis, the main focus is on possible non-linearities in the propagation mechanism. In addition, their main strengths in the present context are two-fold: they can be applied to MS models with exogenous variables, so that we can examine whether they account for asymmetries in the propagation mechanism; and they bear directly on the question of asymmetries in the *business cycle*.

The results of testing for asymmetries in models of the vector process are reported in table 4. The left column is the MS-VECM of Krolzig and Toro (1998). We compare results for this model which does not include oil prices with conditional models involving the first four lags of the five oil price transforms. For the model without oil prices we find evidence of steepness in both output and employment growth at the 5% level. There is also evidence of sharpness at the 10% level from the rejection of the hypothesis that $p_{31} = p_{13}$ (see the definition of Sharpness in section 2.1) because p_{31} is significantly less than p_{13}: the economy is more likely to move from recession to fast growth recovery (p_{13}) – and then to normal growth – than in the reverse direction. The finding of steepness of output and employment in expansions is confirmed for all the oil price measures, while sharpness remains for the LNR and N3OPI measures. For a number of the measures there is evidence of deepness of recessions. For example, when the MS-VECM is conditioned on LNR, recessions are found to be deep in output (at the 10% level) and employment (at the 1% level).

The figures measuring the synchronization show that the regime classification is close to the NBER cycle dating whether or not oil shocks are included. The synchronization frequencies exceed 0.94 for all the models reported in the table. This justifies our interpretation of the SDS tests as bearing on the effects of oil shocks on the asymmetry of the business cycle.

4. Conclusions

The relationship between oil and the macroeconomy has received much attention in the recent literature. In this paper we have argued that a three-state Markov-Switching model that distinguishes between contractions, and divides expansions into 'normal' and rapid recovery growth, is the appropriate model in which to explore the explanatory power of oil prices for business cycle phases, especially recessions, and to investigate the role of oil in generating business cycle asymmetries. We tested the parameter restrictions that rule out SDS asymmetries, and could show that the outcomes are largely unaffected by allowing oil prices to affect the conditional mean of output growth. Our findings are broadly in line with those of Raymond and Rich (1997): oil prices do not appear to be the sole explanation of regime-switching behavior. Fur-

---

[7] On Sichel's interpretation (see previous footnote) the positive skew in the FoD would suggest steepness of expansions.

thermore, the asymmetries detected in the business cycle do not appear to be explicable by oil prices.

While some of the downturns in activity that lead to recessions can be attributed to dramatic changes in the price of oil, the findings of the asymmetry tests are consistently that post-War US economic growth is characterized by steepness of expansions. Whether or not allowance is made for the effects of oil price shocks, business cycle transitions from the state of recession to expansion are more violent than movements in the reverse direction. This finding runs counter to the conventional wisdom (e.g., the quotation from Mitchell) that recessions are more violent (i.e. steeper) than expansions.

Acknowledgement. Financial support from the UK Economic and Social Research Council under grant L138251009 is gratefully acknowledged by both authors. We are grateful to James Hamilton, Baldev Raj and two anonymous referees for helpful comments. We also acknowledge commments from participants at the Nuffield College seminar on Economic Theory and Econometrics, especially David Hendry and Neil Shephard. Computations reported in this paper were carried out using the MSVAR package for Ox (see Krolzig, 1998, and Doornik, 1999) and PcGets (see Hendry and Krolzig, 2001).

References

Anderson HM, Vahid F (2001) Predicting the probability of a recession with nonlinear autoregressive leading indicator models. Macroeconomic Dynamics, 5. Forthcoming

Boldin MD (1996) A check on the robustness of Hamilton's Markov switching model approach to the economic analysis of the Business Cycle. Studies in Nonlinear Dynamics and Econometrics 1:35–46

Burns AF, Mitchell WC (1946) Measuring business cycles. New York: NBER

Canova F (1998) Detrending and business cycle facts. Journal of Monetary Economics 41:475–512

Clements MP, Krolzig H-M (1998) A comparison of the forecast performance of Markov-switching and threshold autoregressive models of US GNP. Econometrics Journal 1:C47–75

Clements MP, Krolzig H-M (2000) Business cycle asymmetries: Characterisation and testing based on Markov-switching autoregressions. mimeo, Department of Economics, University of Warwick

Diebold FX, Rudebusch GD (1996) Measuring business cycles: A modern perspective. The Review of Economics and Statistics 78:67–77

Diebold FX, Rudebusch GD, Sichel DE (1993) Further evidence on business cycle duration dependence. In Stock J, Watson M (eds) Business Cycles, Indicators, and Forecasting, pp. 255–280: Chicago: University of Chicago Press and NBER

Doornik JA (1999) Object-oriented matrix programming using Ox. London: Timberlake Consultants Press. 3rd edition

Filardo AJ (1994) Business–cycle phases and their transitional dynamics. Journal of Business and Economic Statistics 12:299–308

Filardo AJ, Gordon SF (1998) Business cycle durations. Journal of Econometrics 85:99–123

Friedman M (1969) The optimum quantity of money and other essays. Chicago: Aldine

Friedman M (1993) The 'plucking model' of business fluctuations revisited. Economic Inquiry 31:171–177

Hamilton JD (1983) Oil and the macroeconomy since World War II. Journal of Political Economy 91:228–248

Hamilton JD (1989) A new approach to the economic analysis of nonstationary time series and the business cycle. Econometrica 57:357–384

Hamilton JD (1996) This is what happened to the oil price-macroeconomy relationship. Journal of Monetary Economics 38:215–220

Hamilton JD (2000) What is an oil shock?. mimeo, Department of Economics, UCSD, La Jolla, California

Hamilton JD, Lin G (1996) Stock market volatility and the business cycle. Journal of Applied Econometrics 11:573–593

Hamilton JD (1990) Analysis of time series subject to changes in regime. Journal of Econometrics 45:39–70

Hansen BE (1992) The likelihood ratio test under nonstandard conditions: testing the Markov switching model of GNP. Journal of Applied Econometrics 7:S61–S82

Hansen BE (1996) Erratum: The likelihood ratio test under nonstandard conditions: testing the Markov switching model of GNP. Journal of Applied Econometrics 11:195–198

Hendry DF, Krolzig H-M (2001) Automatic econometric model selection with PcGets. London: Timberlake Consultants Press

Hess GD, Iwata S (1995) Measuring business cycle features: University of Kansas, Research Papers in Theoretical and Applied Economics No. 1995-6.

Hooker MA (1996) Whatever happened to the oil price-macroeconomy relationship?. Journal of Monetary Economics 38:195–213

Johansen S (1995) Likelihood-based inference in cointegrated vector autoregressive models. Oxford: Oxford University Press

Krolzig H-M (1996) Statistical analysis of cointegrated VAR processes with Markovian regime shifts. SFB 373 Discussion Paper 25/1996, Humboldt Universität, Berlin

Krolzig H-M (1997) Markov switching vector autoregressions: Modelling, statistical inference and application to business cycle analysis: Lecture Notes in Economics and Mathematical Systems, 454. Springer-Verlag, Berlin

Krolzig H-M (1998) Econometric modelling of Markov-switching vector autoregressions using MSVAR for Ox. Discussion paper, Institute of Economics and Statistics, University of Oxford: http://www.econ.ox.ac.uk/research/hendry/krolzig

Krolzig H-M (2001) Business cycle measurement in the presence of structural change: International evidence. International Journal of Forecasting 17:349–368

Krolzig H-M, Hendry DF (2001) Computer automation of general-to-specific model selection procedures. Journal of Economic Dynamics and Control 25:831–866

Krolzig H-M, Sensier M (2000) A disaggregated Markov-switching model of the business cycle in UK manufacturing. Manchester School 68(3):442–460

Krolzig H-M, Toro J (1998) A new approach to the analysis of shocks and the cycle in a model of output and employment. Working paper eco 99/30, EUI, Florence

Lee K, Ni S, Ratti A (1995) Oil shocks and the macroeconomy: The role of price variability. Energy Journal 16:39–56

Luukkonen R, Saikkonen P, Teräsvirta T (1988) Testing linearity against smooth transition autoregressive models. Biometrika 75:491–499

Luukkonen R, Teräsvirta T (1991) Testing linearity of economic time series against cyclical asymmetry. Annales d'économie et de statistique 20/21:125–142

McConnell MM, Perez-Quiros GP (2000) Output fluctuations in the United States: What has changed since the early 1980s?. American Economic Review 90:1464–1476

McQueen G, Thorley S (1993) Asymmetric business cycle turning points. Journal of Monetary Economics 31:341–362

Mitchell WC (1927) Business cycles: The problem and its setting. New York: National Bureau of Economic Research

Mork KA (1989) Oil and the macroeconomy when prices go up and down: An extension of Hamilton's results. Journal of Political Economy 97:740–744

Newey WK, West KD (1987) A simple positive semi-definite heteroskedasticity and autocorrelation-consistent covariance matrix. Econometrica 55:703–708

Ravn MO, Sola M (1995) Stylized facts and regime changes: Are prices procyclical?. Journal of Monetary Economics 36:497–526

Raymond JE, Rich RW (1997) Oil and the macroeconomy: A Markov state-switching approach. Journal of Money, Credit, and Banking 29:193–213

Sichel DE (1993) Business cycle asymmetry. Economic Inquiry 31:224–236

Sichel DE (1994) Inventories and the three phases of the business cycle. Journal of Business and Economic Statistics 12:269–277

Teräsvirta T, Anderson HM (1992) Characterizing nonlinearities in business cycles using smooth transition autoregressive models. Journal of Applied Econometrics 7:119–139

Tong H (1995) Non-linear time series. A dynamical system approach. Oxford: Clarendon Press. First published 1990

Tong H, Lim KS (1980) Threshold autoregression, limit cycles and cyclical data. Journal of The Royal Statistical Society B 42:245–292

Markov switching in disaggregate unemployment rates*

Marcelle Chauvet[1], **Chinhui Juhn**[2], **Simon Potter**[†3]

[1] Department of Economics University of California, Riverside, CA 92521, chauvet@mail.ucr.edu.
[2] Department of Economics, Univesity of Houston, Houston, TX 77204, cjuhn@uh.edu.
[3] Domestic Research, Federal Reserve Bank of New York, New York, NY 10045, simon.potter@ny.frb.org.

First Version Received: December 2000/Final Version Received: June 2001

Abstract. We develop a dynamic factor model with Markov switching to examine secular and business cycle fluctuations in the U.S. unemployment rates. We extract the common dynamics amongst unemployment rates disaggregated for 7 age groups. The framework allows analysis of the contribution of demographic factors to secular changes in unemployment rates. In addition, it allows examination of the separate contribution of changes due to asymmetric business cycle fluctuations. We find strong evidence in favor of the common factor and of the switching between high and low unemployment rate regimes. We also find that demographic adjustments can account for a great deal of secular changes in the unemployment rates, particularly the abrupt increase in the 1970s and 1980s and the subsequent decrease in the last 18 years.

Key words: Markov switching, unemployment, common factor, asymmetries, business cycle, baby boom, Bayesian methods

JEL classification: C32, E32

1. Introduction

The U.S. economic performance during the 1990s expansion was in some aspects unprecedented. Not only was this the longest expansion in U.S. history, inflation and unemployment were unusually low far into the business cycle,

---

* We would like to thank the editors and two referees for numerous useful comments and suggestions.

† The views expressed in this paper are those of the authors and do not necessarily reflect the views of the Federal Reserve Bank of New York or the Federal Reserve System.

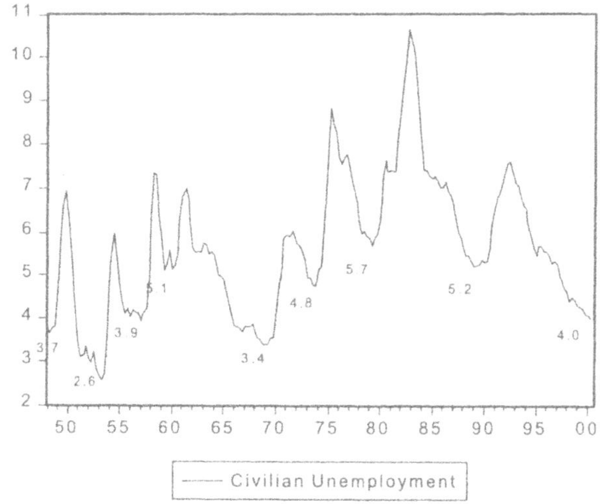

Fig. 1. Civilian Unemployment (SA), and NBER-Dated Recessions

even in the presence of the 2000–2001 slowdown. In particular, the unemployment rate reached its lowest levels since before the 1970 recession.

This paper examines the secular and business cycle movements in unemployment over the past 50 years. In particular, we focus on a variety of features that can be observed in Figure 1, which shows the U.S. total civilian unemployment rate along with shaded bands indicating the NBER-dated recessions. One observes several interesting patterns in the unemployment fluctuations. First, there is the usual cyclical movement related to the phases of the business cycle. Unemployment decreases slowly during expansions, reaching its lowest level around the beginning of recessions. During recessions unemployment rises sharply, reaching a maximum a couple of months after the economic trough. Second, unemployment exhibits a different secular pattern before and after 1969. In particular, unemployment fluctuations display a long upswing through the 1970s and early 1980s, with a high of over 10% at the end of the 1982 recession.

We develop a common factor model with Markov switching to analyze these secular and business cycle fluctuations in the U.S. unemployment rate.[1] In particular, we consider extracting the common dynamics amongst a collection of disaggregate unemployment rates which, given appropriate labor force weights, sum to the total unemployment rate. The framework proposed allows analysis of the contribution of demographic factors to secular changes in unemployment rates. In particular, we focus on the impact of the entry into the

[1] Linear dynamic factor models have been widely applied in economics. A classical exposition is Geweke (1977) and one of the most popular applications is Stock and Watson's (1989), who build coincident and leading indicators of the U.S. economy. Diebold and Rudebusch (1996) propose adding Hamilton's (1989) Markov switching model to this framework in order to capture asymmetries over the business cycle.

labor force and the subsequent aging of the baby-boom generation.[2] In addition, it allows examination of the separate contribution of changes in unemployment rates due to asymmetric business cycle fluctuations.

The behavior of unemployment over the business cycle has attracted a great deal of attention from economists using nonlinear time series models.[3] With a few exceptions[4] this large literature has focused on some measure of aggregate unemployment. The focus of this paper is to extend the nonlinear analysis of unemployment rates to the disaggregate level. There are two main motivations for this. The first is that some of the multiple regimes that have been found in the unemployment rate may be explained by demographic factors, particularly the baby boom. The second motivation is that nonlinear models ask a great deal of a single time series in terms of identifying Markov switching regimes. For example, in Neftci's (1984) original analysis the evidence for asymmetry in the total unemployment was marginal. If the regimes are actually present, one would expect to find a common switch in disaggregate series. This would increase both the accuracy of the switch estimates as well as the evidence for their presence.

With respect to demographic factors, the significant increase in the number of births in the 1950s and early 1960s is often acknowledged as changing several aspects of the economy. As far as the overall unemployment rate is concerned, because younger labor market participants tend to have higher unemployment rates than older ones, their entry into the labor market produced an increase in the unemployment rate in the 1970s and 1980s, while their subsequent aging induced a decrease in the 1990s.[5] Our approach is to model a latent unemployment rate that captures common labor market conditions across groups, and then re-aggregate this latent unemployment rate using the time-varying labor force weights of the different age groups. This allows us to decompose changes in unemployment between baby-boom type effects and changes in the overall functioning of the labor market.

We find strong statistical evidence in favor of the common factor structure and of the switching between high and low unemployment rate regimes. In particular, the latent factor exhibits the stylized business cycle asymmetries found in unemployment. The factor displays a fast and steep growth and a slow and long decline, associated with the phases of the business cycle. In addition, the high unemployment state is less persistent and more volatile compared to the low unemployment phase. We also find that demographic adjustments can account for a great deal of secular changes in the U.S. unemployment rates, particularly the abrupt increase in unemployment in the 1970s and 1980s and

[2] Another potential application of our methods is to explain the skill-biased technological change in the 1970s and 1980s, and its differential effects on education groups (see Juhn, Murphy and Topel 1991). Alternatively, one might consider unemployment grouped by sex and race to examine secular changes in the labor market behavior of these groups, particularly the increasing participation of women in the labor force.

[3] See for example, Neftci (1984), Rothman (1993), Boldin (1994), Franses (1995), Montgomery, Zarnowitz, Tsay, and Tiao (1998), Abbring, Berg and Ours (1999), Vredin and Warne (2000), or Skalin and Teräsvirta (2001).

[4] Rothman (1993) and Abbring, Berg, Ours (1999).

[5] Some of the important studies in this subject include Perry (1970) and Gordon (1982). More recently, Shimer (1998) uses an accounting style analysis, which suggests that the aging baby boomer is an important cause of the reduction in unemployment in the 1990s. These results are corroborated in Katz and Krueger (1999).

the subsequent decrease in the last 18 years. The baby boom effect induces a steep increase in the unemployment rate at the beginning of recessions in the 1970s and 1980s as the labor force weights of young labor market participants were increasing at the time that these switches to the high unemployment regime occurred. On the other hand, the impact of age on the unemployment rate was substantially smaller in the 1990 recession, which is related to the subsequent aging of the baby-boom generation.

The model is estimated and analyzed using Bayesian methods. In particular, the Gibbs sampling is used to simulate and estimate the model while the Savage-Dickey Generalized Density Ratio is used to calculate Bayes factors, which allow evaluation of the sample evidence in favor of the Markov switches.

The organization of the paper is as follows. Section 2 develops the statistical model for disaggregate unemployment rates. Section 3 describes some Bayesian techniques to estimate and test the model. Section 4 discusses the features of the data on unemployment rates disaggregate by age. Section 5 discusses the prior used and the results. Section 6 offers some concluding remarks and directions for future research. The appendix summarizes the complete set of priors and conditional distributions used in the analysis.

2. Statistical model and methods

2.1. Common factor model

Let $\mathbf{U}_t$ be the $K \times 1$ vector of unemployment rates for different age groups used to estimate the common factor, C_t. The statistical model is:

$$\mathbf{U}_t = \lambda C_t + \mathbf{V}_t, \tag{1}$$

where λ is the $K \times 1$ vector of factor loadings, which measures the sensitivity of group k's unemployment rate to the $1x1$ underlying factor C_t, and the $K \times 1$ random vector $\mathbf{V}_t$ represents a possibly autocorrelated measurement error. The common factor is given by the Markov switching model:

$$C_t = \begin{cases} \alpha_1 + \phi_{1p}(L)C_{t-1} + \sigma_1\varepsilon_t & \text{if } s_t = 1 \\ \alpha_2 + \phi_{2p}(L)C_{t-1} + \sigma_2\varepsilon_t & \text{if } s_t = 2 \end{cases}, \tag{2}$$

with $P[s_{t+1} = 1 \mid s_t = 1] = \rho_{11}$ and $P[s_{t+1} = 2 \mid s_t = 2] = \rho_{22}$. The regime specific means are defined as:

$$\eta(1) = \frac{\alpha_1}{1 - \phi_{11} - \cdots - \phi_{1p}}, \quad \eta(2) = \frac{\alpha_2}{1 - \phi_{21} - \cdots - \phi_{2p}}.$$

We identify state 1 as the high unemployment phase and state 2 as the low unemployment phase, that is, $\eta(1) > \eta(2)$. Further, we consider the observed asymmetries in unemployment of sharp increases during recessions followed by slow decreases during expansions using restrictions on the autoregressive coefficients in the two regimes. These restrictions are easier to describe in the case of a first order process. In order for unemployment to increase quickly when it switches from state 2 to 1, ϕ_{11} needs to be relatively small so that α_1 is close in size to $\eta(1)$. Alternatively, when there is a switch from state 1 to state 2, unemployment declines slowly if ϕ_{21} is close to 1 and, therefore, α_2 is very different from $\eta(2)$.

The measurement error vector $\mathbf{V}_t$ has an autoregressive structure:

$$\mathbf{V}_t = \Theta_1 \mathbf{V}_{t-1} + \cdots + \Theta_q \mathbf{V}_{t-q} + \mathbf{M}_t, \tag{3}$$

where the innovations to the common factor, $\varepsilon_t \sim IIDN(0,1)$, and the measurement errors, $\mathbf{M}_t \sim IIDN(\mathbf{0}, \Sigma_K)$, are independent of each other at all leads and lags, and Σ_K is diagonal. In addition, the autoregressive matrices are diagonal:

$$\Theta_i = \begin{bmatrix} \theta_{1i} & \cdots & 0 \\ \vdots & \ddots & \vdots \\ 0 & \cdots & \theta_{1K} \end{bmatrix}.$$

2.2. Latent unemployment

Given our collection of K different age groups, we construct demographic weights for each category by:

$$\omega_{kt} = \frac{L_{kt}}{\sum_{k=1}^{K} L_{kt}}, \tag{4}$$

where L_{kt} is the total civilian labor force for age group k at time t. The overall unemployment rate for all groups UR_t is given by the estimate of the total number of workers unemployed, TU_t, divided by the total civilian labor force, $\sum_{k=1}^{K} L_{kt}$:

$$UR_t = \frac{TU_t}{\sum_{k=1}^{K} L_{kt}} = \frac{\sum_{k=1}^{K} L_{kt} U_{kt}}{\sum_{k=1}^{K} L_{kt}}, \text{ or}$$

$$UR_t = \sum_{k=1}^{K} \omega_{kt} U_{kt},$$

where U_{kt} is the unemployment rate for age group k. The latent aggregate unemployment rate implied by the common factor model is:

$$\mathcal{U}_t = C_t \sum_{k=1}^{K} \omega_{kt} \lambda_k, \tag{5}$$

The average or "natural rate" of unemployment fluctuates between the "high-mismatch" average,

$$\mathcal{U}_t(1) = \eta(1) \sum_{k=1}^{K} \omega_{kt} \lambda_k, \tag{6}$$

and the "low-mismatch" average,

$$\mathcal{U}_t(2) = \eta(2)\sum_{k=1}^{K}\omega_{kt}\lambda_k. \tag{7}$$

That is, $\mathcal{U}_t(1)$ and $\mathcal{U}_t(2)$ correspond to demographically adjusted high and low bounds for average unemployment. In the empirical analysis, these bounds allow examination of periods in which average unemployment exceeds the high-mismatch and low mismatch averages in the sample.

Notice that, in contrast with an analysis of the aggregate unemployment rate, our estimate of $\{C_t, s_t\}$ is not influenced by variations over time in the demographic weights. In the case where the labor force weights are constant over time, we have:

$$\mathcal{U}_t - \mathcal{U}_\tau = (C_t - C_\tau)\sum_{k=1}^{K}\omega_k\lambda_k, \quad \text{for } \tau < t, \tag{8}$$

or, alternatively, the factor loadings are equal across groups at unity:

$$\mathcal{U}_t - \mathcal{U}_\tau = (C_t - C_\tau). \tag{9}$$

In both cases, demographic changes have no effect on the change in latent aggregate unemployment and there would be little advantage from examining disaggregate unemployment rates. This should be compared to the more general case in which the factor loadings vary across k or the demographic weights change over time. In these cases, changes in aggregate latent unemployment can be split into 2 different contributions – the ones arising from changes in the common factor and the ones from demographic changes:

$$\begin{aligned}\mathcal{U}_t - \mathcal{U}_\tau &= (C_t - C_\tau)\sum_{k=1}^{K}\omega_{kt}\lambda_k && \text{Factor Effect}\\ &\quad + C_\tau\sum_{k=1}^{K}(\omega_{kt} - \omega_{k_\tau})\lambda_k && \text{Demographic Effect}\end{aligned} \tag{10}$$

2.3. State space form

The model can be written in state space form where we assume that $p = q + 1$ for simplicity of notation. First we define the following:

1. Let $\mathbf{U}_t^* = (\mathbf{I}_k - \Theta(L))\mathbf{U}_t$.
2. Let $\mathbf{C}_t^* = [C_t, \ldots, C_{t-p+1}]'$.
3. Define the $K \times (q+1)$ matrix $\mathbf{H}$ by:

$$\mathbf{H} = \begin{bmatrix} \lambda_1 & -\lambda_1\theta_{11} & \cdots & -\lambda_1\theta_{q1} \\ \lambda_2 & -\lambda_2\theta_{12} & \cdots & -\lambda_2\theta_{q2} \\ \vdots & \vdots & \ddots & \vdots \\ \lambda_K & -\lambda_K\theta_{1K} & \cdots & -\lambda_K\theta_{qK} \end{bmatrix}.$$

4. Define the $p \times p$ matrices $\mathbf{A}_i$ by:

$$\mathbf{A}_i = \begin{bmatrix} \phi_{i1} & \phi_{i2} & \cdots & \phi_{ip} \\ 1 & 0 & \cdots & 0 \\ 0 & 1 & \ddots & \vdots \\ 0 & \ddots & 1 & 0 \end{bmatrix}.$$

The state space form has measurement equation:

$$\mathbf{U}_t^* = \mathbf{HC}_t^* + \mathbf{M}_t \tag{11}$$

and transition equation:

$$\mathbf{C}_t^* = \begin{cases} \mathbf{a}_1 + \mathbf{A}_1\mathbf{C}_{t-1}^* + \mathbf{W}_1\varepsilon_t & \text{if } s_t = 1 \\ \mathbf{a}_2 + \mathbf{A}_2\mathbf{C}_{t-1}^* + \mathbf{W}_2\varepsilon_t & \text{if } s_t = 2, \end{cases} \tag{12}$$

where $\mathbf{W}_i = [\sigma_i, 0, \ldots, 0]'$ and $\mathbf{a}_i = [\alpha_i, 0, \ldots, 0]'$ are $(p \times 1)$ vectors.

Below we will also sometimes summarize the conditional mean coefficients in each regime by the $p \times 1$ vector $\boldsymbol{\phi}_i = (\phi_{1i}, \ldots, \phi_{pi})$, or by the $(p+1) \times 1$ vector $\boldsymbol{\beta}_i = (\alpha_i, \phi_{1i}, \ldots, \phi_{pi})$. Let φ represent all the parameters of the common factor model with Markov switching and χ represent the (smaller by $\boldsymbol{\beta}_2, \sigma_2, p_{11}, p_{22}$) set of parameters of the common factor model without Markov switching.

As is true of all single factor models there is an identification issue between the factor loadings and the scaling of the innovation to the common factor (see Chauvet 1998). We normalize one of the elements of the factor loading vector to 1. Also, unlike Stock and Watson (1989), we do not demean and standardize the observable variables before the analysis. Thus, not only will $\boldsymbol{\lambda}$ be estimated from the joint dynamics of the observed time series it will also depend on information on the relative means and variances of the unemployment rates. In order to capture movements between low and high unemployment regimes, it is crucial to keep the mean information in the series.

3. Bayesian methods

If the sequence $\{s_t\}$ were known, estimation by classical or Bayesian methods would be standard. Both methods use the Kalman filter to construct the likelihood function.

3.1. Kalman filter

The Kalman filter iterations are given by:

1. **Prediction Step:** The conditional mean of the factor is,

$$\mathbf{C}_{t+1|t}^* = \begin{cases} \mathbf{a}_1 + \mathbf{A}_1\mathbf{C}_{t|t}^* & \text{if } s_t = 1 \\ \mathbf{a}_2 + \mathbf{A}_2\mathbf{C}_{t|t}^* & \text{if } s_t = 2 \end{cases}.$$

The conditional variance of the factor is,

$$\mathbf{P}_{t+1|t} = \begin{cases} \mathbf{A}_1\mathbf{P}_{t|t}\mathbf{A}_1' + \mathbf{W}_1\mathbf{W}_1' & \text{if } s_t = 1 \\ \mathbf{A}_2\mathbf{P}_{t|t}\mathbf{A}_2' + \mathbf{W}_2\mathbf{W}_2' & \text{if } s_t = 2 \end{cases}.$$

Using the conditional mean of the factor and the measurement equation (11), we obtain the conditional forecast error:

$$\mathbf{U}_{t+1}^* - \hat{\mathbf{U}}_{t+1|t}^* = \mathbf{H}(\mathbf{C}_{t+1}^* - \mathbf{C}_{t+1|t}^*) + \mathbf{M}_{t+1},$$

and its conditional variance:

$$E[(\mathbf{U}_{t+1}^* - \hat{\mathbf{U}}_{t+1|t}^*)(\mathbf{U}_{t+1}^* - \hat{\mathbf{U}}_{t+1|t}^*)'] = \mathbf{H}\mathbf{P}_{t+1|t}\mathbf{H}' + \Sigma_K.$$

2. **Updating Step:** First, the Kalman gain matrix is constructed:

$$\mathbf{G}_{t+1} = \mathbf{P}_{t+1|t}\mathbf{H}'\{E[(\mathbf{U}_{t+1}^* - \hat{\mathbf{U}}_{t+1|t}^*)(\mathbf{U}_{t+1}^* - \hat{\mathbf{U}}_{t+1|t}^*)']\}^{-1}.$$

Then, as new information about the factor is obtained after observing $\mathbf{U}_{t+1}^*$, the Kalman gain is used to include it in the conditional mean of the factor:

$$\mathbf{C}_{t+1|t+1}^* = \mathbf{C}_{t+1|t}^* + \mathbf{G}_{t+1}(\mathbf{U}_{t+1}^* - \hat{\mathbf{U}}_{t+1|t}^*),$$

and to update the conditional variance:

$$\mathbf{P}_{t+1|t+1} = (\mathbf{I}_p - \mathbf{G}_{t+1}\mathbf{H})\mathbf{P}_{t+1|t}.$$

3.2. Posterior draws of Markov states and common factor

The main estimation problem in the model proposed is that the switches in the Markov chain are not observable. As is well-known, this causes a computational problem for standard maximum likelihood approaches, since one has to keep track of the 2^T possible values of the Markov sequence in the sample. Kim (1994) suggests an maximum likelihood approach using an approximation that truncates the exponential increasing number of terms at each iteration in the Kalman filter. On the other hand, Bayesian simulation techniques can be used to obtain the exact likelihood function of the common factor Markov switching model, as proposed by Albert and Chib (1993) and Shephard (1994).

In this paper our focus is on Bayesian methods to extract the sample evidence about the Markov sequence. In our model it is not possible to work out analytically the properties of the posterior even if the common factor and Markov states were directly observed. In these cases, Bayesians have increasingly turned to simulation methods. These methods are based on the intuition that, given a large enough random sample from a distribution, it is possible to figure out the properties of that distribution (e.g. its mean, median, variance, etc.). Geweke (1999) and Chib (2001a, 2001b) provide recent surveys of the methods used for developing such posterior simulators.[6] The advantage of posterior simulators in our case is that they can also be developed to generate draws of the unobservables, which greatly simplifies the estimation problem.

[6] A textbook-type explanation of the method can also be found in Kim and Nelson (1999).

Posterior simulators for many models can be developed by successively drawing from a sequence of conditional posterior distributions. To motivate such methods, let X and Y be random variables and suppose that we are interested in the features of their joint distribution, $p(X, Y)$. Assume that $p(X, Y)$ is difficult to simulate, but that we can easily obtain draws from the conditional distributions $p(X|Y)$ and $p(Y|X)$. Consider the strategy where one selects an initial value, $Y^{(0)}$, and then successively draws $X^{(j)}$ from $p(X|Y^{(j-1)})$, and $Y^{(j)}$ from $p(Y|X^{(j)})$. The resulting sequence, $X^{(j)}$, $Y^{(j)}$ for $j = 1, \dots, J$ will, under weak conditions, converge to a sample from $p(X, Y)$ as J increases. In practice, this means we can discard $\underline{J}$ initial draws to mitigate startup effects. We can then treat $X^{(j)}$, $Y^{(j)}$ for $j = \underline{J} + 1, \dots, J$ as an approximate sample from $p(X, Y)$, which can be used to estimate features of interest. This is a simple example of a Gibbs sampler, which belongs to a more general class of techniques known as Markov Chain Monte Carlo methods.

Many commonly-used econometric models with latent variables can be easily estimated using Gibbs sampling algorithms. In our particular model, the Gibbs sampler generates random draws of $\{s_t\}$, which allows analysis as if the sequence were known. However, in order to obtain inferences we also need to obtain a random draw of the common factor.

3.2.1. *Common factor*

The recursion to generate the random draw of the common factor is as follows (see Fruhwirth-Schnatter, 1994, Carter and Kohn, 1994, or Shephard, 1994):

1. The last iteration of the Kalman filter gives:

$$\mathbf{C}_T^* \sim N(\mathbf{C}_{T|T}^*, \mathbf{P}_{T|T}).$$

   Thus, using standard methods a realization $\tilde{\mathbf{C}}_T^*$ can be drawn from this multivariate normal. Then, the draw of the most recent value of the common factor is given by:

$$\tilde{C}_T = \mathbf{e}\tilde{\mathbf{C}}_T^*.$$

   where $\mathbf{e} = [1, 0, \dots, 0]$ is a $p \times 1$ selection vector. In practice, one only needs to draw from the univariate normal with mean given by the first element of $\mathbf{C}_{T|T}^*$ and variance by the first diagonal element of $\mathbf{P}_{T|T}$.
2. Given a draw at $t+1$ based on draws from $t+2$ to T the information from the Kalman filter iterations is incorporated as if the filter were running backwards combining prior information from its initial forward run with the 'sample' information generated by the random draw:

$$f_t = \tilde{C}_{t+1} - \begin{cases} \alpha_1 + \phi_{1p}(L)C_{t|t} & \text{if } s_t = 1 \\ \alpha_2 + \phi_{2p}(L)C_{t|t} & \text{if } s_t = 2 \end{cases},$$

$$p_t = \begin{cases} \boldsymbol{\phi}_1'\mathbf{P}_{t|t}\boldsymbol{\phi}_1 + \sigma_1^2 & \text{if } s_t = 1 \\ \boldsymbol{\phi}_2'\mathbf{P}_{t|t}\boldsymbol{\phi}_2 + \sigma_2^2 & \text{if } s_t = 2 \end{cases},$$

$$\mathbf{g}_t = \begin{cases} \mathbf{P}_{t|t}\boldsymbol{\phi}_1/p_t & \text{if } s_t = 1 \\ \mathbf{P}_{t|t}\boldsymbol{\phi}_2/p_t & \text{if } s_t = 2 \end{cases},$$

$$\mathbf{C}^*_{t|T} = \mathbf{C}^*_{t|t} + \mathbf{g}_t f_t,$$

$$\mathbf{P}_{t|T} = \begin{cases} (\mathbf{I}_p - \mathbf{g}_t\boldsymbol{\phi}_1')\mathbf{P}_{t|t} & \text{if } s_t = 1 \\ (\mathbf{I}_p - \mathbf{g}_t\boldsymbol{\phi}_2')\mathbf{P}_{t|t} & \text{if } s_t = 2 \end{cases}.$$

Thus, after observing the whole sample we obtain $\mathbf{C}^*_t \sim N(\mathbf{C}^*_{t|T}, \mathbf{P}_{t|T})$, and standard methods can be used to obtain a random draw.

3. This iteration stops with $\mathbf{C}^*_p \sim N(\mathbf{C}^*_{p|T}, \mathbf{P}_{p|T})$, which is used to simultaneously draw the first p observations of the common factor.

3.2.2. *Markov states*

1. Given this realization of the common factor, the methods described in Chib (1996) can be directly applied to investigate the pattern of Markov states contained in the draw of the dynamic factor. Similarly to the analysis of the common factor, the recursion starts by filtering the "observations" on the common factor to construct a sequence of prior and posterior distributions for the Markov state.

In our case, we assume that the chain starts in the low mismatch state 2. Thus, we have $S_1 = \cdots = S_p = 2$. The prior distribution for the state at time $p+1$ is then:

$$P[S_{p+1} = 2 \mid S_1 = \cdots = S_p = 2] = \hat{b}_{p+1} = \rho_{22}.$$

The relevant sample information is contained in the likelihood for $\tilde{C}_{p+1}$, which takes on the value:

$$\ell_1(\tilde{C}^{p+1}) = (2\pi\sigma_1^2)^{-0.5}\exp[-0.5(\tilde{C}_{p+1} - \alpha_1 - \phi_{1p}(L)\tilde{C}_p)^2/\sigma_1^2]$$

if $S_{p+1} = 1$, and:

$$\ell_2(\tilde{C}^{p+1}) = (2\pi\sigma_2^2)^{-0.5}\exp[-0.5(\tilde{C}_{p+1} - \alpha_2 - \phi_{2p}(L)\tilde{C}_p)^2/\sigma_2^2]$$

if $S_{p+1} = 2$. Thus, the posterior distribution $P[S_{p+1} = 2 \mid S_1 = \cdots = S_p = 2, \tilde{C}^{p+1}]$ is given by:

$$\hat{b}_{p+1} = \frac{\ell_2(\tilde{C}^{p+1})\rho_{22}}{\ell_2(\tilde{C}^{p+1})\rho_{22} + \ell_1(\tilde{C}^{p+1})(1-\rho_{22})}.$$

This posterior is used to form a prior for $S_{p+2} = 2$ from:

$$\hat{b}_{p+2} = b_{p+1}\rho_{22} + (1 - b_{p+1})(1 - \rho_{11}).$$

This process continues through the end of the sample and we obtain:

$$b_T = P[S_T = 2 \mid S_1 = \cdots = S_p = 2, \tilde{C}^T].$$

Next, the posterior distribution over the last sample value of the Markov state is used to generate a draw of S_T. This draw is easy to obtain from the generation of a uniform random variable. If the draw is less than or equal to the posterior probability that $S_T = 2$, then we have $\tilde{S}_T = 2$, otherwise $\tilde{S}_T = 1$.

Similarly to the draw of the common factor, a sequence of draws of $\{S_t\}$ is also generated going backwards through the sample. From the Markov property and the exogeneity of the Markov chain, none of the future realizations of the observed time series $\{\tilde{C}_s : s > t\}$ conditional on observing the value of tomorrow's state, s_{t+1} are relevant for the estimate of today's state. Using this restriction and ignoring the dependence on estimated parameters and the restriction on the initial states, we have:

$$\begin{aligned}
P[S_{T-1} &= 2 \mid S_T = 2, \tilde{C}^{T-1}] \\
&= \frac{P[S_{T-1} = 2, S_T = 2 \mid \tilde{C}^{T-1}]}{P[S_T = 2 \mid \tilde{C}^{T-1}]} \\
&= \frac{P[S_{T-1} = 2 \mid \tilde{C}^{T-1}] P[S_T = 2 \mid S_{T-1} = 2]}{\hat{b}_T} \\
&= \frac{b_{T-1} p_{22}}{\hat{b}_T},
\end{aligned}$$

and also:

$$\begin{aligned}
P[S_{T-1} &= 2, S_T = 2 \mid \tilde{C}^T] \\
&= P[S_{T-1} = 2 \mid S_T = 2, \tilde{C}^T] P[S_T = 2 \mid \tilde{C}^T] \\
&= P[S_{T-1} = 2 \mid S_T = 2, \tilde{C}^{T-1}] b_T \\
&= p_{22} \frac{b_{T-1}}{\hat{b}_T} b_T.
\end{aligned}$$

This last expression can be used to generate a smoothed probability $\tilde{b}_t$ by averaging out over the values of S_T:

$$\tilde{b}_{T-1} = b_{T-1} \left(p_{22} \frac{\tilde{b}_T}{\hat{b}_T} + (1 - p_{11}) \frac{1 - \tilde{b}_T}{1 - \hat{b}_T} \right).$$

The first expression gives a direct method for drawing $\tilde{S}_{T-1}$ using a random uniform number. This iteration is repeated until the draw of $\tilde{S}_{P+1}$ using $P[S_p = 2, S_{p+1} = 2 \mid \tilde{C}^T] = 1$ is obtained.

3.3. Estimation by Gibbs sampler

We initialize the Gibbs sampler running the Kalman filter on the observed data with the following parameters: a Markov sequence given by the NBER business cycle dates, factor loadings proportional to the sample means of the unemployment rates, measurement error equal to 1/4 of the observed variances of the unemployment rates with autoregressive coefficients equal to 1/3, and the prior means used for the common factor dynamic model and loadings. The results of the Kalman filter are then used to draw a initial sequence of realizations for the common factor $\{\tilde{C}_t\}$. Given this sequence and the sequence of Markov states, it is relatively simple to update the draws of the remaining parameters using the Gibbs sampler with appropriate choices of prior distributions.

A summary of our choices is as follows: for the parameters of C_t we use a restricted normal inverted gamma prior; for the factor loadings $\boldsymbol{\lambda}$ we use independent normal priors; for the measurement error variances, $\{\sigma_{kk}\}$ we use independent normal inverted gamma priors; for the autoregressive coefficients in the measurement error process we use restricted independent normal priors; for the transition probabilities we use a Beta distribution. Section 5.1 contains information of the exact prior distributions used and the appendix contains more detailed information on the priors and the implied conditional posteriors. Here we focus on some of the restrictions imposed on the parameters.

For both the parameters of C_t and the measurement error processes we impose a stationarity condition. In the case of the measurement error process the roots of the individual lag polynomials $1 - \theta_{kq}(L)$ all lie outside the unit circle. For the common factor Markov switching model we use the sufficient condition that the roots of each lag polynomial $1 - \phi_{ip}(L)$ lie outside the unit circle. For both sets of restrictions we use simple rejection sampling.

In addition to the stationarity restriction, we also impose the restriction that $\eta(1) > \eta(2) > 0$. Since the regime specific means are nonlinear functions of the underlying autoregressive parameters and the intercept, the restriction is imposed sequentially as follows. First, we draw $\boldsymbol{\beta}_2$ and check whether the stationarity and non-negativity conditions are satisfied. If they are not we make a new draw. This process continues until a satisfactory draw is obtained. Next, we draw $\boldsymbol{\beta}_1$ and check whether both the stationarity and mean inequality conditions hold. Again, we reject this draw if it does not satisfy the conditions, continuing until a statisfactory draw is obtained.

3.4. Evidence for Markov switching

We assess the observed sample evidence in favor of a Markov switching in the common factor model by comparing the average (often called the marginal) likelihood of the observed time series with and without switching. The ratios of these two average likelihoods is the Bayes factor and it provides a direct 'test' of the usefulness of the additional complexity of the Markov switching model. On the other hand, classical testing of Markov switching models is a somewhat unresolved area due to various non-standard aspects of the model. We do not attempt to solve these issues here. Instead, we provide some classical-type information by calculating F-statistics at each iteration of the Gibbs sampler. Note that under the null hypothesis of no Markov switching effect and uninformative priors we would expect these statistics to be draws from a F-distribution with appropriate degrees of freedom. Since we are not using non-informative priors the exact sampling distribution of this sequence of F-statistics is unknown.[7] However, we focus on the minimum value of this statistic across iterations of the Gibbs sampler.

Although the calculation of marginal likelihoods involves multiple integration, it can be simplified using the following tricks. The Bayes factor is the marginal likelihood of the 'no-switching model' divided by the marginal likelihood of the 'switching model':

$$B_{\text{No Switching vs. Switching}} = \frac{\int l(\mathbf{U}|\chi, \{C_t\})b(\chi,)d\{C_t\}\, d\chi}{\int l(\mathbf{U}|\varphi, \{s_t\}, \{C_t\})b(\varphi, s_1 = 2)\, d\{C_t\}\, d\{s_t\}\, d\varphi},$$

if this ratio is larger than 1 the sample favors the simple model with no switching. Notice that a ratio of 0.05 is not equivalent to a classical critical value. Instead, it implies that the Markov switching model is 20 times more likely than the simple model, given the observed data on unemployment rates.

Using the basic likelihood identity (see Chib 1995) we have:

$$\int l(\mathbf{U}|\varphi, \{s_t\}, \{C_t\})b(\varphi, s^p = 2)\, d\{C_t\}\, d\{s_t\}\, d\varphi$$

$$= \frac{l(\mathbf{U}|\varphi, \{s_t\}, \{C_t\})b(\varphi, s^p = 2)}{p(\varphi|\mathbf{U})},$$

for all points in the parameter space. In particular, consider the transformation of the parameter space for the Markov swtiching common factor model from $(\boldsymbol{\beta}_1, \sigma_1, \boldsymbol{\beta}_2, \sigma_2, p_{11}, p_{22})$ to $(\boldsymbol{\beta}_1, \sigma_1, \boldsymbol{\beta}_2 - \boldsymbol{\beta}_1, \sigma_2/\sigma_1, \tau)$. If we evaluate the transformation at $\boldsymbol{\beta}_2 - \boldsymbol{\beta}_1 = 0, \sigma_2/\sigma_1 = 1$, then there is no information in the likelihood function about $\{s_t\}$. As discussed in Koop and Potter (1999), one can use this lack of identification to simplify marginal likelihood calculations using the Savage-Dickey Density ratio. In this case, conditional on the generated sequence of $\{\tilde{C}_t, \tilde{s}_t\}$ we have:

$$\frac{\int l(\{\tilde{C}_t, \tilde{s}_t\} \,|\, \boldsymbol{\beta}_1, \sigma_1)b(\boldsymbol{\beta}_1, \sigma_1)\, d\boldsymbol{\beta}_1\, d\sigma_1}{\int l(\{\tilde{C}_t, \tilde{s}_t\} \,|\, \boldsymbol{\beta}_1, \sigma_1, \boldsymbol{\beta}_2, \sigma_2)b(\boldsymbol{\beta}_1, \sigma_1, \boldsymbol{\beta}_2, \sigma_2)\, d\boldsymbol{\beta}_1\, d\sigma_1\, d\boldsymbol{\beta}_2\, d\sigma_2}$$

$$= \frac{p(\boldsymbol{\beta}_2 - \boldsymbol{\beta}_1 = 0, \sigma_2/\sigma_1 = 1 \,|\, \{\tilde{C}_t, \tilde{s}_t\}, \mathbf{U}, \boldsymbol{\varphi}^-)}{b(\boldsymbol{\beta}_2 - \boldsymbol{\beta}_1 = 0, \sigma_2/\sigma_1 = 1 \,|\, \boldsymbol{\varphi}^-)},$$

where $\boldsymbol{\varphi}^-$ signifies the parameter space excluding the parameters of the common factor model.[8] Using the methods of Koop and Potter (2000), the LHS of this expression can be directly calculated at each iteration of the Gibbs sampler, for normal inverted gamma prior distributions that are independent across regimes. If this quantity is averaged across draws of $\boldsymbol{\varphi}^-$ and $\{\tilde{C}_t, \tilde{s}_t\}$ from the Gibbs sampler we will have:

$$\frac{p(\boldsymbol{\beta}_2 - \boldsymbol{\beta}_1 = 0, \sigma_2/\sigma_1 = 1 \,|\, \mathbf{U})}{b(\boldsymbol{\beta}_2 - \boldsymbol{\beta}_1 = 0, \sigma_2/\sigma_1 = 1)},$$

[7] The informative priors on the parameters of the Markov switching model used here rule out some of the computationally based non-standard problems directly.

[8] In practice, we use different priors between the no switching and switching models, which require a generalization of the density ratio. For simplicity, we ignore this complication here.

which is the Savage Dickey ratio for the Bayes factor of a 'no-switching common factor' versus a 'switching common factor model'.

Our choice of the prior distribution presents a difficulty when implementing this approach, since the prior imposes some nonlinear restrictions on the parameter space. Instead of attempting to directly incorporate these restrictions in the calculation of the conditional marginal likelihood, we calculate the conditional marginal likelihood for the unrestricted case. In practice, the differences in the conditional marginal likelihoods are so large that the computer is rarely able to distinguish the conditional Bayes factor from zero. Since we find few violations of the nonlinear restrictions on the parameter space, an adjustment for the restrictions on the prior would not change the overall result of strong support for the Markov switching model in the data.

4. Data description

We use unemployment rates for seven age groups for the period from 1948Q1 to 2000Q2.[9] The age groups are 16–19, 20–24, 25–34, 35–44, 45–54, 55–64, and 65 and over. We construct the unemployment rates from the three-month averages of the estimated total unemployment for each group, divided by the three-month average of the estimated labor force for each group:

$$UR_{kt} = \frac{TU_{kt}}{L_{kt}}.$$

These underlying data are not seasonally adjusted. We adjusted the age-specific unemployment rates using a seasonal factor given by the ratio of the published seasonally adjusted to the unadjusted total civilian unemployment rates. We also constructed weights for each group given by equation (4). Note that these weights are not seasonally adjusted. Our adjustment procedure produces an overall unemployment rate that is virtually identical to the published series. This would obviously not be the case if we also seasonally adjusted the labor force weights.

Our focus in on the impact of demographic changes related to the entry into the labor market and subsequent aging of the baby-boom generation, which is illustrated in Figure 2. In particular, the figure shows the time path of the civilian labor force for different age groups. The aging of the baby boomers can be observed in the pattern of changes in the age composition of the labor force over time. The wave of young workers (age 16–19) had its peak at the end of the 1970s. Ten years later, some of these workers fell into the 25–35 age category that peaked in 1990. Currently, the majority of the workers is now between 35–44.

What are the implications of these demographic changes in the labor market? In order to answer this question it is important to understand how the unemployment rate behaves differently across different age groups. Table 1 contains some sample statistics on unemployment rates for different age groups, while Table 2 contains information on the relative weights of each group in the

[9] This is the earliest available starting point for high frequency and disaggregate unemployment rates in the United States. For a descriptive analysis of unemployment statistics over 120 years, see Denman and McDonald (1996).

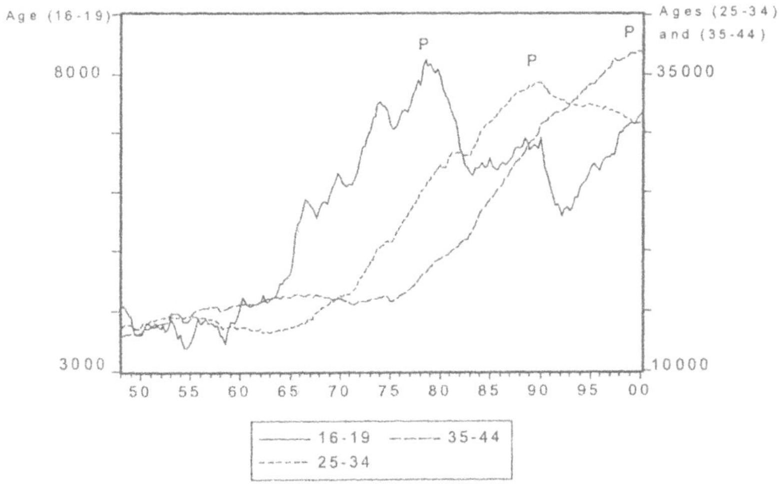

Fig. 2. Civilian Labor Force by Age Groups

Table 1. Statistics for unemployment rates

U_{kt}\Statistic	Mean	St. Dev.	Min	Max
16–19	15.5	3.6	6.3	25.0
20–24	9.0	2.4	3.9	16.0
25–34	5.6	1.7	2.2	10.8
35–44	4.0	1.2	1.8	8.2
45–54	3.6	1.0	1.8	6.7
55–64	3.7	1.0	1.7	6.2
65+	3.6	0.8	1.7	6.1

labor force, with the weights scaled by 100. The unemployment rate for teenagers is much higher and more volatile than for the other age groups. In fact, the mean and variance of the unemployment rate decrease steadily as workers age. For example, teenagers have an average unemployment rate of 15.5%, workers between 35–45 have an average of 4%, while the aggregate rate is 5.7% (Table 1).

As a result of these differences, secular changes in the relative participation of young workers in the labor force has had a significant impact on aggregate unemployment. In particular, as can be seen in Figures 1 and 2, the long secular upswing in the aggregate unemployment rate coincides with the entry of young workers into the labor market. The participation of teenagers in the labor market increased substantially in the 1960s reaching a peak in the mid 1970s, while the participation of workers between 35–45 fell substantially during this period. The subsequent aging of the baby boom generation in the

Table 2. Statistics for labor force weights

ω_{kt}\Statistic	Mean	St. Dev.	Min	Max
16–19	7.3	1.4	5.1	10.7
20–24	11.8	2.0	8.4	15.3
25–34	24.2	3.2	18.7	29.6
35–44	22.7	2.2	17.6	27.5
45–54	18.7	2.2	14.8	21.8
55–64	11.8	1.7	8.8	14.2
65+	3.6	1.0	2.5	5.3

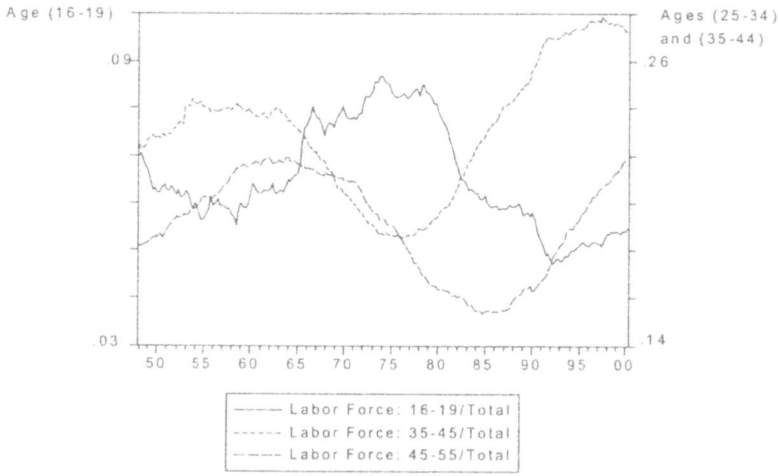

Fig. 3. Participation in the Labor Force by Age (SA)

1980s and 1990s is associated with a reduced fraction of teenagers in the labor force and a substantial increase in the proportion of workers between age 35 and 55 (Figure 3 and Table 2).

Finally, we present the contemporaneous correlation matrix for the unemployment rates ordered from the youngest to the oldest (Table 3). It is interesting to notice how the unemployment rates are correlated between groups close in age, and much less so when comparing younger workers with older workers. The reason is that unemployment rates for younger workers are very volatile over the entire sample, and display particularly accentuated oscillations over the business cycle. On the other hand, the volatility of unemployment decreases monotonically as workers age. Table 1 shows that the standard deviation of teenagers' unemployment is more than 3 times higher than the standard deviation for workers age 35 or older. In addition, the unemployment rates for older workers exhibit much smaller oscillations around

Table 3. Correlation matrix for unemployment rates

	16–19	20–24	25–34	35–44	45–54	55–64	65+
16–19	1						
20–24	0.88	1					
25–34	0.84	0.96	1				
35–44	0.79	0.92	0.97	1			
45–54	0.68	0.86	0.91	0.95	1		
55–64	0.50	0.70	0.76	0.84	0.92	1	
65+	0.28	0.43	0.39	0.45	0.53	0.64	1

business cycle turning points. As argued by Shimer (1998), this may be explained by the fact that although younger workers do not have trouble finding jobs, they are more frequently fired.[10]

Anticipating our empirical results, the resulting dynamic factor model is broadly consistent with the sample moments given in Table 1 for the group of workers 35–44. Notice that this is not only the mid-group, but it is also the one with the highest relative participation in the labor force. On the other hand, as it turns out to be somewhat striking, given the contemporaneous correlation between unemployment rates, our measure of latent unemployment constructed from the factor loadings and demographic weights tracks almost exactly the overall unemployment rate.

5. Priors and results

5.1. Properties of the prior distribution

We start by considering the choice of the hyperparameters of the normal-inverted gamma priors for the common factor parameters in each regime, under the restriction used in the estimation that the lag length is 1. These priors are the most important ones for interpretation of the sample evidence. We begin by eliciting a prior that is relatively noninformative, but accords with our subjective prior beliefs. To simplify matters, the prior covariances are assumed to be zero for all the conditional mean parameters in the model. As we work with one lag in each regime, this does not seem controversial. Since we are examining unemployment rates, it does not make economic sense to assume that the prior means are zero. Instead, we specify the prior means in terms of common empirical findings regarding asymmetries in the unemployment rate.

The prior is specified in two steps. First we describe the unrestricted prior, then we discuss various restrictions on the prior that are imposed as in Ge-

[10] Young workers in the U.S. have a mean and median unemployment duration smaller than older workers.

weke (1986). For the low unemployment regime, we specify a mean of 0.4 for the intercept, and of 0.8 for the autoregressive parameter. The respective variances of these parameters are 1 and 0.3. For the high unemployment regime, we specify a mean of 2.5 for the intercept, and of 0.5 for the autoregressive parameter. The variances of these parameters are 0.8 and 0.95, respectively. These are the priors used in generating candidate random draws from the conditional posterior. These draws must satisfy stationarity as well as the restriction $\eta(1) > \eta(2) > 0$. Finally, the degrees of freedom for the inverted gamma priors are 3 for both regimes, and the prior mean of the variance is set to 0.1.[11]

We simulate from this combined normal inverted gamma prior for two regimes in order to obtain some prior features of interest. The prior means of η are around 1% for the low unemployment regime, and around 13.5% for the high unemployment regime. These values are reasonable, given that the η's are upper and lower bounds under the AR(1) assumption. About 32% of the joint priors have $\eta(1) > 6\%$ and $\eta(2) < 4\%$.

For the factor loadings, we use a normal prior centered at 1 with a diagonal variance matrix, individual variance of 4 for unemployment rates of workers age 25 and over, and variance 1 for the unemployment rates of workers 16–19 and 20–24. Once again, this is an uninformative choice. Naturally, we impose the degenerate prior that the factor loading is 1 for the unemployment rates of workers age 35–44 in order to normalize the dynamic factor.

For the measurement error innovation variance, we use the minimally informative inverted gamma prior with degrees of freedom 3 and mean 1. For the autogressive structure of the measurement errors, we use a more informative Gaussian prior. The prior mean is set to zero and the variance is a diagonal matrix. The standard deviation of the autoregressive coefficient for the group age 25 and older is set to 0.07, while for the 16–19 and 20–24 groups it is equal to 0.1. These priors are based on the fact that the Current Population Survey currently follows a "4 month in 8 month out, 4 month in" rotation for households. Thus, the measurement error in the survey across households should not be too strong.

For the parameters of the Markov chain transition matrix, we use a common beta prior. For the probability of unemployment staying in the low regime p_{22} or staying in the high regime p_{11}, the parameters are (9, 1). This is equivalent to having observed about 10 observations of the Markov chain. Thus, it will be easily dominated by the sample information if there are repeated switches. Using standard formula for the beta distribution, this implies a very vague prior on the expected duration $1/(1 - p_{22})$ or $1/(1 - p_{11})$, since the first moment does not exist. The median duration obtained from the simulation is 13.6 quarters, with a probability equal to 0.09 that the duration is longer than 25 years, and a probability of 0.08 that it is less than 1 year.

5.2. Empirical results

The model is estimated with the order of the autogressive parameters $q = 1$, $p = 1$. The unemployment rate of the age group 35–44 is chosen as the vari-

[11] The variance for the conditional mean parameters already takes into account the prior mean for the variance of the errors.

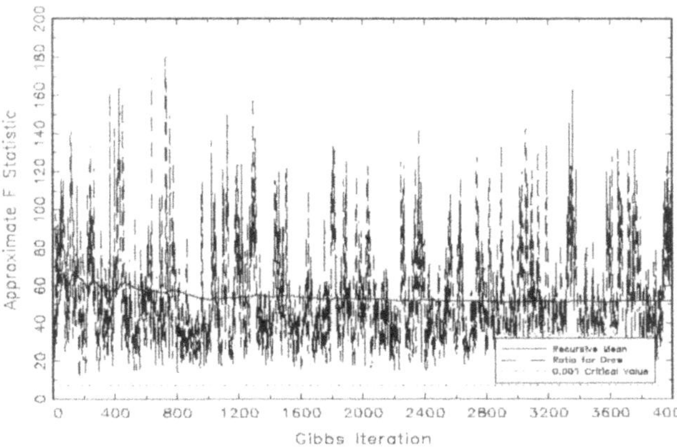

Fig. 4. Approximate F-Statistics at Each Gibbs Iteration

able with factor loading equal to unity. The Gibbs sampler was run with a burn-in phase of 200 iterations and a further 4000 iterations. Repeated runs of the sampler with different initial conditions produced very few changes in the posterior features suggesting that the sampler has converged.

As noted above, the difference in marginal likelihoods is so large between a model with switching and no switching (a Bayes factor of 10^{19} in favor of switching) that there is little information in the conditional Bayes factors. Figure 4 shows evidence on the F-Statistics calculated at each iteration of the Gibbs sampler. Here we can see that the F-statistics are uniformly higher than a 0.1% critical value of around 7 obtained from a F-distribution.

The resulting latent unemployment is highly correlated with total unemployment rate (0.995). In addition, the latent factor is also centered with the actual unemployment rate. With respect to the posterior mean of the factor loadings, they show a pattern consistent with the differences in means and standard deviations reported in Table 1. In particular, young labor market participants have the highest factor loading, and the loadings decline with age.[12]

Figure 5 plots the actual unemployment rate with posterior means of the demographically adjusted bounds, calculated from equations (6) and (7). The unemployment rate fluctuates inside the high-mismatch and low mismatch averages almost the entire sample. In two main instances the bounds are violated, which correspond to periods in which the unemployment rate reached its minimum and maximum values in the sample. One was in the early 1950s, when unemployment rates were very low (2.6%). The other was in the early 1980s, when unemployment rates peaked at 10.7%. The role of the demographic adjustment to the upper and lower bounds can also be seen in this figure. The high and low mismatch averages display a hump in the 1970s, reflecting the entry and subsequent aging of the baby boom in the labor market.

[12] Similar patterns are also found in the posterior means of the autogressive model for the individual measurement errors.

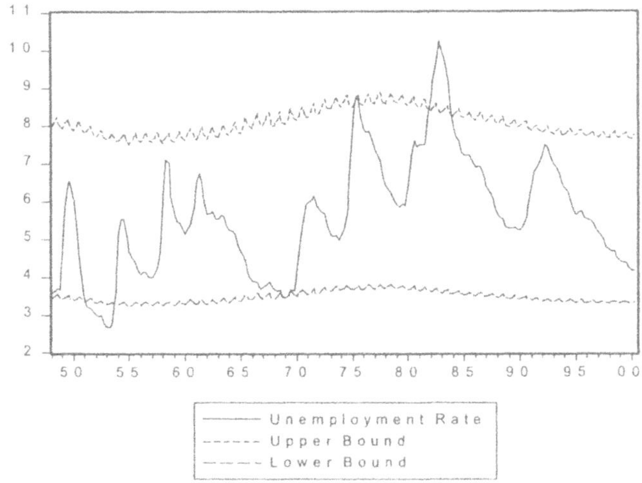

Fig. 5. Unemployment Rate, High and Low Mismatch Averages

In order to further investigate the subsequent influence of the aging baby boomers on unemployment, we compare changes in the unweighted and weighted latent unemployment factors. First, recall that the weighted latent unemployment can be decomposed into a factor effect and a demographic effect, as described in Section 2.2. We consider the change in unemployment for 3 cases: from the earlier dates 1978, 1982, and 1992 to the present (2000). For example, comparing unemployment in 2000 and 1982, equation (10) becomes:

$$\mathcal{U}_{2000} - \mathcal{U}_{1982} = (C_{2000} - C_{1982}) \sum_{k=1}^{K} \omega_{kt}\lambda_k \qquad \text{Factor Effect}$$

$$+ C_{1982} \sum_{k=1}^{K} (\omega_{k2000} - \omega_{k1982})\lambda_k \qquad \text{Demographic Effect}$$

For changes in unemployment from 1978 and 1982 to the present, we find as a demographic effect a reduction of 75 basis points in the latent unemployment rate. This is is very close to the ones obtained in Shimer's (1998) analysis of the actual unemployment rates. Since 1992, there has been a mild demographic induced reduction in the latent unemployment of 10 basis points.

Second, consider the case in which demographic changes have no effect on the change in latent aggregate unemployment, that is, the factor without demographic or factor loading weights, as described in equations (8) and (9). Since we normalize the factor loading of the 35–44 year old group to unity, the factor without demographic\factor loading weights is a measure of the underlying state of the labor market for this group. In this case, equation (8) becomes:

$$C_t\left(\sum_{k=1}^{K} \omega_{kt}\lambda_k - 1\right),$$

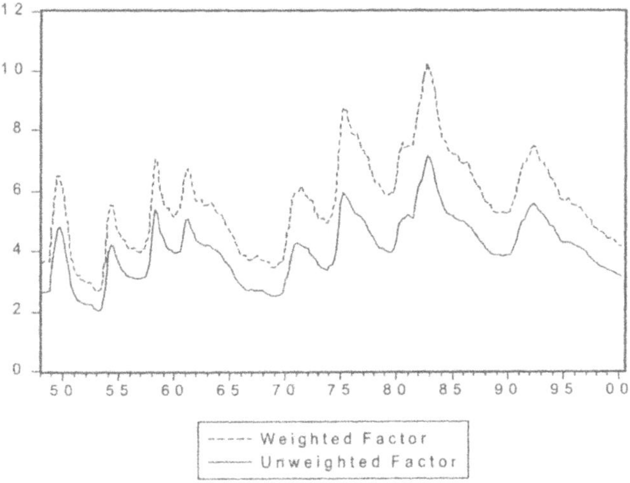

Fig. 6. Weighted and Unweighted Factors

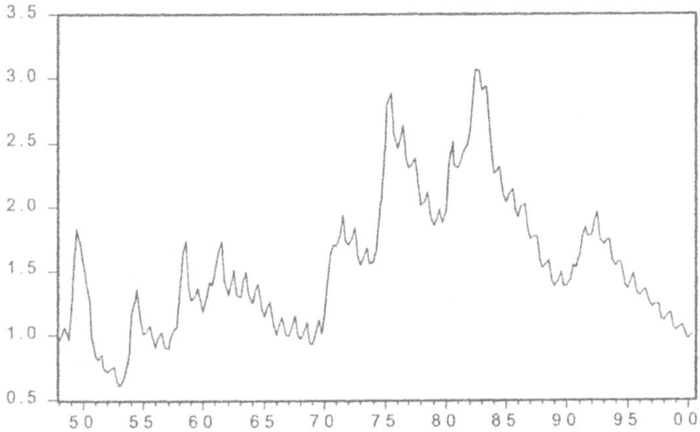

Fig. 7. Difference Between Weighted Factor and Unweighted Factor

which gives the difference between latent unemployment and a hypothetical labor market where all participants are in the 35–44 age group. Figure 6 shows the factor with and without demographic\factor loading weights, while Figure 7 plots the difference between these two variables, which corresponds to the series derived from the equation above.

There are some interesting findings from this analysis. First, changes in the composition of different age workers raise the aggregate unemployment rate from a minimum of 0.61% in the early 1950s to a maximum of 3.07% in 1982. The average impact of age composition on unemployment is 1.55% with a standard deviation of 0.54%. The entry of the baby boom into the labor market in the 1960s and 1970s increased the aggregate unemployment rate by about 1.8%.[13] The subsequent aging of the baby boomers has decreased unemployment by around 1.7%.[14] These findings are also similar to the ones obtained by Shimer's (1998).

A second interesting observation is that the baby boom effect induces a steep increase in the unemployment rate at the beginning of recessions in the 1970s and 1980s. In particular, the values of the difference between the unweighted and weighted factors doubled during the 1970, the 1975, and 1980–82 recessions. The reason is that the labor force weights of young labor market participants were increasing at the time that these switches to the high unemployment regime occurred. One can also observe that in the 1990 recession the impact of age on the unemployment rate was substantially smaller.

The properties of the dynamic factor stochastic model are very similar to those expected and broadly consistent with the sample moments given in Table 1 for the group of workers 35–44. Notice that this is not only the mid-group, but currently is also the one with the highest relative participation in the labor force. If we evaluate the parameters at their posterior means, the implied model is:

$$C_t = \begin{cases} 1.41 + 0.75C_{t-1} + \varepsilon_{1t} & \text{if } s_t = 1 \\ 0.16 + 0.94C_{t-1} + \varepsilon_{2t} & \text{if } s_t = 2 \end{cases},$$

with $P[s_{t+1} = 1 \mid s_t = 1] = \rho_{11} = 0.81$ and $P[s_{t+1} = 2 \mid s_t = 2] = \rho_{22} = 0.93$, $\varepsilon_{1t} \sim N(0, 0.48)$ and $\varepsilon_{2t} \sim N(0, 0.15)$.

However, analysis of the posterior means can be misleading, since they ignore the amount of uncertainty about each parameter and their joint variation. In order to gain some insight into the importance of this, we compare the posterior means of $\eta(1)$ and $\eta(2)$ and the average duration in each regime to those implied by the model evaluated at the posterior means of the parameters. In the high unemployment state, $\eta(1) = 5.81$ (compared to $\alpha_1/(1 - \phi_1) = 5.64$), while $\eta(2) = 2.55$, in state 2 (compared to $\alpha_2/(1 - \phi_2) = 2.66$). For the posterior mean of duration, state 2 lasts 16.9 quarters (compared to $1/(1 - \rho_{22}) =$ 14.3 quarters), while state 1 lasts 5.9 quarters (compared to $1/(1 - \rho_{11}) = 5.3$). Thus, the posterior means provide a reasonably accurate summary of the differences between regimes in terms of average dynamics.

Now, consider the following experiments with impact multipliers to illustrate the asymmetries in unemployment, which consist of sharp increases followed by long slow declines as implied by the model. Assume that the dynamic factor is in regime 1 with an unemployment rate of 5.5%, and that it switches to the low unemployment regime (state 2) with no future shocks. At first unemployment stays high ($\alpha_2 + \phi_2 \times 5.5 = 5.33$) and then it gradually declines. After 4 years, which is the typical duration of the low missmatch regime, the unemployment rate is equal to $[\alpha_2/(1 - \phi_2)] + \phi_2^{16} \times [5.5 - \alpha_2/(1 - \phi_2)] =$ 3.7. That is, it drops 63% of the way to the long run low unemployment level.

---

[13] More specifically, since the baby boomers correspond to births between 1946 and 1964, here we calculate the average difference between the two factors using sample from 1962 to 1983. This period corresponds to the years in which the first and last generations of the baby boomers were between age 16–19.

[14] This is calculated using sample from 1981 on, which corresponds to the year in which the first generation of the baby boomers reached the age of 35.

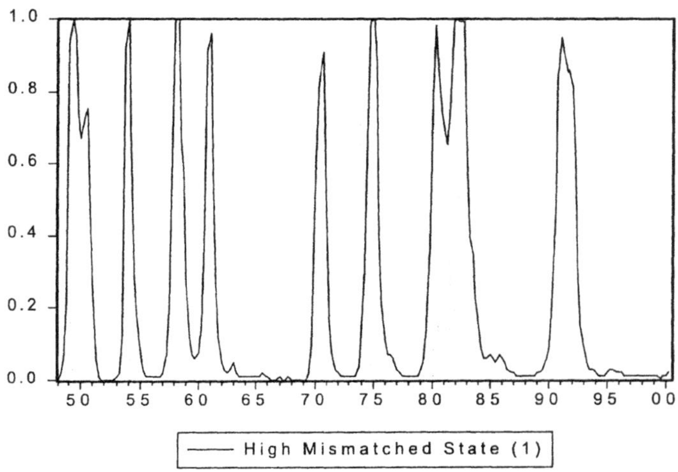

Fig. 8. Posterior Probabilities of High Mismatched State (1)

In contrast, if we start the dynamic factor in regime 2 with an unemployment rate of 2%, upon a switch to regime 1 unemployment immediately jumps to $(\alpha_1 + \phi_1 \times 2) = 2.91$. After 6 quarters, which is the average duration of the high mismatch regime, unemployment reaches a level of $[\alpha_1/(1-\phi_1)] + \phi_1^6 \times [2 - \alpha_1/(1-\phi_1)] = 5.0$, which corresponds to a 82% increase of the way to the long run high unemployment level.

One final aspect of interest in the estimated model is the large diference in the size of the shocks hitting the high unemployment regime versus the low unemployment regime. This difference implies that one should expect quite smooth downward movements in unemployment but more irregular upward movements, which is depicted in Figure 6. The asymmetries found in unemployment are also summarized in Figure 8, which plots the posterior mean of the high mismatch state. Unemployment switches to the high phase right at the beginning of recessions, and switches back to a low unemployment regime a couple of quarters after economic troughs, which illustrates the fast and steep growth of unemployment and its slower and more gradual decline around business cycle turning points. In addition, the high unemployment state is less persistent and corresponds to periods in which unemployment is more volatile, compared to the low unemployment state.

Overall, as shown by the Bayes factor and the collection of F-statistics displayed in Figure 4, there are large differences between the two regimes of unemployment. Furthermore, these differences are sensible and economically important.

6. Conclusions

This paper examines the secular and business cycle movements in unemployment over the past 50 years. We develop a common factor model with Markov switching to analyze disaggregate unemployment rates of workers grouped by age. We find a strong statistical evidence in favor of the common factor structure and of the switching between high and low unemployment rate regimes. In particular, the latent factor exhibits the stylized asymmetries in unemployment associated with the phases of the business cycle. In addition, the model captures the low frequency fluctuations in the U.S. unemployment rate associated with secular demographic changes. We find that demographic adjustments to the unemployment rate can account for a great deal of secular changes in the U.S. unemployment rates. In particular, they explain some of the increases in unemployment in the 1970s and 1980s, and the subsequent decrease in the last two decades.

The framework we have constructed is being extended in two main ways. First, we are examining the introduction of a second factor, in order to model short term fluctuations in disaggregate unemployment rates. In particular, the factor is identified by including changes in inflation rates and in output amongst the observed variables to identify business cycle patterns. The model implies a time-varying Phillips curve associated with the phases of the business cycle. Second, we are extending the framework to include a more detailed demographic decomposition of the total unemployment rate, using observations on unemployment rates by age, sex, education, and race.

7. Appendix

This appendix gives information on the prior distributions used in the Gibbs sampler and the resulting conditional posterior distributions.

1. **Factor Loadings:** we assume that the factor loadings are a priori normally distributed and independent of each other with mean $\mu(\underline{\lambda}_k)$ and precision $\tau(\underline{\lambda}_k)$. Conditional on $\{\tilde{C}_t\}$, $\Theta(L), \Sigma_K$ we draw the $K \times 1$ vector of factor loadings λ from (independent) normal distributions. For the generic loading λ_k we have the sample information:

$$\left[\sum_{t=q+1}^{T} C_{kt}^{*2}\right]^{-1}, \quad \sum_{t=q+1}^{T} C_{kt}^{*} U_{kt}^{*},$$

where $C_{kt}^{*} = \tilde{C}_t - \theta_{1k}\tilde{C}_{t-1} - \cdots - \theta_{qk}\tilde{C}_{t-q}$. Thus, the conditional posterior is normal with mean:

$$\frac{\tau(\underline{\lambda}_k)\mu(\underline{\lambda}_k) + \sum_{t=q+1}^{T} C_{kt}^{*} U_{kt}^{*}/\sigma_{kk}}{\tau(\underline{\lambda}_k) + \sum_{t=q+1}^{T} C_{kt}^{*2}/\sigma_{kk}}$$

and precision:

$$\left[\tau(\underline{\lambda}_k) + \sum_{t=q+1}^{T} C_{kt}^{*2}/\sigma_{kk}\right].$$

For one of the elements of λ we impose the prior belief that it is equal to 1.

2. **Innovation Variance to Measurement Error:** we assume that the innovation variances to the measurement errors are a priori independent inverted Gamma distributions with degrees of freedom of $\underline{\xi}$ and scale $\underline{s}^{-2}$. Conditional on $\{\tilde{C}_t\}$, $\Theta(L), \boldsymbol{\lambda}$ we draw the posterior of the measurement error innovations variances as independent gamma distributions. For the generic measurement error variance σ_{kk} we have the sample information:

$$\sum_{t=q+1}^{T} (U_{kt}^* - \lambda_k C_{kt}^*)^2, \quad T - q,$$

which is combined with the prior degrees of freedom of ξ and "prior sum of squares" $\underline{\xi s}^2$ to obtain the posterior degrees of freedom $\underline{\xi} + T - q$ and sum of squares $\underline{\xi s}^2 + \sum_{t=p+1}^{T} (U_{kt}^* - \lambda_k C_{kt}^*)^2$.
3. **Measurement Error Autoregressive Parameters:** we assume that the measurement error autoregressive parameters are truncated normal with the truncation determined by the stationarity condition. Since we use rejection sampling to implement the truncated prior, we start by describing the proposal distribution. The location and scale parameters of the truncated normal are given by the vector $\mu(\underline{\theta}_k)$ and matrix $\tau(\underline{\theta}_k)^{-1}$. Thus, without the stationarity condition we would have the Gaussian prior. Conditional on $\{\tilde{C}_t\}, \lambda, \Sigma_K$ we draw a proposed set of the measurement autoregressive coefficients from independent multivariate Gaussian distributions. For the generic measurement error autoregression k the sample information is:

$$[\mathbf{Z}_k'\mathbf{Z}_k]^{-1}, \quad \mathbf{Z}_k'\mathbf{W}_k,$$

where $\mathbf{W}_k = [\bar{U}_{kq+1}, \ldots, \bar{U}_{kT}]'$ and

$$\mathbf{Z}_k = \begin{bmatrix} \bar{U}_{kq} & \cdots & \bar{U}_{k1} \\ \bar{U}_{kq+1} & \cdots & \bar{U}_{k2} \\ \vdots & \vdots & \vdots \\ \bar{U}_{kT-1} & \cdots & \bar{U}_{kT-q} \end{bmatrix},$$

and $\bar{U}_{kt} = U_{kt} - \lambda_k C_t$. This is combined with the unrestricted Gaussian "prior" on the autoregressive coefficients in the standard way to obtain a normal distribution with variance matrix:

$$[\tau(\underline{\theta}_k) + \mathbf{Z}_k'\mathbf{Z}_k/\sigma_{kk}]^{-1}$$

and mean:

$$[\tau(\underline{\theta}_k) + \mathbf{Z}_k'\mathbf{Z}_k/\sigma_{kk}]^{-1}[\tau(\underline{\theta}_k)\mu(\underline{\theta}_k) + \mathbf{Z}_k'\mathbf{W}_k/\sigma_{kk}].$$

This distribution is used to generate draws until the stationarity condition is satisfied.
4. **Bayes Factor Calculation:** conditional on $\{\tilde{C}_t\}$, $\{s_t\}$ we calculate the marginal likelihood of $\{\tilde{C}_t\}$ under both the Markov switching model and the no switching model priors. As discussed in the main text this is an approximate calculation.

5. **Dynamic Factor Model Parameters:** as noted in the main text, assuming that $\{\boldsymbol{\beta}_i, \boldsymbol{\sigma}_i\}$ are a priori distributed normal inverted gamma and independently of each other simplifies the calculation of Bayes factors considerably. Conditional on $\{\tilde{C}_t\}$, $\{s_t\}$ we make candidate draws of the autoregressive model parameters for the two regimes from the posterior distributions, which are inverted-gamma normal distribution. These draws are made sequentially starting with the low unemployment regime first as described in the main text. Denote the prior precision matrix of $\boldsymbol{\beta}_i$ by $\tau(\underline{\beta}_i)\sigma_i^2$ and its prior mean by $\mu(\underline{\beta}_i)$. Let the prior degrees of freedom of σ_i^{-2} be $\underline{\nu}_i$ and its mean be $\underline{s}_i^{-2}$. The sample information is contained in the draw of the common factor and the Markov states. Let $y_{it} = 1(s_t = i)\tilde{C}_t$ and define the vector $\mathbf{y}_i^{\cdot} = [y_{i1+p}, \dots y_{iT}]'$ and the matrix:

$$\mathbf{X}_i = \begin{bmatrix} 1 & y_{ip} & \cdots & y_{i1} \\ \vdots & \vdots & \cdots & \vdots \\ 1 & y_{iT-1} & \cdots & y_{iT-p} \end{bmatrix}.$$

The posterior degrees of freedom of the variance in regime i are:

$$\bar{\upsilon}_i = \underline{\nu}_i + \sum_{t=1}^{T} 1(s_t = i).$$

The posterior scale of the inverted gamma is given by:

$$\begin{aligned}\overline{\upsilon s}_i^2 &= \underline{\nu}_i\underline{s}^2 + \upsilon s^2 + [\mu(\bar{\boldsymbol{\beta}}_i) - \boldsymbol{\beta}_i]'\mathbf{X}_i'\mathbf{X}_i[\mu(\bar{\boldsymbol{\beta}}_i) - \mathbf{X}_i] \\ &\quad + [\mu(\bar{\boldsymbol{\beta}}_i) - \mu(\underline{\boldsymbol{\beta}}_i)]'\tau(\underline{\beta}_i)[\mu(\bar{\boldsymbol{\beta}}_i) - \mu(\underline{\beta}_i)],\end{aligned}$$

where the posterior mean of $\boldsymbol{\beta}_i$ is:

$$\mu(\bar{\boldsymbol{\beta}}_i) = \tau(\bar{\boldsymbol{\beta}}_i)[\tau(\underline{\beta}_i)\mu(\underline{\beta}_i) + \mathbf{X}_i'\mathbf{y}_i],$$

the posterior precision matrix is:

$$\tau(\bar{\boldsymbol{\beta}}_i) = \tau(\underline{\beta}_i) + \mathbf{X}_i'\mathbf{X}_i$$

and sample sum of squared errors is:

$$\upsilon s^2 = [\mathbf{y}_i - \mathbf{X}_i\hat{\boldsymbol{\beta}}_i]'[\mathbf{y}_i - \mathbf{X}_i\hat{\boldsymbol{\beta}}_i].$$

In addition,

$$\hat{\boldsymbol{\beta}}_i = [\mathbf{X}_i'\mathbf{X}_i]^{-1}\mathbf{X}_i'\mathbf{y}_i.$$

The candidate draws are obtained by first drawing a value of σ_i^2 from a Gamma distribution with posterior degrees of freedom and scale given above. This draw is then used to obtain the posterior variance of $\boldsymbol{\beta}_i$ as $\sigma_i^2\tau(\bar{\boldsymbol{\beta}}_i)^{-1}$. This variance together with the mean described above is used to obtain a candidate draw of $\boldsymbol{\beta}_i$. If the draw is rejected, we draw σ_i^2 and $\boldsymbol{\beta}_i$ again and repeat until a succesful draw is obtained.

6. **Markov States:** conditional on $\{\tilde{C}_t\}, p_{11}, p_{22}, \beta_1, \beta_2, \sigma_1, \sigma_2$, we draw the sequence $\{s_t\}$ as discussed in the main text using the methods of Chib (1996) with the restriction that $S_1 = \cdots = S_p = 2$.
7. **Transition Probabilities:** we assume that the transition probabilities are a priori independent with a Beta distribution. Under the Beta distribution prior, the posterior is also in the Beta family. We focus on updating the transition probabilities for state 1, as the case for state 2 follows analagously. The Beta density is proportional to:

$$p_{11}^{\delta_{11}-1}(1-p_{11})^{\delta_{12}-1}, \quad \underline{\delta}_{11} > 0,\ \delta_{12} > 0.$$

The updating of the parameters of the Beta distribution is direct with:

$$\bar{\delta}_{11} = \underline{\delta}_{11} + \sum_{t=p+1}^{T} P[S_t = 1, S_{t-1} = 1 \mid \tilde{C}^T],$$

$$\bar{\delta}_{12} = \underline{\delta}_{12} + \sum_{t=p+1}^{T} P[S_t = 2, S_{t-1} = 1 \mid \tilde{C}^T].$$

8. **Common Factor:** conditional on $\Theta(L), \lambda, \Sigma_K, \beta_1, \beta_2, \sigma_1, \sigma_2$, the Kalman filter is run on the observed data. The Kalman filter is initialized at the stationary distribution for $\{C_t\}$ implied by $\tilde{\boldsymbol{\beta}}_2, \sigma_2$. Then, using the recursions described above, a draw of $\{\tilde{C}_t\}$ is obtained and we return to step 1 above. We also calculate various features of the latent unemployment rate using the draw of the common factor and factor loading.

References

Abbring JH, Berg GJVD, Ours JCV (1999) Business cycles and compositional variation in U.S. unemployment. Tinbergen Institute Working Paper 97-050/3

Albert J, Chib S (1993) Bayes inference via Gibbs sampling of autoregressive time series subject to markov mean and variance shifts. Journal of Business and Economic Statistics 11:1–15

Boldin M (1994) Dating turning points in the business cycle. Journal of Business 1:97–131

Carter C, Kohn P (1994) On Gibbs sampling for state space models. Biometrika 81:541–553

Chauvet M (1998) An econometric characterization of business cycle dynamics with factor structure and regime switches. International Economic Review 39(4):969–96

Chib S (1995) Marginal likelihood from Gibbs output. Journal of American Statistical Association 90:1313–1321

Chib S (1996) Calculating posterior distributions and modal estimates in Markov mixture models. Journal of Econometrics 75:79–97

Chib S (2001a) Monte Carlo methods and Bayesian computation: Overview. In: Fienberg SE, Kadane JB (eds) International Encyclopedia of the Social and Behavioral Sciences: Statistics, Amsterdam: Elsevier Science, in press

Chib S (2001b) Markov Chain Monte Carlo methods: Computation and inference. In: Heckman JJ, Leamer E (eds) Handbook of Econometrics, vol. 5, Amsterdam: North Holland, in press

De Jong P, Shephard N (1995) The simulation smoother for time series models. Biometrika 82:339–350

Denman J, McDonald P (1996) Unemployment statistics from 1881 to the present day. Labour Market Trends 5–18

Diebold FX, Rudebusch GD (1996) Measuring business cycles: A modern perspective. Review of Economics and Statistics 78:67–77

Franses PH (1995) Quarterly U.S. unemployment: Cycles, seasons and asymmetries. Empirical Economics 20:717–725

Fruhwirth-Schnatter S (1994) Data augmentation and dynamic linear models. Journal of Time Series Analysis 15:183–202

Geweke J (1977) The dynamic factor analysis of economics time series model. In: Aigner D, Goldberg A (eds) Latent Variables in Socioeconomic Models, 365–383. Amsterdam: North-Holland

Geweke J (1986) Exact inference in the inequality contrained normal linear regression model. Journal of Applied Econometrics 1:127–142

Geweke J (1999) Using simulation methods for Bayesian econometric models: Inference, development and communication. Econometric Reviews 18:1–126

Gordon R (1982) Inflation, flexible exchange rates and the natural rate of unemployment. In: Martin Baily edited Workers, Jobs and Inflation Brookings 89–152

Hamilton J (1989) A new approach to the economic analysis of nonstationary time series and the business cycle. Econometrica 57:357–384

Juhn CK, Murphy M, Topel R (1991) Why has the natural rate of unemployment increased over time? Brookings Papers On Economic Activity 75–126

Katz LF, Krueger AB (1999) New trend in unemployment? Brookings Review 4:4–8

Kim CJ (1994) Dynamic linear models with Markov-switching. Journal of Econometrics 60:1–22

Kim C-J, Nelson C (1999) State space models with regime switching: Classical and Gibbs-sampling approaches with applications. Cambridge: MIT Press

Koop G, Potter SM (1999) Bayes factors and nonlinearity: Evidence from economic time series. Journal of Econometrics 88:251–281

Koop G, Potter SM (2000) Nonlinearity, structural breaks or outliers in economic time series? In: Nonlinear Econometric Modeling in Time Series Analysis, William Barnett (ed) Cambridge: Cambridge University Press 61–78

Montgomery AL, Zarnowitz V, Tsay RS, Tiao GC (1998) Forecasting the U.S. unemployment rate. Journal of the American Statistical Association 442:478–493

Neftci S (1984) Are economic time series asymmetric over the business cycle. Journal of Poltical Economy 92:307–328

Rothman P (1993) Further evidence on the asymmetric behavior of unemployment rates over the cycle. Journal of Macroeconomics 13:291–298

Shephard N (1994) Partial non-gaussian state space. Biometrika 81:115–131

Shimer R (1998) Why is the unemployment rate so much lower? In: Bernanke B, Rotemberg JJ (eds) NBER Macroeconomics Annual, Cambridge, MIT Press 11–61

Skalin J, Teräsvirta T (2001) Modelling asymmetries and moving equilibria in unemployment rates. Forthcoming in Macroeconomic Dynamics

Stock JH, Watson MW (1989) New indices of coincident and leading indicators. In: Blanchard O, Fischer S (eds) NBER Macroeconomics Annual, Cambridge, MIT Press

Vredin A, Warne A (2000) Unemployment and inflation regimes. Mimeo, Research Department, Sveriges Riksbank

III The Business Cycle in Other Countries

A Markov–switching vector equilibrium correction model of the UK labour market

Hans-Martin Krolzig[1], **Massimiliano Marcellino**[2], **Grayham E. Mizon**[3]*

[1] Department of Economics and Nuffield College, Oxford University, Manor Road Building, Oxford OX1 3UQ, U.K.
[2] Istituto di Economia Politica, Università Bocconi and IGIER
[3] Economics Department, University of Southampton, Southampton SO17 1BJ U.K.

First Version Received: December 2000/Final Version Received: August 2001

Abstract. There is a wide literature on the dynamic adjustment of employment and its relationship with the business cycle. In this paper we present a statistical model that offers a congruent representation of part of the UK labour market since the mid 1960s. We use a cointegrated vector autoregressive Markov-switching model in which some parameters change according to the phase of the business cycle. Output, employment, labour supply and real earnings are found to have a common cyclical component. The long run dynamics are characterized by one cointegrating vector relating unemployment to trend-adjusted real wages and output. Despite there having been many changes affecting this sector of the UK economy, the Markov-switching vector-equilibrium-correction model with three regimes (representing recession, normal growth, and high growth) provides a good characterization of the sample data, and performs well relative to alternative linear and nonlinear models. The results of an impulse-response analysis highlight the dangers of using VARs when the constancy of the estimated coefficients has not been established, and demonstrate the advantages of generating regime dependent responses.

Key words: Business Cycles, Employment, Impulse-Response Analysis, Cointegration, Regime Shifts, Markov Switching.

JEL classification: E32, E37, C32, E24

---

* We are grateful to the guest editors, James Hamilton and Baldev Raj, and two anonymous referees for valuable comments and suggestions on a previous version of this paper. We also thank David Hendry for useful discussions during the preparation of this version of the paper. Financial support from the UK Economic and Social Research Council under grant L116251015 is gratefully acknowledged by the first and third authors.

1. Introduction

There have been numerous studies analyzing the time series relationships between wages, prices, productivity and unemployment in the UK (recent examples include Clements and Mizon, 1991, Mizon, 1995, Sgherri and Wallis, 2000 and Marcellino and Mizon, 2000). Most of these studies have found evidence of structural change, and have modelled it via split-sample analysis with a single break occurring around 1979, possibly with additional dummy variables to capture the effects of other changes affecting the UK labour market.

As an alternative to this deterministic approach to structural change and regime shifts, in this paper we develop a small model of part of the UK labour market using a multivariate Markov-switching vector equilibrium correction model (MS-VECM). This methodology is well suited to model the domestic and international cyclical swings that affected the UK economy, and it allows for changing relationships among the labour market variables across different phases of the business cycle. The results we obtain are easily interpretable, from both an economic and an econometric perspective. First, we find an equilibrium relationship that indicates that unemployment increases with deviations of the real wage from its overall trend, and decreases during expansions. Second, switches in the regimes are closely related to changes in the phases of the UK business cycle: the first regime is associated with recessions, the second and the third regimes with periods of normal and sustained growth respectively. Third, the MS-VECM provides a congruent statistical representation for the data, and the restrictions that lead to a standard linear model are strongly rejected. Fourth, the MS-VECM performs well in forecasting.

Another important characteristic of our MS-VECM is that the contemporaneous covariance matrix of the residuals is also regime switching, and substantial differences across regimes emerge. Hence, standard impulse response analysis is likely to lead to severely misleading results. We show that this is indeed the case, and derive the appropriate response functions for each regime. Moreover, the standard approach focuses on the response of the system to Gaussian innovations, even though other shocks could affect the system. In particular, changes in the phase of the cycle is what some economists have in mind when they refer to 'cyclical shocks', namely, investigating the dynamics of some variables in the transition from boom to bust, or vice versa. Within our framework, we also present response functions for this type of shock.

The structure of the paper is the following. Section 2 describes the data and some of the major changes that have taken place in the UK labour market. The specification of a Vector Equilibrium Correction Model (VECM) with non-constant parameters for the period 1965–2001 is described in section 3, and the particular form of the MS-VECM used in this paper is presented in section 4, which also contains the empirical results: firstly for the cointegrated VAR in section 4.1, and then for the MS-VECM in section 4.2. Section 5 contains a comparison of the impulse response functions of the alternative models, and illustrates the susceptibility of such analyses to non-constant parameters. The forecasting performance of the alternative models is evaluated in section 6. Section 7 summarizes and provides conclusions.

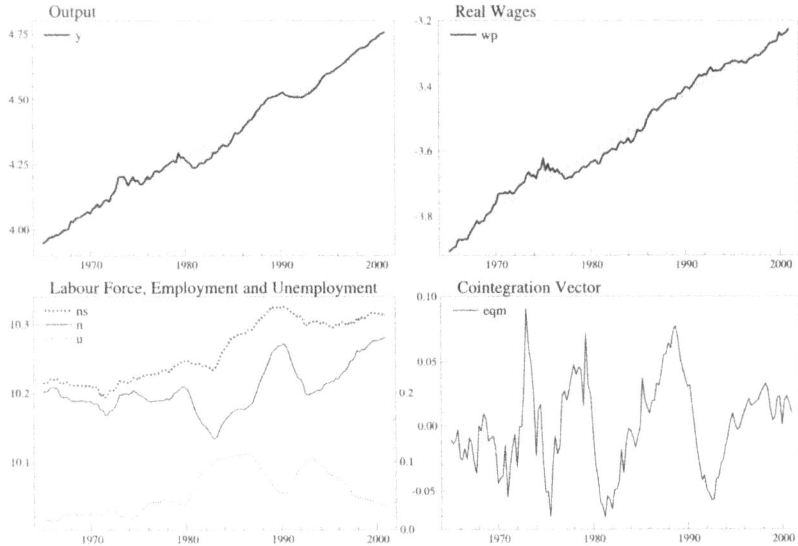

Fig. 1. The variables under analysis and the restricted equilibrium.

2. The data

The seasonally adjusted quarterly data for the UK are similar to those used in Clements and Mizon (1991), Mizon (1995) and Marcellino and Mizon (2000), extended to cover the period 1965(1)–2001(1). The original sources for these data are "Economic Trends" and "Monthly Digest of Statistics" published by the UK Office of National Statistics – more details are contained in the data appendix A.

The output variable, y_t, is the log of total constant price value added. Employment and the labour force, n_t and ns_t, are the logs of the number of employees and the total labour force in the whole economy respectively. The earnings variable, e_t, is the log of the ratio of wages and salaries to the number of employees. The price variable, p_t, is the log of the value added deflator.[1] The real wage, wp_t, is given by the log of real earnings ($wp_t = e_t - p_t$). This broad definition of the real wage is in line with earlier studies by Hall (1986) and Hall (1989). The variables are graphed in Figure 1. The first two panels of which show the strong trend in both output and real wages. The third panel shows the evolution of employment and the labour force, as well as their difference $u_t = (ns_t - n_t)$ as a measure of unemployment. The fourth panel graphs the restricted equilibrium relationship that is estimated in section 4.1 and used in section 4.2.

Notable events affecting the UK labour market in the sample period include the following. There was a big increase in real wages in 1975 associated with the ending of a period of statutory wage and price control. Unemployment increased strongly throughout most of the sample period, with some

[1] Similar results are obtained with the retail price index.

business cycle fluctuations. The decline in 1966 is related to the introduction of the "selective employment tax", which aimed to increase employment in manufacturing industries, though it was subsequently reduced by 50% in 1971. The substantial reductions in unemployment in 1974 and 1988/89 were mainly the delayed consequences of pre-election expansionary policies. 1974 was a turbulent year in the UK labour market with numerous strikes and the 3 Day Week restrictions leading to a change of government, followed by a strong increase in unemployment. There was also a major policy regime shift in late 1979 from broadly Keynesian full-employment to monetarist anti-inflation policies. A number of legislative changes were introduced in the early 1980s with the general effect of liberalizing the labour market. As a result of this and the tight monetary policy adopted to reduce the aggregate rate of inflation, there was a substantial increase in unemployment in the early and late 1980s. In addition, throughout the sample period there was an increase in female labour participation, which in turn led to more part-time working. The UK economy experienced a recession in the early 1990s, and sterling was forced out of the European Exchange Rate Mechanism in September 1992. Following the resulting devaluation there was steady growth in GDP, an increase in employment, and since the size of the labour force changed little from 1993 there was a steady reduction in unemployment to the end of the sample period. Overall there was less volatility in wages, prices, GDP, employment and unemployment post-1980 than pre-1980. Hence difficulties are likely to be experienced in attempting to develop VAR models with constant parameters for a small number of labour market variables. However, a MS-VECM may be better able to represent these events via changes in some of its parameters across regimes.

3. Modelling cointegrated systems with non-constant parameters

Clements and Hendry (1999) showed that unmodelled shifts in deterministic variables, such as intercepts and trends, are the major cause of forecast failure in econometric models, and that these shifts are detectable by conventional tests for parameter constancy such as those in Chow (1960). On the other hand, changes in short run adjustment coefficients and in the equilibrium coefficients are difficult to detect. Hence, we focus here on changes in the mean growth rates of the N variables in $\mathbf{x}_t$ and in the means of the r equilibrium relationships $\boldsymbol{\beta}'\mathbf{x}_t$. In particular, we consider a VECM for the I(1) variables $\mathbf{x}_t$ with intercept shifts introduced:

$$\Delta\mathbf{x}_t = \mathbf{v}(s_t) + \boldsymbol{\alpha\beta}'\mathbf{x}_{t-1} + \mathbf{u}_t, \quad \mathbf{u}_t|s_t \sim \mathsf{NID}(\mathbf{0}, \boldsymbol{\Sigma}), \tag{1}$$

where s_t denotes the unobservable regime indicator variable $s_t \in \{1, \dots, M\}$, $\boldsymbol{\alpha}$ and $\boldsymbol{\beta}$ are $N \times r$ matrices of rank r, and for simplicity only one period lags are introduced into the system and the error covariance matrix is assumed constant. Note that the intercept v is a function of the underlying state:

$$\mathbf{v}(s_t) = \mathbf{v}_{s_t} = \begin{cases} \mathbf{v}_1 & \text{if } s_t = 1 \\ \vdots & \\ \mathbf{v}_\mathrm{M} & \text{if } s_t = M. \end{cases} \tag{2}$$

and can be decomposed into:

$$\mathbf{v}(s_t) = \boldsymbol{\beta}_\perp(\boldsymbol{\alpha}_\perp'\boldsymbol{\beta}_\perp)^{-1}\boldsymbol{\alpha}_\perp'\mathbf{v}(s_t) + \boldsymbol{\alpha}(\boldsymbol{\beta}'\boldsymbol{\alpha})^{-1}\boldsymbol{\beta}'\mathbf{v}(s_t)$$
$$= \boldsymbol{\beta}_\perp\boldsymbol{\delta}^*(s_t) + \boldsymbol{\alpha}\boldsymbol{\mu}(s_t)$$

when $\boldsymbol{\alpha}_\perp$ and $\boldsymbol{\beta}_\perp$ are $N \times (N-r)$ matrices such that $\boldsymbol{\alpha}_\perp'\boldsymbol{\alpha} = \mathbf{0}$ and $\boldsymbol{\beta}_\perp'\boldsymbol{\beta} = \mathbf{0}$. This means that there are $(N-r)$ linearly independent but state-dependent drifts $\boldsymbol{\delta}^*(s_t)$, and r linearly independent but state-dependent equilibrium means $\boldsymbol{\mu}(s_t)$ in the system. Hence, the process (1) can be represented as:

$$\Delta\mathbf{x}_t - \boldsymbol{\beta}_\perp\boldsymbol{\delta}^*(s_t) = \boldsymbol{\alpha}(\boldsymbol{\beta}'\mathbf{x}_{t-1} - \boldsymbol{\mu}(s_t)) + \mathbf{u}_t, \quad \mathbf{u}_t|s_t \sim \mathsf{NID}(\mathbf{0}, \boldsymbol{\Sigma}). \tag{3}$$

In (3), both $\Delta\mathbf{x}_t$ and $\boldsymbol{\beta}'\mathbf{x}_t$ are expressed as deviations about their regime- and time-dependent means, $\boldsymbol{\beta}_\perp\boldsymbol{\delta}^*(s)$ and $\boldsymbol{\mu}(s)$ respectively. Hence, each regime is characterized by an attractor of the system defined by the equilibrium value of the cointegration vector and the drift. Such a formulation is closely related to the notion of multiple equilibria in dynamic economic theory (see e.g. Cooper and John, 1988).

Two implications of the condition $\mathsf{E}[\Delta\mathbf{x}_t\,|\,s] = \boldsymbol{\beta}_\perp\boldsymbol{\delta}^*(s)$ with $s_t = s_{t-1} = \cdots = s$ are worth noting. First, the mean growth rate of the equilibria $\boldsymbol{\beta}'\mathbf{x}_t$ is zero, i.e.,

$$\mathsf{E}[\Delta\boldsymbol{\beta}'\mathbf{x}_t\,|\,s] = \mathsf{E}[\boldsymbol{\beta}'\Delta\mathbf{x}_t\,|\,s] = \boldsymbol{\beta}'\mathsf{E}[\Delta\mathbf{x}_t\,|\,s] = \boldsymbol{\beta}'\boldsymbol{\beta}_\perp\boldsymbol{\delta}^*(s) = \mathbf{0}. \tag{4}$$

Second, if we interpret $\boldsymbol{\beta}_\perp'\mathbf{x}_t$ as stochastic trends in the system, then their mean growth rate in regime $s_t = s_{t-1} = \cdots = s$ is given by $\boldsymbol{\delta}^*(s)$, i.e.,

$$\mathsf{E}[\Delta\boldsymbol{\beta}_\perp'\mathbf{x}_t\,|\,s] = \mathsf{E}[\boldsymbol{\beta}_\perp'\Delta\mathbf{x}_t\,|\,s] = \boldsymbol{\beta}_\perp'\mathsf{E}[\Delta\mathbf{x}_t\,|\,s] = \boldsymbol{\beta}_\perp'\boldsymbol{\beta}_\perp\boldsymbol{\delta}^*(s) = \boldsymbol{\delta}^*(s).$$

Considering instead the stochastic trends represented by $\boldsymbol{\alpha}_\perp'\mathbf{x}_t$, as in Gonzalo and Granger (1995), then their expected change is

$$\mathsf{E}[\Delta\boldsymbol{\alpha}_\perp'\mathbf{x}_t\,|\,s] = \mathsf{E}[\boldsymbol{\alpha}_\perp'\Delta\mathbf{x}_t\,|\,s] = \boldsymbol{\alpha}_\perp'\mathsf{E}[\Delta\mathbf{x}_t\,|\,s] = \boldsymbol{\alpha}_\perp'\boldsymbol{\beta}_\perp\boldsymbol{\delta}^*(s) = \boldsymbol{\alpha}_\perp'\mathbf{v}(s).$$

When the changes in $\mathbf{v}(s_t)$ are due to a small number of deterministic shifts at known dates, their effects can be captured by including in the model an appropriate set of dummy variables. This is a common approach in empirical modelling of macroeconomic time series, and Clements and Mizon (1991) provide an example in the context of a small econometric model of the UK labour market. A similar approach can be adopted when there are changes in $\boldsymbol{\alpha}$ and $\boldsymbol{\beta}$ as well as the intercepts. However, in this latter case, when the sub-samples permit, a valuable alternative is to conduct a split sample analysis of the data. Again with reference to the UK labour market, Marcellino and Mizon (2000) distinguish between the pre- and post-Thatcher period, finding evidence of substantial differences between the two sub-periods.

When the regime shifts are stochastic rather than deterministic both previous approaches can lead to biased, or at least inefficient, results. In this case, it is possible to enlarge the system by adding variables that are related to the regime shifts, such as policy variables, energy and raw material prices, and demographic and social indicators. Yet, it is difficult to jointly model the resulting enlarged set of variables, and conditioning on the regime shift related variables may not be valid and even if it were would not solve the forecasting problem (see Marcellino and Mizon, 2001a for more details).

Therefore, a multivariate generalization of the univariate Markov-switching model originally proposed by Hamilton (1989) provides a viable alternative. The general idea behind the class of MS models is that some of the parameters depend upon a stochastic, unobservable regime indicator variable $s_t \in \{1, \dots, M\}$. The stochastic process for generating the unobservable regimes is an ergodic Markov chain, defined by the transition probabilities:

$$p_{ij} = \Pr(s_{t+1} = j \mid s_t = i), \quad \sum_{j=1}^{M} p_{ij} = 1 \quad \forall i, j \in \{1, \dots, M\}. \tag{5}$$

By inferring the probabilities of the unobserved regimes conditional on an available information set, it is then possible to reconstruct the regimes. For an ergodic Markov chain, regime shifts are persistent if $p_{ij} \neq p_{ii}$ for some $i \neq j$, but not permanent if $p_{ii} \neq 1$ for all i. Further, (3) and (5) define a MSI-VECM (see Krolzig, 1997) when MSI refers to a Markov-switching intercept. The MSI-VECM exhibits equilibrium as well as error correction mechanisms: in each regime disequilibria are adjusted by the *vector equilibrium correction mechanism*; since the regimes themselves are generated by stationary, irreducible Markov chain; *errors* arising from regime shifts themselves are *corrected* towards the stationary distribution of the regimes.

Markov-switching models of multiple time series (see Krolzig, 1997, for an overview) provide a powerful statistical tool for extracting the common component from a group of economic time series representing the business cycle. In their investigation of the interaction of the UK business cycle with changes in the industrial structure of the UK economy during the last three decades, Krolzig and Sensier (2000) propose a Markov-switching vector equilibrium correction model with three regimes representing recession, normal growth and high growth. In their model the regime shifts simultaneously affect the common growth rate and the sectoral equilibrium allocation of industrial production identifying a common cycle which is closely related to traditional datings of the UK business cycle. Hence, an MSI-VECM appears to be a promising alternative specification for a small model of the UK labour market.

4. An MSIH-VECM for real wages, output, and employment

Following Krolzig (1997) we adopt a Markov-switching vector equilibrium correction model with shifts in the drift $\boldsymbol{\delta}(s_t)$ and in the equilibrium mean $\boldsymbol{\mu}(s_t)$:

$$\begin{aligned} \Delta \mathbf{x}_t - \boldsymbol{\delta}(s_t) &= \boldsymbol{\alpha}(\boldsymbol{\beta}' \mathbf{x}_{t-1} - \boldsymbol{\mu}(s_t) - \boldsymbol{\gamma}(t-1)) \\ &\quad + \sum_{k=1}^{p-1} \boldsymbol{\Gamma}_k (\Delta \mathbf{x}_{t-k} - \boldsymbol{\delta}(s_t)) + \mathbf{u}_t, \end{aligned} \tag{6}$$

and the error variance is allowed to change across states $\mathbf{u}_t | s_t \sim \mathsf{NID}(\mathbf{0}, \boldsymbol{\Sigma}(s_t))$. Krolzig (1997) denotes this model by MSIH-VECM, where the H refers to heteroscedasticity in the error process. Note that $\boldsymbol{\beta}'\boldsymbol{\delta}(s) = \mathbf{0}$ since $\mathsf{E}[\Delta \mathbf{x}_t \mid s] = \boldsymbol{\delta}(s) = \boldsymbol{\beta}_\perp \boldsymbol{\delta}^*(s)$ from (4). The vector $\mathbf{x}_t$ includes output (y_t), real wages (wp_t), employment (n_t), and the labour force (ns_t), where the latter is included in the system to capture some changes in demographic and social conditions, such as different birth rates and female participation rates. As discussed in section 2, other variables might affect and modify the relationships between y_t, wp_t, n_t and ns_t. Within the framework of the MSIH-VECM in (6) their effects are captured by $\boldsymbol{\delta}(s_t)$, $\boldsymbol{\mu}(s_t)$ and $\boldsymbol{\Sigma}(s_t)$. As in (5), the unobservable regime variable s_t is governed by a Markov chain with a finite number of states (3 in our case), defined by the transition probabilities p_{ij}.

Each regime, m, is associated with a particular attractor (μ_m, δ_m). Regime shifts in δ_m are interpreted as changes in the state of the business cycle, regime shifts in μ_m as changes in the equilibrium mean $\boldsymbol{\mu}(s_t)$. Note that changes in the equilibrium mean's deterministic trend, γt, are not considered. In the results presented below we find one equilibrium relationship indicating that unemployment (proxied by $ns - n$) increases with 'excess real wages' and decreases with 'excess income'. Hence, changes in μ_m reflect changes in equilibrium unemployment, real wages and income, the latter two trend adjusted.

We now estimate the MSIH-VECM in (6) using the data described in section 2. The estimation method used is the two-stage procedure suggested by Krolzig (1996): first we investigate the cointegration properties of the system; then we present the results from estimating the MSIH-VECM. On the first stage, the cointegration properties of the MS-VECM can be analyzed by applying Johansen's maximum likelihood procedure (see Johansen, 1995) to a finite-order vector autoregressive approximation of the underlying DGP. On the second stage, conditional on the estimated cointegrated matrix, the maximum likelihood estimation of the parameters of the MS-VECM can be based on a version of the Expectation-Maximization (EM) algorithm discussed in Hamilton (1990) and Krolzig (1997). The computations are carried out with the MSVAR class for Ox, see Krolzig (1998) and Doornik (1999).

4.1. Cointegration analysis

The cointegration properties of the data are studied within a linear VAR representation using the maximum likelihood procedure of Johansen (1995) for the sample period 1965(1) to 2001(1). The VAR(p) is here considered as an approximation of the VARMA representation of a MSI-VAR process. Thus the following cointegration analysis is a limited information maximum likelihood technique.

Starting with a VAR(6) and deleting lags which were not significant according to a likelihood ratio (LR) test, led us to a VAR(4). Although the AIC information criterion leads to the choice of a VAR(2) there is more evidence of mis-specification in the VAR(2) than the VAR(4). The Johansen procedure for cointegration analysis as implemented in PcGive (see Johansen, 1988 and Doornik and Hendry, 2001) is then applied to the VECM representation of a VAR with four lags of $\mathbf{x}_t$, a constant, and a linear trend restricted to lie in the cointegration space:

$$\Delta \mathbf{x}_t = \mathbf{v} + \sum_{k=1}^{3} \boldsymbol{\Gamma}_k \Delta \mathbf{x}_{t-k} + \boldsymbol{\alpha}(\boldsymbol{\beta}'\mathbf{x}_{t-1} - \boldsymbol{\gamma}(t-1)) + \mathbf{u}_t. \tag{7}$$

The results of the cointegration tests are shown in Table 1, with the trace test statistics accepting the hypothesis $r = 1$ at the 10%. There is no remaining autocorrelation (vector AR 1–5 test: $F(80, 396) = 0.91$ with a p-value of 0.69) but there is strong evidence of non-normality in the residuals (vector normal-

Table 1. Johansen cointegration likelihood ratio test

eigenvalue	H_0 : rank $= r$	trace test	pvalue
0.1743	$r = 0$	60.711	[0.088]
0.1389	$r \leq 1$	33.699	[0.307]
0.0690	$r \leq 2$	12.621	[0.767]
0.0178	$r \leq 3$	2.536	[0.913]

ity test $\chi^2(8) = 51.34$ with a p-value of 0.00). The latter is most likely the result of the many outliers present in the estimated VAR. Although this can result in under-estimation of cointegrating rank, our subsequent results which allow for Markov switching between three separate regimes suggest that this is not the case.

We then identify the cointegrating vector by applying a set of non-rejected restrictions, the LR test for which is $\chi^2(2) = 1.55$ with a p-value of 0.46. The equilibrium indicates that unemployment (proxied by $ns - n$) increases with positive deviations of the real wage from a linear trend, and with negative deviations of output from a linear trend. After mean adjustment this equilibrium has the form:

$$eqm_t = ns_t - n_t - \underset{(0.19)}{0.85}\,(wp_t - \underset{(-)}{0.0048}\,t) + \underset{(0.21)}{1.91}\,(y_t - \underset{(-)}{0.0056}\,t) - \underset{(0.003)}{10.89} \tag{8}$$

The coefficients of the trends are restricted to coincide with the average growth of the variables over the period under analysis, about 2% per year for the real wage and 2.2% for output. Hence, unemployment decreases with the output gap as predicted by Okun's law, and increases when the accumulated growth of the real wage exceeds its average level (which, it is worth noting, coincides with the average growth of productivity $(y - n)$, about 2% per year).

From an economic point of view, the equilibrium is coherent with models of imperfectly competitive goods and labour markets, where the wage is set in a bargaining process between unions and firms, and the latter determine the level of employment given the wage, and the price level given the wage and demand, see e.g. Kaufman (1994). This theoretical framework is more strictly followed by Sgherri and Wallis (2000) in the development of a small scale structural model of the UK, to be used for the evaluation of monetary policy rules.

Equation (9) reports the estimated coefficients of the equilibrium for each variable in the VECM – the estimated lag coefficients and constants have been omitted for simplicity. The only coefficient of the equilibrium that appears to be statistically significant, that in the GDP equation, has an appropriate sign. However, the equilibrium indirectly affects wp_t, n_t and ns_t through their dependence on lags of y_t.

$$\begin{aligned} \widehat{\Delta wp_t} &= \underset{(0.04)}{0.05}\ eqm_{t-1}, & \widehat{\Delta ns_t} &= \underset{(0.014)}{0.002}\ eqm_{t-1}, \\ \widehat{\Delta n_t} &= \underset{(0.015)}{0.002}\ eqm_{t-1}, & \widehat{\Delta y_t} &= -\underset{(0.04)}{0.14}\ eqm_{t-1}. \end{aligned} \tag{9}$$

Table 2. Persistence of regimes

	Ergodic Probability	Duration	Observations
Regime 1	0.1231	2.73	17.8
Regime 2	0.6355	16.62	89.0
Regime 3	0.2414	4.82	35.2

4.2. The MS-VECM

The cointegration results from the last section are now used in the second stage of our analysis. We adopt an MSIH-VECM with 3 regimes and 2 lags (MSIH(3)-VECM(2)) model, with shifts in the intercept $\mathbf{v}$ and the error variance $\mathbf{\Sigma}$. Two lags is the outcome of an HQ model selection procedure for the lag length p, which is coherent with the result for the VAR in levels, while the number of regimes is fixed a priori, with the aim of capturing periods of low, normal, and high growth. Hence, the resulting model is

$$\Delta \mathbf{x}_t = \mathbf{v}(s_t) + \boldsymbol{\alpha}(\boldsymbol{\beta}'\mathbf{x}_{t-1} - \boldsymbol{\gamma}(t-1)) + \boldsymbol{\Gamma}\Delta \mathbf{x}_{t-1} + \mathbf{u}_t, \tag{10}$$

where $(\boldsymbol{\beta}'\mathbf{x}_{t-1} - \boldsymbol{\gamma}(t-1))$ is the mean-adjusted full sample estimate as defined in (8) and $\mathbf{u}_t|s_t \sim \mathsf{NID}(\mathbf{0}, \mathbf{\Sigma}(s_t))$.

The estimated parameters of the MS-VECM defined in equation (10) using data from 1965(4) to 2000(1) are presented in Table 4. Note that regime 1 is characterized by contraction in output, employment and labour supply, while all three variables expand in regime 3. Interestingly, regime 2 is associated with jobless growth: output increases at a rate of 2.4% a year while employment stagnates. The matrix of transition probabilities is given by

$$\mathbf{P} = \begin{bmatrix} 0.6333 & 0.0731 & 0.2936 \\ 0.0383 & 0.9398 & 0.0218 \\ 0.0862 & 0.1211 & 0.7927 \end{bmatrix},$$

where $p_{ij} = \Pr(s_{t+1} = j \,|\, s_{t-1} = i)$. These estimates indicate that regime shifts are persistent, with no regime being permanent. However, there is a 94% probability of staying in the normal growth regime, which has an estimated duration of 4 years: Recessions on the other hand have duration of 8 months and only occur in steady state 12% of the time.

The resulting regime probabilities are given in Figure 2: Regime 1 depicts very clearly the double dip recessions of 1973:2–1974:1 [0.9987]/1974:4–1975:2 [0.9498] and 1979:1–1979:1 [0.9750]/1979:4–1980:4 [0.9846], and the recession in the early nineties, 1990:3–1991:2 [0.8832]. The figures in square brackets are the average regime probabilities for the quoted periods. Regime 1 also captures an outlier in 1971:1 [1.0000]. Whilst regime 3 characterizes high-growth episodes – Regime 2 represents by default 'normal' growth. It is particularly noticeable that the period up to 1985 was characterized by 'boom and bust' policies, whereas that after 1985 was one of normal growth with the exception of the recession of the early 1990s. As in the Hamilton (1989) model of the US business cycle, the regime classification of the MS-VECM is close to traditional business cycle datings. In figure 2 the contraction periods issued by

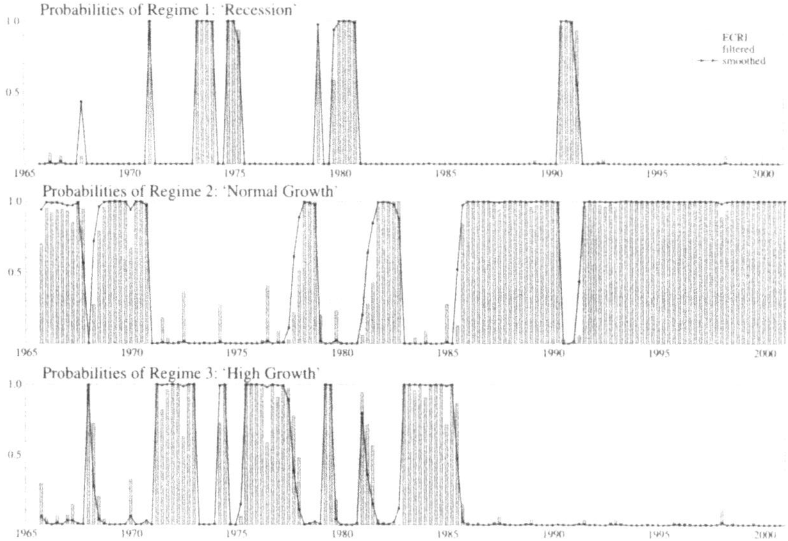

Fig. 2. Regime probabilities of the MS-VECM.

the Economic Cycle Research Institute (ECRI) are superimposed on the smoothed and filtered probabilities of the MS-VECM. The dating of the cycle is very similar to the one produced by the ECRI: using the ex-post (smoothed) regime probabilities, the coverage of UK recessions by regime 1 and expansions by regimes 2 and 3 is 0.9005. The timing of the major recessions is also similar to that obtained following the method suggested by Breunig and Pagan (2001) and Harding and Pagan (2001). We conclude that the MSIH(3)-VECM(2) model is a valid statistical representation of the UK business cycle and that the detection of business cycle turning points is very precise.

Table 3 reports the results of Wald specification tests regarding the significance of the regime shifts in the intercepts of the equations for the individual variables separately, and in the system as a whole, respectively. Under the null hypothesis of $\mathbf{v}_1 = \mathbf{v}_2 = \mathbf{v}_3$ etc., the unrestricted regime-dependent variances ensure the statistical identification of the model under the null hypothesis. The tests are nuisance parameter free so that classical likelihood theory can be invoked, and the asymptotic null distribution of the Wald test is $\chi^2(q)$ where q is the number of linearly independent restrictions. The regime-shifts in equilibrium means and mean growth rates of the system are statistically highly significant. There is not only strong support for recurring recessions and expansions, but also for the presence of a third regime. Running tests for the equations of the system separately helps to characterize the regimes. In the case of recessions (regime 1) versus normal growth (regime 2), the hypothesis $v_{k1} = v_{k2}$ can be rejected very strongly for Δy_t, Δn_t and Δns_t. Comparing the second and the third regime, there is a significant change in the intercepts of all variables, though this is less strong for those of Δy_t and Δwp_t. Finally, it is worth noting that real wage growth has the least evidence for being affected by regime shifts.

Table 3. Wald specification tests

Null hypothesis	Test statistic	Δy_t	Δn_t	Δns_t	Δwp_t	System
$\nu_1 = \nu_2$	$\chi^2(1)$	56.445 [0.0000]	49.950 [0.0000]	9.062 [0.0026]	0.516 [0.4723]	$\chi^2(4) = 175.39$[0.0000]
$\nu_2 = \nu_3$	$\chi^2(1)$	2.526 [0.1120]	16.666 [0.0000]	27.320 [0.0000]	2.388 [0.1223]	$\chi^2(4) = 42.87$[0.0000]
$\nu_1 = \nu_2 = \nu_3$	$\chi^2(2)$	59.265 [0.0000]	98.953 [0.0000]	45.106 [0.0000]	3.218 [0.2001]	$\chi^2(8) = 279.24$[0.0000]

Note: The numbers in brackets represent the marginal significance level of Wald test statistic. The regime-identifying assumption of the system test is that $\Sigma_1 \neq \Sigma_2 \neq \Sigma_3$.

Table 4. ML estimation results for the MS-VECM, 1965(4)–2001(1)

	Δy_t	Δn_t	Δns_t	Δwp_t
Regime-dependent intercepts ($\times 10^2$)				
ν_1	−0.888 (0.197)	−0.498 (0.055)	−0.278 (0.079)	0.414 (0.373)
ν_2	0.607 (0.089)	−0.016 (0.042)	−0.015 (0.041)	0.690 (0.132)
ν_3	0.991 (0.237)	0.271 (0.062)	0.327 (0.061)	0.291 (0.261)
Short-run dynamics				
Δy_{t-1}	−0.213 (0.082)	−0.105 (0.030)	−0.115 (0.032)	−0.176 (0.121)
Δy_{t-2}	0.052 (0.072)	0.036 (0.021)	0.009 (0.024)	−0.032 (0.116)
Δn_{t-1}	0.151 (0.435)	1.072 (0.173)	0.425 (0.175)	0.059 (0.629)
Δn_{t-2}	0.569 (0.383)	−0.271 (0.168)	−0.342 (0.166)	−0.526 (0.558)
Δns_{t-1}	0.391 (0.461)	−0.801 (0.192)	−0.338 (0.189)	0.294 (0.660)
Δns_{t-2}	−0.311 (0.391)	0.326 (0.178)	0.382 (0.171)	0.804 (0.556)
Δwp_{t-1}	0.137 (0.067)	0.138 (0.029)	0.126 (0.028)	−0.131 (0.100)
Δwp_{t-2}	0.060 (0.062)	0.046 (0.023)	0.051 (0.024)	0.097 (0.091)
Equilibrium correction				
eqm_{t-1}	−0.054 (0.024)	0.033 (0.012)	0.030 (0.011)	0.034 (0.034)
Standard errors ($\times 10^2$)				
σ_1	0.6950	0.1599	0.2778	1.2872
σ_2	0.4671	0.3020	0.2712	0.7311
σ_3	1.1963	0.3054	0.2899	1.0982
Regime 1: correlation				
Δy_t	1.0000	−0.5479	−0.2741	0.6186
Δn_t	−0.5479	1.0000	0.7359	−0.7246
Δns_t	−0.2741	0.7359	1.0000	−0.4411
Δwp_t	0.6186	−0.7246	−0.4411	1.0000
Regime 2: correlation				
Δy_t	1.0000	0.3602	0.2334	0.1615
Δn_t	0.3602	1.0000	0.9354	−0.2595
Δns	0.2334	0.9354	1.0000	−0.2420
Δwp_t	0.1615	−0.2595	−0.2420	1.0000
Regime 3: correlation				
Δy_t	1.0000	0.0050	−0.1686	0.4343
Δn_t	0.0050	1.0000	0.8997	0.1752
Δns_t	−0.1686	0.8997	1.0000	0.0332
Δwp_t	0.4343	0.1752	0.0332	1.0000

Fitting	MS-VECM	linear VECM	MS-DVAR	linear DVAR
logLik	2374.9886	2317.9406	2361.6400	2304.3041
AIC	−32.2674	−31.9428	−32.1358	−31.8071
HQ	−31.5569	−31.5199	−31.4591	−31.4180
SC	−30.5189	−30.9020	−30.4705	−30.8496

From Table 4 it is clear that not only are the estimated intercepts $\mathbf{v}(s_t)$ different across regimes, but there are also changes in $\mathbf{\Sigma}(s_t)$ – note in particular the changes in $cov(u_{\Delta y}, u_{\Delta wp})$. This suggests that the correlations between the variables, conditional on the past, differ across regimes, and so the use of a constant parameter VECM could lead to severely misleading results. A likelihood ratio test of the linear VECM(2) against the MSIH(3)-VECM(2) strongly rejects the linearity hypothesis (LR(28) = 114.10), even when the upper bound of Davies (1977) is invoked. Further, the AIC and the HQ criterion favour of the non-linear VECM.

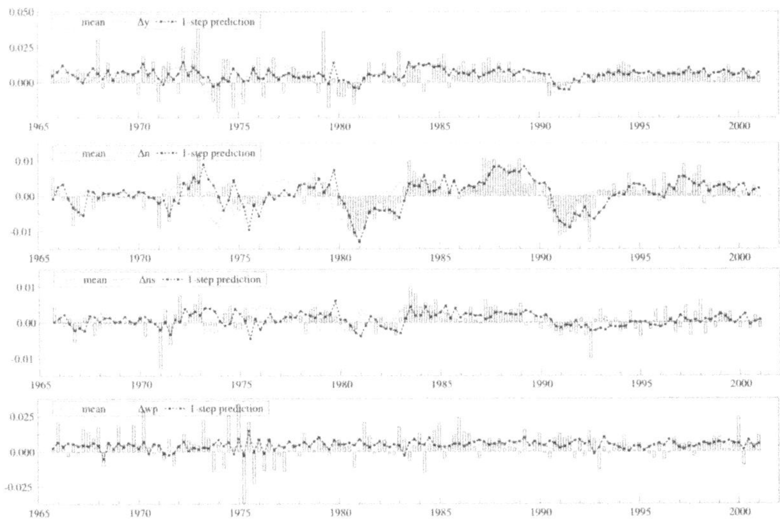

Fig. 3. Fit of the MS-VECM.

We note also that the estimated adjustment coefficients for the MSIH(3)-VECM(2) show that all variables other than real wages respond to the equilibrium, which contrasts with the results for the VECM(3) in (9). The estimated response of labour supply to the equilibrium term though has a perverse sign.

Additional evidence in favour of the MSIH(3)-VECM(2) is provided by the plots of the actual, one-step predictions, and mean values for each variable given in Figure 3 where the fit of the model is seen to be good. Also Figures 4 and 5 show the residuals to be non-autocorrelated, homoscedastic, and normally distributed, in contrast to those of the VAR(4), and so provide further support for the model. Thus the regime inference of our model appears to be based on a congruent econometric model of the inter-relationship between real wages, income, employment and labour supply. As the regime inference is a by-product of the parameter estimation of the MS-VECM, our model overcomes the problems in Acemoglu and Scott (1994) where conditional models of employment dynamics in the UK are considered, but the probability of a recession is derived from a non-congruent Markov-switching model of UK output growth.

5. Impulse-response analysis

In this section we analyze the dynamic properties of the MSIH-VAR underlying the MSIH-VECM by calculating the impulse response functions (IRF). First we compare the results for the MSIH-VAR and a linear VAR. We then show that the differences reported in sub-section 5.1 are essentially replicated when Choleski decompositions for various orderings of the variables are used. Finally, we follow the approach in Krolzig and Toro (1998) to evaluate changes in the MSIH-VAR responses across regimes.

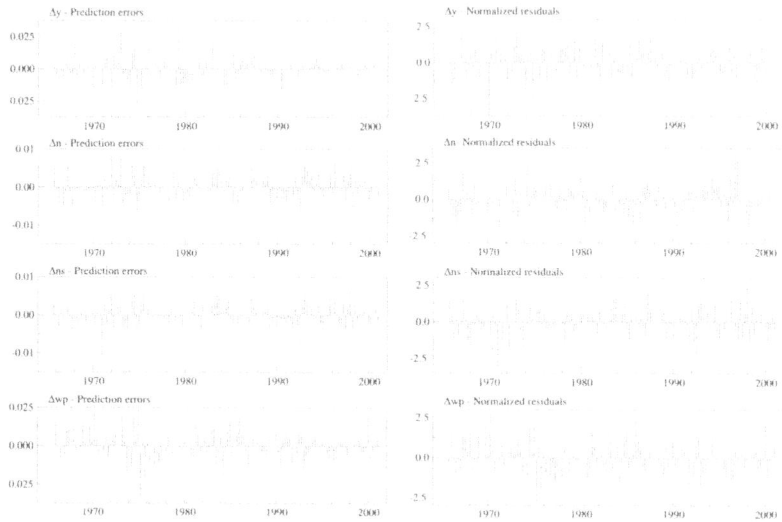

Fig. 4. Residuals of the MS-VECM.

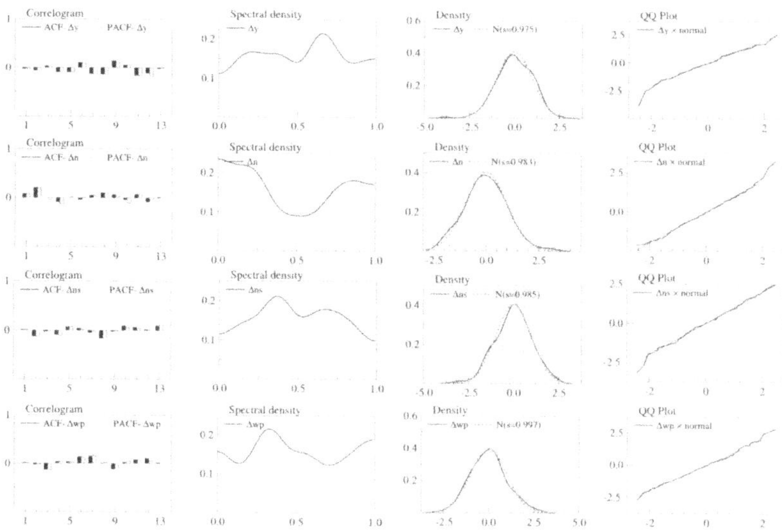

Fig. 5. Statistical properties of the normalized residuals.

5.1. MSIH-VAR and VAR

In Figure 5 we compare the results for the MSIH-VAR and a standard VAR. Cumulative impulse response functions (IRFs) are calculated for unit impulses to the innovations for each of the variables, without orthogonalizing

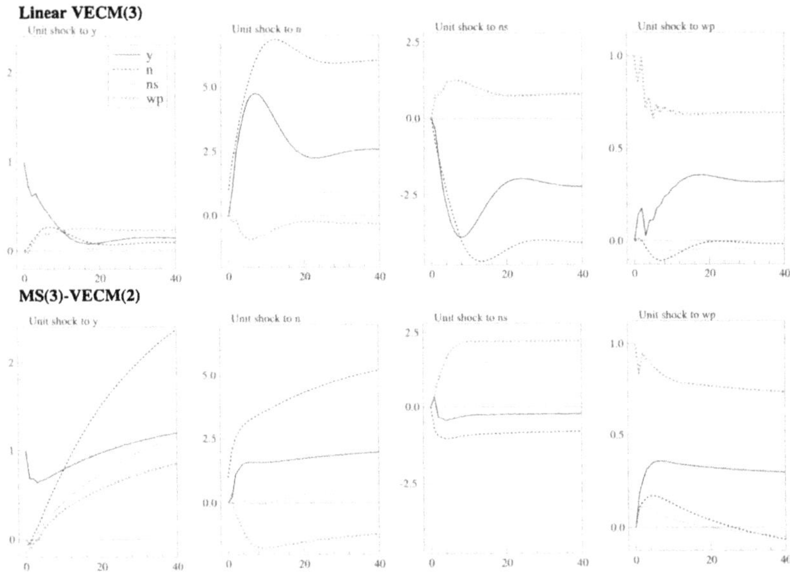

Fig. 6. Impulse Response Functions, MS-VAR and standard VAR.

the variables. We do this both for simplicity and because we want to focus on possible differences in the responses between models and across regimes.

Inspection of Figure 6 reveals that the shape and timing of each variable's response to unit impulses in each of the innovations are very different for the two models. Hence, the MS properties have a noticeable effect on the estimated long run relationships between the variables. We might expect further differences to emerge if orthogonalized innovations were used. However, these results should be interpreted with care because, from the previous section, the covariance matrix of the error term is regime dependent, so that orthogonalized IRFs will differ across regimes. In the next subsection we evaluate whether this is the case.

5.2. Keynesian and classical orthogonalizations

We consider two alternative orderings of the variables: *y-n-wp-ns* and *ns-n-y-wp*. The former can be related to a standard Keynesian model where increased demand leads to increased production, which requires an increase in labour demand. Unemployment falls as only a part of the employment growth is sustained by an increased labour force participation. As nominal wages tend to be more sluggish than prices, the real wage falls initially, over time wages adjust to the increased level of labour productivity. The latter ordering is more in line with a classical model in which changes in the labour supply drive labour input and production, which in turn affect the real wage.

Analyzing orthogonalized IRFs is standard in the case of linear VARs (see, *inter alia*, Hamilton, 1994, §11.4). For the MSIH-VECM proposed in section 4, the presence of regime-dependent heteroscedasticity requires special

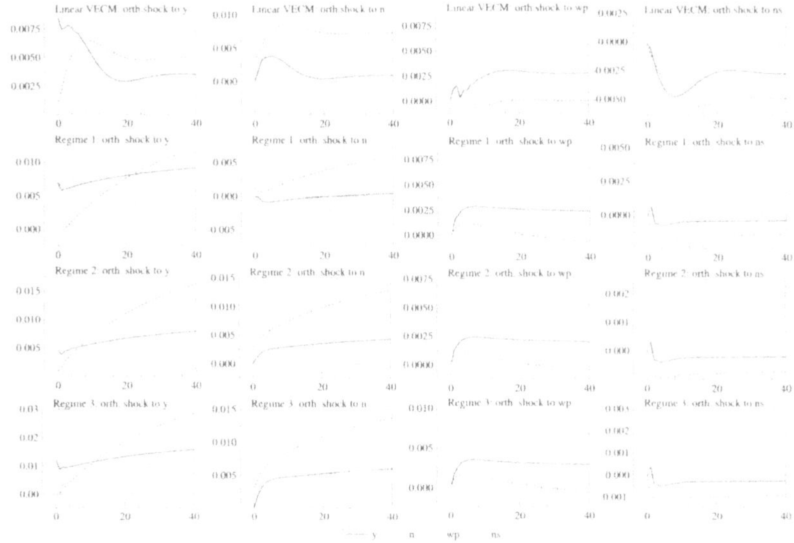

Fig. 7. Impulse Response Functions: Keynesian Orthogonalization.

attention. As the covariance matrix of the error vector is regime dependent, so are the corresponding Choleski decompositions and the associated orthogonalized impulses. Thus for each of the two orderings of the variables, we get three IRFs describing the response of the variables dependent on the state of the system when the shock occurs.

Starting with the IRFs for the Keynesian ordering given in Figure 7, the main difference across regimes to a shock to the y equation innovation appears to be in the response of wp. The reactions to a shock in wp are rather limited and similar in all three regimes. Note that there appears to be a positive long run effect on productivity $(y - n)$ in the linear VAR, but less so in the MSIH-VECM. A shock to ns has similar effects across the three regimes, but is less marked than in the linear VAR.

Turning to IRFs for the classical ordering given in Figure 8, the response to a shock in y are similar to the former case, but with fewer changes across regimes. The effects of an impulse to wp are also very similar across the three regimes. However, there are very marked differences in the responses to shocks in ns and n, and each set is very different from the corresponding Keynesian set.

In summary, the most relevant result for our purposes is the finding of substantial differences in the IRFs that emerge across regimes and relative to the linear VAR, independently of the chosen orthogonalization. In the next subsection we explore an alternative approach to analyze the source and propagation of shocks.

5.3. IRF of regime shifts

Standard IRF analysis focuses on the response of the system to Gaussian innovations, but other shocks could affect the system. In particular, changes in

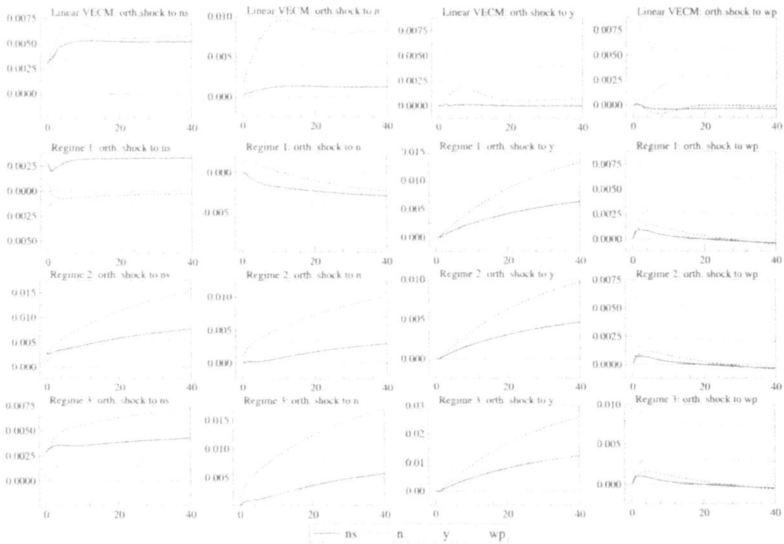

Fig. 8. Impulse Response Functions: Classical Orthogonalization.

the phase of the cycle is probably what some economists have in mind when they refer to 'cyclical shocks', for example, investigating the dynamics of some variables in the transition from boom to bust, or vice versa. Within the MSIH-VAR framework we can deal with both types of shock.

The impulse responses with respect to transitions of the state variables depend on the properties of the VAR, combined with those of the hidden Markov chain. In fact, these effects are due to: (i) changes in the current state and hence changes to the conditional expectation of a future regime; and (ii) the autoregressive transmission of intercept shifts. A formal mathematical derivation of these responses is presented in the appendix of Krolzig and Toro (1998).

In Figure 9 we characterize the behaviour of the variables for the system for each of the three regimes when compared to the ergodic regime probability distribution, and present the responses to changes in the phase of the cycle. A first characteristic that emerges from the IRFs on the diagonal of Figure 9 is the difference in the responses of n and ns. Indeed, there is increasing unemployment in the recession (regime 1), and decreasing unemployment in the high growth regime. Further all variables react negatively in a recession, but they all respond positively in an expansion. These asymmetries in behaviour can be given a theoretical rationale – see Krolzig and Toro (1998) for an overview of some theoretical models.

Consider now the path taken by the variables when there is a change in regime. We observe that moving from a recession to a period of normal or of high growth leads to all variables reacting positively and in a permanent manner to the shocks, though real wages are least affected. Also, the transitions from a high growth period to a normal period or to a recession are similar. Further, the transitions from normal growth to both recession and to

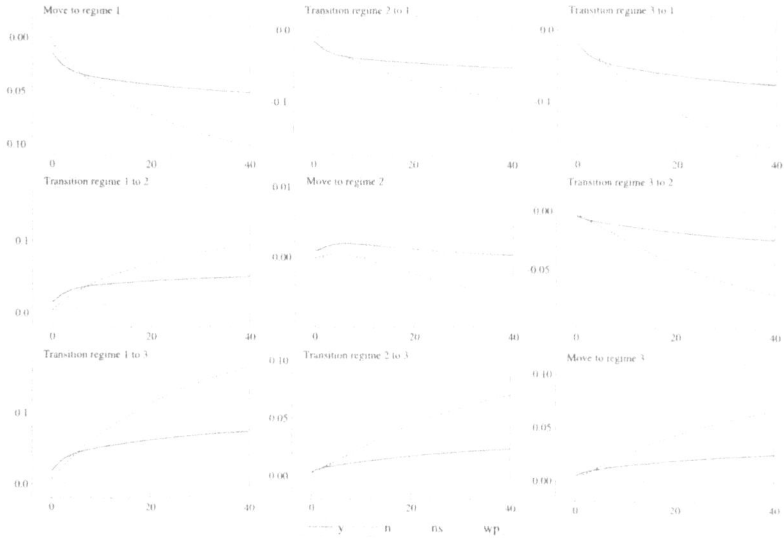

Fig. 9. The Response of the System after Shifts in Regime.

high growth are very different. Finally, transitions from normal growth to high growth is the mirror image (but with negative coefficients) of the responses to a change from high to normal growth. This results from the fact that in our model the mean and variance of the process are state-dependent, but the autoregressive parameters are constant across regimes.

6. Forecasting performance

From the above results the MS-VECM appears to provide a good representation for the in-sample behaviour of all four variables wp_t, y_t, ns_t and n_t, and a significant improvement with respect to standard linear specifications – see the statistics on model fit in Table 4. While regime-switching models tend to be superior to linear models in capturing certain features of the business cycle, their superiority from a forecasting perspective is often less convincing (see, *inter alia*, Clements and Krolzig, 1998). We now evaluate whether the MS-VECM of the UK labour market performs as well out in forecasting.

Krolzig (2000) developed a general approach to predict multiple time series subject to Markovian shifts in the regime. Consider the MS(M)-VECM($p-1$) model

$$\Delta \mathbf{x}_t = \mathbf{M}\xi_t + \boldsymbol{\alpha}\boldsymbol{\beta}'\mathbf{x}_{t-1} - \boldsymbol{\alpha}\gamma(t-1) + \sum_{k=1}^{p-1} \boldsymbol{\Gamma}_k \Delta \mathbf{x}_{t-k} + \mathbf{u}_t,$$

where $\mathbf{M} = [\mathbf{v}_1 : \cdots : \mathbf{v}_M]$ and ξ_t is the M-dimensional state vector consisting of indicator variables $I(s_t = i) = 1$ for $s_t = i$ and 0 otherwise. The one-step predictor can be derived from the corresponding MSIH(M)–VAR(p) representation given by

$$\mathbf{x}_t = \mathbf{M}\xi_t - \boldsymbol{\alpha}\gamma(t-1) + \sum_{k=1}^{p} \mathbf{A}_k \mathbf{x}_{t-k} + \mathbf{u}_t, \tag{11}$$

where $\mathbf{A}_1 = \mathsf{I}_N + \boldsymbol{\alpha}\boldsymbol{\beta}' + \boldsymbol{\Gamma}_1$ and $\mathbf{A}_j = \boldsymbol{\Gamma}_j - \boldsymbol{\Gamma}_{j-1}$ for $1 < j \leq p$ with $\boldsymbol{\Gamma}_p = \mathbf{0}_N$. Hence we have that

$$\mathsf{E}[\mathbf{x}_{t+1} \mid \mathbf{x}_t, \ldots, \mathbf{x}_0] = \mathbf{MP}\hat{\xi}_{t|t} - \boldsymbol{\alpha}\gamma t + \sum_{k=1}^{p} \mathbf{A}_k \mathbf{x}_{t+1-k}, \tag{12}$$

where $\mathbf{P}$ is the transposed matrix of transition probabilities and $\hat{\xi}_{t|t}$ is the vector of filtered regime probabilities at time t. The predictor for the MSIH(M)-DVAR($p-1$) model follows from (12) by setting $\boldsymbol{\alpha} = \mathbf{0}$.

We compare 5 models: an MS-VECM and a linear VECM, plus an MS-DVAR and a standard VAR in first differences (DVAR), and finally a VAR in the second differences of variables (DDVAR), which is a forecasting device that exploits the fact that very few variables accelerate/decelerate indefinitely. In fact, DVARs and DDVARs can provide good forecasts during periods of structural changes, in particular when there are shifts in equilibrium means and mean growth rates – see Clements and Hendry (1999) for a general exposition and Marcellino and Mizon (2001b) for an example relative to the Italian labour market.

The models are estimated using data for the periods 1965(4)–1991(1) and 1965(4)–1998(1), and produce forecasts for the periods 1991(2)–2001(1) and 1998(2)–2001(1) respectively. The models are compared on the basis of the root mean square prediction errors (RMSPE) and the mean absolute prediction error (MAPE) for each of the 12 and 40 quarters forecast horizons. This choice leaves a sufficiently long estimation period to guarantee structural stability of the MS-VECM as a business cycle model, reasonable long-run properties, and strong convergence of the EM estimation procedure.

Table 5 reports the MAPE and RMSPE of the one-step prediction errors in forecasting y_t, n_t, n_t, and wp_t for each of the five models. From Table 5 it is evident that the MSIH(3)-VECM(2) performs well for both forecast periods. Over the 1998(2)–2001(1) period, the MS-VECM performs extremely well for all four variables. It consistently dominates the linear VECM. The outcome of the DDVAR is overall disappointing.

Hence we conclude that the MSIH-VECM provides a good characterization of the four variables modelled in a period of much change, can forecast well, and has an appealing economic interpretation.

7. Conclusions

In this paper we have estimated an MSIH-VECM for a small set of UK labour market variables, and found that it provides a good characterization of the sample data over the period 1965(4)–2001(1) despite there having been many changes affecting this sector of the UK economy. In addition, the switches between the three regimes are closely related to changes in the phases of the UK business cycle. Having found evidence for the existence of three

Table 5. One-step prediction errors

1998(2)–2001(1)	MAPE ($\times 10^2$)				RMSPE ($\times 10^2$)			
Model	*y*	*n*	*ns*	*wp*	*y*	*n*	*ns*	*wp*
MSI(3)-VECM(2)	0.2686*	0.2179*	0.2063*	0.5639*	0.3392*	0.2774*	0.2395*	0.7633*
MSI(3)-DVAR(2)	0.4245	0.2508	0.2480	0.6448	0.4909	0.3094	0.2891	0.8437
Linear VECM(3)	0.3042	0.2482	0.2512	0.5851	0.3685	0.3024	0.2777	0.7855
Linear DVAR(3)	0.2985	0.2486	0.2513	0.6026	0.3641	0.3029	0.2778	0.8011
Linear DDVAR(2)	0.3897	0.2648	0.2589	0.6536	0.4762	0.3384	0.3040	0.8756

1991(2)–2001(1)	MAPE ($\times 10^2$)				RMSPE ($\times 10^2$)			
Model	*y*	*n*	*ns*	*wp*	*y*	*n*	*ns*	*wp*
MSI(3)-VECM(2)	0.3889	0.2692*	0.3056	0.6062	0.5049	0.3343*	0.3676	0.8088
MSI(3)-DVAR(2)	0.5020	0.2944	0.3116	0.5636*	0.6183	0.3673	0.3804	0.7304*
Linear VECM(3)	0.4394	0.2835	0.2940	0.6487	0.5191	0.3463	0.3361	0.8241
Linear DVAR(3)	0.3236*	0.2806	0.2907*	0.6604	0.4182*	0.3450	0.3328*	0.8367
Linear DDVAR(2)	0.4078	0.3091	0.2919	0.7689	0.4791	0.3767	0.3460	0.9945

Note: The model with the lowest prediction error is indicated by*.

separate regimes the results in this paper also highlight the dangers of using impulse response analysis for VARs when the constancy of the estimated coefficients has not been established. This supports the arguments in Ericsson, Hendry and Mizon (1998) and Hendry and Mizon (2000) that great care is needed in using and interpreting impulse response functions. Reassuringly, the MSIH-VECM forecasts better than the linear VECM and models in first and second differences of variables, thus indicating the importance of representing some of the changes. Indeed, our analysis of a small model of the UK labour market illustrates that MS-VECMs do not only offer valuable economic insights having economically interpretable equilibria and regimes shifts that are closely related to changes in the phases of the business cycle, they are also useful statistical forecasting devices.

Data appendix

The data are quarterly seasonally adjusted for the period 1965(1) to 2001(1). From the basic series described in Table A1 the following variables were

Table A1. Definitions of variables

			Source (Mnemonic)
WS	wages and salaries	£m at current prices, SA	E Trends (ROYJ)
EE	number of employees in employment	000s, SA	E Trends (BCAJ)
ET	size of total workforce in industry	000s, SA	E Trends (DYDC)
Y	Gross Value Added at basic prices	index, 1995 prices, SA	E Trends (CGCE)
P	Implicit deflator of GVA	SA	E Trends (CGBV)
U	Unemployment benefit claimants	% of total labour force, SA	E Trends (BCJE)

constructed: log earnings $e = \log(WS/EE)$; log producer price $p = \log(P)$; log real wages $wp = (e - p)$; log labour force $ns = \log(ET/(1 - 0.01 * U))$.

References

Acemoglu D, Scott A (1994) Asymmetries in the cyclical behaviour of UK labour markets. Economic Journal 104:1303–1323

Breunig R, Pagan AR (2001) Some simple methods for assessing Markov switching models. mimeo, Australian National University

Chow GC (1960) Tests of equality between sets of coefficients in two linear regressions. Econometrica 28:591–605

Clements MP, Hendry DF (1990) Forecasting non-stationary economic time series. Cambridge, Mass.: MIT Press. The Zeuthen Lectures on Economic Forecasting

Clements MP, Krolzig HM (1998) A comparison of the forecast performance of Markov-switching and threshold autoregressive models of US GNP. Econometrics Journal 1:C47–C75

Clements MP, Mizon GE (1991) Empirical analysis of macroeconomic time series. VAR and structural models. European Economic Review 35:887–932

Cooper R, John A (1988) Coordinating coordination failures in Keynesian models. Quarterly Journal of Economics 103:441–463

Davies RB (1977) Hypothesis testing when a nuisance parameter is present only under the alternative. Biometrika 64:247–254

Doornik JA (1999) Object-oriented matrix programming using Ox. London: Timberlake Consultants. 3rd edn

Doornik JA, Hendry DF (2001) Modelling dynamic systems using PcGive 10: Volume II. London: Timberlake Consultants Press

Ericsson NR, Hendry DF, Mizon GE (1998) Exogeneity, cointegration and economic policy analysis. Journal of Business and Economic Statistics 16:370–387

Gonzalo J, Granger C (1995) Estimation of common long memory components in cointegrated systems. Journal of Business and Economic Statistics 13:27–35

Hall SG (1986) An application of the Granger and Engle two step estimation procedure to United Kingdom aggregate wage data. Oxford Bulletin of Economics and Statistics 48:213–228

Hall SG (1989) Maximum likelihood estimation of cointegrating vectors. Oxford Bulletin of Economics and Statistics 51:213–218

Hamilton JD (1989) A new approach to the economic analysis of nonstationary time series and the business cycle. Econometrica 57:357–384

Hamilton JD (1990) Analysis of time series subject to changes in regime. Journal of Econometrics 45:39–70

Hamilton JD (1994) State-space models. In Engle R, McFadden D (eds) Handbook of Econometrics, Vol. 4. Amsterdam: North–Holland

Harding D, Pagan AR (2001) A comparison of two business cycle dating methods. mimeo, Australian National University

Hendry DF, Mizon GE (2000) Reformulating empirical macro-econometric modelling. Oxford Review of Economic Policy 16:138–159

Johansen S (1988) Statistical analysis of cointegration vectors. Journal of Economic Dynamics and Control 12:231–254

Johansen S (1995) Likelihood-based inference in cointegrated vector autoregressive models. Oxford: Oxford University Press

Kaufman BE (1994) The economics of labor markets. Fort Worth: The Dryden Press. 4th edition

Krolzig H-M (1996) Statistical analysis of cointegrated VAR processes with Markovian regime shifts. SFB 373 Discussion Paper 25/1996, Humboldt Universität zu Berlin

Krolzig H-M (1997) Markov switching vector autoregressions. Modelling, statistical inference and application to Business Cycle Analysis. Berlin: Springer

Krolzig H-M (1998) Econometric modelling of Markov-switching vector autoregressions using MSVAR for Ox. Discussion paper, Institute of Economics and Statistics, University of Oxford: http://www.econ.ox.ac.uk/research/hendry/krolzig

Krolzig H-M (2000) Predicting Markov-switching vector autoregressive processe. Economics discussion paper 2000-W31, Nuffield College, Oxford

Krolzig H-M, Sensier M (2000) A disaggregated Markov–switching model of the UK business cycle. Manchester School 68:442–460

Krolzig H-M, Toro J (1998) A new approach to the analysis of shocks and the cycle in a model of output and employment. Working paper eco 99/30, EUI, Florence

Marcellino M, Mizon GE (2000) Modelling shifts in the wage-price and unemployment-inflation relationships in Italy, Poland, and the UK. Economic Modelling 17:387–413

Marcellino M, Mizon GE (2001a) Small system modelling of real wages, inflation, unemployment and output per capita in Italy 1970–1994. Journal of Applied Econometrics 16:359–370

Marcellino M, Mizon GE (2001b) Small system modelling of real wages, inflation, unemployment and output per capita in Italy 1970–1994. Discussion Papers in Economics and Econometrics no. 0106, Economics Department, Southampton University

Mizon GE (1995) Progressive modelling of macroeconomic time series: the LSE methodology. In Hoover KD (ed) Macroeconometrics: Developments, Tensions and Prospects, pp. 107–169. Dordrecht: Kluwer Academic Press

Sgherri S, Wallis KF (2000) Policy analysis with macroeconometric models: inflation targetry in a small structural model. mimeo, Department of Economics, University of Warwick

Plucking models of business cycle fluctuations: Evidence from the G-7 countries*

Terence C. Mills and Ping Wang

Department of Economics, Loughborough University, Loughborough, Leicestershire, LE11 3TU, U.K. (e-mail: T.C.Mills@lboro.ac.uk; P.Wang@lboro.ac.uk)

First Version Received: September 2000/Final Version Received: May 2001

Abstract. Friedman's 'plucking' model, in which output cannot exceed a ceiling level but is occasionally plucked downward by recessions, is tested using Kim and Nelson's formal econometric specification on output data from the G-7 countries. Considerable support for the model is obtained, leading us to conclude that during normal periods, output seems to be driven mostly by permanent shocks, but during recessions and high-growth recoveries, transitory shocks dominate. During these periods macroeconomic models that emphasise demand-oriented shocks, rather than real business cycle type models, may thus be more appropriate.

Key words: Business cycle asymmetry, state space models, G-7 countries, Markov switching.

1. Introduction

The recent interest in business cycle asymmetry has brought back into fashion the "plucking model" suggested by Milton Friedman more than 30 years ago. Friedman (1964, 1993) pointed out that the amplitude of cyclical contractions in U.S. output tended to be strongly correlated with succeeding expansions, but that these expansions were uncorrelated with the amplitude of subsequent contractions, thus producing an asymmetry between succeeding phases of the business cycle. To capture this asymmetry, Friedman developed a physical analogy in which the path of output may be thought of as an elastic string

* This paper forms part of the ESRC funded project (Award No. L1382511013) "Business Cycle Volatility and Economic Growth; A Comparative Time Series Study", which itself is part of the *Understanding the Evolving Macroeconomy* research programme. We have benefited from the comments of two anonymous referees, but all remaining errors are clearly our own.

stretched tautly and attached to two points on the irregular underside of a board, which might be held at an angle to represent secular growth. The board represents an upper limit, or ceiling, to output, and the string may be plucked downwards at irregular intervals to represent recessionary shocks. The size of these shocks will vary across recessions, but output will always rebound to the ceiling level, so that recessions can only have temporary effects on output and subsequent expansions are limited in size. Friedman (1993) provided some basic statistical evidence to support the plucking model, but Goodwin and Sweeney (1993) were the first to systematically test the two empirical regularities implied by it: cyclical asymmetry and a ceiling to output. Using output data from eight OECD countries, they find that correlation techniques provide only weak support for asymmetry but, using a frontier production approach, they find much stronger evidence in favour of an output ceiling. However, Goodwin and Sweeney's major indicator of, and criterion for, business cycle asymmetry is the traditional third moment statistic for skewness. Their models therefore cannot accommodate regime shifts, which, since these are regular features of business cycles, may lead to misspecification and possibly erroneous inferences.

Kim and Nelson (1999a) extend the analysis to provide a framework that enables both asymmetry and an output ceiling to be captured within a single model containing shifts in regime. Their nonlinear model incorporates asymmetric movements of output away from trend and asymmetric persistence of shocks during recessionary and normal times. This framework is able to estimate the importance of downward shocks to both trend and cycle, and to test the plucking hypothesis against symmetric trend-plus-cycle alternatives such as Clark (1987). Kim and Nelson show that the stochastic behaviour of U.S. output is well characterised by Friedman's plucking model, i.e., output is occasionally plucked down by recession and the cyclical or transitory component exhibits asymmetric behaviour.

The purpose of this paper is to further our understanding of asymmetric output movements by applying Kim and Nelson's (1999a) framework to the G-7 countries and to present cross-country comparisons in the spirit of Goodwin and Sweeney's (1993) investigation of Friedman's plucking model. One restriction in this framework is that asymmetry in trend is captured through a regime dependent innovation variance. We also investigate an extension of the framework by introducing an asymmetric discrete shock in the trend as well as the cycle. Section 2 thus develops the model specification used in this paper, section 3 presents our results and section 4 concludes.

2. Model specification

The novel feature of Kim and Nelson's specification is that they allow first-order Markov switching variables in both the trend and cycle components, thus allowing both plucking and asymmetric fluctuations around a stochastic trend. In their framework, the logarithm of real output, y_t, is decomposed into two unobserved components:

$$y_t = \tau_t + c_t \tag{1}$$

where τ_t is the trend and c_t is the transitory component. Regime shifts and asymmetric deviations of y_t from its trend are modelled by assuming that innovations to the transitory component are a mixture of two different types of shocks:

$$
\begin{aligned}
&c_t = \phi_1 c_{t-1} + \phi_2 c_{t-2} + \pi_{S_t} + u_t, \\
&\pi_{S_t} = \pi S_t, \quad \pi \neq 0, \\
&u_t \sim N(0, \sigma^2_{u,S_t}), \quad \sigma^2_{u,S_t} = \sigma^2_{u,0}(1 - S_t) + \sigma^2_{u,1} S_t, \quad S_t = 0 \text{ or } 1.
\end{aligned}
\tag{2}
$$

Here π_{S_t} is an asymmetric discrete shock, which is dependent upon an unobserved variable, S_t, an indicator variable that evolves according to a first-order Markov-switching process as in Hamilton (1989):

$$P[S_t = 0 \mid S_{t-1} = 0] = p$$

$$P[S_t = 1 \mid S_{t-1} = 1] = q$$

During 'normal times', $S_t = 0$ and the economy is near to potential or trend output. During 'recessions', however, $S_t = 1$ and the economy is hit by a transitory shock, possibly with a negative expected value if $\pi < 0$. If this is the case, then aggregate demand or other disturbances are 'plucking' output down below its trend ceiling level. Equation (2) allows for the possibility that the variance of the symmetric shock u_t may be different in the two regimes. In the absence of such shocks, c_t evolves as a second order autoregressive process and hence can display both persistence and pseudo-cyclical behaviour.

The specification of the trend component is consistent with Friedman's (1993) suggestion that potential output may be approximated by a random walk, with various types of disturbances producing perturbations to it:

$$
\begin{aligned}
&\tau_t = g_{t-1} + \tau_{t-1} + v_t, \\
&g_t = g_{t-1} + w_t, \\
&v_t \sim N(0, \sigma^2_{v,S_t}), \quad w_t \sim N(0, \sigma^2_w), \\
&\sigma^2_{v,S_t} = \sigma^2_{v,0}(1 - S_t) + \sigma^2_{v,1} S_t.
\end{aligned}
\tag{3}
$$

The stochastic trend τ_t is thus subjected to two shocks – to its level, through v_t, and to its growth rate, through w_t. Specifying trend growth, g_t, to be stochastic allows the possibility of, for example, productivity slowdowns in output. The above specifications again allow for the possibility that the variance of the level shock may be different across regimes. On the other hand, the variance of g_t is assumed not to be systematically different across regimes.

The model can be given the state-space representation

$$y_t = [1 \quad 1 \quad 0 \quad 0] \begin{bmatrix} \tau_t \\ c_t \\ c_{t-1} \\ g_t \end{bmatrix} = H\xi_t \qquad \text{Observation equation}$$

$$\xi_t = \begin{bmatrix} 0 \\ \pi_{S_t} \\ 0 \\ 0 \end{bmatrix} + \begin{bmatrix} 1 & 0 & 0 & 1 \\ 0 & \phi_1 & \phi_2 & 0 \\ 0 & 1 & 0 & 0 \\ 0 & 0 & 0 & 1 \end{bmatrix} \xi_{t-1} + \begin{bmatrix} v_t \\ u_t \\ 0 \\ w_t \end{bmatrix}$$

$$= \bar{\mu}_{s_t} + F\xi_{t-1} + V_t \qquad \text{State equation}$$

where

$$E(V_t V_t') = Q_{S_t}$$

and

$$Q_{S_t} = \begin{bmatrix} \sigma^2_{v,S_t} & 0 & 0 & 0 \\ 0 & \sigma^2_{u,S_t} & 0 & 0 \\ 0 & 0 & 0 & 0 \\ 0 & 0 & 0 & \sigma^2_{w,S_t} \end{bmatrix}$$

Estimation can be carried out by approximate maximum likelihood (Kim, 1994) using the GAUSS routines supplied by Kim (see Kim and Nelson, 1999a, 1999b, chapter 5).

3. Data and results

We analyse the logarithms of quarterly real GDP (output) for the G-7 countries. All of the data come from Datastream, which in turn takes the data from different sources. The sources of the U.K., U.S., German and Japanese data are the respective national accounts, while the Canadian, French and Italian data are provided by the International Monetary Fund. The sample periods are as follows: Canada, 1957:1–1999:4; France, 1965:1–1999:4; Germany, 1960:1–1999:4; Italy, 1970:1–1999:4; Japan, 1955:2–1999:4; U.K., 1955:1–1999:4; U.S., 1950:1–2000:1.

Table 1 summarises the results for the U.S. and the U.K., where model 1 is the unrestricted version described above and models 2 and 3 are restricted versions that impose $\sigma^2_w = 0$ and $\sigma^2_{u,1} = \sigma^2_{u,0} = 0$, respectively. Note that, unlike Kim and Nelson (1999a, Table 1, note (b)), unrestricted estimates of these latter variances were always positive, albeit very small, so that no regularity conditions were violated.

Looking first at the results for the U.S., we find that, not surprisingly, they are very similar to those reported by Kim and Nelson (1999a), although they use a somewhat different sample period to that employed here (they use 1951:1–1995:3). The sum of the autoregressive cycle coefficients, $\phi_1 + \phi_2$, for the transitory component is 0.7147, a little smaller than that reported by Kim and Nelson, (0.7969), suggesting that once output is plucked down by negative transitory shocks, their effects decay relatively faster after incorporating recent data. The estimated coefficients yield a pair of complex autoregressive roots

Table 1. Estimated models for U.S. and U.K.

	U.S.			U.K.		
Parameter	Model 1	Model 2	Model 3	Model 1	Model 2	Model 3
q	0.9330 (0.0452)	0.9271 (0.0428)	0.9214 (0.0442)	0.9706 (0.0194)	0.9708 (0.0192)	0.9708 (0.0190)
p	0.9649 (0.0254)	0.9393 (0.0367)	0.9554 (0.0252)	0.9531 (0.0368)	0.9535 (0.0354)	0.9535 (0.0352)
ϕ_1	1.3285 (0.1266)	1.5643 (0.1084)	1.3189 (0.1095)	1.4723 (0.2314)	1.4770 (0.2074)	1.4770 (0.2021)
ϕ_2	−0.6138 (0.1181)	−0.7125 (0.0861)	−0.6350 (0.1298)	−0.6860 (0.2246)	−0.6916 (0.1991)	−0.6916 (0.1942)
$\sigma_{u,0}$	0.0014 (0.0013)	0.0001 (0.0034)	–	0.0003 (0.0021)	<0.0001 (<0.0001)	–
$\sigma_{u,1}$	0.00005 (0.0013)	0.00004 (0.0012)	–	<0.0001 (0.0003)	<0.0001 (0.0001)	–
$\sigma_{v,0}$	0.0050 (0.0009)	0.0051 (0.0005)	0.0051 (0.0007)	0.0031 (0.0004)	0.0032 (0.0003)	0.0032 (0.0003)
$\sigma_{v,1}$	0.0115 (0.0013)	0.0113 (0.0010)	0.0115 (0.0013)	0.0120 (0.0008)	0.0120 (0.0008)	0.0120 (0.0008)
σ_w	0.0008 (0.0004)	–	0.0008 (0.0004)	<0.0001 (<0.0001)	–	<0.0001 (<0.0001)
π	−0.0099 (0.0027)	−0.0062 (0.0015)	−0.0098 (0.0027)	−0.0039 (0.0022)	−0.0039 (0.0021)	−0.0039 (0.0020)
Log L'lihood	607.359	605.473	607.211	528.842	528.840	528.840

implying a period of 11 quarters. Comparing the likelihood values for the two models, the LR test statistics for the hypothesis $\sigma_w^2 = 0$ is 3.77, rejecting the null at a p-value of 0.052, a slightly stronger rejection than Kim and Nelson, for whom the test statistic was 3.44. We thus conclude that U.S. trend growth has not been constant. Like Kim and Nelson, the LR statistic for the joint hypothesis that $\sigma_{u,1}^2 = \sigma_{u,0}^2 = 0$ allows us to accept the null at a very high p-value (0.30), thus implying that the discrete shock explains most of the dynamics in the transitory component. During normal times, the economy is thus subject to mostly permanent shocks and is operating near its trend ceiling. During recessions and the recovery periods that follow, however, the transitory component plays a major role in producing output fluctuations. Note that $\hat{\pi} = -0.01$ and is clearly significantly negative.

The estimated model is thus consistent with Kim and Nelson (1999a) and their interpretation bears repeating. The estimate $\hat{p} = 0.9554$ implies that the expected duration of a 'normal' regime is 22 quarters, while $\hat{q} = 0.9214$ implies an expected duration of recession of 13 quarters. The steady state probabilities of being in a normal or recessionary regime are 0.64 and 0.36, respectively.

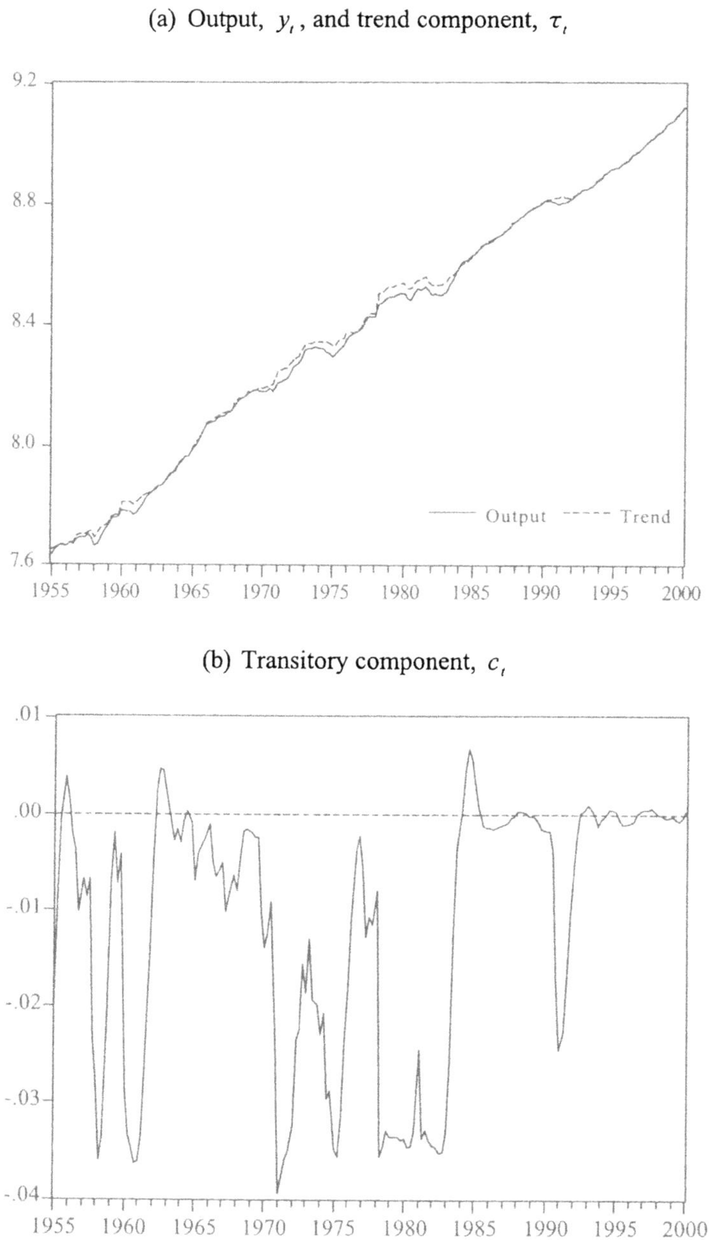

Fig. 1. Plucking model decompositions for the U.S.

(c) Probabilities of negative shocks to c_t

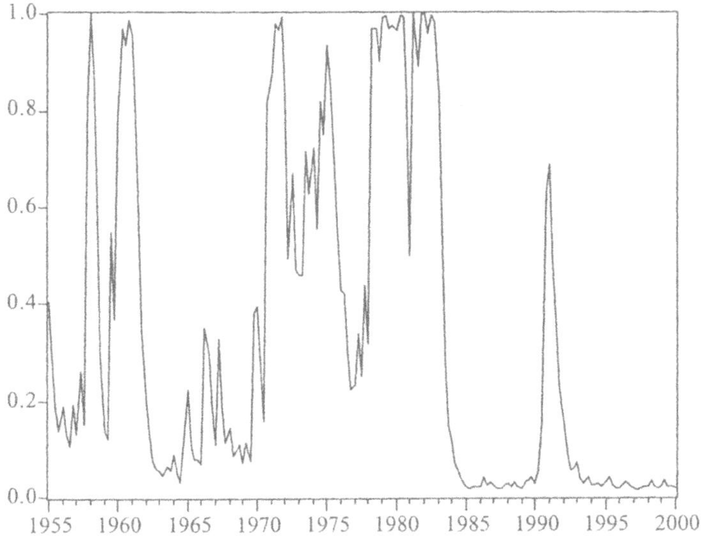

Fig. 1. Continued

(The expected duration of a normal regime, for example, is given by $1/(1-p)$, while the steady state probability is $(1-p)/(2-p-q)$). The onset of a recession thus produces a sequence of negative transitory shocks which 'pluck' output down, although with $\phi_1 + \phi_2 = 0.71$, their effects decay reasonably quickly. Near the end of the recession, and in the absence of further negative shocks, the fast-decaying negative shocks give rise to a third, high-recovery phase, moving the economy back near the trend ceiling again. There is thus, à la Sichel (1994), three distinctive phases of business cycle dynamics: a normal, a recessionary, and a high growth, recovery phase.

Figure 1(a), which shows y_t and estimates of the trend ceiling component, τ_t, reveals that most of the time the U.S. economy is operating at or near to the trend ceiling. Kim and Nelson (1999b) provide details of the construction of estimates: the first five years of each sample are used to obtain initial values of the filter and these observations are thus omitted from the plots. Figures 1(b) and 1(c) show estimates of the transitory component, c_t, and the filtered probability of a negative shock to the transitory component, i.e., the probability that $S_t = 1$ conditional on information up to $t-1$.

The transitory component and the probability of negative shocks correlate well with recessionary periods, as discussed in Kim and Nelson (1999a). These periods are shown, in conventional fashion, as shaded areas on Figures 1(b) and (c) and are constructed from the business cycle chronologies presented as Table D1 of Artis, Kontolemis and Osborn (1997). It is important to note that they are constructed from monthly data on industrial production, and so are determined independently of the output data being investigated here.

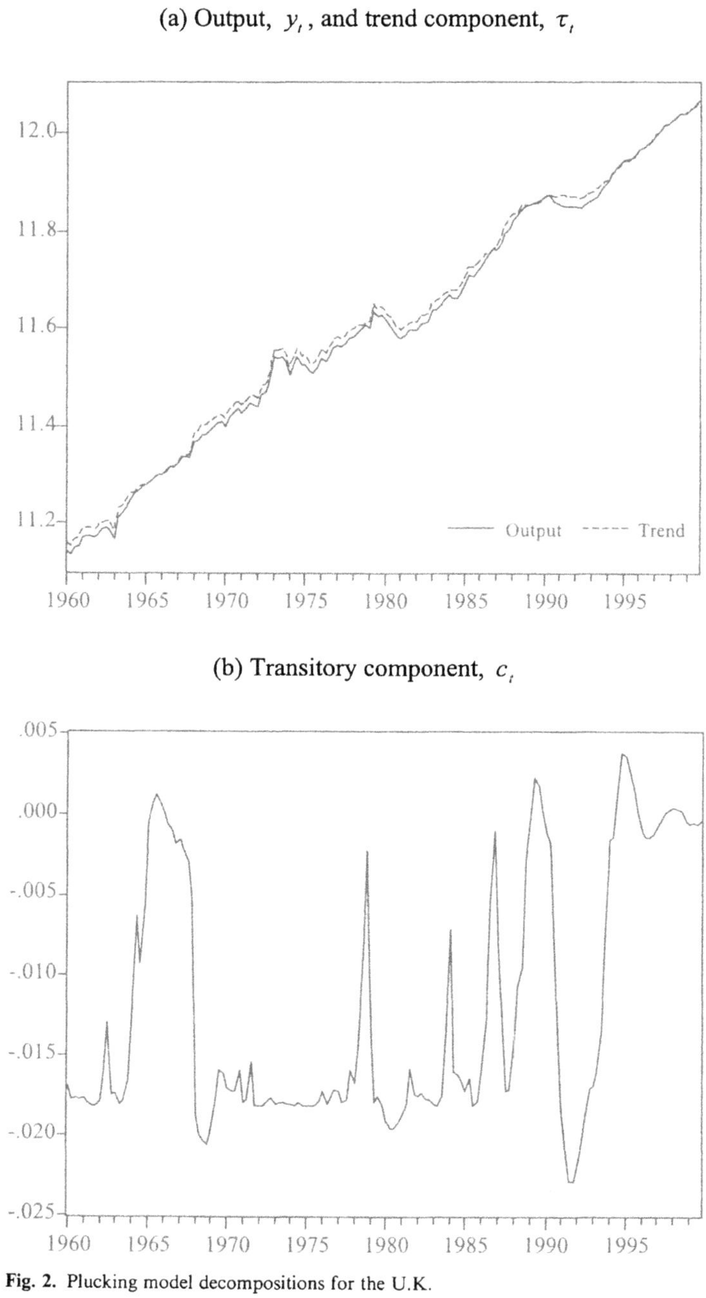

Fig. 2. Plucking model decompositions for the U.K.

(c) Probabilities of negative shocks to c_t

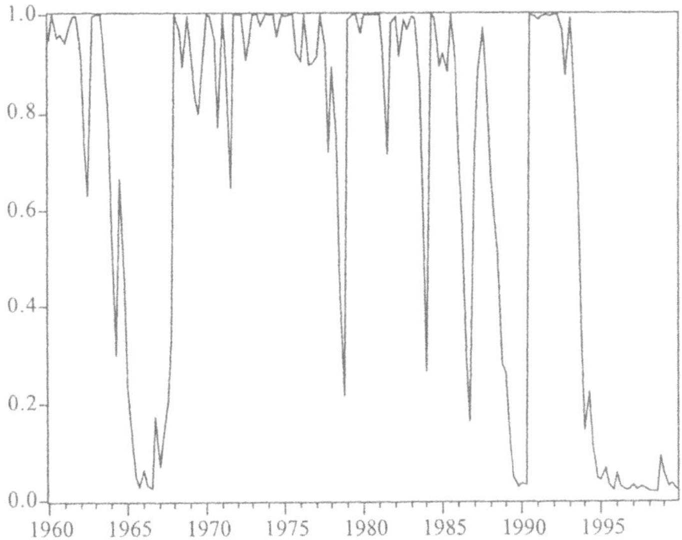

Fig. 2. Continued

Nevertheless, recessions tend to be accompanied by large (negative) values or rapidly increasing negative values of the transitory component and high or rapidly increasing probabilities of negative shocks to the component. The figures also show that, apart from a brief period in the early 1990s (no doubt a consequence of the Gulf war and the accompanying oil price shocks), the economy has been running at ceiling output since 1985. This is consistent with the view that this is the longest period of sustained expansion in U.S. economic history, typically attributed to the fact that macroeconomic policy has kept inflation firmly under control (Romer, 1999).

For the U.K. the sum of the AR coefficients is $\phi_1 + \phi_2 = 0.7863$, a little higher than for the U.S. The estimated coefficients again imply complex roots with a period of 13 quarters. Testing $\sigma_w^2 = 0$ by comparing models 1 and 2 produces an LR statistic of 0.004, which therefore strongly supports the hypothesis that the variance of trend growth rate is zero. This suggests that the trend component is only subject to level shocks and that over this period trend growth has been constant, unlike the U.S. Comparing models 1 and 3 provides a test of the joint hypothesis that $\sigma_{u,1}^2 = \sigma_{u,0}^2 = 0$. The LR statistic of 0.004 obviously accepts the hypothesis, implying that, as in the U.S., discrete shocks explain most of the dynamics in the transitory component. The estimate of the impact of such shocks is $\hat{\pi} = -0.004$, which is again negative but rather smaller than for the U.S., while the estimates of $\hat{q}$ and $\hat{p}$ imply expected durations of 34 and 22 quarters for recession and normal phases respectively, with steady state probabilities of 0.61 and 0.39. The implications of these estimates are seen in Figure 2. Figures 2(a) and 2(b) show that, unlike the U.S.,

Table 2. Estimated unrestricted models for the other G-7 countries

Parameters	Canada	France	Italy	Germany	Japan
q	0.6144 (0.3359)	0.7312 (0.1970)	0.5539 (0.1604)	0.8257 (0.1186)	0.2945 (0.2447)
p	0.9866 (0.0138)	0.9439 (0.0758)	0.9786 (0.0242)	0.9716 (0.0249)	0.8974 (0.1194)
ϕ_1	1.5411 (0.2520)	0.4964 (0.4467)	1.4931 (0.1404)	−0.0234 (0.1062)	1.0827 (0.1842)
ϕ_2	−0.5852 (0.2253)	0.3363 (0.3776)	−0.6116 (0.1675)	0.5223 (0.1748)	−0.2196 (0.1870)
$\sigma_{u,0}$	0.0043 (0.0021)	0.0015 (0.0034)	0.0013 (0.0023)	0.00001 (0.0002)	0.0069 (0.0012)
$\sigma_{u,1}$	0.00001 (0.0003)	0.0057 (0.0049)	<0.0001 (0.0004)	0.0083 (0.0041)	<0.0001 (0.0002)
$\sigma_{v,0}$	0.0073 (0.0013)	0.0056 (0.0016)	0.0051 (0.0009)	0.0093 (0.0008)	0.0001 (0.0018)
$\sigma_{v,1}$	0.0047 (0.0024)	0.0054 (0.0066)	0.0034 (0.0008)	0.0161 (0.0049)	0.0180 (0.0059)
σ_w	0.0006 (0.0004)	0.0012 (0.0005)	0.0008 (0.0003)	0.0003 (0.0004)	0.0015 (0.0005)
π	−0.0145 (0.0044)	−0.0081 (0.0036)	−0.0103 (0.0029)	−0.0128 (0.0087)	−0.0030 (0.0051)
Log L'lihood	490.94	418.23	365.59	427.32	511.20

output has consistently been below its ceiling level for the great majority of the sample period. Only since the mid-1990s has a lengthy period of 'normal' growth been achieved, which corresponds well with contemporary views of the behaviour of the U.K. economy (Bean and Crafts, 1996). The last five years of the sample are clearly unusual, for Figure 2(c) shows that only the mid-1960s approximate in terms of the prolonged absence of negative shocks. Recessionary periods, again taken from Artis, Kontolemis and Osborn (1997), are again closely associated with large negative values of, and the probability of negative shocks to, the transitory component.

Table 2 reports unrestricted estimates of the model for the other G-7 countries, while Table 3 reports estimates of restricted models, where insignificant parameters have been set to zero. All restrictions are accepted at very high p-values, as can be seen by comparing the respective log-likelihoods in the two tables. Figures 3 to 7 present similar sets of plots to those presented for the U.S. and the U.K., again using recessionary periods constructed from the chronologies provided by Artis, Kontolemis and Osborn (1997).

Compared with the U.S. and the U.K., these models provide a variety of interpretations. Like the U.S., but unlike the U.K., estimates of p are always greater than q, implying that recessions have shorter expected durations and

Table 3. Estimated restricted models for the other G-7 countries

Parameters	Canada	France	Italy	Germany	Japan
q	0.6143 (0.2229)	0.6871 (0.2781)	0.5582 (0.1509)	0.8339 (0.1186)	0.3728 (0.2870)
p	0.9866 (0.0138)	0.9305 (0.1195)	0.9824 (0.0201)	0.9774 (0.0232)	0.9275 (0.0870)
ϕ_1	1.5411 (0.2399)	0.8557 (0.1035)	1.5458 (0.1271)	–	0.9004 (0.0654)
ϕ_2	−0.5953 (0.2149)	–	−0.6705 (0.1404)	0.5886 (0.1677)	–
$\sigma_{u,0}$	0.0043 (0.0020)	–	–	–	0.0072 (0.0012)
$\sigma_{u,1}$	–	–	–	0.0095 (0.0050)	–
$\sigma_{v,0}$	0.0073 (0.0013)	0.0059 (0.0010)	0.0054 (0.0005)	0.0097 (0.0008)	–
$\sigma_{v,1}$	0.0047 (0.0023)	0.0091 (0.0033)	0.0035 (0.0007)	0.0170 (0.0046)	0.0184 (0.0067)
σ_w	0.0006 (0.0003)	0.0010 (0.0005)	0.0008 (0.0003)	–	0.0017 (0.0006)
π	−0.0145 (0.0042)	−0.0068 (0.0038)	−0.0094 (0.0021)	–	–
Log L'lihood	490.94	417.96	365.58	426.11	509.84

lower steady state probabilities than normal phases. These probabilities vary from 0.37 for Japan to 0.83 for Germany, and all are much lower than for the U.S. and the U.K. Estimates of shock persistence, $\phi_1 + \phi_2$, range from 0.5886 for Germany to 0.9458 for Canada, and for Japan and France the transitory components exhibit exponential rather than pseudo-cyclical behaviour. Only for France and Italy can the 'trend ceiling' hypothesis $\sigma_{u,1}^2 = \sigma_{u,0}^2 = 0$ be accepted. For Japan and Canada only $\sigma_{u,1}^2 = 0$, so that just 'normal' symmetric shocks effect the transitory component, whereas the situation is reversed for Germany, which is affected only by symmetric recessionary shocks. On the other hand, regime dependent level shocks are observed for all countries, and only for Germany is $\sigma_w^2 = 0$, so that, like the U.K., trend growth has remained constant. The evidence in favour of 'plucking' is somewhat mixed – although π is always negative, it is not significantly so for Japan or Germany. For Japan, the estimate of q is insignificantly different from zero. A linear symmetric model was therefore also fitted, which produced a log likelihood of 502.82, which is well below the value of 511.20 obtained in Table 2. We thus conclude that a model with asymmetric dynamics best models Japanese output, although the low value for q perhaps makes it difficult to lend a business cycle interpretation to the switching process.

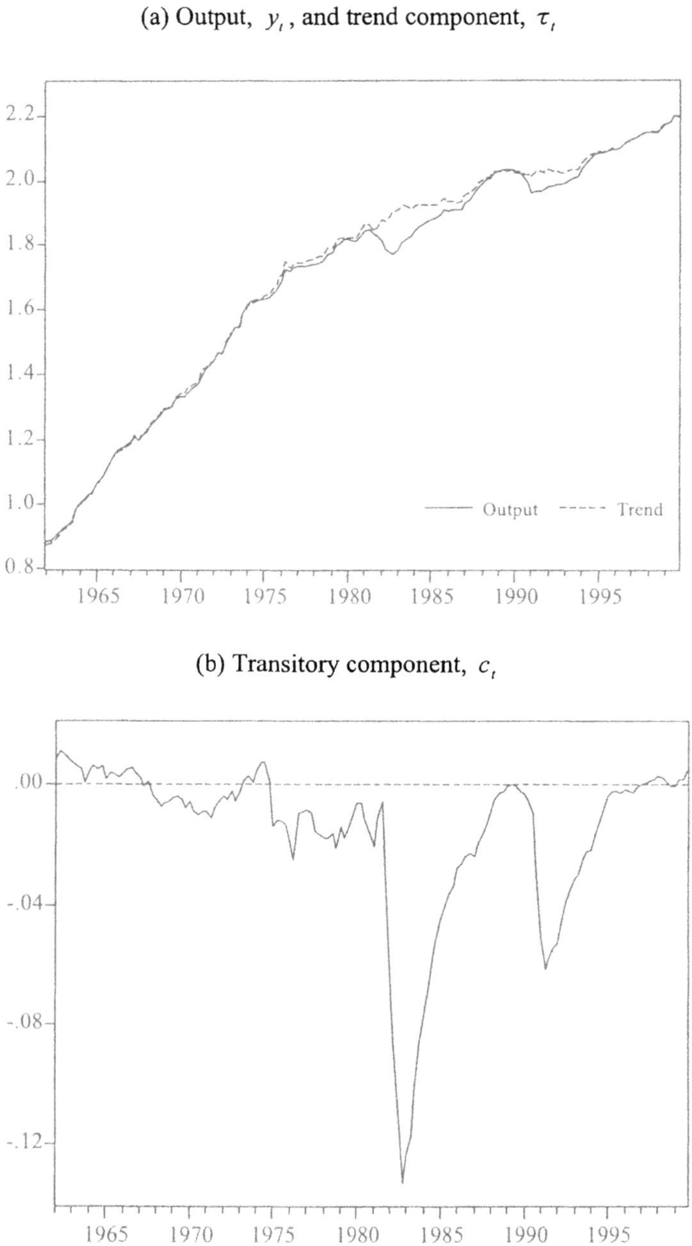

Fig. 3. Plucking model decompositions for Canada

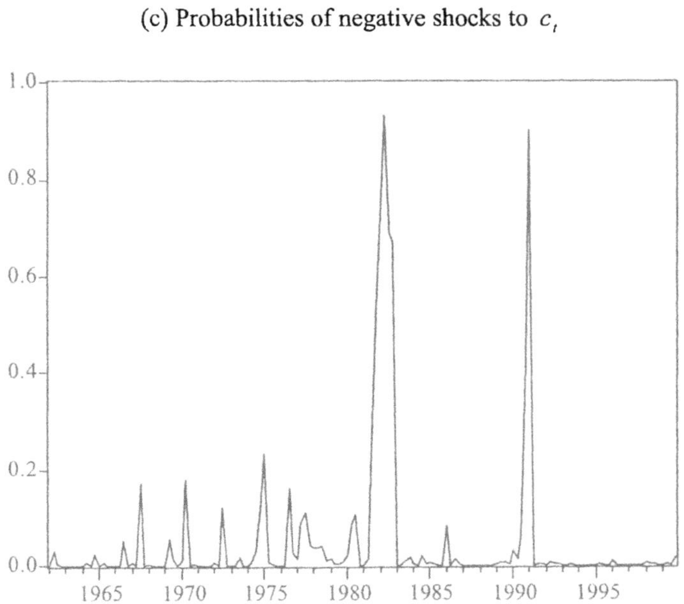

Fig. 3. Continued

Figure 3 shows that Canadian output has been close to its ceiling value except for two major episodes – throughout most of the 1980s and, like the U.S. and the U.K., during the early 1990s. The onset of these two episodes correspond to recessions found in the business cycle chronology for Canada, and are seen to be a consequence of two major negative shocks to the transitory component of output. Canada was particularly affected in the early 1980s by shifts in international trade patterns and also by labour market rigidities caused by provincial disparities and structural differences. As noted above, Canada has the greatest shock persistence of all the G-7 countries, and this is seen in the length of the two recessions.

From Figure 4, we see that France has been consistently below its output ceiling, with the large deviations in the 1970s being a consequence of it adapting only with difficulty to wage and oil shocks. The 1981–83 decline was related to the succession of exchange rate crises that eventually led to a major shift in macroeconomic policy by the Mitterand administration, who then followed more market-oriented policies which produced a more stable growth path (Sicsic and Wyplosz, 1996). These episodes correspond well with the business cycle chronology found for France.

By comparison, Germany has tended to be rather closer to trend, although with some rather volatile fluctuations during the late 1960s and early 1970s (see Figure 5). These were probably a consequence of the recession of 1966–67, which produced a fall in employment as well as in output. This, in turn, led to significant changes in work practices and a subsequent loss of discipline by both unions and employers associations, manifesting itself in wildcat strikes,

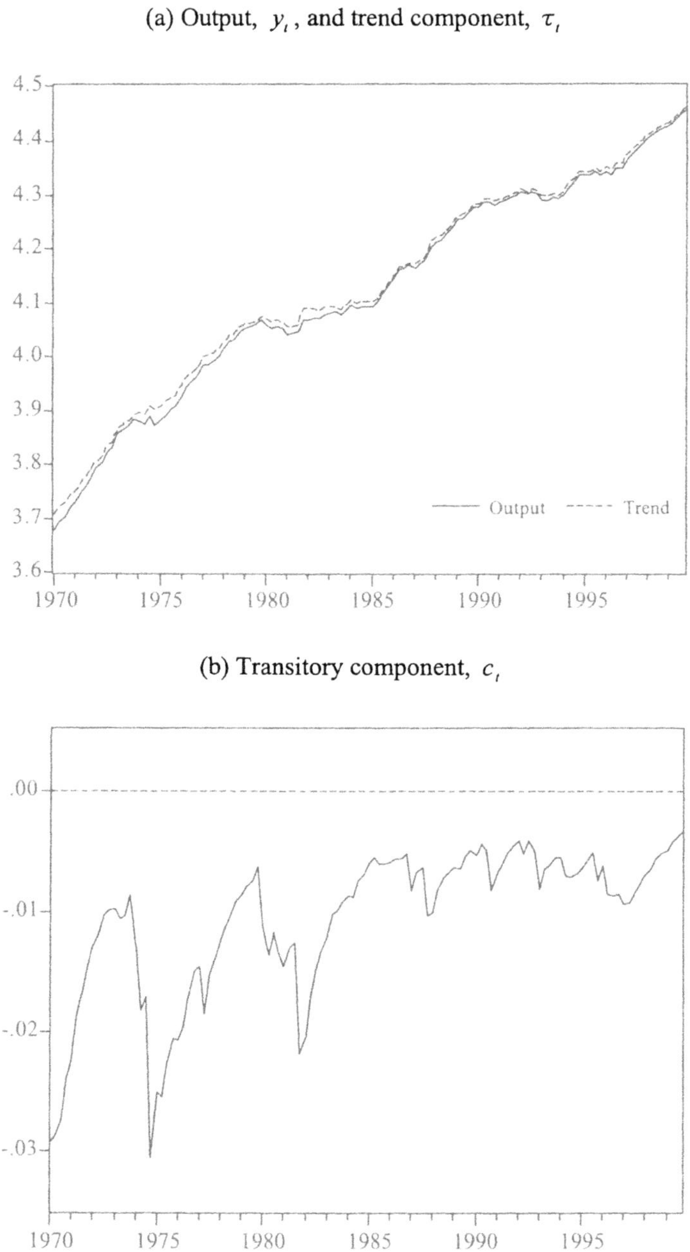

Fig. 4. Plucking model decompositions for France

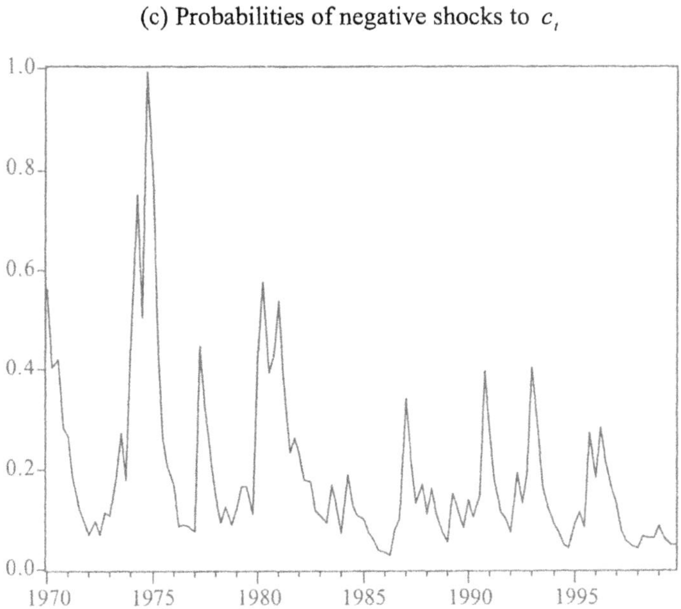

Fig. 4. Continued

which were exacerbated by an appreciation of the exchange rate. Such instability ended after the floating of the Deutschmark in 1973 and the adoption by the Bundesbank of a tight non-accommodating monetary policy (see Carlin, 1996). Recessions have thus been short and shallow and, in contrast to the other countries in the G-7, do not map particularly closely with the cyclical chronology obtained by Artis, Kontolemis and Osborn (1997).

Italy, whose sample period only begins in 1970, was well below its ceiling until the mid-1980s, but since then has been very close to trend except for 1992 to 1995 (see Figure 6). The poor performance during late 1970s and early 1980s undoubtedly had its origins earlier, for the social and institutional developments of the previous decade, which led to a succession of weak government coalitions, made the Italian economy more vulnerable to exogenous shocks, particularly as the country was also hit by waves of terrorism. The stable performance throughout the 1980s was a reflection of a new commitment to exchange rate stability, industrial restructuring and improved labour relations. Nevertheless, government borrowing remained out of control and this precipitated the poor performance of the early 1990s (Rossi and Toniolo, 1996). The business cycle chronology for Italy maps closely with the size of the transitory component and the probability of negative shocks, with the instability of the late 1970s and early 1980s captured particularly well.

Finally, from Figure 7, Japan has always been close to trend, but this masks the fact that throughout the first half of the 1990s the transitory component has been negative, reflecting the long recession after the stock market crash at the start of the decade. As output moved back to its ceiling level in 1997,

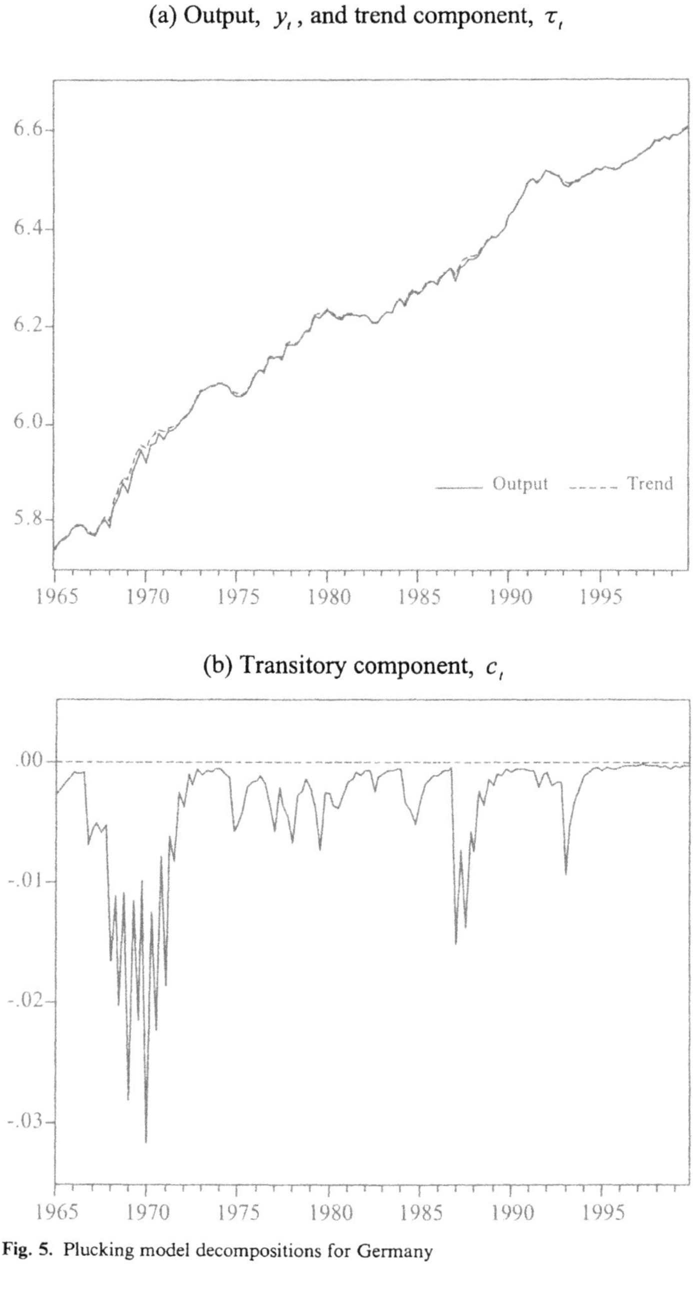

Fig. 5. Plucking model decompositions for Germany

(c) Probabilities of negative shocks to c_t

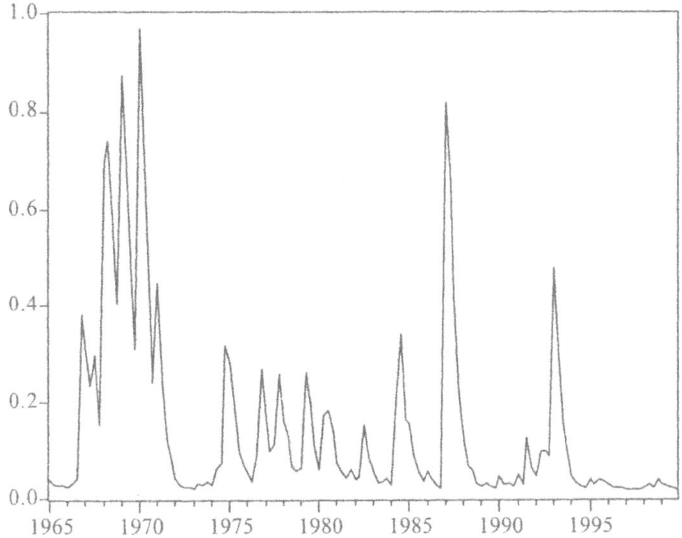

Fig. 5. Continued

a large negative shock (associated with the major tax increase in that year) tipped the economy back into recession again, in which it has remained. This episode is not captured by Artis, Kontolemis and Osborn (1997), as their sample period ended in 1993, but the oil price induced slow down in 1975 and the recession of the early 1990s clearly are.

As suggested by Kim and Nelson (1999a, footnote 5), we also estimated a more general model in which recessions are allowed to have permanent as well as transitory effects. This was done by replacing (3) with

$$\tau_t = g_{t-1} + \tau_{t-1} + \theta S_t + v_t$$

The coefficient θ was found to be insignificant for the U.S., in line with Kim and Nelson, and also for the U.K. and Italy. For Japan and Germany, θ was significantly positive, which is not readily interpretable in this framework. When S_t is included in the trend specification for Canada, the estimate of π in the cycle becomes insignificant, while θ enters significantly. This perhaps suggests that a model of the type proposed by Lam (1990) might be more appropriate for Canada. When S_t is included in the trend specification for France, both coefficients are significant, but the estimate of π becomes positive. Except for France, for which the positive estimate of π makes such estimates uninterpretable, the estimated trends, transitory components and negative shock probabilities are virtually identical to those plotted previously and we therefore conclude that such an extension is unnecessary.

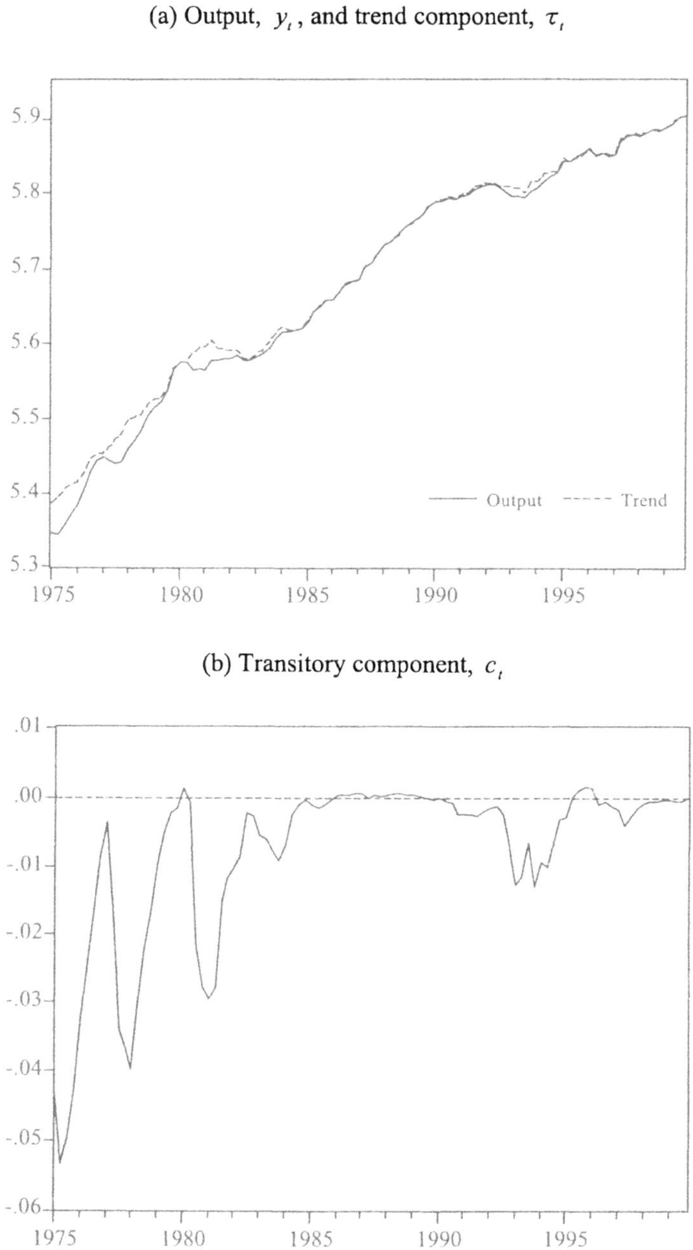

Fig. 6. Plucking model decompositions for Italy

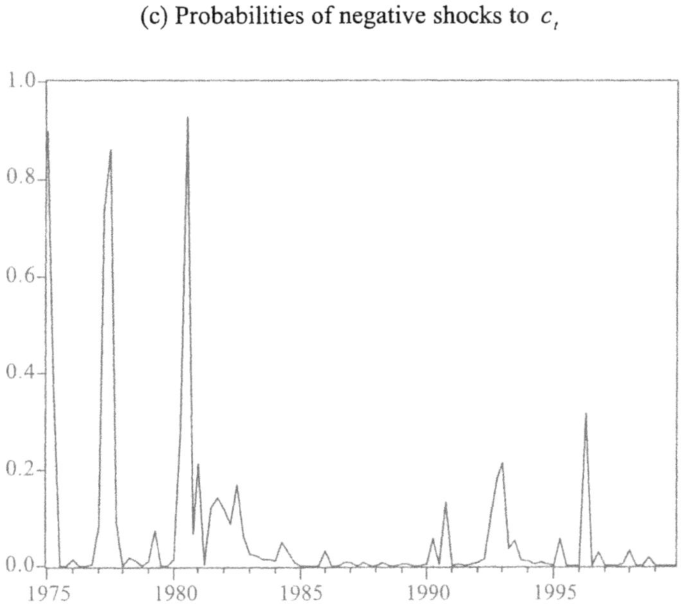

Fig. 6. Continued

4. Conclusions

Friedman's plucking model, as rigorously formulated by Kim and Nelson (1999a, b), offers an interesting approach to investigating asymmetries in business cycles. On fitting this model to output data from the G-7 countries, we have found a fair degree of support for it. Negative asymmetric discrete shocks are found to influence the transitory component of output of each country, so that there does seem to be evidence for the downward recessionary 'plucks' envisaged by Friedman (1964, 1993). The evidence of a ceiling level for output is less widespread, being accepted for the U.S., the U.K., France and Italy, but not for Canada, Japan and Germany. The hypothesis of constant trend growth can only be accepted for the U.K. and Germany and typically both normal and recessionary symmetric shocks influence trend output. It would appear that recessionary shocks tend to have only transitory effects and do not enter significantly into the trend component.

The deviations of actual from estimated trend output for each country accords well with macroeconomic history, particularly with the business cycle chronology determined independently by Artis, Kontolemis and Osborn (1997). The length and depth of recessions nevertheless vary widely and only for the U.K. is the expected duration of a recession longer than that of a 'normal' period. In general, though, our results for the wider set of G-7 economies are consistent with those found by Kim and Nelson (1999a) for the U.S. Output during normal times seems to be driven mostly by permanent shocks, but during recessions and high-growth recoveries, transitory shocks dominate,

(a) Output, y_t, and trend component, τ_t

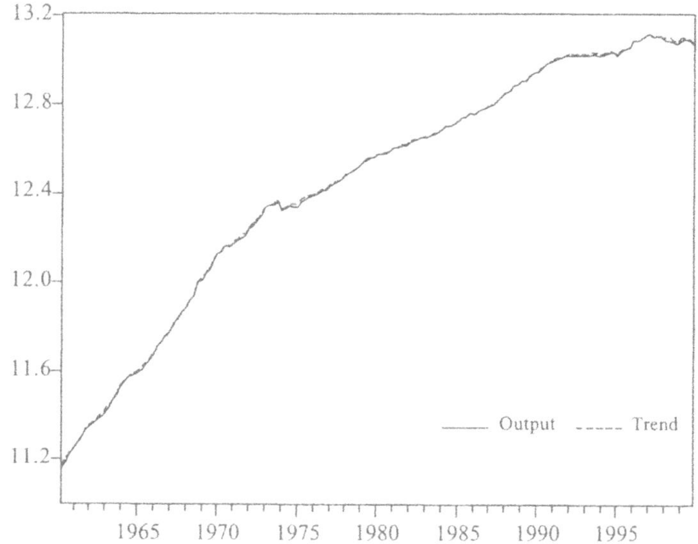

(b) Transitory component, c_t

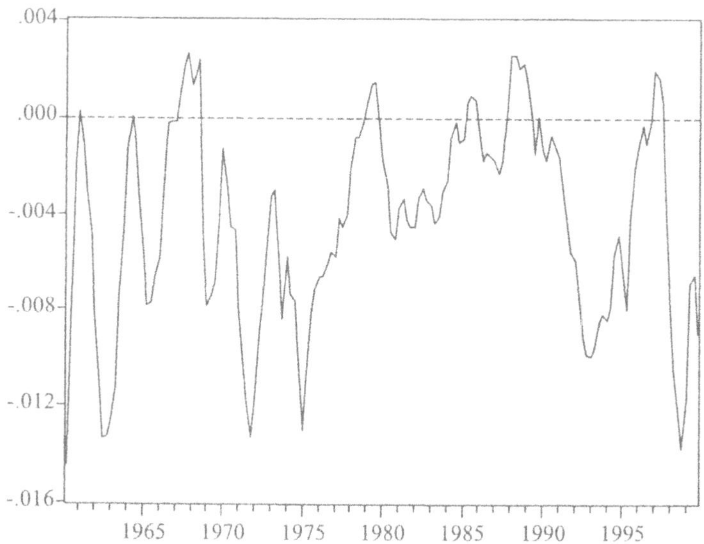

Fig. 7. Plucking model decompositions for Japan

(c) Probabilities of negative shocks to c_t

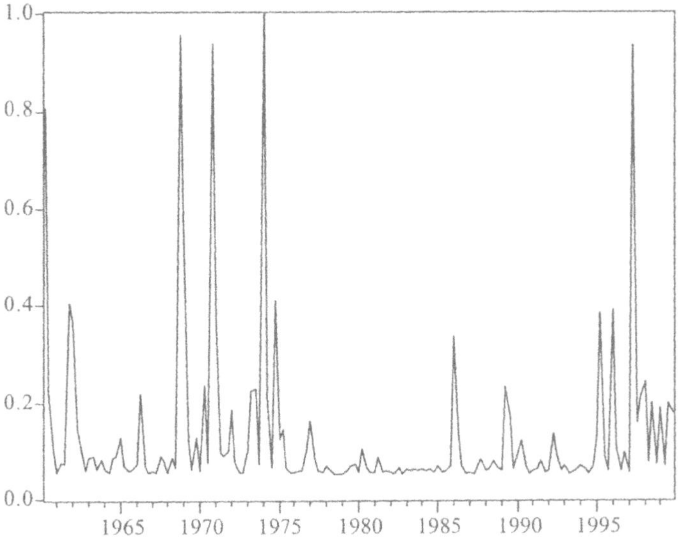

Fig. 7. Continued

so that during these periods macroeconomic models that emphasise demand-oriented shocks, rather than real business cycle type models, may be more appropriate.

References

Artis MJ, Kontolemis ZG, Osborn DR (1997) Business cycles for G7 and European countries. Journal of Business 70:249–279

Bean C, Crafts N (1996) British economic growth since 1945: relative economic decline ... and renaissance? In: Crafts N, Toniolo G (eds.) Economic growth in Europe since 1945. Cambridge University Press, Cambridge, pp. 131–172

Carlin W (1996) West German growth and institutions, 1945–90. In: Crafts N and Toniolo G (eds.) Economic growth in Europe since 1945. Cambridge University Press, Cambridge, pp. 455–497

Clark PK (1987) The cyclical component of the U.S. economic activity. Quarterly Journal of Economics 102:797–814

Friedman M (1964) Monetary studies of the National Bureau. The National Bureau Enters its 45th Year, 44th Annual Report, pp. 7–25

Friedman M (1993) The 'plucking model' of business fluctuations revisited. Economic Inquiry 31:171–177

Goodwin TH, Sweeney RJ (1993) International evidence on Friedman's theory of the business cycle. Economic Inquiry 31:178–193

Hamilton JD (1989) A new approach to the economic analysis of nonstationary time series and the business cycle. Econometrica 57:357–384

Kim CJ (1994) Dynamic linear models with Markov-switching. Journal of Econometrics 60:1–22

Kim CJ, Nelson CR (1999a) Friedman's plucking model of business fluctuations: tests and estimations of permanent and transitory components. Journal of Money, Credit and Banking 31:317–334

Kim CJ, Nelson CR (1999b) State-space models with regime switching: Classical and Gibbs-sampling approaches with applications. MIT Press, Cambridge, Mass.

Lam P-S (1990) The Hamilton model with a general autoregressive component: Estimation and comparison with other models of economic time series. Journal of Monetary Economics 26:409–432

Romer CD (1999) Changes in business cycles: Evidence and explanations. Journal of Economic Perspectives 13(2):23–44

Rossi N, Toniolo G (1996) Italy. In: Crafts N, Toniolo G (eds.) Economic growth in Europe since 1945. Cambridge University Press, Cambridge, pp. 427–454

Sichel DE (1994) Inventories and the three phases of the business cycle. Journal of Business and Economic Statistics 12:269–277

Sicsic P, Wyplosz C (1996) France, 1945–92. In: Crafts N, Toniolo G (eds.) Economic growth in Europe since 1945. Cambridge University Press, Cambridge, pp. 210–239

IV Financial Applications

Is there an asymmetric effect of monetary policy over time?

A Bayesian analysis using Austrian data.

Sylvia Kaufmann*

Oesterreichische Nationalbank, Economic Analysis Division, P.O. Box 61, A-1011 Vienna, and University of Vienna, Department of Economics, Hohenstaufengasse 9, A-1010 Vienna
(e-mail: sylvia.kaufmann@oenb.co.at)

First Version Received: December 2000/Final Version Received: May 2001

Abstract. The present paper assesses whether monetary policy effects are asymmetric over the business cycle by estimating a univariate model for GDP including additionally the first difference of the 3-month Austrian interest rate as a measure for monetary policy. The asymmetry of the effects is captured by allowing for state-dependent parameters where the latent state variable follows a Markov switching process. The model is estimated within a Bayesian framework using Markov Chain Monte Carlo simulation methods. Model selection and specification tests are performed by means of marginal likelihood. The results document significant negative effects of monetary policy during periods of below-average growth, while the effect seems insignificant during periods of normal or above-average growth. These results corroborate those derived in theoretical models assuming price rigidities and implying a convex supply curve. Additionally, the concern of using appropriate state-identifying restrictions is raised to obtain an unbiased posterior inference. Finally, the analysis concludes by assessing the robustness of the results with respect to alternative measures of monetary policy.

Key words: Asymmetry, monetary policy, Markov switching, Markov Chain Monte Carlo, marginal likelihood

JEL Classification: C11, C15, C22, E52

1. Introduction

In the literature there are basically two theoretical explanations given for asymmetric effects of monetary policy to arise over time. The models presented pre-

* I thank two anonymous referees for constructive comments, and for the editor's and co-editor's additional suggestions. Of course, remaining omissions and errors are mine. Finally, the views expressed in the paper are strictly those of the author and do in no way commit the OeNB.

dict that monetary policy is more effective during recessions than during expansions. One strand builds on downward price rigidity. Ball and Mankiw (1994) present a model in which firms change their prices regularly and, if paying a menu cost, can make special adjustments in response to shocks. Asymmetries arise if a positive trend inflation is added to the model. The approach implies a convex short-run aggregate supply curve. During expansion – i.e. at the relatively steep part of the supply curve – monetary policy actions, measured by their influence on the aggregate demand curve, result mainly in price changes rather than output changes whereas in recessionary periods – at the flat part of the supply curve – monetary policy actions mainly affect output. Tsiddon (1993) shows that given fixed costs of changing a nominal price an increase in the average rate of monetary expansion leads to a decrease in the lag of price adjustment in response to a positive shock.

The second approach is based on the external finance premium – the difference between external (by issuing debt or equity) and internal (e.g. retained earnings) finance. During tight-monetary periods informational frictions in the credit market worsen and enhance the effects of monetary policy on the real economy (see Bernanke and Gertler, 1995, for an overview). Two potential channels are identified to magnify monetary policy actions. The deteriorating effect of a monetary contraction on borrowers' net worth (balance sheet) increases interest rates even further through an increase in the external finance premium. In Bernanke and Gertler (1989) asymmetric information gives rise to agency costs of financing real capital investments which is reflected in the external finance premium. Farmer (1985, 1988) builds a model of financial contracting in the presence of asymmetric information and limited collateral: increases in interest rates lead firms to write contracts in which layoffs occur more frequently. Recently, Kiyotaki (1998) and Kiyotaki and Moore (1997a, 1997b) present a model in which credit constraints arise because creditors cannot force debtors to repay debts unless they are secured by collateral. The credit system becomes a propagation mechanism by which the effects of shocks persist and amplify through the interactions between collateral, borrowers' net worth and credit limits. Relatively small shocks to technology or to wealth distribution can then generate large persistent fluctuations in output and employment. Finally, credit market imperfections give rise to an endogenous regime-switching mechanism between different equilibrium states in the business cycle model of Azariadis and Smith (1998).

Aggregate empirical evidence in favour of asymmetric effects of monetary policy is presented in several papers, including Cover (1992), Karras (1996a, 1996b) and Lenz (1997) among others. Cover presents a two step procedure. The first step consists in estimating a money-supply process to identify the endogenous component of monetary policy. The residuals of this equation are interpreted as the innovation in monetary policy, i.e. the monetary policy shock. These are included in the second equation estimating the output process of the system where the specification allows for different effects of negative and positive values of monetary policy shocks. A test of equal effects of positive and negative values is rejected. The evidence thus supports the view that negative money supply shocks have a larger and more important effect on output than positive shocks. The same system of equations is estimated in Karras (1996a, 1996b) and Lenz (1997) simultaneously using nonlinear least squares methods. The evidence supports again differential effects of positive and negative monetary policy shocks.

Garcia and Schaller (1995) and Kakes (1998) take another approach and investigate the asymmetric effect of monetary policy applying the Markov switching model presented in Hamilton (1989, 1990). Based on a univariate model for the growth rates of output and industrial production, respectively, they find evidence for a statistically significant asymmetric effect of interest rate changes over the business cycle. Peersman and Smets (2001) investigate industrial production of the countries participating in the Eurosystem. They document an overall negative effect of unexpected monetary policy innovations for most of the countries, asymmetric effects in individual countries are reported for France, Germany, and Spain only, however.

The present paper presents evidence on Austria in this line of research. The model is estimated within a Bayesian framework using Markov Chain Monte Carlo (MCMC) simulation methods (see Smith and Roberts, 1993, and Chib and Greenberg, 1996, for an overview on MCMC methods). There are few MCMC applications to Markov switching models to macroeconomic data in particular. Kim and Nelson (1998) estimate a dynamic factor model with Markov switching to get a coincident index of the business cycle and to assess duration dependence. Within the same setting, Kaufmann (2000) infers business cycle turning points, performs additionally model selection by means of marginal likelihoods and applies diagnostic measures to assess the model fit. An overview of additional applications to economic data is also found in Kim and Nelson (1999). The present paper uses the permutation sampler derived in Frühwirth-Schnatter (2001a) to estimate the model. Model selection and specification tests are performed by means of marginal likelihoods using results of Frühwirth-Schnatter (2001b) who presents a detailed analysis on marginal likelihoods for mixture and Markov switching models.

The analysis uses quarterly data on Austrian GDP and the first difference of the 3-month interest rate as a measure for monetary policy covering the period from 1976 to 1998. As the Austrian Schilling was pegged to the German Mark from 1981 onwards, monetary policy stance coming from Germany is most likely to be reflected in Austrian interest rates.[1] We can infer two regimes that refer to periods of below- and above-average growth, respectively. The effect of interest rate increases seems to be significantly negative in periods of below-average growth. The inference on the posterior state probabilities can be related to specific business cycle periods. One classification however, seems to be an artifact of the effect that the anticipated introduction of the luxury tax had on sales in the last quarter of 1977 and the first quarter of 1978. But restricting the sample to exclude this outlier does not change the basic evidence in favour of the switching specification. Rather, the results are refined and the relation of the latent state variable to business cycle periods becomes more obvious. Additional results document the usefulness of the random permutation sampler to find adequate state identifying restrictions. It turns out that poor constraints, i.e. constraints that do not uniquely identify the states, may bias the results considerably. Moreover, the results are robust with respect to the measure of monetary policy stance. The inference changes only marginally when using the interest rate level rather than its first difference. In the spirit of Bernanke and Mihov (1998), a final investigation using the residuals of a structural vector

[1] Indeed, the correlation between the Austrian and German interest rate is above 0.97 for the sample 1981 through 1998, and the one between the first differences is near 0.7 and above 0.9 for the observation period beginning in 1981 and 1990, respectively.

autoregression (SVAR) as a measure for domestic monetary policy shocks obtains only marginal negative effects on real activity, that are not asymmetric over time, however. A fact that reflects the close integration of the Austrian with the German economy.

The next section specifies the model and presents the assumption about the prior distributions completing the Bayesian specification. Section 3 summarizes the sampling scheme. An estimator of the model likelihood is given in section 4. The results are discussed in section 5, and the robustness analysis follows in section 6. Finally, section 7 concludes by comparing the results to those reported in a selection of papers analyzing European countries, and closely related to the present one.

2. Model specification, prior specification

Let $y^N = (y_1, \ldots, y_N)$ represent an $N \times 1$ vector of observable variables. The general form of the model investigated here takes the following form:

$$y_t = X_t \beta_{S_t} + \varepsilon_t, \quad \varepsilon_t \sim \text{i.i.d.}\mathcal{N}(0, \sigma_{S_t}), \tag{1}$$

where X_t is $R \times 1$, and may also contain lagged dependent variables besides usual explanatory variables, $X_t = (1, y_{t-1}, \ldots, y_{t-p}, x_t, \ldots, x_{t-q})$. The specification investigated later allows the time-varying parameters β_{S_t} and σ_{S_t} to take on one out of 2 values depending on the regime prevailing in period t, $\beta_{S_t} = \beta_j$ and $\sigma_{S_t} = \sigma_j$ iff $S_t = j$, $j = 1, 2$. The process governing the latent state variable S_t is assumed to be Markovian of order one with transition probabilities $\eta_{ij} = P(S_t = j \mid S_{t-1} = i)$, where $\sum_{j=1}^{2} \eta_{ij} = 1$.

Within the present paper we will analyze whether a real macroeconomic variable, specifically the growth rate of GDP, is affected by monetary policy actions, and whether these effects are asymmetric over time. The motivation behind the latent specification of the state process is the fact that the prevailing economic regime is usually not directly observed, and the Markovian property captures the fact that economic regimes are thought to persist for some time. The persistence of regimes might differ, however, which is reflected by the transition probabilities.

Note that as it stands, the model needs a restriction to uniquely define the states and the state specific parameters. Usually, economic intuition or the purpose of the analysis itself yield such a restriction. In our case, thinking of asymmetry over time, a natural identification would be to associate the first state with periods of economic slowdown and a second state with periods of economic recovery, i.e. ordering the state specific parameters according to some element of β:

$$\beta_{1,i} < \beta_{2,i}, \tag{2}$$

where i is either value out of $1, \ldots, R$. Obviously, there is a problem of choosing the parameters with respect to which the states are identified. Potentially, the states might even be very poorly separable in terms of β, but well separable in terms of the persistence parameters η_{ii}, $i = 1, 2$. In such cases, a restriction on η, like $\eta_{11} < \eta_{22}$, would identify the state specific parameters. Sometimes, even a combination of the two might be appropriate (see Kaufmann and Frühwirth-

Schnatter, 2000, for an example). If there is a priori no known well-separating, identifying restriction, the simulations of the random permutation sampler (Frühwirth-Schnatter, 2001a) can be post-processed in an explorative manner to find an adequate one (see the next section and section 5).

We conclude the model specification by a discussion of its hierarchical structure. For ease of exposition, we introduce the following notation. The vector $S^N = (S_1, \ldots, S_N)$ gathers all state variables up to time N, and a corresponding realization is denoted by $s^N = (s_1, \ldots, s_N)$. The vector $\eta = (\eta_{1\cdot}, \eta_{2\cdot})$, with $\eta_{i\cdot} = (\eta_{i1}, \eta_{i2})$, collects the transition probabilities. The vector $\phi = (\beta, \sigma, \eta)$ collects all model parameters, where $\beta = (\beta_1, \beta_2)$ and $\sigma = (\sigma_1, \sigma_2)$. The "augmented parameter vector" $\theta = (\phi, S^N)$ includes additionally the vector of the latent state variables. Conditional on a known realization for S^N, the data likelihood factorizes as

$$L(y^N|\phi, s^N) = \prod_{t=1}^{N} f(y_t|y^{t-1}, \phi, s_t), \tag{3}$$

where the one-step ahead predictive distribution is Gaussian

$$f(y_t|y^{t-1}, \phi, s_t) = \sqrt{\frac{1}{2\pi\sigma_{s_t}}} \exp\left\{-\frac{(y_t - X_t\beta_{s_t})^2}{2\sigma_{s_t}}\right\}. \tag{4}$$

The density of the prior distribution of s^N, $\pi(s^N|\eta)$, depends only on the transition distribution η, and is proportional to

$$\pi(s^N|\eta) \propto \prod_{t=1}^{N} \eta_{s_t, s_{t-1}} \pi(s_0) = \prod_{j=1}^{2}\prod_{i=1}^{2} \eta_{ij}^{N_{ij}} \pi(s_0),$$
$$N_{ij} = \#\{s_t = j \,|\, s_{t-1} = i\}. \tag{5}$$

In order to use Bayesian estimation we need to specify a prior distribution for the parameter vector ϕ, $\pi(\phi)$. We have to use proper prior distributions as improper priors on state dependent parameters will lead to improper posterior distributions in the case where no observation will be assigned to a specific state. Thus, we assume the following conjugate prior distributions:

- The parameters β, σ and η are independent *a priori*, $\pi(\phi) = \pi(\beta)\pi(\sigma)\pi(\eta)$.
- β is assumed normal $\mathcal{N}(b_0, B_0^{-1})$.
- σ_1, σ_2 are independent *a priori*. The natural prior is inverse Gamma, $\sigma_i \sim IG(g_0, G_0)$, $i = 1, 2$.
- $\eta_{1\cdot}, \eta_{2\cdot}$ are independent *a priori*, and are assumed to have a Dirichlet prior distribution, $\eta_{i\cdot} \sim D(e_1, e_2)$.

Note that the Dirichlet prior specification of the transition probabilities is equivalent to a Beta distribution in the present two states specification, $\eta_{i\cdot} \sim \text{Beta}(e_1, e_2)$. The Dirichlet specification enables a straightforward extension to more than 2 states, however. Moreover, the state independent hyperparameters render the prior invariant to state permutations, i.e. the labeling of the states can be interchanged (state 1 becomes state 2 and vice versa) without affecting the mass of the prior. This property combined with the fact that the prior integrates to one, makes it readily available for the estimation of the marginal likelihood $L(y^N)$ using the bridge sampling techniques discussed in detail for mixture and switching models in Frühwirth-Schnatter (2001b).

3. The sampling scheme

The estimation of the model parameters and of the latent state variable is based on MCMC simulation methods using the permutation sampler proposed in Frühwirth-Schnatter (2001a). The method uses the Gibbs sampling technique to obtain an inference on the posterior distribution of θ by simulating successively out of the conditional posterior distributions of the appropriately blocked parameter vector:

(i) $\pi(S^N|\phi, y^N)$
(ii) $\pi(\eta|s^N)$
(iii) $\pi(\beta|\sigma, s^N, y^N)$
(iv) $\pi(\sigma|\beta, s^N, y^N)$

Steps (i) and (ii) are by now standard in the literature. Albert and Chib (1993) derived a single-move sampler for the latent state variable vector S^N. Here instead we sample S^N in a multi-move manner as described in detail in Chib (1996), Carter and Kohn (1994) and Shephard (1994). Then, for given S^N, η is sampled out of its posterior distribution, which is a product of independent Dirichlet distributions,

$$\pi(\eta|s^N) = \prod_{i=1}^{2} \pi(\eta_{i\cdot}|s^N) = \prod_{i=1}^{2} D(e_{i1} + N_{i1}, e_{i2} + N_{i2}). \tag{6}$$

The derivation of (iii) and (iv) reduces to standard Bayesian analysis. (iii) is based on a regression with heteroskedastic errors. We rewrite equation (1) as

$$y_t = S_t^1 \cdot X_t\beta_1 + S_t^2 \cdot X_t\beta_2 + \varepsilon_t, \quad \varepsilon_t \sim \mathcal{N}(0, \sigma_{s_t}) \tag{7}$$

where $S_t^j = 1$ iff $S_t = j$ and 0 otherwise, $j = 1, 2$. Combining the prior distribution with (7), the conditional posterior distribution of β is multivariate normal,

$$\pi(\beta|\sigma, s^N, y^N) = \mathcal{N}(b, B), \tag{8}$$

where $b = B(Z'Wy + B_0b_0)$ and $B = (Z'WZ + B_0)^{-1}$. The vector $y = y^N$ gathers all left-hand variables in (7) and Z is the predictor matrix of the system,

$$Z = \begin{bmatrix} S_1^1 \cdot X_1 & S_1^2 \cdot X_1 \\ \vdots & \vdots \\ S_N^1 \cdot X_N & S_N^2 \cdot X_N \end{bmatrix}.$$

The weighting matrix W takes into account the heteroskedastic nature of the observations, $W = \text{diag}(w_1, \dots, w_N)$, where $w_t = \sigma_{s_t}^{-1}$.

Step (iv) samples the variances $\sigma = (\sigma_1, \sigma_2)$. Given all other model parameters, s^N, and the observations, the posterior distribution of σ is a product of independent inverse Gamma distributions:

$$\pi(\sigma|\beta, s^N, y^N) = \prod_{i=1}^{2} \pi(\sigma_i|\beta, s^N, y^N) = \prod_{i=1}^{2} IG(g_i, G_i), \tag{9}$$

where $g_i = g_0 + 0.5 \cdot \sum_{t=1}^{N} S_t^i$ and $G_i = G_0 + 0.5 \cdot \sum_{t=1}^{N} S_t^i (y_t - Z_t\beta)^2$, with Z_t denoting the tth row of the matrix Z.

Throughout, we sample out of the unconstrained posterior, i.e. the sampled values are accepted irrespective of whether the restriction in (2) is fulfilled or not. If the restriction is violated, a permutation (defined by ρ) completes the sampler that reorders the parameters accordingly to fulfill the restriction. For the two states specification, this amounts to interchanging the values of the state dependent parameters and of the state vector itself as well:

$$\begin{aligned}
(\beta_1, \beta_2) &:= (\beta_2, \beta_1), \\
(\sigma_1, \sigma_2) &:= (\sigma_2, \sigma_1), \\
s^N &:= (\rho(s_0), \rho(s_1), \dots, \rho(s_N)), \\
\eta &:= (\tilde{\eta}_{1\cdot}, \tilde{\eta}_{2\cdot}), \quad \begin{aligned} \tilde{\eta}_{1\cdot} &:= (\eta_{22}, \eta_{21}) \\ \tilde{\eta}_{2\cdot} &:= (\eta_{12}, \eta_{11}). \end{aligned}
\end{aligned} \tag{10}$$

If a suitable identifying restriction is not available or is not known a priori, then post-processing the MCMC output of a random permutation sampler in an exploratory way often proves to be a useful tool in finding such a restriction. To this aim, the permutation step consists in a random permutation of the sampled values in order to explore the unrestricted posterior distribution of the model parameters.

4. Model selection

Normally, the number of autoregressive lags, p, of distributed lags of the exogenous variable, q, as well as the number of states, K, are not known a priori. For given K, selection of the order parameters p and q could be based on likelihood ratio tests or on some information criteria like AIC or SIC. Testing the null of $K = 1$ versus the non-nested alternative $K = 2$ raises non-trivial problems, however. As some parameters are not identified under the null, the likelihood ratio test statistic departs from its standard χ^2 distribution (Hansen, 1992, 1996). Within the Bayesian context we circumvent these problems by estimating the marginal likelihood $L(y^N)$, a measure that is independent of specific parameter values. A direct model comparison is then feasible by means of Bayes factors.

To apply the bridge sampler described and investigated in detail in Frühwirth-Schnatter (2001b) we need an arbitrary function $\alpha(\phi)$ such that $\int \alpha(\phi)\pi(\phi|y^N)q(\phi)\,d\phi > 0$, where $q(\phi)$ is a distribution with known density that approximates in a simple manner the posterior distribution of the parameters. The estimate of the marginal likelihood is then based on the following identity:

$$1 = \frac{\int \alpha(\phi)\pi(\phi|y^N)q(\phi)\,d\phi}{\int \alpha(\phi)q(\phi)\pi(\phi|y^N)\,d\phi} = \frac{\int \alpha(\phi)\pi^*(\phi|y^N)q(\phi)\,d\phi}{L(y^N)\int \alpha(\phi)q(\phi)\pi(\phi|y^N)\,d\phi}, \tag{11}$$

where we use the fact that $L(y^N)$ is the normalizing constant of the unnormalized posterior distribution:

$$\pi(\phi|y^N) = \frac{L(y^N|\phi)\pi(\phi)}{L(y^N)} = \frac{\pi^*(\phi|y^N)}{L(y^N)}. \tag{12}$$

Let E_f denote expectation with respect to the density f, then (11) can be rewritten:

$$L(y^N) = \frac{E_q(\alpha(\phi)\pi^*(\phi|y^N))}{E_\pi(\alpha(\phi)q(\phi))}. \tag{13}$$

If we have a sample out of each density q and π, $\tilde{\phi}^{(l)}$, $l = 1, \ldots, L$, and $\phi^{(m)}$, $m = 1, \ldots, M$, respectively, (13) can be estimated by

$$\hat{L}(y^N) = \frac{\hat{E}_q}{\hat{E}_\pi} = \frac{L^{-1}\sum_{l=1}^{L}\alpha(\tilde{\phi}^{(l)})\pi^*(\tilde{\phi}^{(l)}|y^N)}{M^{-1}\sum_{m=1}^{M}\alpha(\phi^{(m)})q(\phi^{(m)})}. \tag{14}$$

From the several alternatives at hand, the present investigation uses the optimal bridge function (Meng and Wong, 1996, Frühwirth-Schnatter, 2001b) for $\alpha(\phi)$, and $q(\phi)$ is constructed by a mixture of the densities given in (6), (8) and (9):

$$q(\phi) = 1/U\sum_{u=1}^{U}\pi(\eta|s^{N(u)})\pi(\beta|y^N, s^{N(u)}, (\eta,\sigma)^{(u)})\pi(\sigma|y^N, s^{N(u)}, (\eta,\beta)^{(u)}), \tag{15}$$

where the elements (u) entering the mixture in (15) are chosen randomly from the simulations of the MCMC output. Out of (15) we simulate the L values $\tilde{\phi}^{(l)}$, $l = 1, \ldots, L$, while the M values $\phi^{(m)}$, $m = 1, \ldots, M$, used to evaluate (14) are directly chosen (randomly) from the MCMC output.

5. Results

The model described so far is applied to quarterly real GDP growth and the first difference of the Austrian 3-month interest rate to assess whether the effects of monetary policy are asymmetric over time. GDP is seasonally adjusted. The data cover the period from the first quarter of 1976 to the last quarter of 1998. Figure 3, bottom panel, depicts the series used in the analysis. The most general version of the model investigated allows for state dependent parameters except the autoregressive ones. The explicit specification of equation (1) is:

$$y_t = \mu_{S_t} + \sum_{i=1}^{p} \beta_{yi} y_{t-i} + \sum_{i=1}^{q} \beta_{mS_t,i} x_{t-i} + \varepsilon_t, \quad \varepsilon_t \sim \text{i.i.d.}\mathcal{N}(0, \sigma_{S_t}), \tag{16}$$

where y_t stands for the growth rate of GDP and x_t represents the measure for monetary policy, in particular the first difference of the interest rate. Including only lags of the interest rate reflects the usual identifying assumption that GDP reacts with a lag to monetary policy actions.

For the estimation, the hyperparameters of the prior distribution were set according to:

- $\beta \sim \mathcal{N}(0, I)$, where I is the identity matrix, and $\beta = (\mu_1, \mu_2, \beta_{y,1}, \ldots, \beta_{y,p}, \beta_{m1,1}, \ldots, \beta_{m2,q})$.
- $\sigma_i \sim IG(1, 2)$, $i = 1, 2$,
- $\eta_{i\cdot} \sim D(1, 1)$, $i = 1, 2$.

These priors reflect rather vague information on the model parameters. The unit scale of the variance for β can be justified by the fact that GDP growth rates and the (first difference of the) interest rate are the variables investigated.[2] Nevertheless, the results discussed later are robust with respect to the scale of the prior as they do not change significantly when it is increased to 4. Note moreover, that we do not restrict the prior to the stationary space for the autoregressive process. It turns out that the sampler by itself yields autoregressive coefficients characterizing a stationary process with coefficient estimates well below one for all model specifications investigated. An alternative would be to use a truncated prior that restricts the parameter space to ensure a stationary autoregressive process. However, in this case, the prior would not integrate to one which would have to be accounted for when estimating the marginal likelihood.

In a first round, we compute the marginal likelihood for various choices of the order p and q, the highest order being 4 and 6, respectively. It proved to be very hard however, to find an identifying restriction that uniquely discriminated between the states across all model specifications. Therefore, we use the random permutation sampler to explore the unconstrained posterior distribution of the parameters, and the best parsimonious model specification is chosen according to the marginal likelihood estimated by means of bridge sampling. Table 1 summarizes the marginal likelihoods for the various lag order specifications. The estimates are based on 6,000 iterations of the sampler after an initial burn-in phase of 2,000 iterations to get rid of the dependence on initial conditions. 1,000 sampled values are selected randomly to form the importance density in (15). The appropriate parsimonious representation in terms of marginal likelihood sets $p = 2$ and $q = 1$. The bottom panel of the table documents that the marginal likelihood is improved for the specification that assumes a state-independent variance, the log of the Bayes factor being 1.68 in favour of

[2] The scale allows quarterly effects of a 100 basis-point increase in the interest rate up to $+/-2\%$ in quarterly GDP growth (which amounts to $+/-8\%$ on an annualized basis) within the 95% confidence interval.

Table 1. Marginal likelihoods (standard errors in parenthesis) estimated by the bridge sampler for given lag orders p and q of the 2-states model. The estimation is based on the random permutation sampler. Throughout, 1,000 out of the 6,000 sampled values of the posterior distribution are randomly selected to construct the mixture density $q(\phi)$

q / p	6	5	4	3	2	1
4	−128.519 (0.012)	−129.601 (0.011)	−130.284 (0.012)	−128.724 (0.013)	−126.429 (0.009)	−123.931 (0.012)
3	−126.318 (0.011)	−127.369 (0.011)	−128.007 (0.011)	−127.629 (0.011)	−125.402 (0.008)	−122.882 (0.008)
2	−124.698 (0.009)	−125.697 (0.011)	−126.308 (0.011)	−125.899 (0.011)	−124.934 (0.009)	**−122.401** (0.008)
1	−122.955 (0.010)	−123.869 (0.009)	−124.731 (0.010)	−124.156 (0.009)	−122.885 (0.009)	−123.621 (0.006)
$\sigma_1 = \sigma_2,\ p = 2,\ q = 1$: **−120.723** (0.007)						

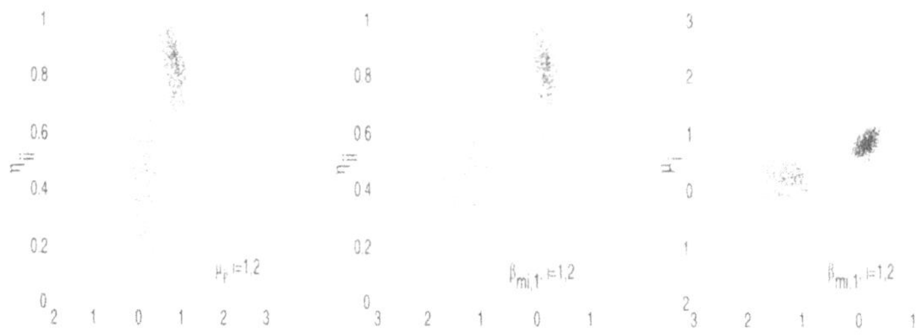

Fig. 1. Markov switching model with the interest rate difference for $p = 2$, $q = 1$, and no switching variances. Scatter plots of sampled values for μ_i and $\beta_{mi,j}$ against persistence η_{ii}, $i,j = 1,2$, and against each other, panel (a), (b) and (c) respectively.

the constant variance specification. Thus, in the following we will discuss the results of a 2-state, constant variance model specification with $p = 2$ and $q = 1$.

To find an adequate state-identifying restriction, the MCMC output of the random permutation sampler is post-processed in an exploratory manner. Figure 1 provides scatter plots of the sampled values for μ and β against persistence and against each other, respectively. Whereas it seems difficult to discriminate the states by means of the persistence parameters η_{ii} or the constant μ_i, $i = 1,2$, panel (b) and (c) clearly reveal that the states might be identified by means of $\beta_{mi,1}$. The constrained permutation sampler was then used to infer the state-dependent parameters and the posterior state probabilities by assuming $\beta_{m1,1} < \beta_{m2,1}$.

Table 2 summarizes the posterior distribution of all model parameters, and figure 2 displays the marginal posterior distributions of the state dependent parameters. Although the posterior distributions overlap in some cases, the states seem to be well-discriminated using the restriction on $\beta_{mi,1}$. Mean, standard error and median of the posterior distribution (see table 2) are simply

Table 2. Markov switching model with interest rate difference for $p = 2$ and $q = 1$. Posterior distribution of the model parameters.

par	mean	sd	median	95% conf.int.	
μ_1	0.2041	0.3135	0.2153	−0.4414	0.7767
μ_2	0.8650	0.1851	0.8593	0.5268	1.2332
β_{y1}	−0.0861	0.1050	−0.0858	−0.2964	0.1238
β_{y2}	−0.0814	0.1085	−0.0802	−0.3011	0.1228
$\beta_{m1,1}$	−1.4040	0.3604	−1.3794	−2.1715	−0.7700
$\beta_{m2,1}$	0.1509	0.1537	0.1474	−0.1438	0.4591
σ	0.5231	0.1041	0.5094	0.3559	0.7627
η_{11}	0.4370	0.1749	0.4351	0.1141	0.7767
η_{12}	0.5630	0.1749	0.5649	0.2228	0.8856
η_{21}	0.1934	0.1045	0.1810	0.0319	0.4326
η_{22}	0.8066	0.1045	0.8190	0.5673	0.9681

marginal likelihood: −120.723 (0.007)
marginal likelihood with $\beta_{m1,i} = \beta_{m2,i}$: −127.898 (0.007)
marginal likelihood with $K = 1$: −128.081

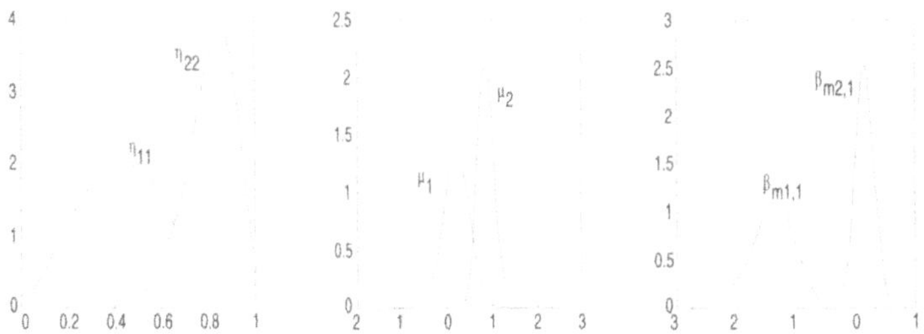

(a) (b) (c)

Fig. 2. Markov switching model with interest rate difference for $p = 2$ and $q = 1$. Identified model with $\beta_{m1,1} < \beta_{m2,1}$. Posterior distribution for η_{ii}, μ_i and $\beta_{mi,1}$, $i = 1, 2$, panel (a), (b) and (c), respectively.

computed by taking the mean, the standard deviation and the median of the retained MCMC output values, respectively. The 95% confidence interval is estimated using the lower and the upper 2.5th percentiles. State 1 seems to pertain to a below-average growth state (0.8% on an annualized basis) with low persistence, the mean persistence to remain in the prevailing state being lower than the mean probability to switch. State 2 relates to above-average growth periods and displays a considerable persistence. Our hypothesis of a stronger effect of monetary policy during periods of subdued economic performance is not rejected by the results, $\beta_{m1,1}$ being much lower than $\beta_{m2,1}$, and significantly negative. The bottom panel of table 2 reports the marginal likelihood of the estimated model along with marginal likelihoods of additional restricted specifications. In any case, the model with state dependent parameters outperforms a specification assuming state-independent effects of monetary policy ($\beta_{m1,i} = \beta_{m2,i}$) and one assuming overall state-independent parameters ($K = 1$), the log of the Bayes factor being 7.18 and 7.34 in favour of the switching specification, respectively.

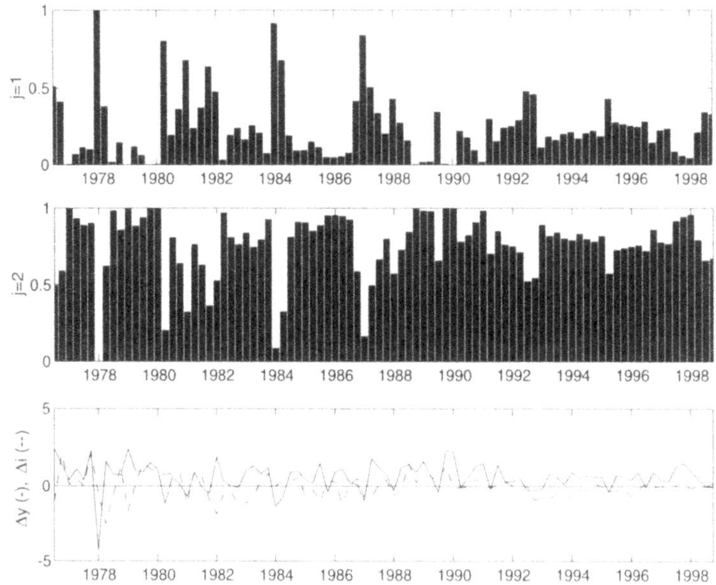

Fig. 3. Markov switching model with interest rate difference for $p = 2$ and $q = 1$. Posterior state probabilities with a plot of GDP growth and the interest rate difference.

Finally, the posterior smoothed state probabilities $P(S_t|y^N)$ are depicted in figure 3 along with the series for GDP growth and the interest rate difference. They are computed by averaging over the 6,000 paths for s^N, each simulated while iterating over the MCMC sampler. At first sight, it is not obvious that the states relate to specific business cycle periods. However, the prevalence of state one clusters around periods of economic slowdown. This relates in particular to the dates around 1980/81, 1983/84 and 1986/87. The classification of the first quarter of 1978 to state 1 is an artifact due to the effect that the anticipated introduction of a luxury tax (a tax on mostly imported goods) had on sales. Finally, as the economic slack of the years 1992/1993, quite strong in major EU countries, fell out only moderately in Austria, the sampler fails to clearly classify it to one of the two states.

6. Robustness analysis

6.1. Using a different restriction

In the previous section we emphasized the use of the random permutation sampler to find a unique state-identifying restriction. Many macroeconomic applications however, estimate a constrained model based on a restriction which is thought to be appropriate on a priori grounds. A usual restriction for the present model would be $\mu_1 < \mu_2$. Figure 4 depicts the posterior distribution of the state dependent parameters using the output of the permutation sampler based on $\mu_1 < \mu_2$. Panel (b) reflects the fact that the states are not well

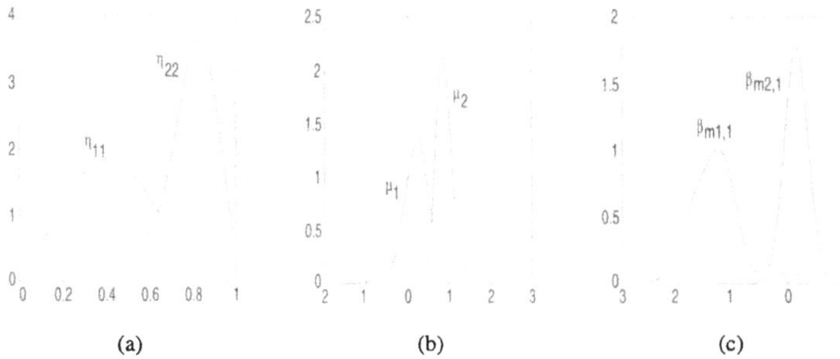

Fig. 4. Markov switching model with interest rate difference for $p = 2$ and $q = 1$. Identified model with $\mu_1 > \mu_2$. Posterior distribution for η_{ii}, μ_i and $\beta_{mi,1}$, $i = 1, 2$, panel (a), (b) and (c), respectively.

discriminated on the grounds of μ as their posterior distributions overlap over a considerable range. It happens then that sampled values for $\beta_{m1,1}$ and $\beta_{m2,1}$ are wrongly classified after permutation, which leads to multimodal posterior distributions for the $\beta_{mi,1}$'s. Three major concerns arise due to this multimodality. First, there would be an upward and a downward bias in the mean estimate of $\beta_{m1,1}$ and $\beta_{m2,1}$, respectively, if these simulated values were used to compile table 2. Second, the decrease in precision (reflected in an increased estimate of the standard deviation) pertains to the other parameters as well, and leads to fatter tailed posterior distributions for μ and η (see panel (a) and (b)). Third, estimates of the marginal likelihood would also be biased as the importance density $q(\phi)$ builds on a normal approximation of the posterior distribution. This would interfere with model selection and might potentially bias the results towards a no switching specification.

6.2. Estimating the model without the outlier

To assess the influence of the outlier in GDP growth in the first quarter of 1978, we estimate the model for the restricted sample period beginning in 1978/2. The best specification in terms of marginal likelihood sets $p = 1$ and $q = 1$. The results are displayed in table 3. Basically, the Markov switching specification still outperforms the specification assuming state-independent parameters on the interest rate difference and a no-switching specification. Interestingly, the mean growth and variance parameters change only marginally. The influence on the parameters is reflected by a significant reduction in the interest rate effect during periods of below-average growth, the mean estimate decreases (in absolute value) from -1.4 to -0.6. Moreover, both identified states now display significant persistence, the mean persistence of remaining in state 1 and state 2 being 0.63 and 0.67, respectively. Figure 5 displays the posterior distributions of the state-dependent parameters. Overlapping distributions for the persistence parameter reflect the estimation of two states with nearly equal persistence. Moreover, the effect of estimating the model without the outlier on $\beta_{m1,1}$ is reflected in a rightward shift of its posterior distribution. Finally, note that the mean estimated posterior probability of state 1 (see figure 6) now relates more clearly to periods of economic slack as a whole, and not just to some

Table 3. Markov switching model with interest rate difference for $p = 1$ and $q = 1$. Sample period 1978/2–1998/4. Posterior distribution of the model parameters.

par	mean	sd	median	95% conf.int.	
μ_1	0.2403	0.2143	0.2469	−0.1967	0.6220
μ_2	0.8809	0.2280	0.8745	0.4532	1.3420
β_{y1}	−0.0305	0.1221	−0.0315	−0.2655	0.2089
$\beta_{m1,1}$	−0.5690	0.3084	−0.5317	−1.2836	−0.0666
$\beta_{m2,1}$	0.2844	0.2061	0.2691	−0.0719	0.7445
σ	0.4750	0.1075	0.4623	0.3015	0.7202
η_{11}	0.6287	0.2010	0.6567	0.1928	0.9468
η_{12}	0.3713	0.2010	0.3432	0.0526	0.8064
η_{21}	0.3254	0.1697	0.3068	0.0547	0.7113
η_{22}	0.6746	0.1697	0.6932	0.2886	0.9453

marginal likelihood: −102.674 (0.007)
marginal likelihood with $\beta_{m1,i} = \beta_{m2,i}$: −104.315 (0.004)
marginal likelihood with $K = 1$: −103.734

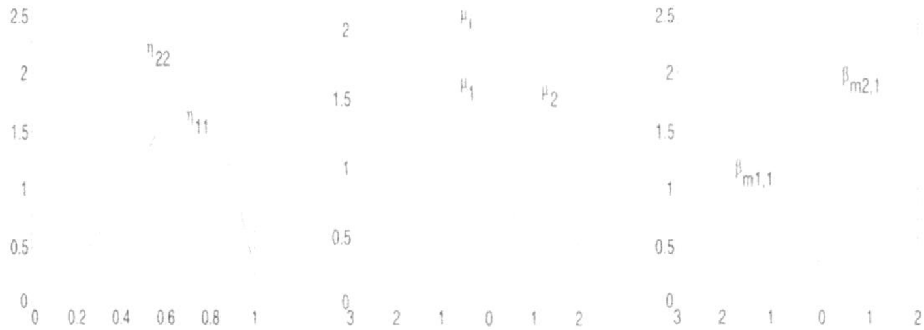

(a) (b) (c)

Fig. 5. Markov switching model with interest rate difference for $p = 1$ and $q = 1$. Sample period 1978/2–1998/4. Identified model with $\beta_{m1,1} < \beta_{m2,1}$. Posterior distribution for η_{ii}, μ_i and $\beta_{mi,1}$, $i = 1, 2$, panel (a), (b) and (c), respectively.

quarters of it as in the model estimated using the whole sample period. To summarize, even if the presence of an outlier in the observation sample (obviously) influences the inference, it is noteworthy that the basic evidence, namely that monetary policy displays asymmetric effects over time, remains unchanged whether we use the whole or only the restricted sample to obtain it.

6.3. Using the interest rate level

Table 4 presents the results we obtained using the interest rate level as a measure for monetary policy stance rather than the first difference. The model specification that performs best in terms of marginal likelihood is the one with order parameters $p = 1$ and $q = 2$. The evidence remains broadly unchanged when compared to the results obtained with the interest rate difference. The states relate both to below- and above-average growth periods, the mean persistence of the former being lower than its switching probability, while the latter displays considerable persistence. A clear significant negative effect of monetary

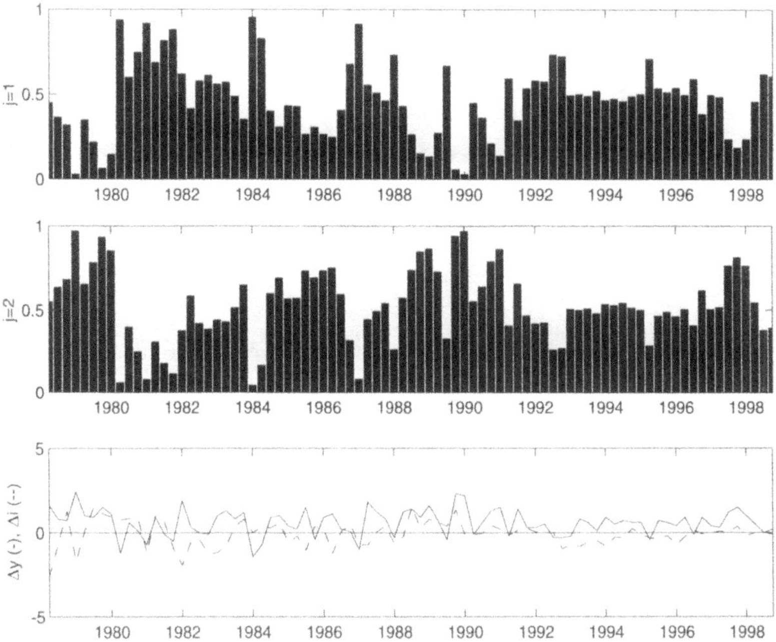

Fig. 6. Markov switching model with interest rate difference for $p = 1$ and $q = 1$. Sample period 1978/2–1998/4. Posterior state probabilities with a plot of GDP growth and the interest rate difference.

Table 4. Markov switching model with interest rate level for $p = 1$ and $q = 2$. β_{mi}, $i = 1, 2$, refers to the sum over the parameters in state i, $\beta_{mi} = \sum_{j=1}^{2} \beta_{mi,j}$.

par	mean	sd	median	95% conf.int.	
μ_1	0.2414	0.7104	0.2408	−1.2116	1.6574
μ_2	0.9416	0.4458	0.9687	0.0260	1.6811
β_{y1}	−0.0832	0.1002	−0.0816	−0.2847	0.1108
$\beta_{m1,1}$	−1.2193	0.4322	−1.2535	−1.9997	−0.1441
$\beta_{m1,2}$	1.1696	0.5017	1.2129	−0.0312	2.0548
$\beta_{m2,1}$	0.0681	0.1674	0.0550	−0.2127	0.4315
$\beta_{m2,2}$	−0.1125	0.2219	−0.0883	−0.6231	0.1752
β_{m1}	−0.0497	0.1543	−0.0280	−0.4317	0.1695
β_{m2}	−0.0444	0.1232	−0.0322	−0.4575	0.0921
σ	0.5531	0.1151	0.5383	0.3696	0.8065
η_{11}	0.4476	0.2076	0.4270	0.0956	0.9709
η_{12}	0.5524	0.2076	0.5730	0.0290	0.9043
η_{21}	0.1854	0.1389	0.1557	0.0151	0.5550
η_{22}	0.8146	0.1389	0.8442	0.4443	0.9849

marginal likelihood: −124.761 (0.007)
marginal likelihood with $\beta_{m1,i} = \beta_{m2,i}$: −127.938 (0.005)
marginal likelihood with $K = 1$: −128.279

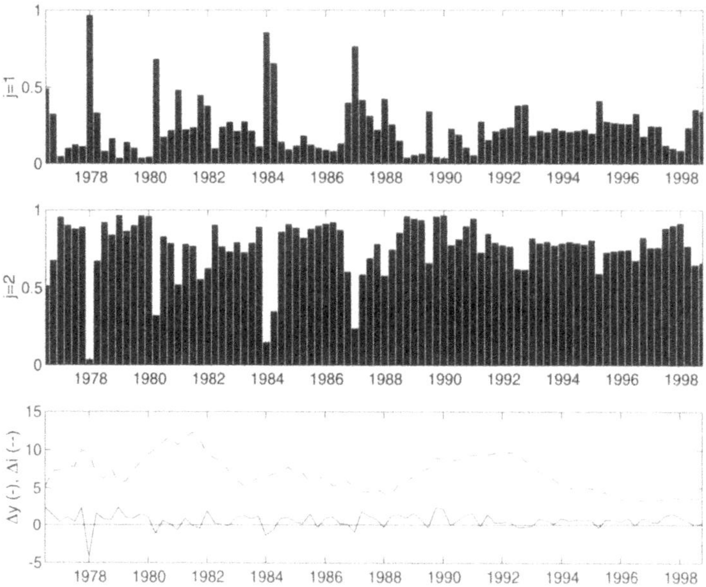

Fig. 7. Markov switching model with interest rate level for $p = 1$ and $q = 2$. Posterior state probabilities with a plot of GDP growth and the interest rate.

policy is recorded for periods of below-average growth only. The total effect of monetary policy, computed as the sum of the coefficients on the interest rate in each state, $\beta_{mi} = \sum_{j=1}^{2} \beta_{mi,j}$, $i = 1, 2$, respectively, seems to be negative on average, the significance of the effect remains doubtful, however. The bottom panel of table 4 documents again that in terms of marginal likelihood a state-dependent specification of the parameters outperforms a specification where the parameters on the interest rate are assumed equal across regimes ($\beta_{m1,i} = \beta_{m2,i}$, $i = 1, 2$) and a specification assuming state-independent parameters ($K = 1$).

Figure 7 depicts the posterior state probabilities obtained by averaging over the sampled values of the MCMC output. Despite the relation to business cycle periods becoming weaker in this setting, single quarters within periods of economic slack represent the first state. The same comment as before apply to the first quarter in 1978 and to the ones around 1992/93.

6.4. Using a policy shock

So far, the use of the first difference of the interest rate and its level as a measure for monetary policy can be justified by the peg of the Austrian Schilling to the German Mark (officially since 1981). Austrian rates follow very closely German ones (the correlation being around 0.9) and basically reflect German policy moves. Nevertheless, there may be a residual part in the moves of domestic interest rates necessary to maintain the peg that accommodate domestic shocks. The magnitude of those moves and their effect as well should be small, however, because of the Austrian economy being quite integrated with the German one. The domestic policy shock is estimated with the use of a SVAR taking into account the relationship of the Austrian with the German economy.[3] The resulting shock series covers the period 1976/4 to 1998/4. Within this setting the lag orders p and q have to be chosen with some caution. It turns out that the specification $p = 1$, $q = 6$ performs best in terms of marginal likelihood. However, most of the parameters are insignificant. This result obtains from the artifact of the data already mentioned before. With the high lag specification the effective sample range for the estimation begins in 1978/2 and thus excludes the outlier at the beginning of the sample. Therefore, the best specification with significant parameters is chosen, i.e. $p, q = 1$.

The results[4] are comparable to the previous ones using the first difference of the interest rate as a measure for monetary policy. The switching specification performs again best, and monetary policy is effective when the low growth regime prevails while it has no effect on real activity during above-average growth periods. The persistence of the first state (η_{11}) is low in comparison with the relatively high one of the second state. However, the posterior state probabilities document that the results are mainly driven by the outlier in the first quarter of 1978.

Therefore, the sample is also restricted to exclude the observations previous to 1978/2, and as expected above, the effect of domestic policy shocks becomes negligible. Table 5 reports that the state independent specification now outper-

Table 5. Markov switching model with domestic policy shock, $p, q = 1$. Sample period 1978/2–1998/4.

par	mean	sd	median	95% conf.int.	
μ_1	0.3936	0.3517	0.4373	−0.3888	0.9394
μ_2	0.6481	0.3772	0.6725	−0.2559	1.3234
β_{y1}	−0.0072	0.1187	−0.0061	−0.2354	0.2277
$\beta_{m1,1}$	−0.3681	0.3832	−0.3264	−1.2328	0.2421
$\beta_{m2,1}$	0.5392	0.4673	0.4299	−0.1279	1.7015
σ	0.5716	0.1102	0.5637	0.3787	0.8114
η_{11}	0.6838	0.2287	0.7317	0.1547	0.9865
η_{12}	0.3162	0.2287	0.2682	0.0135	0.8443
η_{21}	0.3425	0.2231	0.3122	0.0131	0.8185
η_{22}	0.6575	0.2231	0.6877	0.1814	0.9869

marginal likelihood: −103.475 (0.008)
marginal likelihood with $\beta_{m1,i} = \beta_{m2,i}$: −103.932 (0.008)
marginal likelihood with $K = 1$: −103.327

[3] The VAR includes real GDP, the unemployment rate, the consumer price index, the 3-month Austrian interest rate and the nominal effective exchange rate as endogenous variables, and additionally German GDP as exogenous variable. The system is identified by a Cholesky decomposition of the residual covariance matrix. The impulse responses display the expected pattern, and the inclusion of German GDP removes the often encountered price puzzle (see also Valderrama, 2001).

[4] Not displayed in order to save space. The interested reader may refer to the working paper version of the investigation (Kaufmann, 2001).

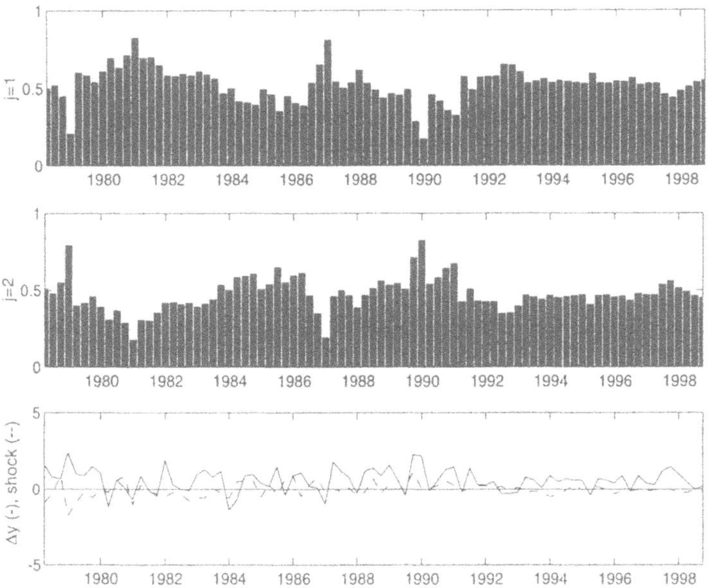

Fig. 8. Markov switching model with domestic policy shock $p, q = 1$. Sample period 1978/2–1998/4. Posterior state probabilities with a plot of GDP growth and the policy shock.

forms the switching one, the log of the Bayes factor being marginally in favour of $K = 1$ with 0.15. This is also reflected by the posterior state probabilities in figure 8 where most of the time the sampler is not able to distinctively discriminate between the regimes. When restricting the specification to $K = 1$ (the detailed results of which are again not displayed in order to save space), the mean estimate of policy shock effects remains marginally significantly negative (-0.35 with a standard error of 0.2).

To summarize again, the inference clearly documents that the main policy impulses come from Germany and are propagated through interest rates. While monetary policy in general has significantly negative effects on real activity during periods of low growth, the overall effects of domestic policy shocks are marginally significant, and not asymmetric over time.

7. Conclusion

The present paper assesses whether the effects of monetary policy in Austria are asymmetric over time. We estimate within a Bayesian framework a univariate model for Austrian GDP including additionally the first difference of the 3-month Austrian interest rate as exogenous variable. To measure asymmetric effects of monetary policy the most general specification allows for state dependent coefficients on the interest rate difference, and state dependent constant and variance as well. We apply the random permutation sampler in a first round to perform model selection by means of marginal likelihoods and to find a suitable, unique state-identifying restriction. The results of the identified parsimonious model document a significant negative effect of monetary policy during periods of below-average growth, while the effect appears to be insignificant during periods of normal- or above-average growth. Obviously, quarters of below-average growth occur during periods of economic slack, which is reflected in the plot of posterior state probabilities. The results thus are in line with theoretical derivations of asymmetric effects of monetary policy building on price rigidities and implying a convex supply curve. The basic evidence is refined and remains broadly unchanged when a restricted sample is used for the inference that eliminates the outlier of GDP growth due to the effect that the anticipated introduction of the luxury tax had on sales in the first quarter of 1978.

An additional investigation demonstrates that identifying restrictions have to be set with great care as relatively poor constraints may lead to multimodal posterior distributions that bias the posterior inference. Moreover, using the interest rate level rather than the first difference of it does not change the results significantly. A negative effect of monetary policy is again recorded during periods of economic slowdown. The significance of the total effect of monetary policy seems doubtful in both states, however. A final exercise uses a domestic policy shock identified with the use of a SVAR that takes into account the relation of Austria's economy with the German one. Still, a marginal negative effect of monetary policy is evidenced that is not asymmetric over time, however.

To conclude, the results presented here are in line with comparable investigations on European countries. In particular, the Austrian results are comparable to those for Germany documented in Kakes (1998), where a significant negative effect of monetary policy is found during recession periods while it is insignificant during boom times. Moreover, when using a monetary policy shock identified by means of a SVAR, the real effect of monetary policy is insignificant for the Netherlands and Belgium, two small European countries that were also closely following the German Mark. This finding is reproduced for Austria in the present paper as well when we restrict the sample to exclude the outlier in GDP growth recorded for the first quarter of 1978. Kakes advocates different policy regimes to explain the insignificant response of the Netherlands and Belgium. For Austria however, this might be due to the fact that unexpected interest rate moves necessary to maintain the peg did not have a major effect on the economy due to the high synchronization of the Austrian business cycle with the German one. The results are also compatible with the ones presented in Peersman and Smets (2001) who investigate the asymmetric effects of monetary policy in the Euro area. When using the first difference of the interest rate, they estimate a negative effect of monetary policy during recession times while it is insignificant during boom times. In particular for Austria, they find an overall significant negative effect of monetary policy measured by a shock identified on the basis of a Euro area wide SVAR, that is not asymmetric over the business cycle, however. Note finally that, interestingly, the posterior state probabilities of the present analysis are following quite closely the ones in Kakes for Germany, and the ones in Peersman and Smets for the European common cycle.

References

Albert JH, Chib S (1993) Bayes inference via Gibbs sampling of autoregressive time series subject to Markov mean and variance shifts. Journal of Business & Economic Statistics 11:1–15

Azariadis C, Smith B (1998) Financial intermediation and regime switching in business cycles. The American Economic Review 88:516–536
Ball L, Mankiw NG (1994) Asymmetric price adjustment and economic fluctuations. The Economic Journal 104:247–261
Bernanke BS, Gertler M (1989) Agency costs, net worth, and business fluctuations. The American Economic Review 79:14–31
Bernanke BS, Gertler M (1995) Inside the black box: The credit channel of monetary policy transmission. Journal of Economic Perspectives 9:27–48
Bernanke BS, Mihov I (1998) Measuring monetary policy. The Quarterly Journal of Economics 113:869–902
Carter CK, Kohn R (1994) On Gibbs sampling for state space models. Biometrika 84:541–553
Chib S (1996) Calculating posterior distributions and modal estimates in Markov mixture models. Journal of Econometrics 75:79–97
Chib S, Greenberg E (1996) Markov chain Monte Carlo simulation methods in econometrics. Econometric Theory 12:409–431
Cover JP (1992) Asymmetric effects of positive and negative money-supply shocks. The Quarterly Journal of Economics 108:1261–1282
Farmer RE (1985) Implicit contracts with asymmetric information and bankruptcy: The effect of interest rates on layoffs. Review of Economic Studies 52:427–442
Farmer RE (1988) Money and contracts. Review of Economic Studies 55:431–446
Frühwirth-Schnatter S (2001a) MCMC estimation of classical and dynamic switching and mixture models. Journal of the American Statistical Association, forthcoming
Frühwirth-Schnatter S (2001b) Model likelihoods and Bayes factors for switching and mixture models. Technical Report 1999-71, revised version January 2001, Vienna University of Economics and Business Administration
Garcia R, Schaller H (1995) Are the effects of monetary policy asymmetric? Scientific Series 95s-6, CIRANO
Hamilton JD (1989) A new approach to the economic analysis of nonstationary time series and the business cycle. Econometrica 57:357–384
Hamilton JD (1990) Analysis of time series subject to changes in regime. Journal of Econometrics 45:39–70
Hansen BE (1992) The likelihood ratio test under nonstandard conditions: Testing the Markov switching model of GNP. Journal of Applied Econometrics 7:S61–S82
Hansen BE (1996) Erratum: The likelihood ratio test under nonstandard conditions: Testing the Markov switching model of GNP. Journal of Applied Econometrics 11:195–198
Kakes J (1998) Monetary transmission and business cycle asymmetry. SOM research report 98C36, University of Groningen
Karras G (1996a) Are the output effects of monetary policy asymmetric? Evidence from a sample of European countries. Oxford Bulletin of Economics and Statistics 58:267–278
Karras G (1996b) Why are the effects of money-supply shocks asymmetric? Convex aggregate supply or "pushing on a string"? Journal of Macroeconomics 18:605–619
Kaufmann S (2000) Measuring business cycles with a dynamic Markov switching factor model: an assessment using Bayesian simulation methods. The Econometrics Journal 3:39–65
Kaufmann S (2001) Is there an asymmetric effect of monetary poliy over time? A Bayesian analysis using Austrian data. Working Paper 45, Oesterreichische Nationalbank, Economic Studies
Kaufmann S, Frühwirth-Schnatter S (2000) Bayesian analysis of switching ARCH models. Journal of Time Series Analysis, forthcoming
Kim CJ, Nelson CR (1998) Business cycle turning points, a new coincident index, and tests of duration dependence based on a dynamic factor model with regime-switching. Review of Economics & Statistics 80:188–201
Kim CJ, Nelson CR (1999) State-space models with regime switching. MIT Press, Cambridge Massachusetts
Kiyotaki N (1998) Credit and business cycles. The Japanese Economic Review 49:18–35
Kiyotaki N, Moore J (1997a) Credit chains. mimeo
Kiyotaki N, Moore J (1997b) Credit cycles. Journal of Political Economy 105:211–248
Lenz C (1997) Asymmetric effects of monetary policy in Switzerland. Swiss Journal of Economics and Statistics 133:441–454
Meng X-L, Wong WH (1996) Simulating ratios of normalising constants via a simple identity. Statistica Sinica 6:831–860

Peersman G, Smets F (2001) Are the effects of monetary policy in the Euro area greater in recessions than in booms? Working Paper 52, European Central Bank
Shephard N (1994) Partial non-Gaussian state space. Biometrika 81:115–131
Smith AF, Roberts GO (1993) Bayesian computation via the Gibbs sampler and related Markov Chain Monte Carlo methods. Journal of the Royal Statistical Society B 55:3–23
Tsiddon D (1993) The (mis)behaviour of the aggregate price level. Review of Economic Studies 60:889–902
Valderrama M (2001) Monetary shocks and investment behaviour in Austria: A microeconometric approach. mimeo, Oesterreichische Nationalbank

A regime-switching approach to the study of speculative attacks: A focus on EMS crises

Maria Soledad Martinez Peria*

The World Bank, 1818 H St., N.W., Room MC 3-451, Washington D.C. 20433
(e-mail: mmartinezperia@worldbank.org)

First Version Received: October 2000/Final Version Received: June 2001

Abstract. This paper implements a regime-switching framework to study speculative attacks against EMS currencies during 1979–1993. To identify speculative episodes, we model exchange rates, reserves, and interest rates as time series subject to discrete regime shifts between two possible states: "tranquil" and "speculative". We allow the probabilities of switching between states to be a function of fundamentals and expectations. The regime-switching framework improves the ability to identify speculative attacks vis-à-vis the indices of speculative pressure used in the literature. The results also indicate that fundamentals (particularly budget deficits) and expectations drive the probability of switching to a speculative state.

Key words: Exchange rates, speculative attacks, EMS, Markov regime-switching models

JEL Classification Codes: F30, F33, C32

* I am indebted to Barry Eichengreen, Richard Lyons, Maurice Obstfeld, and James Powell for their advice and encouragement. I greatly benefited from comments from the editors of this issue, James Hamilton and Baldev Raj, and from suggestions from two anonymous referees. I would also like to thank David Bowman, Jon Faust, Michael Gibson, Clive Granger, Dale Henderson, Chang-Tai Hsieh, Steve Kamin, Andy Levin, Gian Maria Milesi-Ferreti, John Rogers, Tom Rothenberg, Paul Ruud, and Sergio Schmukler for very helpful comments. Furthermore, I received fruitful suggestions from seminar participants at related presentations at the Central Bank of Argentina, Dartmouth College, Duke University, the Federal Reserve Bank of Boston, the Federal Reserve Board, the Inter-American Development Bank, Tufts University, Universidad San Andres, Wellesley College, Wesleyan University, and the World Bank Research Department. Finally, I would like to express my gratitude to Matthew Jones and Gretchen Weinbach for their help with the empirical estimations of the EM algorithm.

1. Introduction

Speculative attacks refer to episodes when currencies come under severe pressure to be devalued. In recent years, both developed and developing countries have experienced speculative attacks on their currencies. The European Monetary System (EMS) was severely undermined by intense speculative pressure in 1992–1993. In December 1994, following a speculative attack on the Mexican peso, the currency was devalued. More recently, turbulence in financial markets crippled many Asian currencies, as well as, the Russian ruble and the Brazilian real.

Two types of models, the so-called "first-generation" and "second-generation" models, dominate the existing theoretical literature on the determinants of speculative attacks and devaluations. The first-generation models (following Flood and Garber (1984a) and Krugman (1979), among others) emphasize the relationship between speculative attacks and economic fundamentals. In these models, countries suffer attacks when they run unsustainable monetary and fiscal policies. Thus, budget and trade deficits, appreciations of the real exchange rate, and/or high unemployment rates typically precede first-generation speculative attacks.[1] On the other hand, the second-generation models (following Flood and Garber (1984b) and Obstfeld (1986, 1994), among others) argue that speculative attacks may be self-fulfilling. In these models, expectations play a crucial role in bringing about speculative attacks.

The empirical literature on currency crises has mostly focused on the study of discrete devaluations in developing economies.[2,3] A number of recent papers, however, have also analyzed speculative attacks – namely, episodes where devaluations may occur or where they may be averted at the expense of sizeable losses in reserves and/or large increases in interest rates. Eichengreen, Rose, and Wyplosz (1995, 1996), ERW hereafter, Kaminsky and Reinhart (1996), and Kaminsky, Lizondo, and Reinhart (1998) are the trailblazers in this literature. These studies focus on speculative attacks in industrial (including EMS) and both developed and developing countries, respectively. In particular, ERW (1995) find that unemployment rates, government budget deficits, and domestic credit growth are unrelated to exchange rate episodes in industrial countries, including EMS members. ERW (1996) conclude that fundamentals do not seem to explain EMS crises.

The papers above pursue a two-step approach to identify and study the determinants of speculative attacks. First, they identify speculative attacks by constructing indices of speculative pressure. These are weighted averages of changes in exchanges rates, interest rates, and reserves, since movements in these variables are associated with periods of speculative pressure. They classify a given episode as a speculative attack if the index is above a certain threshold. Based on this classification, they construct a zero/one variable to capture speculative attack episodes in the sample. Second, they analyze the determinants of the likelihood of speculative attacks by estimating logit or

[1] For a model where unemployment rates may affect the likelihood of a speculative attack see Ozkan and Sutherland (1994).

[2] See Blanco and Garber (1986), Cumby and Van Wijnbergern (1989), Edwards (1989), Frankel and Rose (1996), Goldberg (1994), Klein and Marion (1997), and Martinez Peria (1997).

[3] Ötker and Pazarbaşioğlu (1997) use a probit model to analyze the determinants of devaluations in EMS countries.

probit models, where the zero/one variable capturing attacks is used as the dependent variable.[4]

This paper adopts a different approach to study speculative attacks. Currency markets, especially those under fixed and semi-fixed exchange rate regimes, are characterized by periods of calm, interrupted by episodes of speculative pressure. Given the nature of currency markets, this paper implements a regime-switching model with time-varying transition probabilities to, simultaneously, identify speculative attacks and study the determinants of switching to speculative regimes. Though regime shifts are not directly observable, we can draw probabilistic inferences on these episodes from the behavior of observable variables. In particular, large exchange rate depreciations, sharp falls in reserves, and/or increases in interest rates are symptoms of speculative pressure. Thus, this paper identifies speculative attacks by modeling exchange rates, reserves, and interest rate differentials as time series subject to discrete shifts between "tranquil" and "speculative" regimes.[5]

Following the literature on speculative attacks and devaluations, we model transition probabilities as logistic functions of economic fundamentals[6] Also, we include measures of expectations of devaluation, such as interest rate differentials and survey data on expected exchange rates, to allow for the possibility that market expectations drive speculative attacks.

The approach pursued in this paper has methodological and conceptual advantages. First, this method avoids the arbitrariness of the indices of speculative pressure typically used to identify speculative attacks. Constructing such indices requires that we specify which variables to include and what weights to assign to each variable. Instead, in the regime-switching approach, the parameters estimated in the model and the data reveal the state of the economy at each point in time. Second, the regime-switching approach can simultaneously and directly address the question of what causes shifts from and to speculative episodes. In particular, by modeling transition probabilities as a function of fundamentals and expectations, we are able to study the determinants of speculative attacks, as we identify these episodes. Conceptually, this approach recognizes that tranquil periods are intrinsically different from speculative episodes.

This paper implements the regime-switching approach to study speculative attacks on EMS currencies during the period 1979–1993. We estimate two switching models. In the first case, large movements and high volatility in exchange rate changes identify the unobserved regimes. The second model is a vector autoregressive (VAR) switching model of changes in exchange rates, reserves, and interest rate differentials. In both models, we allow transition probabilities to be a function of fundamentals and expectations.

---

[4] Rather than using a probit model to examine the determinants of speculative attacks (as defined by an index of speculative pressure), ERW (1996) conduct a non-parametric analysis of these episodes. Essentially, they compare the behavior of fundamentals in crises and non-crises episodes via non-parametric tests.

[5] This is not the first paper to examine the behavior of exchange rates using a regime-switching framework. Engel and Hamilton (1990) estimate a two-state Markov switching model with constant transition probabilities to explain the behavior of the U.S. dollar against the German mark, the French franc, and British pound over the period 1973–1988. Weinbach (1995) extends the work of Engel and Hamilton to the time-varying transition probability case. However, neither of these papers focuses on the study of speculative attacks.

[6] These fundamentals include: the growth of domestic credit, the ratio of imports to exports, the real exchange rate, the unemployment rate, and the fiscal deficit.

The empirical results indicate that regime-switching models can accurately describe the behavior of changes in exchange rates, interest rates, and reserves in EMS countries. Furthermore, the regime-switching models (in particular the VAR model) can almost perfectly capture the speculative attacks identified by indices of speculative pressure used in the literature, along with other episodes that these indices missed. Finally, regarding the determinants of speculative attacks, we find some support for both the first-generation and second-generation models of attacks, since both economic fundamentals and expectations affect the likelihood of switching to a speculative regime. In particular, budget deficits appear to be the most important factor driving this probability.

This is not the first paper to estimate a regime-switching model to explain the behavior of EMS exchange rates, reserves, and interest rates. Hsieh (1994) is perhaps the closest study to this paper. He identifies periods of speculative attacks against EMS currencies by estimating separate regime-switching models to describe movements in interest rates, reserves, and exchange rates. While Hsieh's study recognizes the suitability of the regime-switching approach to identify speculative attacks, it stops short of building a model that considers the interaction between different symptoms of speculative pressure and that allows for a study of the determinants of regime switches. Recently, other studies like Engel and Hakkio (1996), Gomez-Puig and Montalvo (1997), and Dahlquist and Gray (2000) have estimated regime-switching models to characterize the behavior of EMS exchange rates (in the case of the first study) and interest rates (in the other two). These papers show that this approach represents a significant improvement over other empirical models used in the target zone literature, like the diffusion-jump model of exchange rates and the drift adjusted method to measure credibility.

While the application of regime-switching models to study EMS crises is not new, this paper makes a number of important contributions to the existing literature. First, this paper recognizes that speculative attacks can manifest not only through changes in exchange rates or interest rates, separately, but rather we allow for attacks to be identified from the joint behavior of reserves, exchange rates, and interest rates. In this sense, the application of a VAR regime-switching model to analyze this problem is new. Second, this paper makes an effort to compare the attacks identified by the regime-switching models with the commonly used indices of speculative pressure. Finally, by allowing transition probabilities to be a function of expectations and economic fundamentals, this paper tries to test whether EMS crises fall under the first or second-generation models of speculative attacks.

The rest of the paper is organized as follows. Section 2 describes the data used. Section 3 discusses the empirical approach pursued. Section 4 presents the empirical results. Section 5 examines the question of how well the switching approach captures attacks. Finally, section 6 concludes.

2. The data

We identify and study the nature of speculative attacks in ERM member countries between 1979 and 1993. The following countries are in our sample: Belgium (1979–1993), Denmark (1979–1993), France (1979–1993), Ireland (1979–1993), Italy (1979–1992), Spain (1989–1993), and the UK (1990–1992). Except for Italy and the UK that abandoned the ERM in 1992, the dates in parentheses correspond to the period of membership in the arrangement up until the widening of the band in 1993. We construct most variables for these countries as differences or ratios to the corresponding German values.

Monthly data for this study are from the IMF's International Financial Statistics and the OECD's Main Economic Indicators publications. Survey data on expected exchange rates come from the Currency Forecasters Digest, a Financial Times publication.

3. Empirical estimation approach

Speculative attacks are typically associated with significant depreciations of the exchange rate. However, attacks can also result in sharp falls of reserves or increases in interest rate differentials, depending on the policy pursued by the government at the time of the attacks. For example, the exchange rate might depreciate if the government is not willing to lose reserves or to raise interest rates to defend the currency. Alternatively, if the government is determined to maintain a fixed parity or band, it might be ready to sell reserves or even increase interest rates to deter the outflow of reserves. Therefore, at a given point in time, a speculative attack can be associated with a depreciation of the exchange rate, a fall in reserves, and/or a rise in interest rates. Also, the volatility of these variables might increase during speculative episodes. On the other hand, these three variables are typically stable during periods of tranquility. Thus, exchange rates, reserves, and interest rates are likely to exhibit a different behavior in periods of tranquility than during speculative attack episodes.

This paper estimates two regime-switching models to identify speculative attacks and to study the determinants of switching between regimes. In the first model, we focus on attacks that resulted in exchange rate devaluations. These periods are identified by modeling exchange rates as time series subject to regime changes. In the second model, we adopt a VAR switching structure to allow speculative attacks to be associated with regime shifts in exchange rates, reserves, and/or interest rates differentials. In both models, we assume time-varying transition probabilities that are logistic functions of fundamentals and expectations.

Model 1: The exchange rate switching model

We assume exchange rate changes, Δe_t, follow the process below:[7]

$$\Delta e_t = \alpha_{s_t,0} + \alpha_{s_t,1}[\Delta e_{t-1}] + \alpha_{s_t,2}[\Delta e_{t-2}] + \alpha_{s_t,3}[\Delta e_{t-3}] + \alpha_{s_t,4}[\Delta e_{t-4}] + \sigma(s_t)\varepsilon_t \tag{1}$$

where ε_t is an i.i.d $N(0,1)$ variable.

According to Equation (1), exchange rate changes behave differently depending on the value of S_t. This variable is an unobserved zero/one indicator that characterizes the regime the economy is in at each point in time (tranquil

[7] The exchange rate variable mentioned above is the percentage change in the exchange rate of each currency with respect to the Deutsche mark.

when $S_t = 0$ or speculative when $S_t = 1$). Thus, exchange rates changes follow an AR(4) process, where the mean, variance, and autoregressive parameters of the equation depend on the state in which the economy resides.[8]

In the original Hamilton (1990) regime-switching model, state transitions follow a first-order Markov process and the probabilities assigned to switching or staying in a given state (called transition probabilities) are assumed to be constant. In this paper, we adopt a variant of Hamilton's model developed by Diebold et al. (1994) in which transition probabilities are allowed to be time-varying. In particular, these probabilities are estimated as logistic functions of a conditioning matrix X_{t-1}, as shown in equations (2)–(5).

$$p_t^{00} = P(s_t = 0/s_{t-1} = 0, x_{t-1}; \beta_0) = \frac{\exp(x'_{t-1}\beta_0)}{1 + \exp(x'_{t-1}\beta_0)} \tag{2}$$

$$p_t^{11} = P(s_t = 1/s_{t-1} = 1, x_{t-1}; \beta_1) = \frac{\exp(x'_{t-1}\beta_1)}{1 + \exp(x'_{t-1}\beta_1)} \tag{3}$$

$$p_t^{01} = (1 - p_t^{00}) = P(s_t = 1/s_{t-1} = 0, x_{t-1}; \beta_0) = 1 - \frac{\exp(x'_{t-1}\beta_0)}{1 + \exp(x'_{t-1}\beta_0)} \tag{4}$$

$$p_t^{10} = (1 - p_t^{11}) = P(s_t = 0/s_{t-1} = 1, x_{t-1}; \beta_1) = 1 - \frac{\exp(x'_{t-1}\beta_1)}{1 + \exp(x'_{t-1}\beta_1)} \tag{5}$$

The probability of remaining in a tranquil (speculative) state, given that the economy was in a tranquil (speculative) state in the previous period, is $p_t^{00}(p_t^{11})$. The probability of switching from a tranquil (speculative) state on date $t-1$ to a speculative state (tranquil) in period t is $p_t^{01}(p_t^{10})$.

By allowing transition probabilities to vary over time, we can study the mechanics underlying shifts from tranquil to speculative regimes explicitly. In particular, the goal is to determine whether economic fundamentals and/or expectations have any effect in bringing about shifts to speculative attack regimes.

Following the theoretical literature on speculative attacks, we include the growth of domestic credit, the ratio of imports to exports, the unemployment rate, the fiscal deficit, and interest rates as potential determinants of the transition probabilities. We express all of these variables as differentials with respect to the corresponding German variable.[9] The ratio of imports to exports is used as a proxy of the current account deficit. We also include a real ex-

[8] Hsieh (1994) found the AR(4) model to be the best specification to describe EMS exchange rate movements. The empirical results reported in Table 1 also support this specification. From this table, it is clear that in most specifications lags 1 and 3 are significant in the model for the tranquil state, and lags 3 and 4 are significant in the model for the crisis state.

[9] We measure all variables relative to Germany, because even though the EMS during the period 1979–1993 was in principle a symmetric system, Germany was, in fact, the anchor country. All realignments within the EMS implied devaluations of the currencies with respect to the Deutsche mark. Standarizing or differencing variables vis-à-vis Germany is the conventional approach used in the literature analyzing EMS crises (see Eichengreen, Rose, and Wyplosz (1995), Engel and Hakkio (1996), Gomez-Puig and Montalvo (1997), Hsieh (1994), and Otker and Pazarbasioglu (1997)).

change rate index to capture the possible deterioration in the competitiveness of a country against Germany. Interest rate differentials are incorporated in the estimation of the transition probabilities as a measure of expectations of devaluation.

Like Diebold et al., we adopt the EM algorithm to obtain maximum likelihood estimates of all the parameters in the exchange rate switching model. The EM algorithm maximizes the incomplete-data log likelihood (that for $\{\Delta e_t\}$ alone) via the iterative maximization of the expected complete-data log likelihood (that for $\{\Delta e_t\}$ and $\{s_t\}$), conditional on the observable data. Given some initial estimate of the parameters and the observed data, the EM algorithm begins by calculating the smoothed state probabilities (i.e., the unconditional probability of a particular state). With the estimated smoothed state and transition probabilities, the algorithm constructs the expected complete-data log likelihood function. This is the "E," expectation part of the algorithm. The expected complete-data log likelihood function is then maximized to obtain an updated parameter estimate. This is the "M," maximization part of the algorithm. Using this updated estimate, the algorithm re-calculates the smoothed probabilities again and substitutes them into the expected likelihood function, which is maximized again. This procedure is repeated until convergence (in the parameter estimates or the likelihood function) is obtained.[10]

Model 2: The VAR switching model

Though most speculative attacks result in sizeable changes in the exchange rate, as discussed above, these episodes can also be associated with substantial losses in reserves and/or increases in interest rate differentials. Consequently, to identify speculative attacks, it is important to take into account the behavior of these three variables. In this model, we assume that changes in exchange rates (Δe_t), reserves (Δr_t), and interest rate differentials (Δid_t) behave according to the following VAR switching structure:

$$\Delta e_t = c_{s_t}^{\Delta e} + \alpha_{s_t}^{\Delta e}[\Delta e_{t-1}] + \delta_{s_t}^{\Delta e}[\Delta r_{t-1}] + \gamma_{s_t}^{\Delta e}[\Delta id_{t-1}] + \sigma(s_t)u_t^{\Delta e} \tag{6}$$

$$\Delta r_t = c_{s_t}^{\Delta r} + \alpha_{s_t}^{\Delta r}[\Delta e_{t-1}] + \delta_{s_t}^{\Delta r}[\Delta r_{t-1}] + \gamma_{s_t}^{\Delta r}[\Delta id_{t-1}] + \sigma(s_t)u_t^{\Delta r} \tag{7}$$

$$\Delta id_t = c_{s_t}^{\Delta id} + \alpha_{s_t}^{\Delta id}[\Delta e_{t-1}] + \delta_{s_t}^{\Delta id}[\Delta r_{t-1}] + \gamma_{s_t}^{\Delta id}[\Delta id_{t-1}] + \sigma(s_t)u_t^{\Delta id} \tag{8}$$

where $u_t^{\Delta e}$, $u_t^{\Delta r}$, and $u_t^{\Delta id}$ are i.i.d. $N(0, 1)$ variables and the superscripts Δe, Δr, and Δid indicate the equation to which the parameters belong.

Once again, S_t is an unobserved zero/one variable that captures the regime (tranquil or speculative) on date t. We can think of the VAR above as really two VARs, one that holds when $S_t = 0$ and one that determines, Δe_t, Δr_t, and Δid_t when $S_t = 1$.

As before, we allow transition probabilities between periods of tranquility and speculative attacks to vary over time. These probabilities follow equations (2) through (5) above. In fact, we model these probabilities as a function of the

---

[10] See Diebold et al. (1994) for a detailed description of the EM algorithm and for the closed form solutions of the maximum likelihood estimates of the parameters.

same X_{t-1} matrix that determines transition probabilities in the exchange rate switching model.[11]

We implement the EM algorithm outlined above to obtain parameter estimates of the VAR regime-switching model. For computational convenience, we apply a Cholesky transformation to equations (6)–(8) so that the model's variance-covariance matrix becomes diagonal. The transformed system is given by equations (6*)–(8*) below:

$$\Delta e_t = c_{s_t}^{*\Delta e} + \alpha_{s_t}^{*\Delta e}[\Delta e_{t-1}] + \delta_{s_t}^{*\Delta e}[\Delta r_{t-1}] + \gamma_{s_t}^{*\Delta e}[\Delta id_{t-1}] + \sigma(s_t)u_t^{*\Delta e} \tag{6*}$$

$$\Delta r_t = c_{s_t}^{*\Delta r} + \alpha 1_{s_t}^{*\Delta r}[\Delta e_t] + \alpha 2_{s_t}^{*\Delta r}[\Delta e_{t-1}] + \delta_{s_t}^{*\Delta r}[\Delta r_{t-1}] + \gamma_{s_t}^{*\Delta r}[\Delta id_{t-1}] + \sigma(s_t)u_t^{*\Delta r} \tag{7*}$$

$$\Delta id_t = c_{s_t}^{*\Delta id} + \alpha 1_{s_t}^{*\Delta id}[\Delta e_t] + \alpha 2_{s_t}^{*\Delta id}[\Delta e_{t-1}] + \delta 1_{s_t}^{*\Delta id}[\Delta r_t] + \delta 2_{s_t}^{*\Delta id}[\Delta r_{t-1}] + \gamma_{s_t}^{*\Delta id}[\Delta id_{t-1}] + \sigma(s_t)u_t^{*\Delta id} \tag{8*}$$

Considering that we are not interested in the actual value of the VAR parameters, but all we care about is whether they are different across states, the Cholesky transformation is harmless. Furthermore, since there is a one to one relationship between the triangular and non-triangular versions of the VAR, and because the coefficients in the transition probabilities are the same in both normalizations, their estimates are unaffected.

Letting $z_{t-1} = (1, \Delta e_{t-1}, \Delta r_{t-1}, \Delta id_{t-1})'$, $w_t = (\Delta e_t, \Delta r_t)'$, $\kappa_{st} = (c_{s_t}^{*\Delta e}, \alpha_{s_t}^{*\Delta e}, \delta_{s_t}^{*\Delta e}, \gamma_{s_t}^{*\Delta e})'$, $\lambda_{st} = (c_{s_t}^{*\Delta r}, \alpha 2_{s_t}^{*\Delta r}, \delta_{s_t}^{*\Delta r}, \gamma_{s_t}^{*\Delta r})'$, $\theta_{s_t} = (\alpha 1_{s_t}^{*\Delta id}, \delta 1_{s_t}^{*\Delta id})'$, and $\mu_{s_t} = (c_{s_t}^{*\Delta id}, \alpha 2_{s_t}^{*\Delta id}, \delta 2_{s_t}^{*\Delta id}, \gamma_{s_t}^{*\Delta id})'$, the individual conditional densities for Δe_t, Δr_t, and Δid_t are given by equations (9)–(11) below:

$$f(\Delta e_t/s_t = j, z_{t-1}; \kappa_j, \sigma(s_j)^{*\Delta e}) = \frac{1}{\sqrt{2\pi}(\sigma_j^{*\Delta e})} \exp\left[\frac{-(\Delta e_t - \kappa_j' z_{t-1})^2}{2(\sigma_j^{*\Delta e})^2}\right] \tag{9}$$

$$f(\Delta r_t/s_t = j, \Delta e_t, z_{t-1}; \alpha 1_j^{\Delta r}, \lambda_j, \sigma(s_j)^{*\Delta r}) = \frac{1}{\sqrt{2\pi}(\sigma_j^{*\Delta r})} \exp\left[\frac{-(\Delta r_t - \alpha 1_j^{\Delta r}[\Delta e_t] - \lambda_j' z_{t-1})^2}{2(\sigma_j^{*\Delta r})^2}\right] \tag{10}$$

[11] The timing of the regime-switching model makes it possible to include the change in the interest rate differential as one of the variables used to identify the regimes and the level of the interest rate differential (which captures expectations of devaluations) as one of the determinants of the transition probabilities, without there being an endogeneity problem. The dynamics of the models are as follows: first, the transition probabilities are determined in the model and then, based on this, the probability of being in a particular state is calculated. This probability, in turn, determines the regime in which the economy resides at times t. For example, interest rate differentials at time $t-1$ help determine the transition probability from a given state at time $t-1$ to another (or the same) state at time t. Based on the transition probabilities and on the behavior of exchange rates, reserves, and interest rate differentials at time t, the unconditional probability that the economy is in a given state is determined. Thus, the sequencing of the model allows us to use interest rate differentials both in the regime-switching and the transition probability parts of the model.

$$f(\Delta id_t/s_t = j, w_t, z_{t-1}; \theta_j, \mu_j, \sigma(s_t)^{*\Delta id})$$
$$= \frac{1}{\sqrt{2\pi}(\sigma_j^{*\Delta id})} \exp\left[\frac{-(\Delta id_t - \theta_j' w_t - \mu_j' z_{t-1})^2}{2(\sigma_j^{*\Delta id})^2}\right] \tag{11}$$

where $j = 0, 1$. Given that the Cholesky transformed VAR has a diagonal error variance-covariance structure, then the conditional density for the model can be calculated as the product of the conditional densities for each of the three equations. In other words, letting $y_t = (\Delta e_t, \Delta r_t, \Delta id_t)'$, $\pi_{s_t} = (\kappa_{s_t}, \alpha 1_{s_t}^{\Delta r}, \lambda_{s_t}, \mu_{s_t}, \theta_{s_t}, \sigma(s_t)^{*\Delta e}, \sigma(s_t)^{*\Delta r}, \sigma(s_t)^{*\Delta id})'$, $\varphi_{s_t} = (\kappa_{s_t}, \sigma(s_t)^{*\Delta e})'$, $\tau_{s_t} = (\alpha 1_{s_t}^{\Delta r}, \lambda_{s_t}, \sigma(s_t)^{*\Delta r})'$, and $v_{s_t} = (\theta_{s_t}, \mu_{s_t}, \sigma(S_t)^{*\Delta id})'$ the conditional density for the VAR follows equation (12) below:

$$f(y_t/s_t = j, w_t, y_{t-1}; \pi_j) = f(\Delta e_t/s_t = j, z_{t-1}; \varphi_j) \times f(\Delta r_t/s_t = j, z_{t-1}, \Delta e_t; \tau_j)$$
$$\times f(\Delta id_t/s_t = j, w_t, z_{t-1}; v_j) \tag{12}$$

Once we obtain an estimate of the conditional density for the VAR, the remaining steps in the EM algorithm are exactly like those for a single equation regime-switching model.

4. Empirical results

To obtain results for both the exchange rate and the VAR switching models, we pool the data for all countries in our sample. Pooling the data is necessary, because the number of switches (or speculative attacks) for each country is small, relative to the number of parameters to be estimated in a model with time-varying transition probabilities. The pooled system is obtained simply by stacking the data for each country and estimating one system for all countries at once, including country dummies in most cases. A limitation of this procedure is that it does not allow for potential correlation across countries. This is discussed in the conclusions as a potential extension to the paper.

4.1. Results from the exchange rate switching model

Table 1 contains the parameter estimates of the switching model based on monthly percentage changes in exchange rates during the period 1979–1993. Model (1.1) presents the estimates of the constant transition probability or Hamilton version of the exchange rate switching model. Model (1.2) refers to the estimates from the exchange rate switching model with time-varying transition probabilities (i.e., the Diebold et al. variant of the model). As noted earlier, the main reason to estimate this model is to test whether the probability of switching from a tranquil period to a speculative regime is driven by fundamentals and/or expectations. In these estimations, the interest rate differential is used as a proxy of expectations of devaluation. Model (1.3) is the same as (1.2), except that we include dummy variables to control for country fixed effects.

Table 1. Exchange rate switching model estimates, 1979–1993

Variables	Model (1.1)		Model (1.2)		Model (1.3)	
Autoregressive Parameters	Coeff.	(T-stat.)	Coeff.	(T-stat.)	Coeff.	(T-stat.)
Tranquil State (TS)						
α_{00} – Constant	0.024	(1.84)	0.024	(1.85)	0.023	(1.77)
α_{01} – $\Delta_{e_{t-1}}$	0.148	(7.65)	0.148	(7.92)	0.15	(8.94)
α_{02} – $\Delta_{e_{t-2}}$	−0.013	(−0.84)	−0.012	(−0.74)	−0.013	(−0.83)
α_{03} – $\Delta_{e_{t-3}}$	0.034	(2.21)	0.033	(2.01)	0.035	(2.08)
α_{04} – $\Delta_{e_{t-4}}$	−0.001	(−0.04)	0.002	(0.12)	0.003	(0.16)
σ_0	0.108	(18.34)	0.099	(18.5)	0.097	(18.51)
Speculative State (SS)						
α_{10} – Constant	1.357	(4.42)	1.197	(4.43)	1.173	(4.03)
α_{11} – $\Delta_{e_{t-1}}$	0.068	(0.91)	0.10	(1.38)	0.128	(1.59)
α_{12} – $\Delta_{e_{t-2}}$	−0.187	(−0.76)	−0.194	(−0.93)	−0.177	(−0.83)
α_{13} – $\Delta_{e_{t-3}}$	0.291	(1.66)	0.266	(1.88)	0.283	(1.95)
α_{14} – $\Delta_{e_{t-4}}$	−0.301	(−2.72)	−0.292	(−2.71)	−0.298	(−2.69)
σ_1	3.679	(8.89)	3.459	(8.25)	3.474	(7.05)
Transition Probability Parameters						
Tranquil State (TS)						
β_{00} – Constant	2.548	(11.98)	6.261	(2.81)	12.715	(2.85)
β_{01} – Domestic Credit Growth	–		0.065	(0.7)	0.133	(1.25)
β_{02} – Trade Balance	–		−0.886	(−1.62)	1.361	(0.61)
β_{03} – Real Exchange Rate	–		−0.03	(−1.41)	−0.045	(−1.35)
β_{04} – Interest Rate Differentials	–		−0.1	(−1.99)	−0.161	(−2.25)
β_{05} – Unemployment Rate	–		0.069	(0.94)	−0.097	(−0.58)
β_{06} – Government Surplus	–		0.11	(2.82)	0.339	(2.86)
Speculative State (SS)						
β_{10} – Constant	0.211	(0.76)	5.243	(1.48)	2.399	(0.21)
β_{11} – Domestic Credit Growth	–		−0.149	(−0.95)	0.026	(0.14)
β_{12} – Trade Balance	–		0.96	(0.79)	−1.835	(−0.67)
β_{13} – Real Exchange Rate	–		−0.053	(−1.52)	−0.01	(−0.19)
β_{14} – Interest Rate Differential	–		−0.061	(−0.52)	−0.126	(−0.65)
β_{15} – Unemployment Rate	–		0.203	(1.56)	−0.378	(−1.03)
β_{16} – Government Surplus	–		0.094	(1.31)	0.192	(0.79)

Likelihood Ratio Tests	Chi-squared statistic	Chi-squared critical value
No regime switching	54.52	9.49
Constant transition probabilities	51.97	21.83
Joint test for country dummies	46.5	23.69

Model (1.1) is the Hamilton (constant transition probability) version of the model. Model (1.2) allows transition probabilities to be time-varying. Model (1.3) includes country dummies. We do not report these parameters, since none of them is individually statistically significant.

We estimate model (1.1), the Hamilton version of the exchange rate switching model, to test two hypotheses. First, we want to test whether exchange rates are subject to regime shifts. Second, we seek to evaluate whether transition probabilities are constant. The problem of testing the hypothesis of no switching is that under the null the parameters in the transition probabilities become unidentified nuisance parameters. When this happens, we cannot assume the standard distributions to conduct our tests. To circumvent this problem we follow Engel and Hamilton (1990) in their "approximate" test of no switching. We test the null of no switching by comparing the log likelihood function from a model where the autoregressive parameters are constrained to be equal across states against the alternative shown in model (1.1), where we allow these parameters to be different across states.[12,13] In both models, the error variance may be different across states. The coefficients $\alpha_{00} - \alpha_{04}$ refer to the constant and autoregressive parameters for the tranquil state, while $\alpha_{10} - \alpha_{14}$ are the corresponding parameters for the speculative state. As shown at the bottom of Table 1, at 5 percent significance, we reject the hypothesis of equal alpha parameters across states. This provides evidence that the exchange rate is subject to regime shifts.

The second hypothesis we test, involving the Hamilton version of the model, is whether fundamentals and expectations play a significant role in determining transition probabilities. The null hypothesis considered (i.e., $\beta_{01} - \beta_{06} = \beta_{11} - \beta_{16} = 0$ in equations (2)–(5)) is a test of the validity of the Hamilton constant probability version of the model (i.e., model (1.1)) versus Diebold et al.'s time-varying transition probability specification (i.e., model (1.2)). The chi-squared statistic for this likelihood ratio test and its critical value appear at the bottom of Table 1. At 5 percent significance, we reject the null that the constant transition probability model is the true model. Therefore, fundamentals and expectations jointly affect the likelihood of switching to and from speculative attack periods.

The parameters β_{01} through β_{06}, in model (1.2), affect the probability of staying in a tranquil period, p_t^{00}, and its complement, p_t^{01}, the likelihood of switching from a stable period to a speculative episode. A log likelihood ratio test confirms that these variables are jointly significant. However, only the interest rate differential and the government surplus are individually significant. The interest rate differential has a negative impact on p_t^{00}. Since this variable is a proxy for expectations, the results indicate that agents' expectations of devaluation play a role in bringing about speculative attacks against EMS currencies. This is consistent with the predictions from the second-generation models. On the other hand, the government surplus has a positive effect on the probability of remaining in a tranquil state (p_t^{00}). Thus, as predicted by the first-generation models, the results indicate that larger government deficits increase the probability of switching from periods of tranquility to speculative attack episodes.

---

[12] Hansen (1992) and Garcia (1998) have developed formal tests to deal with the problem of unidentified nuisance parameters in the context of Markov switching models. However, both of these tests have important limitations. The Hansen test is computationally burdensome and provides a bound for the likelihood ratio statistic, but not a critical value. Garcia's test assumes that the distribution theory proposed by Davies (1987) and Andrews and Ploberger (1994) to deal with the problem of inference in the presence of nuisance parameters under the null can be applied to the Markov-switching model. However, according to Hansen (1991) and Andrews and Ploberger (1994) the sufficient conditions for this to hold are not satisfied in the Markov switching models, since the matrix of second derivatives evaluated at the null appears to be singular.

[13] We do not report the results for the Hamilton version of the model with constrained autoregressive parameters across states, since the only reason behind the estimation of this model is to test the hypothesis of no switching. The results, however, are available upon request.

Table 2. VAR switching model estimates, 1979–1993

Variables	Model (2.1)		Model (2.2)		Model (2.3)	
VAR Parameters	Coeff.	(T-Stat.)	Coeff.	(T-Stat.)	Coeff.	(T-Stat.)
Exchange Rate Equation						
Tranquil State						
$c_0^{*\Delta_{et}}$ – Constant	0.058	(3.67)	0.054	(3.42)	0.055	(3.52)
$\alpha_0^{*\Delta_{et}}$ – $\Delta_{e_{t-1}}$	0.046	(2.65)	0.06	(3.28)	0.051	(2.65)
$\delta_0^{*\Delta_{et}}$ – $\Delta_{r_{t-1}}$	0.0004	(0.21)	0.001	(0.48)	0.001	(0.32)
$\gamma_0^{*\Delta_{et}}$ – $\Delta_{id_{t-1}}$	0.133	(12.39)	0.135	(12.19)	0.132	(10.86)
Speculative State						
$c_1^{*\Delta_{et}}$ – Constant	0.774	(4.16)	0.789	(4.19)	0.79	(3.92)
$\alpha_1^{*\Delta_{et}}$ – $\Delta_{e_{t-1}}$	0.254	(3.64)	0.218	(3.08)	0.214	(2.90)
$\delta_1^{*\Delta_{et}}$ – $\Delta_{r_{t-1}}$	−0.008	(−0.85)	−0.009	(−1.01)	−0.009	(−0.89)
$\gamma_1^{*\Delta_{et}}$ – $\Delta_{id_{t-1}}$	0.044	(1.35)	0.044	(1.37)	0.044	(1.29)
Reserves Equation						
Tranquil State						
$c_0^{*\Delta_{rt}}$ – Constant	1.095	(4.2)	1.092	(4.18)	1.133	(4.29)
$\alpha_{00}^{*\Delta_{rt}}$ – Δ_{e_t}	−3.108	(−4.51)	−2.98	(−4.32)	−3.087	(−4.49)
$\alpha_{01}^{*\Delta_{rt}}$ – $\Delta_{e_{t-1}}$	−0.737	(−2.17)	−0.647	(−1.82)	−0.72	(−1.97)
$\delta_0^{*\Delta_{rt}}$ – $\Delta_{r_{t-1}}$	0.035	(1.15)	0.037	(1.22)	0.033	(1.089)
$\gamma_0^{*\Delta_{rt}}$ – $\Delta_{id_{t-1}}$	−1.03	(−3.16)	−1.054	(−3.17)	−1.058	(−2.98)
Speculative State						
$c_1^{*\Delta_{rt}}$ – Constant	1.417	(0.8)	1.447	(0.8)	1.26	(0.68)
$\alpha_{10}^{*\Delta_{rt}}$ – Δ_{e_t}	−1.374	(−1.72)	−1.374	(−1.65)	−1.41	(−1.52)
$\alpha_{11}^{*\Delta_{rt}}$ – $\Delta_{e_{t-1}}$	−0.089	(−0.06)	−0.153	(−0.103)	−0.157	(−0.1)
$\delta_1^{*\Delta_{rt}}$ – $\Delta_{r_{t-1}}$	−0.301	(−3.79)	−0.296	(−3.67)	−0.289	(−3.51)
$\gamma_1^{*\Delta_{rt}}$ – $\Delta_{id_{t-1}}$	0.347	(0.87)	0.358	(0.89)	0.344	(0.86)
Interest Rates Equation						
Tranquil State						
$c_0^{*\Delta_{idt}}$ – Constant	−0.064	(−3.38)	−0.061	(−3.26)	−0.062	(−3.22)
$\alpha_{00}^{*\Delta_{idt}}$ – Δ_{e_t}	0.181	(3.69)	0.181	(3.65)	0.183	(3.64)
$\alpha_{01}^{*\Delta_{idt}}$ – $\Delta_{e_{t-1}}$	−0.008	(−2.71)	−0.007	(−2.56)	−0.007	(−2.49)
$\delta_{00}^{*\Delta_{idt}}$ – Δ_{r_t}	0.011	(0.42)	0.015	(0.53)	0.027	(0.93)
$\delta_{01}^{*\Delta_{idt}}$ – $\Delta_{r_{t-1}}$	−0.008	(−4.39)	−0.007	(−3.99)	−0.008	(−4.08)
$\gamma_0^{*\Delta_{idt}}$ – $\Delta_{i_{t-1}}$	0.078	(4.13)	0.078	(4.04)	0.084	(3.77)
Speculative State						
$c_1^{*\Delta_{idt}}$ – Constant	0.48	(1.38)	0.456	(1.28)	0.467	(1.31)
$\alpha_{10}^{*\Delta_{idt}}$ – Δ_{e_t}	−0.216	(−0.9)	−0.207	(−0.85)	−0.203	(−0.83)
$\alpha_{11}^{*\Delta_{idt}}$ – $\Delta_{e_{t-1}}$	−0.0188	(−1.53)	−0.018	(−1.48)	−0.018	(−1.42)
$\delta_{10}^{*\Delta_{idt}}$ – Δ_{r_t}	0.169	(0.49)	0.143	(0.41)	0.119	(0.38)
$\delta_{11}^{*\Delta_{idt}}$ – $\Delta_{r_{t-1}}$	−0.029	(−1.54)	−0.031	(−1.58)	−0.031	(−1.61)
$\gamma_1^{*\Delta_{idt}}$ – $\Delta_{i_{t-1}}$	−0.769	(−12.41)	−0.768	(−11.88)	−0.763	(−10.78)
Transition Probability Parameters						
Tranquil State						
β_{00} – Constant	2.276	(14.22)	4.526	(2.75)	5.266	(2.19)
β_{01} – Domestic Credit	–		0.011	(0.14)	0.017	(0.19)
β_{02} – Trade Balance	–		0.556	(1.13)	−0.864	(−0.53)
β_{03} – Real Exchange Rate	–		−0.017	(−1.13)	−0.029	(−1.4)
β_{04} – Interest Rate Differential	–		−0.087	(−1.27)	0.005	(0.06)
β_{05} – Unemployment Rate	–		0.065	(1.18)	0.171	(1.66)
β_{06} – Government Surplus	–		0.072	(1.55)	0.254	(2.95)

Table 2. Continued

Variables	Model (2.1)		Model (2.2)		Model (2.3)	
Speculative State						
β_{10} – Constant	0.541	(2.93)	1.521	(1.04)	−6.632	(−1.83)
β_{11} – Domestic Credit	–		−0.044	(−0.55)	−0.073	(−0.86)
β_{12} – Trade Balance	–		−0.367	(−0.61)	−3.12	(−1.57)
β_{13} – Real Exchange Rate	–		−0.01	(−0.73)	0.039	(1.45)
β_{14} – Interest Rate Differential	–		0.008	(0.11)	−0.011	(−0.12)
β_{15} – Unemployment Rate	–		0.119	(1.54)	0.13	(0.9)
β_{16} – Government Surplus	–		0.082	(1.56)	0.079	(0.79)

Likelihood Ratio Tests	Chi-squared statistic	Chi-squared critical value
No regime switching	45.3	25
Constant transition probabilities	23.8	21.03
Joint test for country dummies	40	23.64

For computational convenience, the exchange rate, reserves, and interest differential equations correspond to the Cholesky transformed version of the model. Model (2.1) is the Hamilton (constant transition probability) version of the model. Model (2.2) allows transition probabilities to be time-varying. Model (2.3) includes country dummies (not shown because none of them is individually significant).

In model (1.2), the parameters $\beta_{10} - \beta_{16}$ affect p_t^{11}, the probability of staying in a speculative episode, and its complement, p_t^{10}, the probability of switching from a speculative to a tranquil state. No regressor affecting p_t^{11} and, therefore, p_t^{10} is significant. A possible explanation for this result (which will be illustrated in section 5) is that speculative attacks are relatively rare, short-lived events. Therefore, with very few and, for the most part, brief speculative episodes, it is hard to estimate the significance of any of these particular parameters.

Model (1.3) in Table 1 is identical to Model (1.2), with the exception that country dummies are added to the latter to control for country fixed effects. Given that no country dummy is individually significant, we do not report their coefficient estimates here. At 5 percent significance, however, a likelihood ratio test rejects the null that country fixed effects are jointly zero. (See the bottom of Table 1.)

When dummies are included, the parameter estimates for the transition probabilities do not change significantly. As in model (1.2), only the interest rate differential and the government surplus (as a % GDP) have a significant impact on the likelihood of switching from a tranquil period to a speculative attack. These variables have the same signs as before.

4.2. Results from the VAR switching model

Table 2 below presents the estimates from the VAR switching model outlined in equations (6)–(8), plus the transition probabilities parameters of equations (2)–(5). For computational convenience, we estimate the Cholesky transformed version of equations (6)–(8), as shown in equations (6*) through (8*).

The VAR switching model enables us to identify and examine the determinants of speculative attacks defined as periods of large movements and high volatility in exchange rates, reserves, and/or interest rates. Thus, the VAR framework allows for the possibility that countries defend from pressures to devalue their currencies by raising interest rates or by selling reserves.

Model (2.1), in Table 2, presents the Hamilton version of the VAR switching model with constant transition probabilities. Model (2.2) corresponds to the estimation of the VAR switching model with time-varying transition probabilities. Model (2.3) is almost identical to model (2.2), except that the former includes country dummies.

As in the exchange rate switching model, we estimate the Hamilton version of the VAR switching model (model (2.1)) to test the null of no switching in exchange rates, reserves, and interest rate differentials. Also, the Hamilton version of the VAR switching model allows us to determine whether the transition probabilities are constant over time.[14] The test for the hypothesis of no regime switching is a likelihood ratio test comparing the Hamilton version of the model with the VAR switching model with autoregressive parameters constrained to be equal across regimes. On the other hand, the test of constant transition probabilities is conducted by comparing the Hamilton version of the model with the Diebold et al. model. At 5 percent significance, we reject both null hypotheses. The corresponding chi-squared statistics and the critical values are at the bottom of Table 2.

Regarding the determinants of the transition probabilities in model (2.2), as mentioned above, we can reject the hypothesis that fundamentals and expectations are jointly insignificant. Thus, these variables jointly determine the likelihood of switching from and to periods of speculative attacks. However, no variable is individually significant.

Model (2.3) extends model (2.2) by including dummy variables to control for country fixed effects. We find that country dummies are jointly significant (see the bottom of Table 2), but none of them is individually significant. Once we allow for country fixed effects, we find that government budget deficits play a significant role in determining the likelihood of switching from a tranquil to a speculative regime.

The regime-switching models estimated so far include the interest rate differential as a measure of expectations of devaluation in the logistic functions for the transition probabilities. Table 3 compares the results from the VAR switching model using, separately, survey data on expected exchange rates and interest rate differentials to capture expectations of devaluation. The purpose of this exercise is to analyze whether the determinants of the transition probabilities are sensitive to the choice of expectations proxy used. Because survey data on expected exchange rates is available since February 1988, we can only estimate the model for the period 1988–1993. Given that we are primarily interested in the effect that expectations have on the transition probabilities, Table 3 only reports the estimated parameters affecting these probabilities.

Both interest rate differentials and expected exchange rates have a negative impact on the probability of staying in a period of tranquility, however, neither of these two expectations proxies is significant. Also, no other variable

[14] The test conducted here is only an approximation to the true test of no switching. See discussion on pages 10–11.

Table 3. VAR switching model estimates, 1988–1993

Variables	Model (3.1)		Model (3.2)	
Transition Probability Parameters	Coeff.	(T-Stat.)	Coeff.	(T-Stat.)
Tranquil State (TS)				
β_{00} – Constant	−58.979	(−0.39)	−28.76	(−0.55)
β_{01} – Domestic Credit Growth	0.016	(0.06)	0.019	(0.07)
β_{02} – Trade Balance	−1.277	(−0.08)	−1.065	(−0.07)
β_{03} – Real Exchange Rate	0.569	(0.38)	0.27	(0.56)
β_{04} – Expectations Proxy	−0.257	(−0.67)	−0.033	(−0.34)
β_{05} – Unemployment Rate	1.581	(0.36)	1.359	(0.39)
β_{06} – Government Surplus	0.797	(0.3)	0.9	(0.24)
Speculative State (SS)				
β_{10} – Constant	−30.776	(−1.18)	−27.911	(−1.29)
β_{11} – Domestic Credit Growth	0.106	(0.19)	0.113	(0.21)
β_{12} – Trade Balance	0.804	(0.22)	0.773	(0.33)
β_{13} – Real Exchange Rate	0.337	(1.25)	0.309	(1.41)
β_{14} – Expectations Proxy	0.06	(0.06)	−0.014	(−0.95)
β_{15} – Unemployment Rate	0.469	(0.85)	0.616	(1.65)
β_{16} – Government Surplus	0.002	(0.01)	0.067	(0.27)

Both model (3.1) and (3.2) correspond to the VAR time-varying transition probabilities regime-switching model. Both models include country dummies in the transition probabilities. Model (3.1) includes the interest rate differential as a proxy for expectations. Model (3.2) includes expected exchange rates (from survey data) as a proxy for expectations of devaluation.

is individually significant in explaining switching probabilities for the period 1988–1993, although, once again, we find that fundamentals and expectations are jointly significant.

The finding that nothing seems to be explaining the EMS crisis over the period 1988–1993 is consistent with what other authors have found. Rose and Svensson (1994), for example, find that realignment expectations remained fairly constant throughout this period. Similarly, Eichengreen and Wyplosz (1993) argue that there is weak evidence that the 1992–1993 EMS crises were the result of deteriorating economic fundamentals. Finally, there can be a purely statistical reason why no variable is individually significant in explaining transition probabilities during 1988–93. Given that this period was in general a tranquil one, with the exception of the 1992–1993 crises, it is possible that there are too few regime switches in the data to identify all the parameters in the model. This may lead to inefficient estimates and, therefore, may explain why no regressor is individually significant during this period.

5. How well do the switching models with time-varying transition probabilities track speculative attacks?

From the estimation of the exchange rate and the VAR switching models, it is possible to recover the estimated probability of a speculative attack at each point in time, given all the observable data. This is the so-called "smoothed" probability of a speculative regime. According to Diebold et al. (1994) the smoothed state probabilities are the EM's algorithm best guess of the state each period. Dahlquist and Gray (2000) also focus on this probability at the time of determining if and when regime switches occurred in the behavior of EMS interest rates.[15] Figures A.1.a–A.14.a, in the appendix, display the unconditional smoothed probabilities that the economy was in a speculative state according to the exchange rate (Figures A.1.a–A.7.a) and VAR (Figures A.8.a–A.14.a) switching models. Figures A.1.b–A.14.b show, for each country, the estimated probability of switching from a tranquil period to a speculative regime (p_t^{01}) and the likelihood of staying in a speculative regime (p_t^{11}), as defined in equations (4) and (3), respectively.

From Figures A.1.a–A.14.a, it is clear that most of the estimated probabilities of speculative attacks are either close to zero or one. Also, these probabilities move rapidly between the two extremes. This seems to ratify the conventional wisdom that speculative attacks appear suddenly and are relatively short-lived events. From Figures A.1.b–A.14.b, we see that the likelihood of switching to a speculative episode (p_t^{01}) increases prior to attacks. Though it is hard to detect a consistent pattern across countries and over time, it appears that the likelihood of staying in a speculative state (p_t^{11}) is quite high in general, yet it tends to drop during periods where the smoothed probability of an attack is close to one. The 1992–93 crisis looks like an exception where both probabilities remain high in multiple periods.

Appendix Tables A.1–A.7 compare the speculative episodes identified by the exchange rate switching, the VAR switching model, and the index of speculative pressure used by Eichengreen, Rose, and Wyplosz (1996) in their study of EMS crises.[16] In the case of the exchange rate and the VAR switching models, we assume the process switches to a speculative state when the predicted probability of a speculative attack is greater than 0.5.[17] Thus, a "Yes" for the exchange rate switching model and the VAR switching model signifies that the probability of an attack predicted by each of these models is larger than 0.5. A "Yes" under the ERW column marks those episodes identified by Eichengreen et al.'s index of speculative pressure. Finally, the last column in these tables shows the dates of the realignments/devaluations of each ERM currency.

A number of well-established speculative attacks appear in the tables. The 1992–1993 crisis shows up for almost every country. Other dates that appear as speculative episodes for the majority of countries correspond to the realignments of October 1981, March 1983, and January 1987. From the experiences of most countries, however, it is clear that speculative attacks need not always coincide with realignments.

The main purpose of this section is to address two questions regarding the speculative attacks identified by the regime-switching methodology used in this paper. First, can this methodology capture those episodes identified by ERW's index of speculative pressure? Second, what other episodes does this methodology identify and can they be classified as speculative attacks?

Table 4 attempts to answer the first question posed above. This table summarizes the findings from appendix Tables A.1–A.7. For each country, Table

---

[15] Alternatively, one could focus on the ex ante probability $Pr[St = i/y_{t-1}, x_{t-1}]$ for forecasting purposes or on the filtered probabilities $Pr[St = i/y_T, x_T]$, which only use the information available up until time $t-1$ and T, respectively.

[16] For both the VAR and the exchange rate switching models, we refer to the time-varying transition probabilities versions of these models.

[17] Since the estimated probability takes values close to zero or one, the classification of observations does not change significantly if we choose 0.6, 0.7, or 0.8 as thresholds.

Table 4. ERW's episodes captured by the exchange rate and VAR switching models

Countries	% of ERW's episodes identified by the exchange rate switching model	% of ERW's episodes identified by the VAR switching model
Belgium	33%	100%
Denmark	50%	75%
France	75%	100%
Ireland	60%	100%
Italy	100%	100%
Spain	100%	100%
UK	100%	100%

ERW's episodes refer to the speculative attacks identified by an index of speculative pressure constructed by Eichengreen, Rose, and Wyplosz (1996) in their study of EMS crises.

Table 5. Number of attacks not in ERW identified by the VAR switching model

Countries	# of attacks not in ERW identified by the VAR switching model	# of attacks not in ERW identified by the VAR model for which there is evidence in the news
Belgium	9	9
Denmark	3	3
France	2	2
Ireland	0	0
Italy	8	6
Spain	2	1
UK	1	0

ERW's episodes refer to the speculative attacks identified by an index of speculative pressure constructed by Eichengreen, Rose, and Wyplosz (1996) in their study of EMS crises.

4 shows the percentage of episodes identified by ERW that the VAR and exchange rate switching models identify. In summary, Table 4 shows that, with the exception of Denmark, the VAR switching model can perfectly capture the episodes identified by ERW's index. On the other hand, the exchange rate switching model can only fully detect those episodes identified by ERW for the cases of Italy, Spain, and the UK. This is not surprising since most speculative attacks against these countries resulted in depreciations of their exchange rates vis-à-vis the deutsche mark.

Table 4 enables us to verify that the VAR switching model can almost perfectly capture those episodes identified by the speculative pressure index used by ERW. The next question is what other episodes does the VAR switching methodology detect? Do these results make sense? The first column in Table 5 lists the number of episodes identified by the VAR switching model that are *not* captured by ERW's index of speculative pressure. The second column in Table 5 reports the number of episodes listed in the first column for which we could find evidence of speculative pressure in the month in questions, in the financial press, or in IMF publications.[18]

The main purpose of Table 5 is to show that indeed most of the episodes the VAR switching model identifies that ERW missed can be truly considered attacks and not type-two errors. Because for those attacks that did not result in realignments, there is no clear observable criteria of whether an attack has taken place, the best one can do is to try to gauge in some way the market perception's of whether an attack occurred. We search through articles in the financial press and in the IMF's reports for accounts of episodes of speculative pressure.[19]

Table 5 shows that out of 25 attacks not identified by ERW, but captured by the VAR switching model, there are only 4 cases for which we could not find evidence of speculative pressure in the news reports searched. Thus, the VAR regime-switching model can identify most of ERW's attacks plus others for which we find evidence in the news.

6. Conclusions

This paper implemented a regime-switching approach with time-varying transition probabilities to study speculative attacks against EMS currencies. We estimated two switching models: an exchange rate and a VAR switching model. The exchange rate switching model identified as speculative attack episodes associated with large movements and volatility in exchange rates. In the VAR switching model, speculative attacks corresponded to episodes of large depreciations of the exchange rate, reserve losses, and/or increases in interest rate differentials.

The regime-switching models allow the data to determine the state in which the economy resides at each point in time. Thus, these models avoid the arbitrary classification of observations that results from using indices of speculative pressure. Also, the estimation of the switching models enable us to study the factors affecting the likelihood that a country will shift from a tranquil state to a speculative regime. Finally, contrary to other studies that neglect the role of expectations in causing speculative attacks, this paper incorporated them explicitly.

A number of conclusions follow from the results obtained in this paper. First, the switching models with time-varying transition probabilities fit the data for exchange rates, reserves, and interest rates for EMS countries very well. Thus, previous models that did not take into account the regime-switching nature of these variables are probably mispecified. Second, this methodology captures most of the conventional episodes of speculative attacks. Third, speculative attacks do not always coincide with currency realignments. Finally, both economic fundamentals and expectations determine the likelihood of

[18] Tables A.8 through A.14 in the appendix contain a list of all episodes identified by the VAR switching model, followed by a list of news or IMF reports surrounding them.

[19] Though they do not cite specific press articles, Eichengreen et al. (1996) also rely on these to justify the episodes their index of speculative pressure identifies.

switching from a tranquil period to a speculative attack. In particular, in both switching models, budget deficits appear to be the most important factor driving the probability of switching to a speculative regime.

There are a number of potential extensions to this paper. One is particularly relevant. Given that currency crises tend to occur at the same time in more than one country, it would be interesting to adapt the regime-switching framework to explore the role of contagion in explaining crises. This issue, however, is left for future research.

References

Andrews D, Ploberger W (1994) Optimal tests when a nuisance parameter is present only under the alternative. Econometrica 62:1383–1414

Blanco H, Garber P (1986) Recurrent devaluations and speculative attacks on the Mexican peso. Journal of Political Economy 94:148–66

Cumby R, van Wijenbergen S (1989) Financial policy and speculative runs with a crawling peg: Argentina 1979–1981. Journal of International Economics 27:111–27

Dahlquist M, Gray S (2000) Regime-switching and interest rates in the European Monetary System. Journal of International Economics 50:399–419

Davies R (1987) Hypothesis testing when a nuisance parameter is present only under the alternative. Biometrika 74:33–43

Dempster A, Laird M, Rubin D (1977) Maximum likelihood from incomplete data via the EM algorithm. Journal of the Royal Statistical Society 39:1–38

Diebold F, Joon-Haeng L, Weinbach G (1994) Regime-switching with time-varying transition probabilities. In: Hargreaves C (ed.) Nonstationary time series analysis and cointegration. Oxford University Press, Oxford, pp. 284–302

Edwards S (1989) Real exchange rates, devaluation, and adjustment: Exchange rate policy in developing countries. MIT Press, Cambridge

Eichengreen B, Wyplosz C (1993) The unstable EMS. Brookings Papers on Economic Activity 1:51–143

———, Rose A, Wyplosz C (1995) Exchange market mayhem: The antecedents and aftermath of speculative attacks. Economic Policy 21:249–96

——— (1996) Speculative attacks on pegged exchange rates: An empirical exploration with special reference to the European Monetary System. In: Canzoneri M, Ethier W, Grilli V (eds.) The new transatlantic economy. Cambridge University press, New York, pp. 191–228

Engel C, Hakkio C (1996) The distribution of exchange rates in the EMS. International Journal of Finance and Economics 1:55–67

———, Hamilton J (1990) Long swings in the dollar: Are they in the data and do markets know it? American Economic Review 80:689–713

Flood R, Garber P (1984a) Collapsing exchange-rate regimes: Some linear examples. Journal of International Economics 17:1–13

——— (1984b) Gold monetization and gold discipline. Journal of Political Economy 92:90–107

Frankel J, Rose A (1996) Currency crashes in emerging markets: An empirical treatment. Journal of International Economics 41:351–66

Garcia R (1998) Asymptotic null distribution of the likelihood ratio test in Markov switching models. International Economic Review 39:763–788

Goldberg L (1994) Predicting exchange rate crises: Mexico revisited. Journal of International Economics 36:413–30

Gomez-Puig M, Montalvo J (1997) A new indicator to assess the credibility of the EMS. European Economic Review 41:1511–1535

Hamilton J (1990) Analysis of times series subject to changes in regime. Journal of Econometrics 45:39–70

——— (1994) Time series analysis. Princeton University Press, Princeton

Hansen B (1991) Inference when a nuisance parameter is not identified under the null hypothesis. Working Paper No. 296, Center for Economic Research, University of Rochester

Hsieh C (1994) Identifying speculative attacks in the European Monetary System. University of California, Berkeley, Mimeo

Jones M (1997) Three essays on central banking: Lender of last resort, currency boards, and the Gold Standard. Ph.D. Dissertation, University of California, Berkeley

Kaminsky G, Reinhart C (1996) Twin crises: The causes of banking and balance of payments problems. International Finance Discussion Paper No. 544, Board of Governors of the Federal Reserve System

———, Lizondo S, Reinhart C (1998) Leading indicators of currency crises. IMF Staff Papers 45:1–48

Klein M, Marion N (1997) Explaining the duration of exchange rate pegs. Journal of Development Economics 54:387–404

Krugman P (1979) A model of balance of payments crises. Journal of Money, Credit and Banking 11:311–25

Martinez Peria M (1997) Understanding devaluations in Latin America: A 'bad' fundamentals approach. Center for International and Development Economics Research, Discussion Paper No. C97-086

Obstfeld M (1986) Rational and self-fulfilling balance of payments crises. American Economic Review 76:72–81

——— (1994) The logic of currency crises. Cahiers Economiques et Monetaires 43:189–213

Ötker I, Pazarbaşioğlu C (1997) Speculative attacks and macroeconomic fundamentals: Evidence from some European currencies. European Economic Review 41:847–860

Ozkan F, Sutherland A (1994) A model of the ERM crisis. Center for Economic Policy Research, Discussion Paper No. 879

Rose A, Svensson L (1994) European exchange rate credibility before the fall. European Economic Review 38:1185–1216

Weinbach G (1995) Can a time-varying Markov switching model better explain exchange rate movements? Board of Governors of the Federal Reserve System, Division of Monetary Affairs, Mimeo

Appendix: Figures and tables

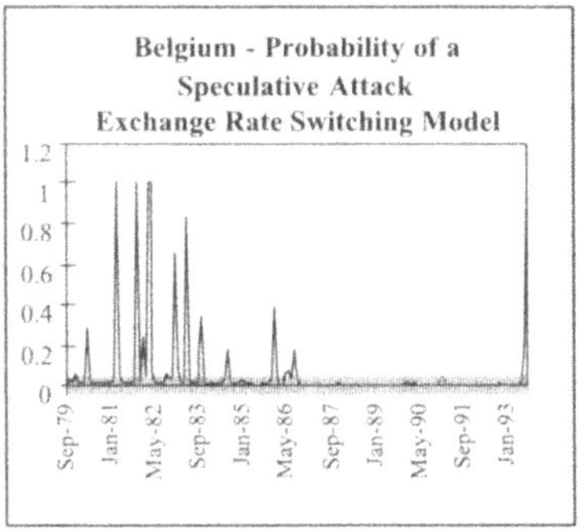

Fig. A.1.a*

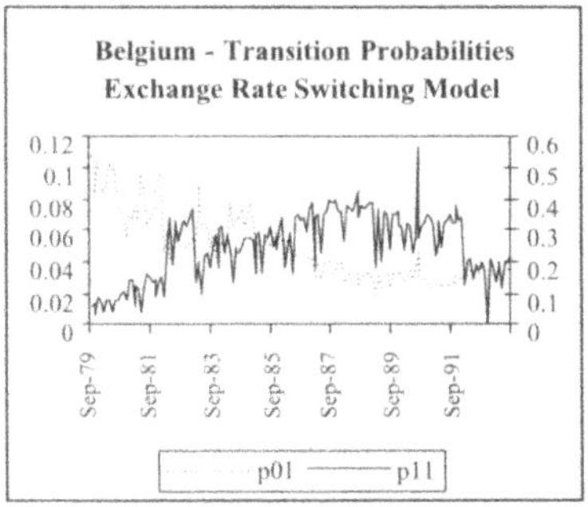

Fig. A.1.b**

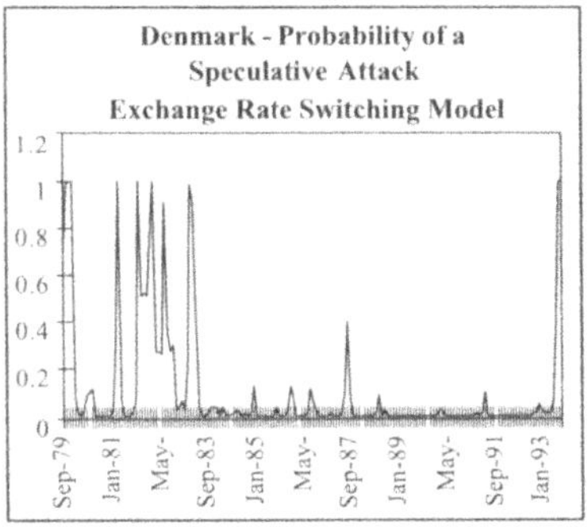

Fig. A.2.a*

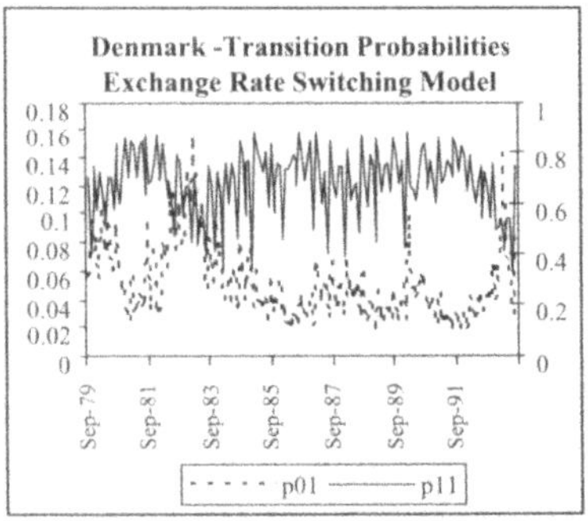

Fig. A.2.b**

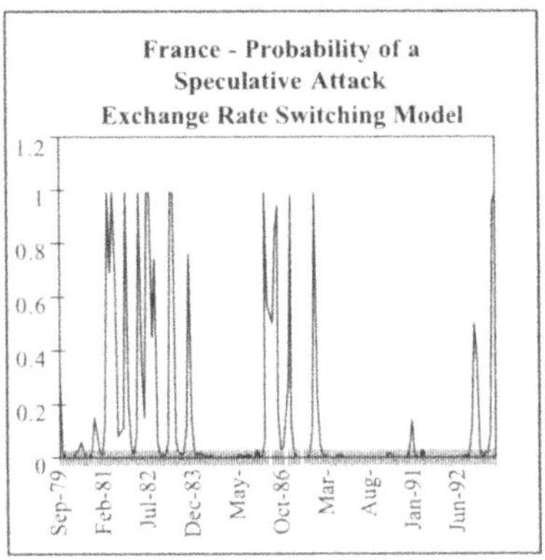

Fig. A.3.a*

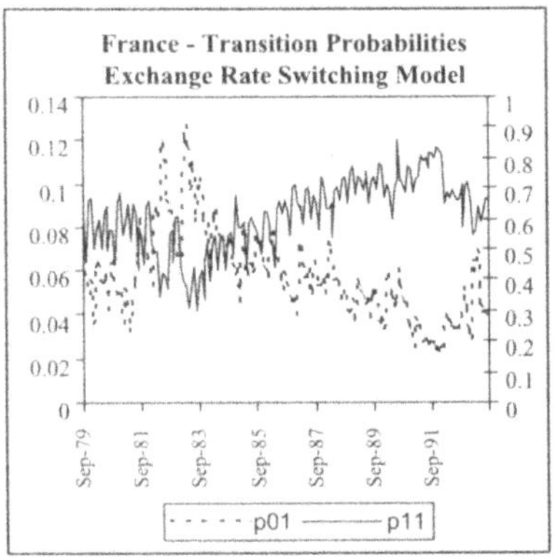

Fig. A.3.b**

* Figures display the estimated probability of a speculative attack according to the exchange rate switching model.

** Figures display the estimated probability of switching from a tranquil period to a speculative attack regime (p01 – left axis) and the probability of staying in a crisis regime (p11 – right axis) according to the exchange rate switching model.

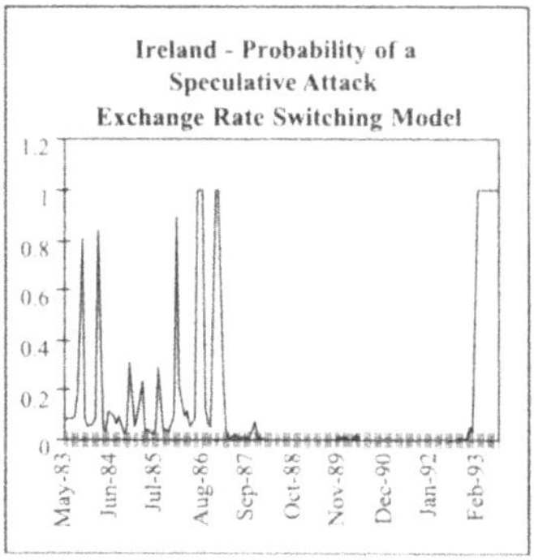

Fig. A.4.a*

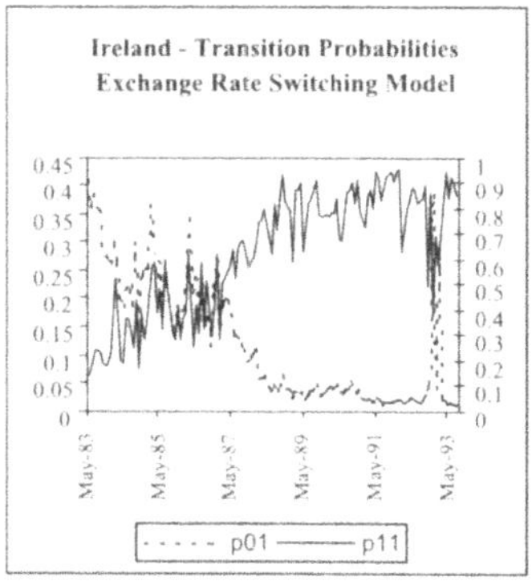

Fig. A.4.b**

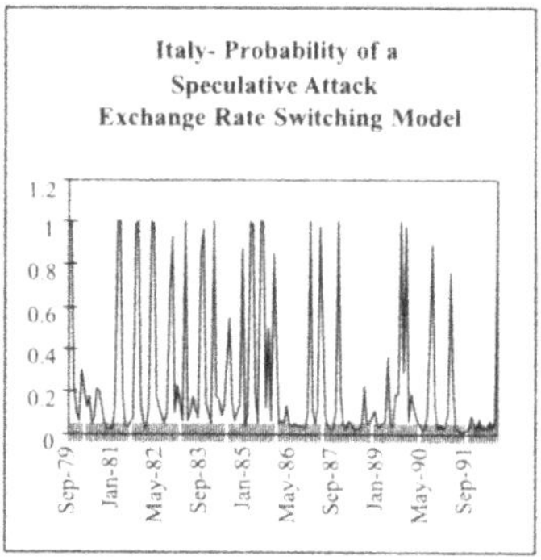

Fig. A.5.a*

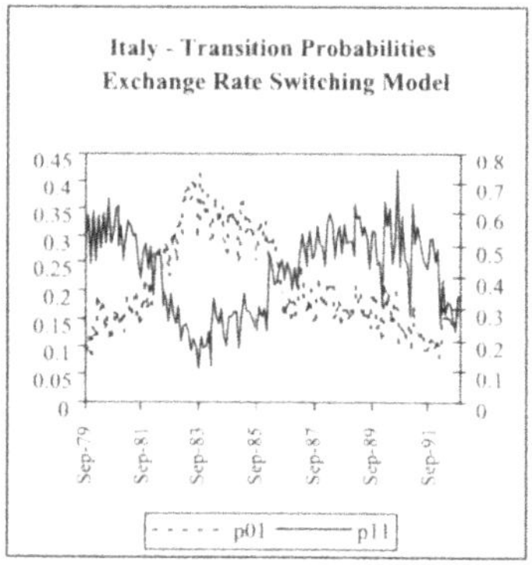

Fig. A.5.b**

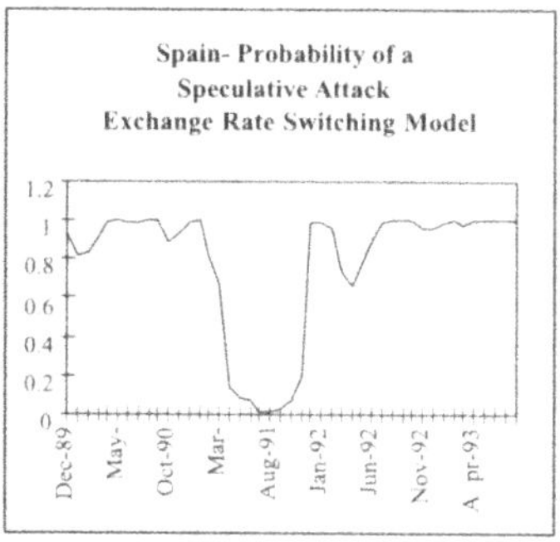

Fig. A.6.a*

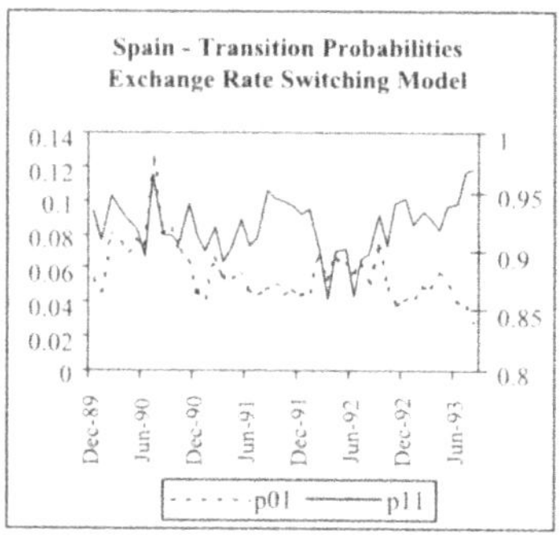

Fig. A.6.b**

* Figures display the estimated probability of a speculative attack according to the exchange rate switching model.

** Figures display the estimated probability of switching from a tranquil period to a speculative attack regime (p01 – left axis) and the probability of staying in a crisis regime (p11 – right axis) according to the exchange rate switching model.

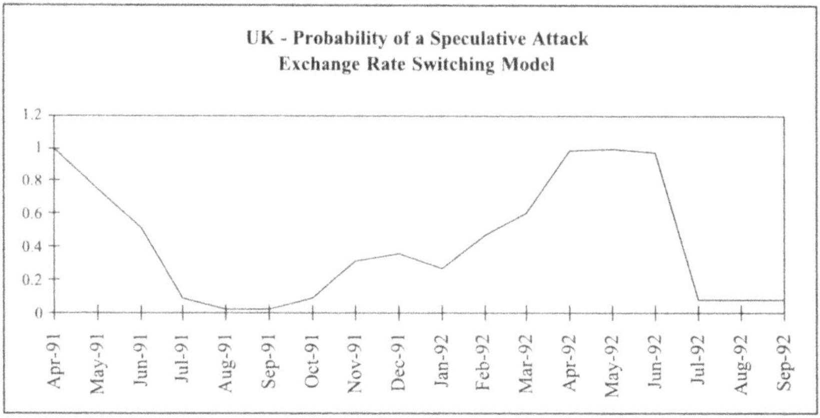

Fig. A.7.a*

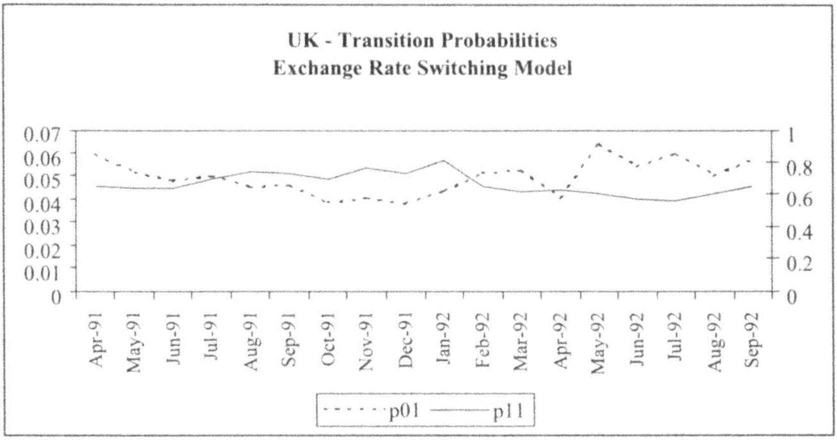

Fig. A.7.b**

* Figure displays the estimated probability of a speculative attack according to the exchange rate switching model.

** Figures display the estimated probability of switching from a tranquil period to a speculative attack regime (p01 – left axis) and the probability of staying in a crisis regime (p11 – right axis) according to the exchange rate switching model.

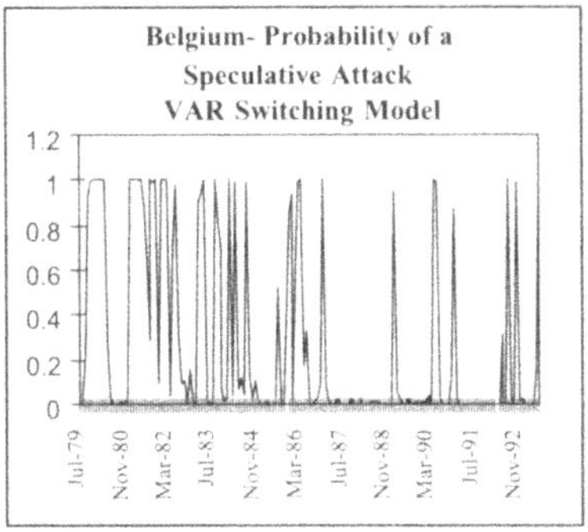

Fig. A.8.a*

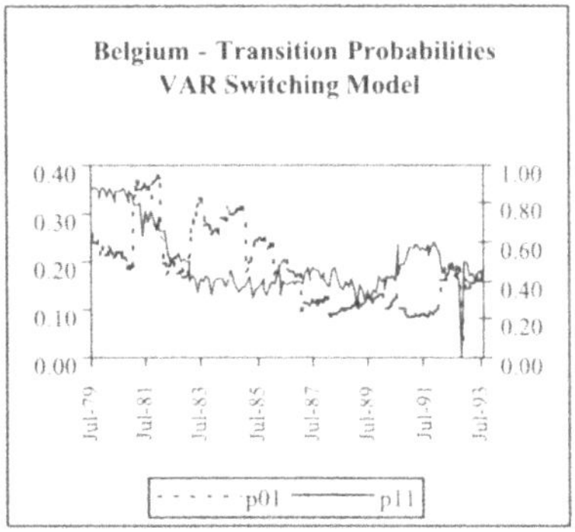

Fig. A.8.b**

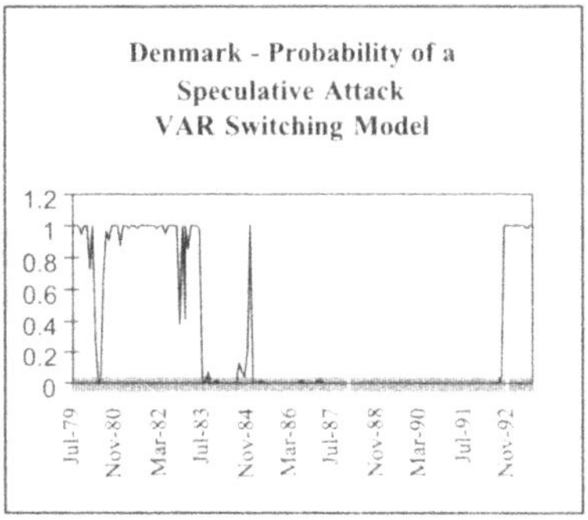

Fig. A.9.a*

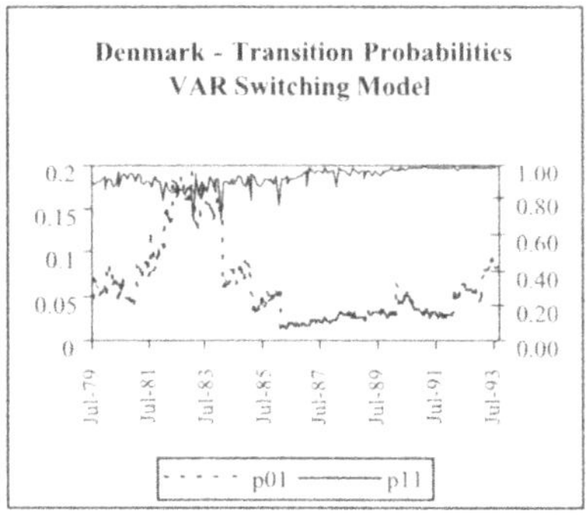

Fig. A.9.b**

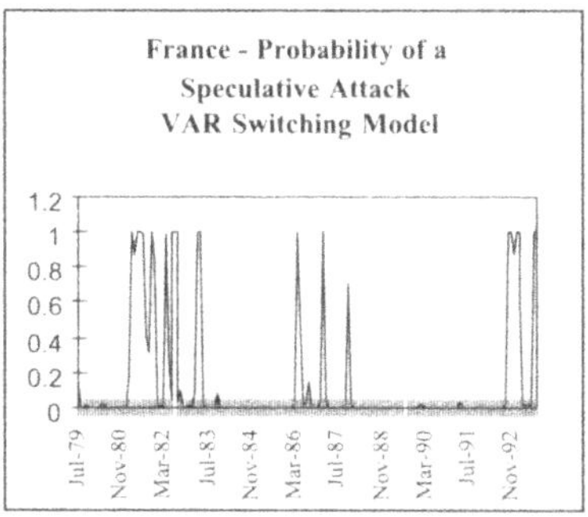

Fig. A.10.a*

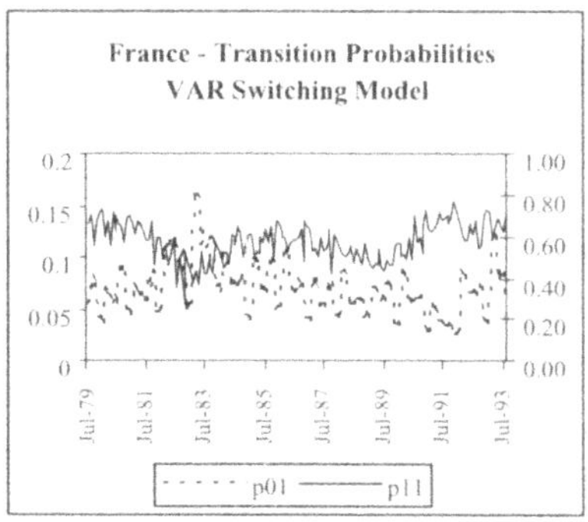

Fig. A.10.b**

* Figures display the estimated probability of a speculative attack according to the VAR switching model.

** Figures display the estimated probability of switching from a tranquil period to a speculative attack regime (p01 – left axis) and the probability of staying in a crisis (p11 – right axis) regime according to the VAR switching model.

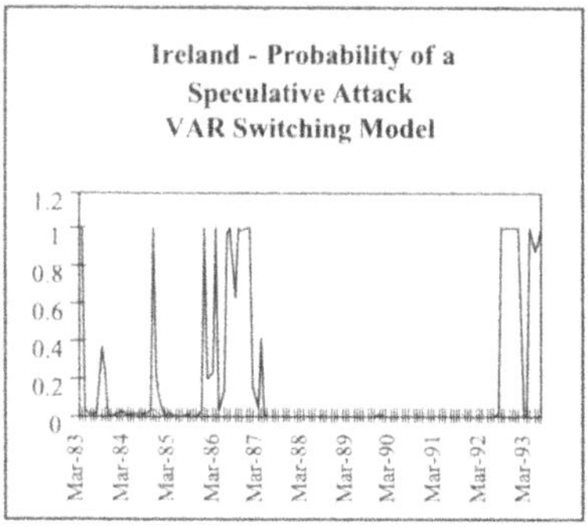

Fig. A.11.a*

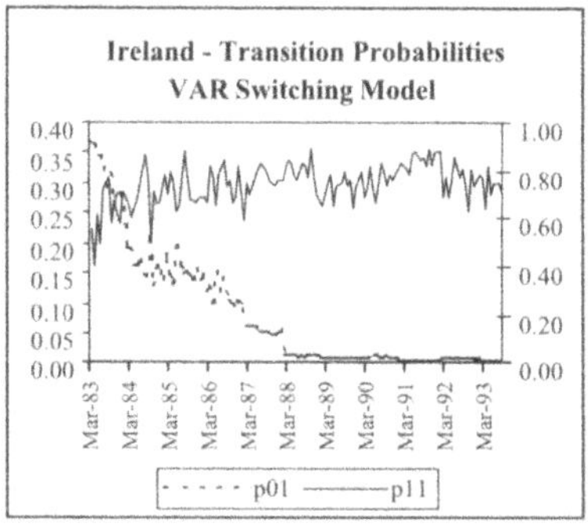

Fig. A.11.b**

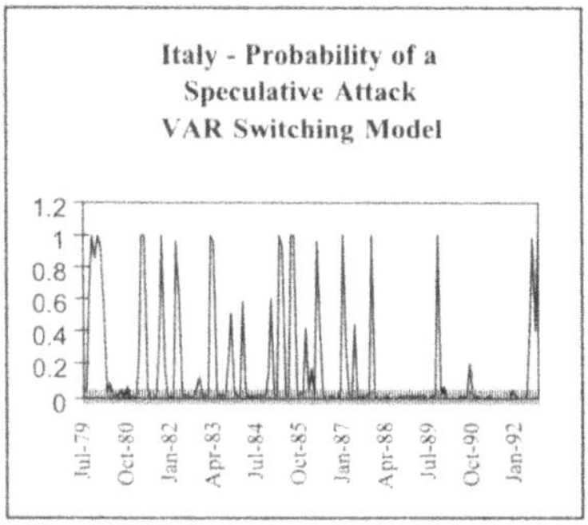

Fig. A.12.a*

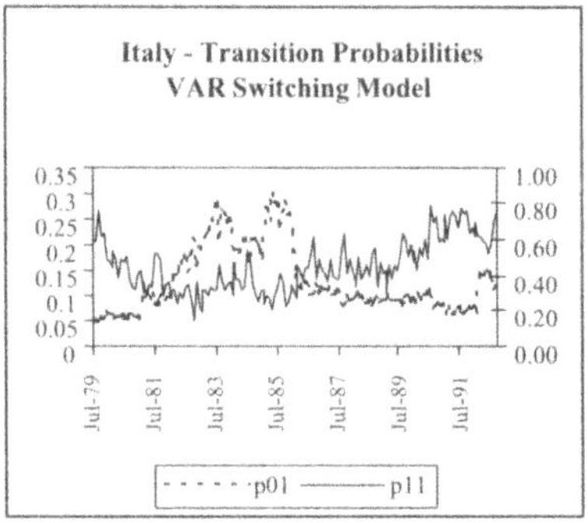

Fig. A.12.b**

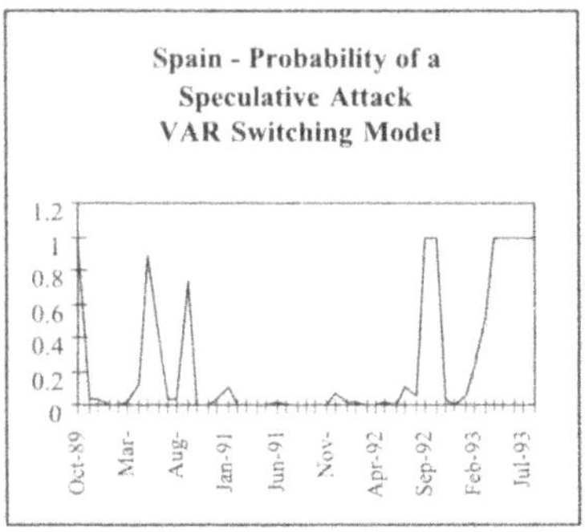

Fig. A.13.a*

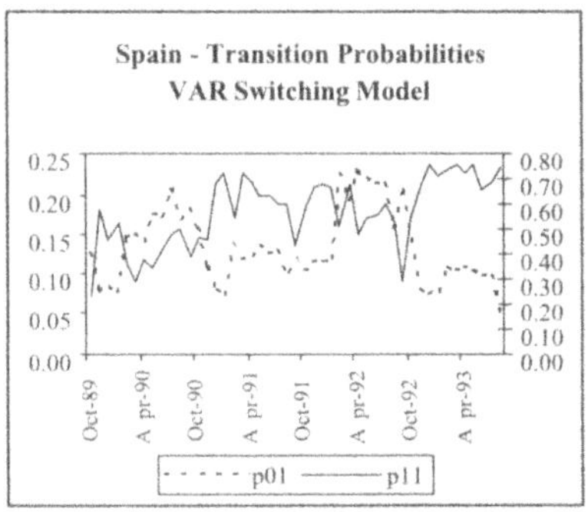

Fig. A.13.b**

* Figures display the estimated probability of a speculative attack according to the VAR switching model.

** Figures display the estimated probability of switching from a tranquil period to a speculative attack regime (p01 – left axis) and the probability of staying in a crisis (p11 – right axis) regime according to the VAR switching model.

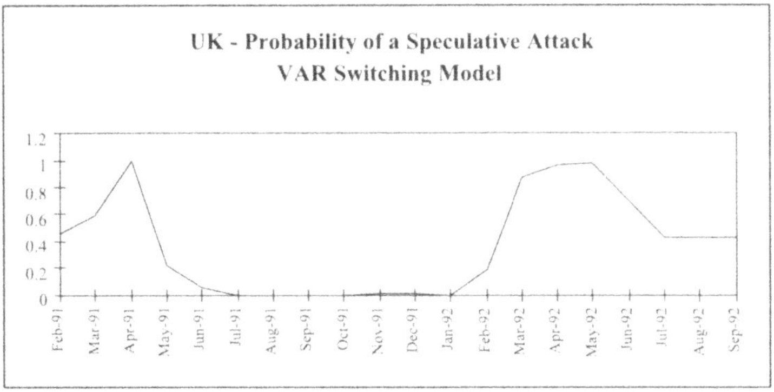

Fig. A.14.a*

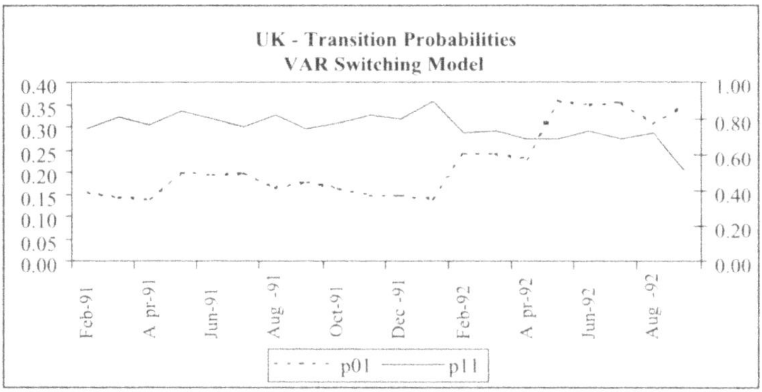

Fig. A.14.b**

* Figure displays the estimated probability of a speculative attack according to the VAR switching model.

** Figures display the estimated probability of switching from a tranquil period to a speculative attack regime (p01 – left axis) and the probability of staying in a crisis (p11 – right axis) regime according to the VAR switching model.

Table A.1. Speculative attack episodes: Belgium

Dates of Speculative Attacks	Attacks identified by the exchange rate switching model	Attacks identified by the VAR switching model	Attacks identified by ERW's index of speculative pressure	Realignment Dates
Sept. 1979–May 1980	No	Yes	No	1979:09:24
Feb. 1981–Jul. 1981	Yes	Yes	No	–
Oct. 1981–Apr. 1982	Yes	Yes	Yes	1981:10:05 & 1982:02:22
Jun. 1982–Jul. 1982	No	Yes	Yes	1982:06:14
Mar. 1983–May 1983	Yes	Yes	No	1983:03:21
Sept. 1983–Nov. 1983	No	Yes	No	–
Mar. 1984–Sept. 1984	No	Yes	No	–
Dec. 1985–May 1986	No	Yes	No	1986:04:07
Jan. 1987	No	Yes	No	1987:01:12
Mar. 1989	No	Yes	No	–
Jun. 1990–Jul. 1990	No	Yes	No	–
Sept. 1992–Dec. 1992	No	Yes	Yes	–
Aug. 1993	Yes	Yes	N/A*	widening of ERM band

ERW's index of speculative pressure refers to the index used by Eichengreen, Rose, and Wyplosz (1996).
* Period not covered by this measure

Table A.2. Speculative attack episodes: Denmark

Dates of Speculative Attacks	Attacks identified by the exchange rate switching model	Attacks identified by the VAR switching model	Attacks identified by ERW's index of speculative pressure	Realignment Dates
Jun. 1979–Dec. 1979	Yes	Yes	Yes	1979:09:24 & 1979:11:30
Jul. 1980–Mar. 1981	Yes	Yes	Yes	–
Oct. 1981–Mar. 1982	Yes	Yes	No	1981:10:05 & 1982:02:22
Jun. 1982–Sep. 1982	Yes	Yes	No	1982:06:14
Mar. 1983–May 1983	Yes	Yes	No	1983:03:21
Apr. 1986	No	No	No	1986:04:07
Jan. 1987	No	No	Yes	1987:01:12
Sept. 1992	No	Yes	Yes	–
Jul. 1993–Aug. 1993	Yes	Yes	N/A*	widening of ERM band

ERW's index of speculative pressure refers to the index used by Eichengreen, Rose, and Wyplosz (1996).
* Period not covered by this measure

Table A.3. Speculative attack episodes: France

Dates of Speculative Attacks	Attacks identified by the exchange rate switching model	Attacks identified by the VAR switching model	Attacks identified by ERW's index of speculative pressure	Realignment Dates
Sept. 1979	No	No	No	1979:09:24
Mar. 1981–Nov. 1981	Yes	Yes	Yes	1981:10:05
Mar. 1982–Sept. 1982	Yes	Yes	Yes	1982:06:14
Mar. 1983–Apr. 1983	Yes	Yes	No	1983:03:21
Apr. 1986–Aug. 1986	Yes	Yes	No	1986:04:07
Jan. 1987	Yes	Yes	Yes	1987:01:12
Nov. 1987	Yes	No	No	–
Sept. 1992–Dec. 1992	No	Yes	Yes	–
Jul. 1993–Aug. 1993	Yes	Yes	N/A*	widening of ERM band

ERW's index of speculative pressure refers to the index used by Eichengreen, Rose, and Wyplosz (1996).
* Period not covered by this measure

Table A.4. Speculative attack episodes: Ireland

Dates of Speculative Attacks	Attacks identified by the exchange rate switching model	Attacks identified by the VAR switching model	Attacks identified by ERW's index of speculative pressure	Realignment Dates
Sept. 1979	N/A*	N/A*	No	1979:09:24
Oct. 1981	N/A*	N/A*	No	1981:10:05
Jun. 1982	N/A*	N/A*	Yes	1982:06:14
Mar. 1983–Jun. 1983	No	Yes	Yes	1983:03:21
Jan. 1986–Aug. 1986	Yes	Yes	Yes	1986:04:07 & 1986:08:04
Dec. 1986–Feb. 1987	Yes	Yes	Yes	1987:01:12
Sept. 1992–Jan. 1993	No	Yes	Yes	–
Feb. 1993–May 1993	Yes	Yes	Yes	1993:02:01
Jul. 1993–Aug. 1993	Yes	Yes	N/A*	widening of ERM band

ERW's index of speculative pressure refers to the index used by Eichengreen, Rose, and Wyplosz (1996).

Table A.5. Speculative attack episodes: Italy

Dates of Speculative Attacks	Attacks identified by the exchange rate switching model	Attacks identified by the VAR switching model	Attacks identified by ERW's index of speculative pressure	Realignment Dates
Sept. 1979–Jan. 1980	Yes	Yes	No	1979:09:24
Mar. 1981–Apr. 1981	Yes	Yes	No	1981:03:23
Sept. 1981–Oct. 1981	Yes	Yes	Yes	1981:10:05
Mar. 1982–Apr. 1982	Yes	Yes	Yes	–
Jun. 1982	No	No	No	1982:06:14
Oct. 1982–Nov. 1982	Yes	No	No	–
Mar. 1983–Apr. 1983	Yes	Yes	No	1983:03:21
Sept. 1983–Oct. 1983	Yes	No	No	–
Feb. 1984	Yes	No	No	–
Dec. 1984	Yes	No	No	–
Mar. 1985–Apr. 1985	Yes	Yes	No	–
Jul. 1985–Aug. 1985	Yes	Yes	No	1985:07:22
Dec. 1985	Yes	No	No	–
Apr. 1986	No	Yes	No	1986:04:07
Jan. 1987–May 1987	Yes	Yes	Yes	1987:01:12
Nov. 1987	Yes	Yes	No	–
Dec. 1989	Yes	Yes	No	1990:01:08
Sept. 1990	Yes	No	No	–
Jul. 1992–Sept. 1992	Yes	Yes	Yes	Exit ERM 1992:09:17

ERW's index of speculative pressure refers to the index used by Eichengreen, Rose, and Wyplosz (1996).

Table A.6. Speculative attack episodes: Spain

Dates of Speculative Attacks	Attacks identified by the exchange rate switching model	Attacks identified by the VAR switching model	Attacks identified by ERW's index of speculative pressure	Realignment Dates
Oct. 1989–Dec. 1989	Yes	Yes	No	–
Apr. 1990–May 1990	Yes	Yes	No	–
Jul. 1990–Mar. 1991	Yes	No	No	–
Dec. 1991–May 1992	Yes	No	No	–
Sept. 1992–Oct. 1992	Yes	Yes	Yes	1992:09:13 & 1992:11:22
Mar. 1993–Aug. 1993	Yes	Yes	N/A*	1995:05:13

ERW's index of speculative pressure refers to the index used by Eichengreen, Rose, and Wyplosz (1996).

* Period not covered by this measure

Table A.7. Speculative attack episodes: UK

Dates of Speculative Attacks	Attacks identified by the exchange rate switching model	Attacks identified by the VAR switching model	Attacks identified by ERW's index of speculative pressure	Realignment Dates
Mar. 1991–Jun. 1991	Yes	Yes	No	–
Mar. 1992–Sept. 1992	Yes	Yes	Yes	Exit ERM 1992:09:16

ERW's index of speculative pressure refers to the index used by Eichengreen, Rose, and Wyplosz (1996).

Table A.8. Evidence of speculative pressure: Belgium

1979:09–1980:05

- A realignment of EMS currencies took place on September 24, 1979. The revaluation of the Deutsche mark (DM) implied a 2 percent devaluation of the Belgian franc against this currency. Source: IMF Annual Report on Exchange Arrangements and Restrictions (IMF AREAR), 1980.

1981:02–1981:07

- The Belgian franc breached its divergence threshold several times in February–March 1980 and again in February 1981 necessitating intervention and tighter monetary measures. Source: IMF AREAR, 1981.

1981:10–1982:03

- On October 5, the DM was revalued by 5.5 percent. This realignment implied a 5.5 percent devaluation of the Belgian franc vis-à-vis the DM. Subsequent to the realignment; the Belgian franc needed continued support. Pressure on the Belgian franc intensified in December. On February 22, 1982 a realignment of the grid took place. The adjustment resulted in a devaluation of the Belgian franc and the Danish krone by 8.5 percent and 3 percent, respectively, against other currencies. Source: IMF AREAR, 1982.

1982:06

- With effect from June 14, 1982, a general realignment took place. The revaluation of the DM implied an effective 4 percent devaluation of the Belgian franc against this currency. Source: IMF AREAR, 1982.

1983:03–1983:04

- The Bundesbank intervened to support the Belgian franc. Source: The Economist, 3/12/1983.
- The Belgian franc was devalued with respect to the DM, Netherlands guilder, and the Danish krone, but revalued against the French franc, Italian lira, and Irish punt. The devaluation of the Belgian franc against the DM was of 4 percent. Source: IMF AREAR, 1984.
- The National Bank of Belgium reportedly spent up to 15 billion Belgian francs in support of the franc. With the franc on the floor of the EMS grid, the Belgian government announced a surprise 2.5 percent increase in interest rates to 14 percent. Source: Financial Times, 3/22/1983.

1983:09–1983:10

- The Belgian central bank raised its discount rate from 9 to 10 percent. The central bank spent 80 billion Belgian francs since August in support of the currency. Source: Financial Times, 11/24/1983.

1984:03–1984:09

- The National Bank of Belgium raised interest rates and intervened heavily in support of the Belgian franc, given that it fell to its floor vis-à-vis the DM. Source: The Economist, 3/10/1984.

Table A.8. Continued

1985:12–1986:07

- On April 5, 1986, the Financial Times reported that the Belgian franc and Italian lira could follow the French franc in a devaluation, given the speculative pressure against these currencies. Source: Financial Times, 4/5/1986.
- With effect from April 7, a realignment of the ERM central rates took place. The realignment implied a 2 percent devaluation of the Belgian franc against the DM. Source: IMF AREAR, 1987.

1987:01

- Speculation forced France, Belgium, and Denmark to raise interest rates to defend their currencies and, also, seriously depleted these countries' reserves. Source: Financial Times, 1/10/1987.
- On January 12, 1987, the Belgian franc was devalued by only 1 percent against the DM in a general realignment. Source: IMF AREAR, 1988.

1989:03

- The National Bank of Belgium raised key interest rates hiking the discount rate by 0.5 points to 8.75 in response to speculative pressure against the franc. Source: Reuters News, 4/21/1989.

1990:06–1990:07

- Belgian foreign currency reserves fell 6.82 billion francs to 233.18 billion francs in the five days to July 20. Source: Reuters News, 7/25/1990.

1992:09–1992:12

- No evidence of a speculative attack. According to Reuters, the Belgian franc remained stable throughout this period. Rates were cut and the Belgian National bank intervened in favor of the lira and the punt.

1993:08

- Belgium tightened monetary conditions to resist speculative attacks against the Belgian franc pushing its central rate up to 7.5 percent from 6.7 percent. Source: Financial Times, 7/23/1993.

Table A.9. Evidence of speculative pressure: Denmark

1979:06–1979:12

- A realignment of EMS currencies took place on September 24, 1979. The Danish krone was devalued by 5 percent. Subsequently, as part of a program to strengthen Denmark's external position, the bilateral intervention limits in that country were raised by 5 percent against the Danish krone, effective November 30, 1979. Between March 1979 and December 1979, the Danish krone reached its lower divergence thresholds on several occasions. Source: IMF AREAR, 1980.

1980:08–1981:03

- With effect, March 23, 1981, Italy devalued the lira by 6 percent against the other currencies participating in the EMS. No other exchange rate adjustment was made, but the system became subject to occasional strain and the Danish krone came under attack. Source: IMF AREAR, 1981.

1981:10

- On October 5, the Deutsche mark and the Netherlands guilder were revalued by 5.5 percent. This realignment implied an effective 5 percent devaluation of the krone against the DM. Source: IMF AREAR, 1982.

1982:02

- The Danish krone came under intense pressure in early 1982 with the result that on February 22, 1982 a realignment of the grid took place. The adjustment resulted in a 3 percent devaluation of the Danish krone against other currencies, respectively. Source: IMF AREAR, 1982.

1982:06

- Following renewed pressure within the EMS; a new realignment was decided upon on June 12. This realignment implied a 4 percent devaluation of the krone against the DM. Source: IMF AREAR, 1982

1983:03

- The Danish krone reached its floor against the DM on March 9, 1983. Source: Financial Times, 3/9/1983.
- The Bundesbank intervened in support of the Danish krone. Source: The Economist, 3/12/1983.
- Pressures on exchange rates within the EMS reappeared. A general realignment took place that implied a 3 percent devaluation of the Danish krone with respect to the DM and the guilder. Source: IMF AREAR, 1984.

1986:04

- The Danish krone was devalued by 2 percent with respect to the DM and the guilder in a general realignment. Source: IMF AREAR, 1986.

1987:01

- Speculation forced France, Belgium, and Denmark to raise interest rates to defend their currencies and seriously depleted their reserves. Source: Financial Times, 1/10/1987.
- A realignment of the central rates with the EMS was implemented on January 12, resulting in an effective 3 percent devaluation of the krone vis-à-vis the DM. Source: IMF AREAR, 1988.

1992:09

- The Danish krone, French franc, and Irish punt fell to their floors in the ERM, prompting central bank intervention, as speculators moved on to new targets after pummeling the pound, lira, and peseta. Source: Financial Times, 9/18/1992.
- The Danish Central bank countered speculative pressure against the krone by tightening money market liquidity. Source: Reuters News, 9/25/1992.

1993:08

- The Danish krone was subject to intense speculative pressure similar to that suffered by the French franc with authorities forced to increase interest rates in its defense. Source: Financial Times, 7/24/1993.

Table A.10. Evidence of speculative pressure: France

1981:03–1981:11

- The French franc came under pressure after the French presidential elections and the monetary authorities of some EMS members intervened heavily in May to support the French franc. The French franc came under pressure again in September. Finally on October 5, a realignment took place that entailed an overall depreciation of 8.1 percent of the franc against the DM and the Netherlands guilder. Source: IMF AREAR, 1982.
- France spent $1.3b defending the franc prior to the October realignment. Source: The Economist, 10/10/1981.

1982:03–1982:09

- Following renewed pressure against the French franc, a realignment was decided on June 14, 1982. This realignment implied an effective devaluation of the franc against the DM of almost 10 percent. Source: IMF AREAR, 1982–83.

1983:03

- A realignment took place on March 21 that implied an 8 percent of the French franc. Source: IMF AREAR, 1984

1986:04

- A realignment occurred that implied a 6 percent devaluation of the franc vis-à-vis the DM. Source: IMF AREAR, 1986.
- The devaluation of the French franc was the first major realignment of the EMS since 1983. Speculative pressure had been mounting since mid-March. Source: Financial Times, 4/7/1986.

1986:09–1987:01

- France raised rates by 1 percent after intense pressure on the franc. Source: Financial Times, 12/ 9/1986.
- Renewed pressure on the French franc forced the Bank of France to raise its 7-day repurchase rate by half a percentage to 8.25 percent. The franc fell to a rate against the DM close to its floor. Source: Financial Times, 12/31/1986.
- France, Belgium, and Denmark had to raise interest rates to defend their currencies. Source: Financial Times, 1/10/1987.
- A realignment of the central rates within the EMS was implemented on January 12. This resulted in an appreciation of the DM, Netherlands guilder, Belgian franc, and Luxembourg franc. Source: IMF AREAR, 1987

1992:09–1992:12

- Germany and France united to defend the French franc from speculative attacks. France pushed its short-term rate sharply higher and both the German Bundesbank and the Bank of France intervened heavily in support of the franc. The Bank of France raised its five to ten day repurchase rate from 10.5 percent to 13 percent triggering a sharp rise in money market rates. Source: Financial Times, 9/24/1992.
- The speculation against the ERM in September was unprecedented. Bundesbank intervention in support of the lira, sterling, and French franc reached 92 billion DMs. Source: Financial Times, 11/16/1992.
- The French franc came under pressure following the Spanish peseta and Portuguese escudo on November 22. Source: Financial Times, 12/12/1992.

1993:07–1993:08

- Massive central bank intervention by the Bundesbank alone failed to give sufficient support to the franc. The Bank of France pushed up its 24 hour lending rate to 10 percent from 7.75 percent. Source: Financial Times, 7/24/1993.

Table A.11. Evidence of speculative pressure: Ireland

1983:03–1983:06
- Following a realignment on March 21, the punt was devalued by 8.53 percent against the DM. Source: IMF AREAR, 1984.

1986:01–1986:08
- In April 1986, a realignment resulted in a devaluation of the punt of 3 percent against the DM. In August, the Irish punt was devalued again, this time by 8 percent. Source: IMF AREAR, 1987

1986:12–1987:01
- The Irish punt was effectively devalued by 3 percent against the DM.

1992:09–93:02
- The Irish punt fell to its floors in the ERM, prompting central bank intervention. Source: Financial Times, 9/18/1992.
- The Irish punt was under intense selling pressure during September 1992. Source: Financial Times, 9/24/1992.
- The Irish punt was unaffected by the November realignment of the peseta and the escudo despite of speculation against this currency. Source: Financial Times, 11/23/1992.
- Ireland was forced to push interest rates to usurious levels in the hope of maintaining the exchange rate parities. Source: Financial Times, 11/12/1992.
- On January 30, 1993, the Irish punt was devalued by 10 percent. Source: IMF AREAR, 1994.

1993:07–08
- The punt plunged 3.5 percent in three days following the recent ERM band widening. Source: Reuters News, 8/ 10/1993.

Table A.12. Evidence of speculative pressure: Italy

1979:09–1980:01
- On September 24, 1979 the lira was effectively devalued by 2 percent against the DM. Source: IMF AREAR, 1980.

1981:03
- The Italian lira came under pressure at the beginning of March. Effective March 23, the Italian lira was devalued by 6 percent against all other EMS currencies. Source: IMF AREAR, 1981.

1981:09–1981:10
- On October 5, the lira was effectively devalued by 8 percent against the DM. Source: IMF AREAR, 1982

1982:03
- Following the devaluation of the Belgian franc (8.5 percent) in February 1982, France and Italy came under attacks. With inflation in France and Italy running at twice the Belgian level speculative attacks shifted towards these most vulnerable members. Source: Financial Times, April 1, 1982.

1982:06
- In June 14, 1982, the lira was effectively devalued by 7 percent against the DM. Source: IMF AREAR, 1982.

1983:03
- Changes in the grid meant that the lira was devalued by 8 percent against the DM. Source: IMF AREAR, 1984.

1985:03–198:04

No evidence.

1985:07
- The central rates of the EMS were realigned. Changes involved a devaluation of 7.8 percent in the bilateral central rates of the Italian lira. Source: IMF AREAR, 1986

1986:04
- The Italian lira and French franc were devalued against all other currencies. The realignment implied an effective 3 percent devaluation of the lira. Source: IMF AREAR, 1987

1987:11

No evidence.

1989:12
- The Bank of Italy sold 161 million marks at the fixed rate, as the lira slid to its 15 month low against the mark. Source: Reuters news, December 15, 1989.
- The lira was devalued by 3.8 percent against its EMS central rates on January 10, 1990. Source: Financial Times, January 10, 1990.

1992:09
- Italy forced up interest rates by 1.75 percent points, the biggest increase in 11 years and drew on international bank credits in an attempt to protect the lira. Source: Financial Times, September 6, 1992.
- On September 13, the central rate of the lira against other currencies was devalued by 7 percent.
- On September 17, the lira was withdrawn from the ERM. Source: IMF AREAR, 1993.

Table A.13. Evidence of speculative pressure: Spain

1989:10–1989:12
- October 24, Spain fights pressure against the peseta. Source: Financial Times, October 24, 1989.
- October 26, The Bank of Spain intervened to support the peseta selling 290 million marks at a fixing rate of 63.8 pesetas. It was the central bank fifth intervention in a week. Source: Reuters news October 26, 1989.
- Bank of Spain sold 96.65 million dollars to brake the Spanish currency decline against the mark. Source: Reuters news October 20, 1989.

1990:04–1990:06
No evidence

1992:09–1992:11
- On September 17, the central rate of the peseta against the central rates of the currencies participating in the ERM of the EMS was devalued by 4.8 percent. Source: IMF AREAR, 1993.
- On November 22, the central rate of the peseta against the central rates of the currencies participating in the ERM of the EMS was devalued by 6 percent. Source: IMF AREAR, 1993.

1993:04–1993:08
- The Bank of Spain raised unofficial intervention rates and intervened strongly on the market to defend the peseta's central parity rate. The Madrid authorities took action by raising intervention rates from 13.35 percent to 14 percent and put aside 45 billion dollars for the peseta's defense. Source: Financial Times, April 23, 1993.
- On May 13, the central rate of the peseta against the central rates of the currencies participating in the ERM of the EMS was devalued by 8 percent. Source: IMF AREAR, 1994.

Table A.14. Evidence of speculative pressure: UK

1991:04–1991:06
No evidence

1992:03–1992:09
- The British government borrowed 7.27 billion pounds of DM and other currencies and sold these for sterling to support the currency. Source: Financial Times, September 4, 1992.
- On September 16, the UK suspended intervention obligations with respect to the exchange and intervention mechanism of the EMS. Source: IMF AREAR, 1993.

Fads or bubbles?

Huntley Schaller[1], **Simon van Norden**[2]

[1] Department of Economics, Carleton University, 1125 Colonel By Drive, Ottawa, Ontario, K1S 5B6, CANADA (e-mail: schaller@ccs.carleton.ca.)
[2] Service de l'enseignment de la finance, Ecole des H.E.C., 3000 Chemin de la Côte Sainte Catherine, Montreal, QC, Canada H3T 2A7

First Version Received: October 2000/Final Version Received: October 2001

Abstract. This paper tests between fads and bubbles using a switching regression to distinguish between competing models. Two main features of the bubbles model distinguish it from the fads model. First, the bubbles model implies that returns are drawn from regimes which differ in the way returns vary with deviations from fundamental prices. Second, the bubbles model implies that deviations from fundamental price will help predict regime switches. Using US data for 1926–89, we find evidence which is consistent with the fads model even when we allow for variation in expected dividend growth rates and expected discount rates. However, the restrictions which the fads model implies for a more general switching-regression specification are rejected. The rejections point in the direction of the bubbles model, although not all of the implications of the bubbles model are supported by the data.

Key words: macroeconomics and financial markets, fads, bubbles, time series econometrics, regime switching

JEL classification: G1, E3, C3.

Introduction

Events of the last five years, but particularly the terrific rise and fall in the value of "dot-com" shares from 1998 to 2001, have again challenged the view that

---

We would like to thank the editors of the journal, James Hamilton and Baldev Raj, two anonymous referees, O. Blanchard and seminar participants at the Econometric Society, Canadian Econometric Study Group, SEDC, Bank of Canada, University of British Columbia, Carleton University and Simon Fraser University for helpful comments. Dr. Schaller thanks the Financial Research Foundation of Canada and the SSHRC for their financial support and the Operations Research Center at MIT for providing a pleasant environment in which to pursue this research. Any errors are our own. We are solely responsible for the views expressed here.

most stock price movements are justified by news about the fundamental value of the underlying firms. This view continues to attract widespread attention despite its ongoing failure to provide coherent explanations for notable market upheavals, such as the 1987 global stock market crash. Furthermore, while there are alternative models of stock price determination, there is little consensus on which of these alternatives gives the most realistic description of the ongoing behaviour we observe in financial markets. This in turn reflects the limited work which has been done comparing the performance of such alternative models.

Two of the main alternatives are the fads model proposed by Summers (1986) and the stochastic bubbles model proposed by Blanchard and Watson (1982). In a world with fads, Cutler, Poterba, and Summers (1991) show that a measure of the deviation of actual price from fundamental price will predict returns. Stochastic bubbles, on the other hand, can lead to regime switching in stock market returns. In this paper, we seek to compare these two alternatives to determine which is more important in describing "non-fundamental" behaviour in stock markets.

We begin by showing that both models can be nested within a switching-regression specification. Each model has testable implications for the switching regression. Using long series from the CRSP database, we find evidence that there is more than just fads in the data. First, regime switches are predictable using a measure of apparent deviations from fundamentals. Second, expected returns (conditional on the size of the deviation in the previous period) are higher in the survival regime than in the collapse regime. The first aspect is quite pronounced and contributes strongly to the rejection of the fads model restrictions. The second aspect is considerably weaker and would not, on its own, lead to the rejection of the fads model restrictions in most of the specifications we consider.

A problem with estimating both fads and bubbles models is that there is no consensus on the correct model of fundamentals. To check the robustness of our results, we use three different techniques for measuring the apparent deviation from fundamentals, each of which is based on successively less restrictive assumptions. For the most part, the qualitative results are similar, regardless of the measure we use.

Our paper is organized as follows. Section I surveys the literature on non-fundamental models of stock prices which is most relevant to this paper. Section II gives a detailed specification of the fads model, then introduces the bubbles model and shows how it leads to a switching-regression specification for stock market returns. Section III discusses estimation of the two models and shows how they imply different parameter restrictions on a general switching-regression specification. Sections IV and V present empirical results for the fads and bubbles models, respectively. Section VI discusses the interpretation of the empirical results and suggests some possible directions for future research.

I. Literature survey

As noted in the survey by Bollerslev and Hodrick (1995), there has been considerable ongoing academic interest in models of the stock market in which price deviates from fundamental price. Some, such as DeLong, Shleifer, Summers, and Waldmann (1989, 1991) argue that presence of a few irrational traders in the market should have important and persistent effects on overall market behaviour. Some, such as Froot and Obstfeld (1991), have argued that apparent deviations from fundamentals may reflect an unexpected non-linearity in the determination of stock prices.

One of the most notable strands in this literature is perhaps that which focusses on the ability of apparent deviations from simple measures of fundamental prices to predict future returns, particularly over long horizons. Summers (1986) points out that if there are fads in the stock market, we may observe long temporary price swings which can be modeled as a slowly decaying stationary component in prices.[1] The decay over time in the transitory component will lead to mean reversion in stock prices. Influential papers documenting this characteristic include Summers (1986), Campbell and Shiller (1987, 1988), Fama and French (1988b) and Cutler, Poterba, and Summers (1991). These papers vary somewhat in the terms used to describe this phenomenum and they focus more on characterizing this apparent behavior of stock prices than in providing a rigorous theoretical underpinning for it. We follow Summers in refering to this behaviour as "fads" and we review its behavior in more detail below. For now, we simply note that in a world with fads, a measure of the deviation of actual price from fundamental price will help predict future returns.

Perhaps the most durable approach to thinking about non-fundamental movements in stock prices is one which is based on the idea of rational agents and multiple expectational equilibria. Such phenomena are frequently referred to as "bubbles" and the origins of such models date back almost as far as the creation of organized financial markets. Rigorous treatments of such behaviour in a rational expectations framework also dates back to early in the tradition of rational expectations modelling, with important contributions by Blanchard (1979), Blanchard and Watson (1982), Tirole (1982, 1985), Obstfeld and Rogoff (1983, 1986) and Diba and Grossman (1988a,b).

It should be noted that many of these articles debated whether bubbles were strictly admissible in a rigorous and fully-rational model. Blanchard and Fischer (1989, p. 238) argue that "[These restrictions] often rely on an extreme form of rationality and are not, for this reason, altogether convincing. Often bubbles are ruled out because they imply, with a very small probability and very far in the future, some violation of rationality, such as non-negativity of prices or the bubbles becoming larger than the economy. It is conceivable that the probability may be so small, or the future so distant, that it is simply ignored by market participants." Moreover, work by Allen and Gorton (1991) and Leach (1991) has shown that restrictions on non-fundamental solutions are not robust to minor changes in assumptions, such as heterogeneous agents and either continuous time or more than two periods in an OLG model.

Our motivation for using the models of speculative behaviour in this paper is the same as Solow (1957, p. 323–324) in using an aggregate production function, which was controversial at the time: "Either this kind of [approach] appeals or it doesn't.... If it does, I think one can draw some ... useful conclusions from the results."

The existence of multiple equilibria in theoretical models has been linked to empirical evidence of regime switching in studies ranging from Lee and Porter

---

[1] The predictability of returns could come from time variation in required returns. Fama (1991), Fama and French (1988b), and Poterba and Summers (1988) discuss the question of interpretation in more detail and provide references to a variety of explanations.

(1984) to Jeanne and Masson (2000). The assumption in most bubble models that a bubbles may either survive or collapse implies that stock market returns come from two distinct regimes, one of which corresponds to surviving bubbles and the other to collapsing bubbles. The bubbles model therefore implies that the relationship between returns and deviations from fundamental price will differ between the two regimes. This observation has lead many researchers to test for evidence of bubbles by testing for certain kinds of regime switching. The multivariate approach we describe below is similar to that used in van Norden and Schaller (1993), van Norden (1996), and Schaller and van Norden (1997a, 1999). An alternative univariate approach has been suggested by Funke, Hall and Sola (1994), and Hall, Psarakakis, and Sola (1999); see van Norden and Vigfusson (1998) for an overview and comparison.

II. Specification of fads and bubbles models

As the above discussion suggests, the fads and bubbles strands in the empirical literature have remained largely distinct. Our aim in this paper to combine both in a more general framework and examine which best characterizes the observed behaviour of stock prices. This requires that we first review the specifications of both models in more detail.

A. The fads model

The following model, used in Fama and French (1988) and Cutler, Poterba, and Summers (1991), can capture both the traditional efficient-markets model and the idea of fads:

$$p_t = p_t^* + e_t \tag{1}$$

$$p_t^* = p_{t-1}^* + \varepsilon_t \tag{2}$$

where p_t is the log of the stock market price in period t, p_t^* is the non-stationary component of the log price, and ε_t is white noise. Under the traditional model, log prices are a martingale, $e_t = 0$ and returns (the difference in log prices) are white noise.[2] We can think of p_t^* as the fundamental price because it does not include a fads element. Under the fads model, prices have a stationary component:

$$e_t = \rho_e e_{t-1} + v_t \tag{3}$$

Thus the fads model can be characterized as a situation in which $\sigma_e^2 > 0$ and $\rho_e > 0$, where σ_e^2 is the variance of e_t. The stationary component e_t in stock prices implies that returns will be predictable.

Cutler, Poterba, and Summers (1991) consider a situation in which a proxy is available for the fundamental price. Because there is no universally accepted

---

[2] Strictly speaking, efficiency in financial markets implies that log prices are a martingale, rather than a random walk. Our presentation of the traditional and fads models follows Cutler, Poterba, and Summers (1991). Later in this section we allow the variance of ε_t to vary over time; then in the traditional model (i.e., when $\sigma_e^2 = 0$) log prices are a martingale.

model of fundamentals, any such proxy is likely to be measured with error. We can model this using an errors-in-variables approach:

$$p_t^f = p_t^* + w_t \tag{4}$$

where p^f is the proxy and w is the measurement error (which is assumed to be serially uncorrelated). Cutler, Poterba, and Summers also suggest the following statistic λ as a way of reflecting the degree of measurement error:

$$\lambda \equiv \frac{\sigma_e^2}{[\sigma_e^2 + \sigma_w^2]} \tag{5}$$

If p^f is a perfect measure of fundamentals (so $\sigma_w^2 = 0$), then $\lambda = 1$; if p^f measures p^* with error, then $\lambda < 1$. In any case, since it is a ratio of variances it is always non-negative.

To see how fads lead to the predictability of returns based on lagged information, use equations (1)–(4) to express returns in terms of differences between the price and the proxy for fundamental price. This suggests regressions of the form:

$$p_{t+1} - p_t = \beta_0 + \beta_b(p_t - p_t^f) + v_{t+1} \tag{6}$$

where $p_{t+1} - p_t$ (the difference in log prices) is the rate of return and $p_t - p_t^f$ is the difference between actual (log) price and a measure p_t^f of the fundamental (log) price.

One example of a proxy for fundamental price is the log of the real dividend. (This is the proxy that Cutler, Poterba, and Summers (1991) use in their empirical work on stock market returns.) Equation (6) is then a regression of returns on the lagged log dividend-price ratio. It is easy to show that (1)–(4) imply that:

$$\operatorname*{plim}_{T\to\infty}(\hat{\beta}_b) = -(1 - \rho_e)\lambda \tag{7}$$

The fads model therefore implies that estimates of β_b should be negative.[3]

In section III, we will show that this fads model represents a special case of a general switching-regression specification. In the same section, we will discuss how to estimate and test the fads model.

B. The bubbles model and regime switching

In this section, we begin by describing the Blanchard-Watson (1982) model of stochastic bubbles. We then follow Schaller and van Norden (1999) in showing how this can fit within the framework of a switching regression.

By stochastic bubbles, we mean bubbles which may either survive or collapse in each period. The existence of stochastic bubbles implies that there are

[3] Equations (6) and (7) correspond to equations (6) and (7) in Cutler, Poterba, and Summers (1991).

two regimes generating stock market returns, one where the bubble collapses and one where it survives. Rational investors take this into account when deciding whether or not to hold an asset. The period-to-period arbitrage condition allows us to impose some structure on asset returns in the surviving and collapsing regimes: in the surviving regime, returns should be sufficiently high to compensate the investor for the possibility that the bubble may collapse. Combined with the historical observation that larger overvaluations are more likely to collapse, this provides us with the essential elements for a regime-switching specification for stock market returns.

We begin by considering a simple asset-pricing model where risk-neutral investors choose between holding an asset that yields $(1 + r)$ and a risky stock. The investors' first-order conditions imply:

$$P_t = (1 + r)^{-1} \cdot (E_t(P_{t+1}) + D_t) \tag{8}$$

where P_t and D_t are the stock's price and dividend at time t and E_t denotes the expectation conditional on information available at time t. One possible solution to this equation defines the fundamental price

$$P_t^* \equiv \sum_{k=0}^{\infty} (1 + r)^{-(k+1)} \cdot E_t(D_{t+k}) \tag{9}$$

All other prices are said to be "bubbly," with the size of the bubble defined as

$$B_t \equiv P_t - P_t^* \tag{10}$$

Since we have assumed that all asset prices, bubbly or not, follow (8), this implies that the bubble must satisfy the condition

$$E_t(B_{t+1}) = (1 + r) \cdot B_t \tag{11}$$

Blanchard (1979) and Blanchard and Watson (1982) consider a particular stochastic solution to (11). They suppose there are two states of nature, one where the bubble survives (state S) and one where it collapses (state C). If the possibility of being in state S is some constant q and being in state C implies $B_t = 0$ then (11) implies

$$E_t(B_{t+1}|S) = \frac{(1 + r)}{q} \cdot B_t \tag{12}$$

The intuition here is that (if $B_t > 0$) agents expect capital losses of B_t in state C, which must be balanced by expected capital gains in state S in order to earn the required rate of return on the bubble.

Historical accounts suggest that the probability of a bubble surviving decreases as the bubble grows. The Blanchard-Watson model can therefore be extended by allowing the probability of survival q to depend on the proportionate size of the bubble

$$q \equiv q(b_t) \tag{13}$$

where $b_t \equiv B_t/P_t$ and

$$\frac{dq(b_t)}{d|b_t|} < 0 \tag{14}$$

Note the use of the absolute value of b_t, since the bubble may be positive or negative.

While some notable market crashes have occurred in a single day, in other cases a collapse may occur over several months.[4] To model this, the Blanchard-Watson model is again generalized to permit the expected value of the bubble, conditional on collapse, to be non-zero, thereby allowing for partial collapses.[5] Assuming that the expected size of a bubble in state C, which we define as $u_t P_t$, depends on the relative size of the bubble in the previous period, so

$$E_t[B_{t+1}|C] = u(b_t) \cdot P_t \tag{15}$$

Further assuming that $u(\cdot)$ is a continuous and everywhere differentiable function and that:[6]

$$u(0) = 0 \tag{16}$$

$$0 \leq \frac{du(b_t)}{db_t} \leq 1 \tag{17}$$

(The differentiability assumption is made because we will need to linearize the model.) The assumptions (16) and (17) are added to ensure that a collapse means that the bubble is expected to shrink.[7] Imposing (16) then gives

$$E[B_{t+1}|S] = \frac{1+r}{q(b_t)} B_t - \frac{1-q(b_t)}{q(b_t)} u(b_t) \cdot P_t \tag{18}$$

This shows that the expected value of the bubble in the surviving state is a decreasing function of the probability of survival $q(b_t)$. In other words, the greater the probability of collapse, the larger the gain on a positive bubble must be in the surviving state in order to compensate the investor for the possibility of collapse.

Note that when $q(b_t) \equiv q$, a constant, and $u(b_t) \equiv 0$, this model reduces to the Blanchard-Watson process.

It is straightforward to derive the expected excess returns R in each regime,

---

[4] The fall in the Tokyo stock exchange in the period following January 1990 or in the NASDAQ after mid-2000 are examples.

[5] Early papers which considered bubbles which either shrink (or partially collapse) include Diba and Grossman (1988b) and Evans (1991).

[6] As with assumptions on $q(b_t)$, the assumptions on $u(b_t)$ are not imposed on the data. Instead, they allow us to determine the expected signs and relative magnitudes of the parameters.

[7] To see this, draw a graph with $u(b_t)$ (which equals $E[B_{t+1}|C]/P_t$) on the vertical axis and b_t on the horizontal axis. The function $u(b_t)$ passes through the origin, since $u(0) = 0$. The 45° line represents a situation where $E[B_{t+1}|C]/P_t = B_t/P_t$; i.e., where a "collapsing" bubble is the same size as the previous period's bubble. Since $0 \leq u' \leq 1$, $u(b_t)$ always lies on or below the 45° line. Thus these assumptions ensure that a collapsing bubble is no larger than the bubble in the previous period.

where excess returns are the rate of return on the bubbly asset less the rate of return on the alternative asset.

$$E_t(R_{t+1}|S) = \frac{1 - q(b_t)}{q(b_t)} [(1 + r)b_t - u(b_t)] \tag{19}$$

$$E_t(R_{t+1}|C) = u(b_t) - (1 + r)b_t \tag{20}$$

Noting that conditional expected excess returns are a function of b_t, we can take first-order Taylor series approximations of $E_t(R_{t+1}|S)$ and $E_t(R_{t+1}|C)$ with respect to b_t around some arbitrary value $\bar{b}$ to obtain:

$$E(R_{t+1}|S) = \beta_{SO} + \beta_{Sb} b_t \tag{21}$$

$$E(R_{t+1}|C) = \beta_{CO} + \beta_{Cb} b_t \tag{22}$$

where

$$\beta_{Sb} \equiv -\frac{1}{q(\bar{b})^2} \cdot \left.\frac{dq(b_t)}{db_t}\right|_{b_t=\bar{b}} \cdot [(1 + r) \cdot \bar{b} - u(\bar{b})] + \frac{1 - q(\bar{b})}{q(\bar{b})} \cdot \left[1 + r - \left.\frac{du(b_t)}{db_t}\right|_{b_t=\bar{b}}\right] . \tag{23}$$

$$\beta_{Cb} \equiv \left[\left.\frac{d_u(b_t)}{db_t}\right|_{b_t=\bar{b}} - (1 + r)\right] \tag{24}$$

Assuming $r \geq 0$, we can then prove that $\beta_{Sb} \geq 0$ and $\beta_{Cb} \leq 0$, and more generally that $\beta_{Sb} \geq \beta_{Cb}$.[8]

By dropping the expectations operator E_t in equations (21) and (22), we can rewrite them as

$$R_{S,t+1} = \beta_{SO} + \beta_{Sb} \cdot b_t + \varepsilon_{S,t+1} \tag{25}$$

$$R_{C,t+1} = \beta_{C0} + \beta_{Cb} \cdot b_t + \varepsilon_{C,t+1} \tag{26}$$

where $\varepsilon_{i,t+1} \sim N(0, \sigma_i)$ for $i = S, C$. To complete the switching-regression model, we need a functional form for $q(b_t)$ which satisfies (14) and which guarantees that the resulting estimates of q will be bounded between 0 and 1. We use the Logit form

$$q(b_t) = \Phi(\beta_{q0} + \beta_{qb} b_t^2) \tag{27}$$

where Φ is the logistic cumulative distribution function. These three equations

[8] The proof for β_{Cb} follows directly from (24). For β_{Sb}, we can use (23) and the fact that $1 \geq q(b_t) \geq 0$ to show that the second term in the expression is always non-negative. Equations (14), (16), and (17) together imply that the first term is also non-negative, so the sum of the two terms will be non-negative.

(25 to 27) form a standard switching-regression model of the type described by Goldfeld and Quandt (1976) and Hartley (1978), and can be estimated by standard maximum likelihood methods.[9] Previous empirical studies of this type include van Norden and Schaller (1993), who examined returns on the Toronto Stock Exchange, and van Norden (1996), who used a similar framework to test for bubbles in foreign exchange markets.

III. Testing the fads & bubbles models

In this section, we show how both the fads and bubbles models nest within and imply parameter restrictions on the general switching-regression specification above. By testing these restrictions jointly and separately, we can make statements about the ways in which each model corresponds, or fails to correspond, to the data.

The fads model implies a number of restrictions on the general switching-regression specification. First, according to the fads model, expected returns (conditional on b_t) should be the same in both regimes. This implies that β_{S0} should equal β_{C0} and that β_{Sb} should equal β_{Cb}. Second, as shown in section I, the fads model implies that returns should be mean reverting. This implies that the estimated value of β_b should be negative. Finally, according to the fads model, b_t should not influence which regime will occur in the subsequent period. This implies that β_{qb} should equal zero. The fads model restrictions can be summarized as follows:

$$\beta_{S0} = \beta_{C0} = \beta_0 \tag{28}$$

$$\beta_{Sb} = \beta_{Cb} = \beta_b \tag{29}$$

$$\beta_{qb} = 0 \tag{30}$$

$$\beta_b < 0 \tag{31}$$

With these restrictions on the switching regression, the fads model differs from a linear regression in only one respect; the variance of the error term may change with the state.[10] The fads model is silent on the question of whether returns should be homoscedastic or heteroscedastic. We decided against im-

[9] For those familiar with Markov switching models, it may be useful to note that this switching model has a related stochastic structure. A two-state Markov switching model has two state-dependent probabilities: $q(t) = \Pr(S(t) = 0 \mid S(t-1) = 0)$ and $p(t) = \Pr(S(t) = 1 \mid S(t-1) = 1)$. The switching model presented here has one state-independent probability $q(t) = \Pr(S(t) = 0)$. This is the special case of the Markov switching model where $q(t) = 1 - p(t)$; i.e., the probability of today's state is independent of yesterday's state. Our specification implies that volatility will be independently distributed between a high and low variance state. However, there is much evidence that stock market volatility shows persistence; that is, periods of high volatility are more likely to be followed by high volatility than are periods of low volatility. For example, see Schwert (1989), who considers a Markov-switching model for stock market variances.

[10] Kim and Kim (1996) also estimate a model of fads which allows for regime-switching in the variance of returns. They find evidence of fads, particularly around the first oil shock and the 1987 crash. Their approach differs substantially from ours in that they do not include any measure of $(p_t - p_t^f)$, the difference between actual and fundamental price, in their specification.

posing the homoscedasticity assumption for two reasons. First, imposing this assumption might result in our rejecting the fads model simply because the switching regression finds significant heteroscedasticity in the data. Second, imposing the homoscedasticity assumption would greatly complicate testing the fads model against the general switching-regression specification alternative since the parameter β_{q0} would be unidentified under the null hypothesis of fads.[11]

We can test the fads model in two basic ways. The first way is to impose the first three restrictions and compare the fit of the resulting regression with the fit of the unrestricted general switching-regression specification. In section IV, we use a likelihood ratio statistic to conduct this joint test.[12] The second way is to impose the first three restrictions (so we are estimating the fads model) and check whether β_b is negative.

The bubbles model also has implications for the general switching-regression specification. First, according to the bubbles model, expected returns (conditional on b_t) should be greater in the states where the bubble survives than in the states where it collapses.[13] This implies that β_{S0} will not necessarily equal β_{C0} and that β_{Sb} should be greater than β_{Cb}. Second, according to the bubbles model, collapses are more likely when bubbles are large in magnitude. This implies that β_{qb} should be positive. The implications of the bubbles model for the general switching-regression specification can be summarized as follows:

$$\beta_{S0} \neq \beta_{C0} \tag{32}$$

$$\beta_{Sb} > \beta_{Cb} \tag{33}$$

$$\beta_{qb} > 0 \tag{34}$$

There are two main ways in which we can test the bubbles model against the fads model. The first we have already discussed above. The fads model implies certain restrictions on the general switching-regression specification. These restrictions are inconsistent with the bubbles model, so if we fail to reject them, we would conclude that there is no significant evidence for the bubbles model. The second sort of test involves the implications which are summarized in the previous three equations. If these parameter restrictions hold, it provides evidence in favour of the bubbles model.[14]

---

[11] See Hansen (1996) for a discussion of hypothesis testing under these conditions.

[12] A number of authors have noted that while Lagrange Multiplier and Wald tests should be asymptotically equivalent to the LR tests, they sometimes give widely divergent results when applied to regime switching models. For example, see Engel and Hamilton (1990). The LR tests are thought to be the most reliable, so we use these for most of the joint hypothesis tests we report.

[13] For $b_t < 0$, the expected returns in the surviving regime should be larger in absolute value (i.e., more negative) than those in the collapsing regime. Of course, the implications for the signs of β_{Sb} and β_{Cb} are the same regardless of whether b_t is positive or negative.

[14] As always, other interpretations, which may involve neither bubbles nor fads, are possible. One particularly interesting study is Driffill and Sola (1998), who consider both "intrinsic bubbles" [Froot and Obstfeld (1991)] and regime switching in dividends. They find that each can account for the main movements in stock prices in the U.S. over the period 1900–87, although a specification which allows for regime switching in dividends (but no bubble) is rejected in favour of a specification which includes both regime switching in dividends and a bubble.

The data we examine for evidence of speculative behaviour is drawn from the Center for Research on Security Prices (CRSP) database. We use the monthly value-weighted price (P) and dividend (D) indices for all stocks from January 1926 to December 1989. R_t is constructed as the difference between gross nominal returns (including dividends) and the monthly yield on Moody's Industrial Bond Index. Since dividends display strong seasonal fluctuations, we follow Fama and French (1988a) in using an average over the twelve-month period ending in the given month to deseasonalize D. Where required for constructing fundamental values, we convert nominal values to real using the Consumer Price Index.

IV. Empirical estimates of the fads model

The fads model is a switching regression of the form:

$$R_{t+1} = \beta_0 + \beta_b \cdot b_t + \varepsilon_{i,t+1}$$

$$\varepsilon_{i,t+1} \sim N(0, \sigma_i), \quad i = S, C$$

$$\Pr(i = S) = \Phi(\beta_{q0})$$

Specifically, this is a standard switching-regression model of the type described by Goldfeld and Quandt (1976) and Hartley (1978), and can be estimated by standard maximum likelihood methods. Given normality of $(\varepsilon_{S,t+1}, \varepsilon_{C,t+1})$, estimates of the β's can be found by maximizing the likelihood function

$$\prod_{t=1}^{T} \left[\Phi(\beta_{q0}) \cdot \varphi\left(\frac{R_{t+1} - \beta_0}{\sigma_S}\right) \cdot \sigma_S^{-1} \right.$$
$$\left. + \{1 - \Phi(\beta_{q0})\} \cdot \varphi\left(\frac{R_{t+1} - \beta_0}{\sigma_C}\right) \cdot \sigma_C^{-1} \right] \tag{35}$$

where φ is the standard normal probability density function (pdf) and σ_S, σ_C are the standard deviations of $\varepsilon_{S,t+1}$, $\varepsilon_{C,t+1}$. This estimation technique takes b_t, which we construct separately, as given. (The construction of b_t is discussed below.)

We use three different approaches to measuring b_t, the proportional derivation of actual stock market price from fundamental price. To motivate the three approaches, consider the classic Gordon (1962) model:

$$P_t = \frac{D_t}{r - g} \tag{36}$$

where g is the dividend growth rate. We can think of the fundamental price in the Gordon world as a function of current dividends, anticipated dividend growth, and anticipated interest rates.

The first measure of the deviation of actual stock market price from fundamental price (b^A) is based on a multiple of current dividends, where the multiple is the sample mean of the price-dividend ratio. The second measure (b^B) is based on a multiple of current dividends plus a multiple of the predicted present value of future dividend changes, where the predictions come from a bivariate VAR of dividend changes and the "spread" (the stock price minus a multiple of current dividends). The third measure is based on $\exp(-\delta_t^c)$ times current dividends, where δ^c is the predicted log dividend-price ratio, where the predictions come from a VAR involving the log dividend-price ratio, the interest rate, and the growth rate of dividends. (These three approaches to measuring b_t are described in more detail in an appendix which is available from the authors.)

A. Assuming the dividend process (b^A)

Table I presents estimates of the fads model. We begin by focusing on the first column of the table which presents parameter estimates based on b_t^A. A major implication of the fads model is that a regression of returns on the apparent deviation of actual prices from fundamental prices should yield a negative coefficient. As the first column shows, the point estimate of this coefficient (denoted β_b) is -0.013 and the t-statistic is -2.1, a result which is consistent with the fads model.[15] To get a sense of the economic significance of the point estimate, consider the value of b_t in September 1987 (one of the larger values in the sample and one of historical interest). With $b_t = .29$, the point estimate implies excess returns will be lower by .37% per month (5% per year).

The result for β_b is consistent with the results of previous studies. As noted above, the regression reported in the first column of Table I is very similar to the Cutler, Poterba, and Summers (1991) test of the fads model. Their estimate of β_b is -0.01 which is close to our estimate.[16]

A number of authors have argued that the evidence of fads is weaker if one takes account of heteroscedasticity. For example, Kim, Nelson, and Startz (1991) argue that most of the evidence for mean reversion comes from the period before World War II, a period during which the volatility of stock market returns was unusually high.[17] We allow for heteroscedasticity by letting disturbances come from a high and low variance regime. As Table I shows, σ_C is about three times as large as σ_S, so heteroscedasticity appears to be a genuine issue in the data.[18] Even after allowing for heteroscedasticity, there is still evidence that returns are predictable, since the results in column one of Table I show β_b to be significantly negative.

---

[15] We report t-ratios based on the inverse of the Hessian. The results that we report are asymptotically consistent and efficient under our assumptions. A number of recent studies [e.g., Kim, Nelson, and Startz (1991), McQueen (1992), Nelson and Kim (1993), and Richardson and Stock (1989)] have found that standard test statistics can be misleading in studies of stock market predictability. In this paper, we use more than 700 non-overlapping observations and account for conditional heteroscedasticity.

[16] Our results correspond most closely to the last row, first column of their Table 6. The sign of their estimate differs because they regress returns on fundamental price minus actual price and we regress returns on actual price minus fundamental price.

[17] See also McQueen (1992) and Nelson and Kim (1993) on heteroskedasticity.

[18] A formal test for the equality of σ_S and σ_C is difficult; see Hansen (1996) and Garcia (1998) for recent progress in this area.

Table I. The fads model: Full sample (1929–1989)

Coefficients	b_t^A	b_t^B	b_t^C
β_0	0.0067 (4.015)	0.0047 (2.691)	0.0051 (2.988)
β_b	−0.0126 (−2.079)	−0.0117 (−2.122)	−0.0077 (−2.547)
β_{q0}	−1.1983 (−7.511)	−1.1951 (−7.469)	−1.1747 (−7.354)
σ_S	0.0392 (21.198)	0.0393 (20.919)	0.0390 (20.535)
σ_C	0.1278 (8.526)	0.1289 (8.460)	0.1274 (8.574)
Joint Test	16.32 (0.0010)	10.82 (0.0127)	4.02 (0.2598)

The coefficients are estimated from a switching regression of the form

$$R_{t+1} = \beta_0 + \beta_b \cdot b_t + \varepsilon_{i,t+1}$$

$$\varepsilon_{i,t+1} \sim N(0, \sigma_i), \quad i = S, C$$

$$\Pr(i = S) = \Phi(\beta_{q0})$$

The figures in parentheses below the point estimates are t-statistics calculated using the inverse of the Hessian. The headings b_t^A, b_t^B, and b_t^C refer to three different measures of apparent deviations from fundamental price which are described more fully in Subsections A, B, and C of Section IV, respectively. The Joint test takes the general switching-regression specification represented by the equations (25)–(27) as the null hypothesis and the coefficient restrictions in equations (28)–(30) as the alternative hypothesis; the likelihood-ratio statistic is distributed χ^2 with three degrees of freedom. The marginal significance levels (p-values) are in parentheses below the Joint test statistics. The switching regression is estimated using the maxlik procedure in GAUSS with a combination of BFGS and BHHH algorithms. For b_t^A, the sample period is 1927–89, because lagged data are not required for the VAR's (which are used to construct b_t^B and b_t^C).

In section III, we discussed two main types of tests of the fads model. The first imposes the fads model restrictions on the general switching-regression specification – the general switching regression specification is equations (25), (26), and (27) – and then tests whether or not β_b is negative. However, this does not test between the fads and bubbles models. The second type of test examines whether the fads model restrictions – equations (28), (29), and (30) – are valid; it is therefore a more useful test in distinguishing between fads and bubbles.

The fads model imposes restrictions on the general switching-regression specification. These restrictions reflect two key differences between the fads model and the bubbles model. First, the bubbles model implies that returns are drawn from two distinct regimes, so that the intercept (β_{S0} and β_{C0}) and slope (β_{Sb} and β_{Cb}) coefficients may differ between regimes. Second, the bubbles model implies that the size of deviations from fundamental price influence the regime from which each stock market return is drawn, so that β_{qb} will not be equal to zero.

As shown in the lower portion of Table I, the likelihood-ratio test statistic for the joint test of the fads model restrictions is 16.3. Since this test has a χ^2 distribution with three degrees of freedom under the null hypothesis of fads, the joint test strongly rejects the fads model restrictions.

B. Alternative measures of deviations from fundamental price (b^B, b^C)

Constructing a measure of the fundamental stock market price is an inherently difficult and potentially contentious task. If we were attempting to test either the fads model or the bubbles model against the null hypothesis that stock market returns are driven exclusively by fundamentals, it would also be an extremely important task. When we are trying to distinguish between the fads model and the bubbles model, it is less clear that our choice of a model of fundamentals is crucial.

Cutler, Poterba, and Summers (1991) argue that a noisy measure of fundamental price will tend to bias tests against finding evidence that non-fundamentals are important. Thus, if we use a noisy measure of fundamental price and still find evidence of either fads or bubbles, their view is that the noisiness of our measure of fundamentals strengthens the case that non-fundamentals matter. Others take a different view. For example, Cecchetti, Lam, and Mark (1990) argue that some of the evidence for fads can be explained by variations in the endowment process. In the present value model which we outline in section II, this might be represented, for example, by variation in the expected growth rate of dividends.

Whether or not the measure of fundamentals makes a difference in testing between fads and bubbles is a question on which the previous literature is largely silent. Our approach is therefore eclectic and empirical: we consider various measures of fundamental price and examine whether they lead to different results.

The results in the first column of Table I assume that the expected dividend growth rate is constant. Our second measure of fundamental price allows for predictable variation in the dividend growth rate. In particular, it incorporates the information available in past dividend changes and stock market prices using a linear projection on this past information.[19]

We refer to the measure of deviation from fundamental price which incorporates predictable time variation in the dividend growth rate as b^B. The results for this measure are presented in column two of Table I. The point estimate of β_b is -0.012 with a t-statistic of 2.1, which is very close to the results using b^A. We can test the fads model against the bubbles model by determining whether the fads model restrictions on the general switching-regression specifi-

[19] If the existence of fads or bubbles leads returns to be predictable, then incorporating this predictability in the measure of fundamental price might bias tests against finding evidence for fads or bubbles. Whether incorporating this predictability into fundamental price would tend to bias the tests relatively more against fads or against bubbles is hard to say.

cation are valid. In the lower portion of Table I, the test statistic for the joint test of these restrictions is 10.8. As in the earlier results, this is a strong rejection of the fads model restrictions.

Fama (1990) and Fama and French (1988) argue that the predictability of returns is due to time variation in expected returns. One way to take this into account is to use excess returns as the dependent variable, as we do in this paper. This captures variations in the rate of return on the alternative asset. A second way to take this into account is to use predictable variation in discount rates in constructing the measure of fundamental price. This may help to capture predictable variation in the interest rate or the risk premium.

We refer to the measure of deviation from fundamental price which incorporates predictable variation in the discount rate (as well as in the dividend growth rate) as b^C. The results for this measure are presented in column three of Table I. The point estimate of β_b is -0.008 with a t-statistic of 2.5. The value of b_t^c is .51 in September 1987, so the point estimate of β_b implies returns will be about .39% lower in October (about 5% lower at annualized rates). This is very close to the results using b^A.

The second type of test is whether the fads model restrictions on the general switching-regression specification are valid. In the lower portion of Table I, the test statistic for the joint test of these restrictions is 4.0. In contrast to the earlier results, the test fails to reject the fads model restrictions.

We can briefly summarize the results for the full sample. The main focus of this paper is testing between fads and bubbles. We do this by testing the restrictions which the fads model imposes on the general switching-regression specification. For two of our three measures of fundamental price, we find strong rejections of the fads model restrictions. Our estimates of the fads model differ from previous research because we allow for state-dependent conditional heteroscedasticity; nevertheless, we still find evidence that returns are predictable, since our estimates of β_b are negative. The evidence that returns are predictable is also robust to allowing for variation in the dividend growth rate and the interest rate in constructing measures of fundamental price.

C. Subperiods

It is often suggested that much of the evidence for the predictability of returns comes from periods which include the 1929 crash and the Great Depression.[20] More generally, time series econometric results are sometimes sensitive to the specific time period over which the estimation is done. In this subsection, we therefore present results for three subperiods – 1929–45, 1946–72, 1973–89. The first includes the 1929 crash, the Great Depression, and World War II; the second includes the post-war boom up until the first major oil shock; and the third covers the most recent period, including the inflation of the 1970's and the 1987 crash.

The results for the period 1929–45 (Table II) are the most surprising. Once allowance is made for state-dependent heteroscedasticity (as our switching regression does), the evidence for fads is very weak. Contrary to the prediction of the fads model, the estimate of β_b is either positive or close to zero, depending

[20] See, for example, Kim, Nelson, and Startz (1991).

Table II. The fads model: 1929–1945

Coefficients	b_t^A	b_t^B	b_t^C
β_0	0.0085 (1.763)	0.0043 (0.730)	0.0007 (0.090)
β_b	0.0056 (0.405)	−0.0003 (−0.017)	−0.0067 (−0.697)
β_{q0}	−0.7387 (−2.427)	−0.7342 (−2.426)	−0.7508 (−2.301)
σ_S	0.0482 (7.643)	0.0513 (9.034)	0.0517 (7.730)
σ_C	0.1490 (5.993)	0.1538 (5.509)	0.1540 (5.611)
Joint Test	12.65 (0.0055)	5.60 (0.1329)	4.02 (0.2596)

See the notes to Table I. For b_t^A, the sample period is 1927–45, because lagged data are not required for the VAR's (which are used to construct b_t^B and b_t^C).

on how we measure fundamental price. In all cases, the t-statistic on β_b is less than one in absolute value.

In the 1946–72 period, the estimates of β_b are all negative and all have t-statistics greater than two in absolute value as shown in Table III. However, when we test the fads model restrictions, they are very strongly rejected regardless of which measure of fundamental price we use.

The results for the period 1973–89 provide the evidence most consistent with the fads model. As shown in Table IV, the estimates of β_b are all negative and all have t-statistics greater than two. Nevertheless, one of the three measures of fundamental price leads to a rejection of the fads model restrictions.

The subperiod results suggest that the evidence for fads we find in the full sample is not coming primarily from the 1930's; the estimates of β_b are more consistent with the fads model during the post-war boom and the period since the 1973 OPEC shock. However, as in the full sample, the subperiod results frequently reject the restrictions implied by the fads model, suggesting that there is more in the data than fads.

We discuss the interpretation of the empirical results for the fads model (and how they relate to the empirical results for the bubbles model) in the conclusion.

V. Empirical estimates of the bubbles model

In this section, we present estimates of the bubbles model derived in section II as well as tests of the restrictions which the bubbles model implies for the general switching-regression specification. The bubbles model differs from the

Table III. The fads model: 1946–1972

Coefficients	b_t^A	b_t^B	b_t^C
β_0	0.0084 (3.742)	0.0066 (3.065)	0.0057 (2.562)
β_b	−0.0180 (−2.462)	−0.0153 (−2.380)	−0.0092 (−2.480)
β_{q0}	−0.2525 (−0.044)	−0.2925 (−0.057)	−0.1803 (−0.025)
σ_S	0.0338 (2.607)	0.0338 (2.787)	0.0340 (2.209)
σ_C	0.0405 (2.108)	0.0408 (2.139)	0.0398 (1.931)
Joint Test	18.79 (0.0003)	19.09 (0.0003)	17.56 (0.0005)

See the notes to Table I.

Table IV. The fads model: 1973–1989

Coefficients	b_t^A	b_t^B	b_t^C
β_0	0.0044 (1.396)	−0.0010 (−0.296)	0.0246 (2.897)
β_b	−0.0493 (−2.333)	−0.0424 (−2.364)	−0.0711 (−2.781)
β_{q0}	−0.7714 (−1.531)	−0.7795 (−1.573)	−0.6324 (−1.617)
σ_S	0.0360 (8.098)	0.0360 (8.240)	0.0337 (8.983)
σ_C	0.0759 (4.666)	0.0763 (4.681)	0.0741 (5.727)
Joint Test	4.04 (0.2570)	8.38 (0.0388)	1.41 (0.7031)

See the notes to Table I.

fads model in two main ways. First, the bubbles model implies that returns are drawn from two distinct regimes. In particular, we show in section II that the bubbles model implies an inequality restriction on the slope coefficients in the surviving and collapsing regimes, namely that $\beta_{Sb} \geq \beta_{Cb}$. Moreover, since returns come from distinct regimes, there is no reason to expect the intercept coefficients (β_{S0} and β_{C0}) to be the same in the two regimes. Second, the bubbles model implies that deviations from fundamental price influence the regime from which the next period's stock market return is drawn. Specifically, the bubbles model in section II suggests that a bubble is more likely to collapse when the actual price is far away from the fundamental price. This implies that β_{qb} will be positive.

A. Assuming the dividend process

As noted in the previous section, the fads models restrictions are frequently rejected; the estimates of the bubbles model parameters in Table V help us to see why. We begin by focusing on the first column of the table, which presents parameter estimates based on b_t^A. The point estimate of β_{S0} is .0074 with a t-statistic of 4.1. If β_{Sb} were zero, this point estimate would translate into positive excess returns of 0.7% per month (9% per year) for a surviving bubble. The point estimate of β_{C0} is $-.0294$ with a t-statistic of -1.4. If β_{Cb} were zero, this point estimate would translate into negative excess returns of about 3% per month (31% per year). The point estimates of the intercept coefficients therefore imply substantial differences in expected returns between the surviving and collapsing regimes. The statistical significance of the difference is weaker; as the lower panel of the table shows, the marginal significance level of the restriction $\beta_{S0} = \beta_{C0}$ is about .08.

The bubbles model in section II implies that β_{Sb} should be greater than β_{Cb}. The point estimate of β_{Sb} is $-.0136$ with a t-statistic of 2.0. The point estimate of β_{Cb} is $-.0554$ with a t-statistic of 1.4. The inequality restriction implied by the bubbles model therefore holds but the point estimates are not sharp enough to reject the null hypothesis that $\beta_{Sb} = \beta_{Cb}$ at conventional significance levels. The economic significance of the coefficient estimates is quite different, though. For example, consider one of the larger values of b_t in our sample, namely the value in September 1929, which was .26. Even at this relatively high value of b_t, the coefficient estimate implies a change in expected returns of only 35 basis points in the surviving regime. In the collapsing regime, the point estimate of β_{Cb} implies a change of 144 basis points.

The bubbles model in section II suggests that bubbles are more likely to collapse when they comprise a large portion of the price of the stock. This implies that β_{qb} should be positive. The point estimate of β_{qb} is 1.71 with a t-statistic of 3.1.

The existence of distinct regimes in the bubbles model (and particularly the fact that the probability of a collapse depends on b_t) means that the relationship between returns and b_t can be highly non-linear. One way to illustrate this is to look at the probability that next period's return will be unusually high or low. In the fads model, expected returns next period depend on b_t; thus if b_t is large this period, there is an increased likelihood that next period's returns will be unusually low. In the bubbles model, a change in b_t has an effect through the slope coefficients (β_{Sb} and β_{Cb}), but there is an additional effect because b_t influences the probability that a given regime will occur. Mathematically, the probability of a return two standard deviations below the mean (a "crash") is:

$$\Pr(R_{t+1} < x) = \Phi\left(\frac{x - \beta_{S0} - \beta_{Sb} b_t}{\sigma_S}\right) q(b_t) + \Phi\left(\frac{x - \beta_{C0} - \beta_{Cb} b_t}{\sigma_C}\right) (1 - q(b_t))$$

Table V. The bubbles model: Full sample (1929–1989)

Coefficients	b_t^A	b_t^B	b_t^C
β_{S0}	0.0074 (4.087)	0.0053 (2.818)	0.0059 (3.228)
β_{Sb}	−0.0136 (−1.976)	−0.0117 (−1.926)	−0.0071 (−2.239)
β_{C0}	−0.0294 (−1.402)	−0.0386 (−1.572)	−0.0253 (−1.349)
β_{Cb}	−0.0554 (−1.361)	−0.0757 (−1.553)	−0.0397 (−1.374)
β_{q0}	−1.7660 (−6.181)	−1.6593 (−5.872)	−1.3227 (−4.815)
β_{qb}	1.7132 (3.071)	1.2068 (2.459)	0.2396 (0.800)
σ_S	0.0406 (19.645)	0.0407 (19.812)	0.0394 (18.165)
σ_C	0.1338 (7.463)	0.1340 (7.475)	0.1271 (7.896)
Tests:			
$\beta_{S0} = \beta_{C0}$	3.0284 (0.0818)	3.1647 (0.0753)	2.7031 (0.1002)
$\beta_{Sb} = \beta_{Cb}$	0.9870 (0.3205)	1.6602 (0.1976)	1.2256 (0.2683)
$\beta_{S0} = \beta_{C0}$ and $\beta_{Sb} = \beta_{Cb}$	3.3819 (0.1844)	3.6452 (0.1616)	3.3148 (0.1906)

The coefficients are estimated from a switching regression of the form represented by the equations (25)–(27). The figures in parentheses below the point estimates are t-statistics calculated using the inverse of the Hessian. The headings b_t^A, b_t^B, and b_t^C refer to measures of apparent deviations from fundamental price; see Subsections A, B, and C of Section IV, respectively. The first two tests are based on Wald statistics using the inverse of the Hessian and are asymptotically distributed χ^2, with one degree of freedom. The third test is based on a likelihood-ratio statistic and is asymptotically distributed χ^2 with two degrees of freedom. Marginal significance levels are listed below the test statistics. The estimation uses the max-lik procedure in GAUSS with a combination of BFGS and BHHH algorithms.

The probability of an unusually high return ("rally") can be defined similarly.

If the non-linearity introduced by the bubbles model is empirically important, the magnitude of the fluctuations in the probability of a crash will be much larger in the bubbles model. Figure I graphs the probabilities of a crash generated by the fads and bubbles models. The scale of the fluctuations is very different. For example, from the beginning of the sample to September 1929, the probability of a crash generated by the fads model increases by only about

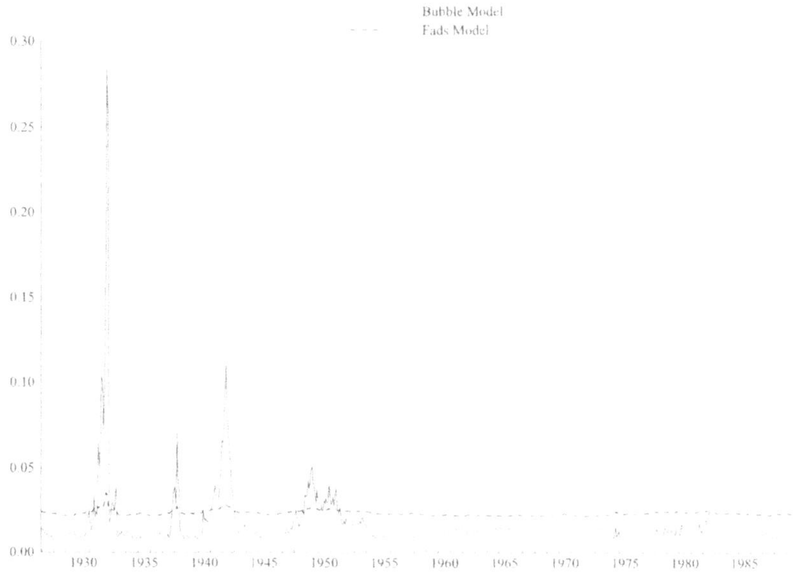

Fig. 1. Probability of a Crash

two-tenths of a percentage point (from .022 to .024). Over the same time span, the probability of a crash generated by the bubbles model rises from about .03 to almost .10. Figure II plots the probability of a rally. In the months leading up to May 1932 (the lowest value of b_t in the sample), the probability of a rally generated by the fads model rises by about one percentage point (from .026 to .036). The probability of a rally generated by the bubbles model rises from about .01 to almost .09.

B. Alternative measures of deviations from fundamental price (b^B, b^C)

The results in the first column of Table V are based on the assumption that the expected dividend growth rate is constant. Our second measure of fundamental price allows for predictable variation in the dividend growth rate. The second column of Table V presents estimates of the bubbles model using b^B. The picture that emerges is broadly similar to the results in the first column of Table V. The point estimate of β_{S0} is positive, while that for β_{C0} is negative and much larger in magnitude. If β_{Sb} and β_{Cb} were zero, the point estimates of the intercept coefficients (β_{S0} and β_{C0}) imply that annualized returns would be about 67% higher in the surviving regime than in the collapsing regime. The marginal significance level for a test of the restriction $\beta_{S0} = \beta_{C0}$ is .08. The point estimate of β_{Cb} is negative and about six times smaller than the point estimate of β_{Sb}. Neither parameter is very precisely estimated, however, so the data fail to reject the restriction $\beta_{Sb} = \beta_{Cb}$. As predicted by the bubbles model in section II, β_{qb} is positive with a t-statistic of about 2.5.

Fig. 2. Probability of a Rally

Our final measure of deviation from fundamental price is b^C which incorporates predictable variation in the discount rate (as well as in the dividend growth rate) in the fundamental price. The results for b^C are presented in column three of Table V. The point estimates of the intercept and slope coefficients in the equations for the surviving and collapsing regimes are similar to those for b^A and b^B. The point estimate of β_{S0} is positive and relatively small in magnitude, while the point estimate of β_{C0} is negative and larger in magnitude. If β_{Sb} and β_{Cb} were zero, the point estimates of the intercept coefficients (β_{S0} and β_{C0}) imply that annualized returns would be about 45% higher in the surviving regime than in the collapsing regime. The marginal significance level for the restriction $\beta_{S0} = \beta_{C0}$ is about .10. As with b^A and b^B, the point estimate of β_{Cb} is negative and smaller than β_{Sb} by about a factor of five. The point estimate of β_{qb} is positive; unlike the estimates of β_{qb} in columns one and two, however, the t-statistic is small.

Intuitively, the bubbles model suggests that: 1) there should be a regime in which the bubble survives and excess returns are positive to compensate the investor for the possibility that the bubble may collapse; 2) in the periods in which a positive bubble collapses, returns should be negative; and 3) the probability of a collapse should increase as the bubble gets larger. The empirical results for the full sample broadly correspond to this description of stochastic bubbles. There is one important exception: simple models of rational bubbles (and the derivations presented in Section II) imply that returns in the surviving regime should be higher when the bubble is larger. This conflicts with our finding that β_{Sb} is negative.

C. Subperiods

For the subperiod which includes the 1929 crash and the Great Depression, the results are broadly similar to those for the full sample. As shown in Table VI, the estimates of β_{S0} are greater than the estimates of β_{C0}, the estimates of β_{Sb} are considerably larger than the estimates of β_{Cb}, and the estimate of β_{qb} is positive. Unlike the full sample, for the period 1929–45, β_{Sb} is either positive or very close to zero.

For the period 1946–72, the estimate of β_{S0} is larger than the estimate for β_{C0} as shown in Table VII. Unlike the full sample, this difference is highly significant; in fact, the difference between β_{S0} and β_{C0} is the main reason the fads model is so strongly rejected during the post-war boom subperiod. The difference in slope coefficients is smaller than in the full sample (and the direction is reversed) and β_{qb} is insignificantly different from zero.

Table VI. The bubbles model: 1929–1945

Coefficients	b_t^A	b_t^B	b_t^C
β_{S0}	0.0110 (1.775)	0.0048 (0.675)	0.0065 (0.372)
β_{Sb}	0.0128 (0.685)	0.0037 (0.217)	−0.0002 (−0.012)
β_{C0}	−0.0427 (−1.297)	−0.0543 (−1.068)	−0.0677 (−1.263)
β_{Cb}	−0.0741 (−1.361)	−0.1046 (−1.232)	−0.0965 (−1.374)
β_{q0}	−1.3388 (−2.773)	−1.3917 (−2.701)	−0.8444 (−0.682)
β_{qb}	1.8821 (2.341)	1.1490 (1.664)	0.1985 (0.239)
σ_S	0.0497 (6.712)	0.0561 (9.065)	0.0510 (2.951)
σ_C	0.1471 (5.231)	0.1676 (4.918)	0.1462 (2.820)
Tests:			
$\beta_{S0} = \beta_{C0}$	2.6087 (0.1063)	1.3002 (0.2542)	2.5374 (0.1112)
$\beta_{Sb} = \beta_{Cb}$	2.1674 (0.1410)	1.5069 (0.2196)	2.1955 (0.1384)
$\beta_{S0} = \beta_{C0}$ and $\beta_{Sb} = \beta_{Cb}$	2.6476 (0.2661)	1.5829 (0.4532)	2.7798 (0.2491)

See the notes to Table V. For b_t^A, the sample period is 1927–45, because lagged data are not required for the VAR's (which are used to construct b_t^B and b_t^C).

Table VII. The bubbles model: 1946–1972

Coefficients	b_t^A	b_t^B	b_t^C
β_{S0}	0.0324 (6.849)	0.0304 (7.146)	0.0296 (7.164)
β_{Sb}	−0.0268 (−2.852)	−0.0237 (−2.824)	−0.0142 (−2.115)
β_{C0}	−0.0013 (−0.300)	−0.0030 (−0.722)	−0.0036 (−0.881)
β_{Cb}	−0.0149 (−1.439)	−0.0132 (−1.264)	−0.0104 (−1.782)
β_{q0}	0.6634 (1.500)	0.5406 (1.351)	0.4315 (1.120)
β_{qb}	−0.3029 (−0.218)	0.1632 (0.151)	0.4462 (0.628)
σ_S	0.0161 (4.784)	0.0161 (4.840)	0.0161 (4.998)
σ_C	0.0382 (17.657)	0.0380 (18.467)	0.0379 (19.116)
Tests:			
$\beta_{S0} = \beta_{C0}$	32.1920 (0.0000)	36.9500 (0.0000)	39.5250 (0.0000)
$\beta_{Sb} = \beta_{Cb}$	0.6562 (0.4179)	0.6187 (0.4315)	0.2066 (0.6494)
$\beta_{S0} = \beta_{C0}$ and $\beta_{Sb} = \beta_{Cb}$	9.0357 (0.0109)	6.5806 (0.0372)	12.7790 (0.0017)

See the notes to Table V.

The results for the period since the first OPEC shock are broadly similar to the full sample results. As shown in Table VIII, the estimate of β_{S0} is greater than the estimate of β_{C0}, the estimate of β_{Cb} is much smaller than the estimate of β_{Sb}, and the estimate of β_{qb} is positive (except when b^C is used).

VI. Conclusion

The objective of this paper is to test which model provides a better description of U.S. stock market returns: a fads model or a bubbles model. Previous authors have shown that the fads model implies that apparent deviations from fundamental price will help to predict stock market returns. Our estimates of the relevant coefficient (β_b) generally support this implication. When we test the restrictions that the fads model imposes on the general switching-regression specification, however, we frequently reject these restrictions.

Table VIII. The bubbles model: 1973–1989

Coefficients	b_t^A	b_t^B	b_t^C
β_{S0}	0.0036 (0.913)	0.0014 (0.406)	0.0231 (2.095)
β_{Sb}	−0.0229 (−0.879)	−0.0245 (−1.051)	−0.0630 (−1.991)
β_{C0}	0.0025 (0.146)	−0.0636 (−1.337)	−0.0399 (1.145)
β_{Cb}	−0.1898 (−1.730)	−0.2431 (−1.765)	−0.1454 (−1.247)
β_{q0}	−1.1542 (−1.685)	−2.4383 (−3.148)	−0.3120 (−0.472)
β_{qb}	1.9339 (0.769)	6.2322 (2.092)	−1.3777 (−0.791)
σ_S	0.0368 (7.934)	0.0395 (13.825)	0.0345 (9.010)
σ_C	0.0749 (5.381)	0.0721 (5.553)	0.0758 (5.702)
Tests:			
$\beta_{S0} = \beta_{C0}$	0.0034 (0.9535)	1.8828 (0.1700)	0.1747 (0.6760)
$\beta_{Sb} = \beta_{Cb}$	2.1251 (0.1449)	2.5809 (0.1082)	0.3984 (0.5279)
$\beta_{S0} = \beta_{C0}$ and $\beta_{Sb} = \beta_{Cb}$	3.1280 (0.2093)	4.9634 (0.0836)	0.6708 (0.7151)

See the notes to Table V.

In our formulation, there are two key differences between the fads model and the bubbles model. The first arises from the fact that the bubbles model imposes a link between the bubbly asset and the alternative asset. This condition of the bubbles model implies that returns must be high in the states where the bubble survives to compensate the investor for the low returns in the states where the bubble collapses.

The point estimates of the parameters which reflect this difference tend to point in the direction of the bubbles model. The fads model implies that the slope and intercept coefficients should be the same in the two regimes. The point estimates suggest economically important differences between the intercept coefficients. If the slope coefficients were zero, the intercept coefficients typically imply that annualized returns in the surviving regime would be 40–70% higher than in the collapsing regime.

The point estimates of the slope coefficients (β_{Sb} and β_{Cb}) are also quite different. The bubbles model implies that the coefficient in the collapsing regime should be negative and smaller than the coefficient in the surviving regime. The point estimate of the coefficient in the collapsing regime is always negative and typically about four to five times smaller than the coefficient in the surviving regime.

The second difference between the fads and bubbles models arises because the bubbles model in section II suggests that a large bubble is more likely to collapse. In our formulation, this implies that the coefficient β_{qb} should be positive. Over the period 1928–89, this is what we find; moreover, the data strongly reject the hypothesis that $\beta_{qb} = 0$ for two of our three measures of fundamental price.

Although the rejections of the fads model point in the direction of the bubbles model, the evidence is not definitive. First, the statistical significance of the differences in the intercept and slope coefficients between regimes is weak. Over the period 1928–89, the marginal significance level of the test for equal intercept coefficients is generally around .10. In the test for equal slope coefficients, the marginal significance level is higher.

Second, intuition (and the derivations in section II) suggest that expected returns should be an increasing function of the size of the bubble in the states where the bubble survives. In our data, the relevant coefficient (β_{Sb}) has the opposite sign.

Taken together, our results suggest that there is more in the data than fads. The specific ways in which the data conflict with the fads model are frequently consistent with the bubbles model, but the evidence in favour of the bubbles model is not decisive.

We see a number of directions for further research. First, this paper examines stock market returns for the U.S. Thus, the usual caveat applies: our findings on fads and bubbles do not necessarily characterize stock market returns in other countries. It would be interesting to see if the patterns we find in U.S. data carry over to other countries. Second, our focus is on aggregate data. Future research might usefully examine returns for individual firms. Third, this paper studies stock market returns. It has been argued that fads and bubbles might affect other assets. Fourth, apparent anomalies in asset markets may arise because of strong assumptions about the constraints faced by agents. For example, Brock and LeBaron (1990) show that in a production economy asset pricing model, the introduction of finance constraints on firms can accentuate mean reversion.[21]

References

Allen F, Gorton G (1993) Churning bubbles. Review of Economic Studies 60:813–836

Blanchard OJ (1979) Speculative bubbles, crashes and rational expectations. Economics Letters 3:387–389

Blanchard OJ, Fischer S (1989) Lectures on macroeconomics. (Cambridge: MIT Press), 1st edition

Blanchard OJ, Rhee C, Summers LH (1993) The stock market, profit and investment. Quarterly Journal of Economics, CVIII, 115–134

[21] There is some empirical evidence to support this idea; see Jog and Schaller (1994). Woodford (1989) shows that imperfect financial intermediation can lead to non-linear (or even chaotic) dynamics. Gomes, Yaron, and Zhang (2001), in contrast, find that finance constraints are unsuccessful in improving the overall statistical ability of investment returns as a pricing factor.

Blanchard O, Watson M (1982) Bubbles, rational expectations and financial markets. In: Wachtel P (ed) Crises in the Economic and Financial Structure. Lexington Books, Lexington MA

Bollerslev T, Hodrick RJ (1995) Financial market efficiency tests. The Handbook of Applied Econometrics, I, Macroeconomics, Pesaran MH, Wickins MR (ed) 415–458

Brock WA, LeBaron B (1990) Liquidity constraints in production-based asset-pricing models. In: Glenn Hubbard R (ed) Asymmetric Information, Corporate Finance, and Investment, Chicago: University of Chicago Press 231–56

Campbell JY, Shiller RJ (1987) Cointegration and tests of present value models. Journal of Political Economy 95:1062–1088

Campbell JY, Shiller RJ (1988) Stock prices, earnings, and expected dividends. Journal of Finance 43:661–676

Campbell JY, Shiller RJ (1988) The dividend-price ratio and expectations of future dividends and discount factors. Review of Financial Studies 1:195–228

Cecchetti SG, Lam P-S, Mark NC (1990) Mean reversion in equilibrium asset prices. American Economic Review 80, 3:398–418

Chirinko RS, Schaller H (1996) Bubbles, fundamentals, and investment: A multiple equation specification testing strategy. Journal of Monetary Economics 38:47–76

Cutler DM, Poterba JM, Summers LH (1991) Speculative dynamics. Review of Economic Studies 58:529–546

De Long JB, Shleifer A, Summers LH, Waldmann RJ (1989) The size and incidence of the losses from noise trading. Journal of Finance July, 681–696

De Long JB, Shleifer A, Summers LH, Waldmann RJ (1990) Noise trader risk in financial markets. Journal of Political Economy 98:703–738

Diba BT, Grossman HI (1988a) Explosive rational bubbles in stock prices?. American Economic Review 78:520–528

Diba BT, Grossman HI (1988b) Rational inflationary bubbles. Journal of Monetary Economics 21:35–46

Driffill J, Sola M (1998) Intrinsic bubbles and regime switching. Journal of Monetary Economics 42:357–373

Engel C, Hamilton JD (1990) Long swings in the exchange rate: Are they in the data and do markets know it?. American Economic Review 80:689–713

Evans GW (1991) Pitfalls in testing for explosive bubbles in asset prices. American Economic Review 81:922–930

Fama EF (1991) Efficient capital markets: II. Journal of Finance 46:1575–1618

Fama EF, French KR (1988a) Dividend yields and expected stock returns. Journal of Financial Economics 22, 1:3–25

Fama EF, French KR (1988b) Permanent and temporary components of stock prices. Journal of Political Economy 96, 2:246–274

Froot KA, Obstfeld M (1991) Intrinsic bubbles: The case of stock prices. American Economic Review 81:1189–1214

Funke M, Hall S, Sola M (1994) Rational bubbles during Poland's hyperinflation: Implications and empirical evidence. European Economic Review 38:1257–76

Galeotti M, Schiantarelli F (1994) Stock market volatility and investment: Do only fundamentals matter?. Economica 61:147–165

Garcia R (1998) Asymptotic null distribution of the likelihood ratio test in Markov switching models. International Economic Review 39:763–788

Goldfeld SM, Quandt RE (1976) Studies in nonlinear estimation. Ballinger, Cambridge, U.S.A.

Gomes JF, Yaron A, Zhang L (2001) Asset pricing implications of firms' financing constraints. Mimeo, Finance Department, Wharton School, University of Pennsylvania

Gordon MJ (1962) The investment, financing and valuation of the corporation. Irwin, Homewood, III

Hall SG, Psarakakis Z, Sola M (1999) Detecting periodically collapsing bubbles: A Markov-switching unit root test. Journal of Applied Econometrics 14(2):143–54

Hamilton JD (1989) A new approach to the economic analysis of nonstationary time series and the business cycle. Econometrica 57(2):357–384

Hansen B (1996) Inference when a nuisance parameter is not identified under the null hypothesis. Econometrica 64(2):413–30

Hartley MJ (1978) Comment on 'estimating mixtures of normal distributions and switching regressions' by Quandt and Ramsey. Journal of the American Statistical Association 738–741

Jeanne O, Masson P (2000) Currency crises, sunspots and Markov-switching regimes. Journal of International Economics 50:327–350

Jog V, Schaller H (1994) Finance constraints and asset pricing: Evidence on mean reversion. Journal of Empirical Finance 1:193–209

Kiefer NM (1978) Discrete parameter variation: Efficient estimation of switching regression model. Econometrica 46:427–434

Kim C-J, Kim M-J (1996) Transient fads and the crash of '87. Journal of Applied Econometrics 11:41–58

Kim MJ, Nelson CR, Startz R (1991) Mean reversion in stock prices? A reappraisal of the empirical evidence. Review of Economic Studies May, 515–525

Kindleberger CP (1989) Manias, panics and crashes: A history of financial crises. (New York: Basic Books, Inc.), Revised Edition

Leach J (1991) Rational speculation. Journal of Political Economy 99:131–144

Lee L-F, Chesher A (1986) Specification testing when score test statistics are identically zero. Journal of Econometrics 31:121–149

Lee L-F, Porter RH (1984) Switching regression models with imperfect sample separation information – with an application on cartel stability. Econometrica 52:391–418

Lucas RE Jr. (1978) Asset prices in an exchange economy. Econometrica 66:429–45

Mehta JS, Swamy PAVB (1975) Bayesian and non-bayesian analysis of switching regression model and of random coefficient regression models. Journal of the American Statistical Association September, 593–602

McQueen G (1992) Long-horizon mean-reverting stock prices revisited. Journal of Financial and Quantitative Analysis 27(1):1–18

Morck R, Shleifer A, Vishny RW (1990) The stock market and investment: Is the market a sideshow?. Brookings Papers on Economic Activity 2:157–215

Nelson CR, Kim MJ (1993) Predictable stock returns: The role of small sample bias. The Journal of Finance 48(2):641–61

Obstfeld M, Rogoff K (1983) Speculative hyperinflations in maximizing models: Can we rule them out?. Journal of Political Economy 91:675–687

Obstfeld M, Rogoff K (1986) Ruling out divergent speculative bubbles. Journal of Monetary Economics 17:349–362

Poterba JM, Summers LH (1988) Mean reversion in stock prices: Evidence and implications. Journal of Financial Economics 22, 1:27–59

Quandt RE, Ramsey JB (1978) Estimating mixtures of normal distributions and switching regressions. Journal of the American Statistical Association 73:730–713

Richardson M, Stock JH (1989) Drawing inferences from statistics based on multi-year asset returns. Journal of Financial Economics 25:323–348

Schaller H, van Norden S (1997a) Regime switching in stock market returns. Applied Financial Economics 7:177–191

Schaller H, van Norden S (1997b) Fads or bubbles?. Bank of Canada working paper 97-2

Schaller H, van Norden S (1999) Speculative behaviour, regime-switching, and stock market crashes. In: Philip Rothman (ed) Nonlinear Time Series Analysis of Economic and Financial Data. Kluwer, 321–356

Scharfstein DS, Stein JC (1990) Herd behaviour and investment. American Economic Review 80:465–479

Schwert GW (1989) Business cycles, financial crises, and stock volatility. Carnegie-Rochester Conference Series on Public Policy 31:83–126

Schwert GW (1989) Why does stock market volatility change over time?. Journal of Finance XLIV(5):1115–1153

Solow RM (1957) Technical change and the aggregate production function. Review of Economics and Statistics 39:312–320

Summers LH (1986) Does the stock market rationally reflect fundamental values?. Journal of Finance XLI(3):591–603

Tirole J (1982) On the possibility of speculation under rational expectations. Econometrica 50:1163–1181

Tirole J (1985) Asset bubbles and overlapping generations. Econometrica 53:1071–1100

van Norden S (1996) Regime switching as a test for exchange rate bubbles. Journal of Applied Econometrics 11:219–251 van Norden S, Schaller H (1993) The predictability of stock market regime: Evidence from the toronto stock exchange. Review of Economics and Statistics 75, 3:505–510

van Norden S, Vigfusson R (1998) Avoiding the pitfalls: Can regime-switching tests reliably detect bubbles. Studies in Non-Linear Dynamics and Econometrics 3, 1:1–22

White H (1980) A heteroscedasticity-consistent covariance matrix estimator and a direct test for heteroscedasticity. Econometrica 48:817–838

Woodford M (1989) Imperfect financial intermediation and complex dynamics. In: WA Barnett, Geweke J, Shell K (ed) Economic Complexity: Chaos, Sunspots, Bubbles, and Nonlinearity. Cambridge University Press, Cambridge MA

Improving GARCH volatility forecasts with regime-switching GARCH

Franc Klaassen*

Department of Economics, University of Amsterdam, Roetersstraat 11, 1018 WB Amsterdam, the Netherlands (e-mail: klaassen@fee.uva.nl)

First Version Received: November 2000/Final Version Received: August 2001

Abstract. Many researchers use GARCH models to generate volatility forecasts. Using data on three major U.S. dollar exchange rates we show that such forecasts are too high in volatile periods. We argue that this is due to the high persistence of shocks in GARCH forecasts. To obtain more flexibility regarding volatility persistence, this paper generalizes the GARCH model by distinguishing two regimes with different volatility levels; GARCH effects are allowed within each regime. The resulting Markov regime-switching GARCH model improves on existing variants, for instance by making multi-period-ahead volatility forecasting a convenient recursive procedure. The empirical analysis demonstrates that the model resolves the problem with the high single-regime GARCH forecasts and that it yields significantly better out-of-sample volatility forecasts.

Key words: GARCH, Markov-switching, variance, forecasting, exchange rates

JEL classification: C52, C53, F31

1. Introduction

Volatility of financial returns is an important aspect of many financial decisions. For example, volatility of exchange rates is a determinant for pricing currency options used for risk management. Hence, there is a need for good volatility forecasts.

Such forecasts are often based on the fact that volatility is time-varying in high-frequency data and that periods of high volatility tend to cluster. To

---

* I thank Harry Huizinga, Frank de Jong, Michael McAleer, Bertrand Melenberg, Theo Nijman, Arthur van Soest, Kenneth West, the editors of this issue, James Hamilton and Baldev Raj, and two referees for very useful and constructive comments.

capture this, many authors use autoregressive conditional heteroskedasticity (ARCH) models, as introduced by Engle (1982) and extended to generalized ARCH (GARCH) in Bollerslev (1986); see Bollerslev, Chou and Kroner (1992) for an overview of the GARCH literature. Such models usually improve the fit a lot compared with a constant variance model and, as Andersen and Bollerslev (1998) claim, GARCH models provide good volatility forecasts.

This paper shows that GARCH forecasts are, nevertheless, too high in volatile periods, using almost twenty years of daily data on U.S. dollar exchange rates versus the British pound, German mark and Japanese yen. This suggests that better volatility forecasts can be obtained by solving that problem. The goal of this paper is to adapt the GARCH model in order to obtain such better forecasts.

The reason for the excessive GARCH forecasts in volatile periods may be the well-known high persistence of individual shocks in those forecasts. Lamoureux and Lastrapes (1990), among others, show that this persistence may originate from structural changes in the variance process. For example, if the variance is high but constant for some time and low but constant otherwise, persistence of such high- and low-volatility homoskedastic periods already results in volatility persistence (see also Timmermann (2000)). A GARCH model, which cannot capture persistence of such periods, puts all volatility persistence in the persistence of individual shocks. This idea is similar to Perron's (1989) work on the mean equation, as he finds that structural breaks in the mean make it more difficult to reject the null of a unit-root, that is, permanent persistence of shocks in the mean.

One possibility to allow for periods with different unconditional variances is, of course, by introducing deterministic shifts into the variance process, but this is rather ad hoc. A popular approach to endogenize changes in the data generating process is the Markov regime-switching model. Hamilton (1989) introduces this model to describe the U.S. business cycle, which is characterized by periodic shifts from recessions to expansions and vice versa. In our context of exchange rate volatility, a Markov process can be used to govern the switches between regimes with different variances. See Kaufmann and Scheicher (1996) for a survey on Markov-switching models.

To solve the problem of the excessive GARCH forecasts in volatile periods, we therefore generalize the GARCH model by allowing for regimes with different volatility levels. We use two regimes and do not consider models with more regimes, because we want to explore whether the introduction of regimes helps solve the problem with the GARCH forecasts and it turns out that two regimes are sufficient for that. Within each regime we use GARCH models to govern the variance. Hence, it is a regime-switching GARCH model. The persistence of both regimes yields an extra source of volatility persistence compared to standard, single-regime GARCH, thereby enhancing the flexibility in describing the volatility persistence of shocks.

The regime-switching GARCH model we develop differs from existing variants. First, it allows for GARCH dynamics, thereby generalizing the regime-switching ARCH models of Cai (1994) and Hamilton and Susmel (1994), and also used by Fong (1998). Because for our data the conditional heteroskedasticity within regimes cannot always be captured by a moderate number of ARCH terms, we need a GARCH term for parsimony. In addition, the data reveal that the variance dynamics differ across regimes. Our model allows for that, which is not the case for their models.

A second difference between our model and existing variants concerns Gray's (1996a) regime-switching GARCH specification, also used in Ang and Bekaert (1998). For that variant we are unable to compute the multi-period-ahead volatility forecasts needed for the detailed forecasting analysis we want to do in the current paper. In contrast, for our version such forecasts can be obtained through a convenient first-order recursive procedure. The idea behind this difference is that, when integrating out the unobserved regimes, we use all available information, whereas Gray uses only part of it; this also explains the better fit for our model. The development of our convenient regime-switching GARCH model is the main contribution of the paper from a theoretical point of view.

The main empirical results are that regime-switching GARCH resolves the problem that standard GARCH forecasts are significantly too high in volatile periods and that regime-switching GARCH forecasts significantly outperform GARCH forecasts in terms of mean squared error. These results hold out-of-sample and for both forecast horizons we examine, namely the one-day and ten-day horizons. This provides evidence for the conjecture raised by West and Cho (1995) that it will be productive to explore models that explicitly account for movement in the variance generating process, for instance, by regime switches.

The next section introduces the regime-switching GARCH model and discusses its properties. Section 3 describes the data used in the empirical application and presents the empirical results. It also contains the out-of-sample forecasting exercise that yields the most important empirical results of the paper. Section 4 concludes.

2. Regime-switching GARCH

In this section we introduce the regime-switching GARCH model, with which we try to improve on the standard, one-regime GARCH volatility forecasts. We describe the model, discuss its properties and relate the model to existing regime-switching ARCH and GARCH models.

2.1. The model

We use the following notation. Let S_t denote the logarithm of a spot exchange rate at time t, that is, the domestic currency price of one unit of foreign currency. We concentrate on the exchange rate change $s_t = 100(S_t - S_{t-1})$, so that s_t is the percentage depreciation of the domestic currency from time $t-1$ to t.

The regime-switching GARCH model consists of four elements, namely the mean, regime process, variance and distribution. Two of them, the regime process and variance are crucial for interpreting the empirical results, as they are directly related to the difference between our model and standard, one-regime GARCH models.

The mean of exchange rate processes is often modeled by a random walk (with drift). For instance, Meese and Rogoff (1983) and MacDonald and Taylor (1992) stress the empirical quality of the random walk over structural models of exchange rate determination, particularly in the short run.

We follow this simple but reasonable approach, also because the focus of our paper is on the volatility rather than the mean:

$$s_t = \mu + \varepsilon_t. \tag{1}$$

The innovation ε_t has zero mean conditional on the information set of the data generating process to be defined below. Thus, μ is the constant conditional mean of s_t. (It is possible to incorporate, for example, autoregressive terms in the conditional mean without making the formulas that follow essentially different.)

As argued in the introduction, the purpose of the regimes with different volatility levels is to explain part of the volatility persistence. This requires that regimes can be persistent. To model this, let $r_t \in \{1, 2\}$ be the (unobserved) variance regime at time t, where the first regime is identified as the low-variance one. Let $p_{t-1}(r_t|\tilde{r}_{t-1}) = p(r_t \mid I_{t-1}, \tilde{r}_{t-1})$ denote the probability of going to regime r_t at time t conditional on the information set of the data generating process, which consists of two parts. The first part, I_{t-1}, denotes the information observed by the econometrician, that is $(s_{t-1}, s_{t-2}, \ldots)$. The second part, $\tilde{r}_{t-1}$, is the regime path $(r_{t-1}, r_{t-2}, \ldots)$, which is not observed by the econometrician. Note that the subscript $t-1$ below an operator (probability, expectation or variance) is short-hand notation for conditioning on I_{t-1}.

As in Hamilton (1989), we assume that r_t follows a first-order Markov process with constant staying probabilities

$$p_{t-1}(r_t|\tilde{r}_{t-1}) = p(r_t|r_{t-1}) = \begin{cases} p_{11} & \text{if } r_t = r_{t-1} = 1 \\ p_{22} & \text{if } r_t = r_{t-1} = 2. \end{cases} \tag{2}$$

If p_{11} and p_{22} are high, this specification results in the regime persistence required above.

The specification of the conditional variance, the third element of the model, represents the main difference between this paper and earlier ones on regime-switching ARCH and GARCH. Using the law of iterated expectations and (1), the conditional variance $V_{t-1}\{s_t\}$ equals $E_{t-1}[V_{t-1}\{\varepsilon_t|\tilde{r}_t\}]$, so that we concentrate on $V_{t-1}\{\varepsilon_t|\tilde{r}_t\}$. Four specifications of the latter variance will be discussed, where the final one turns out to be the most convenient. For the sake of exposition, we confine ourselves to models with only one ARCH and one GARCH term; including more ARCH and GARCH terms is straightforward.

The first specification of the conditional variance is a direct application of the GARCH(1,1) model in a regime-switching context:

$$V_{t-1}\{\varepsilon_t|\tilde{r}_t\} = \omega_{r_t} + \alpha_{r_t}\varepsilon_{t-1}^2 + \beta_{r_t} V_{t-2}\{\varepsilon_{t-1}|\tilde{r}_{t-1}\}, \tag{3}$$

where $V_{t-1}\{\varepsilon_t|\tilde{r}_t\}$ denotes the variance of ε_t conditional on observable information I_{t-1} and on the regime path $\tilde{r}_t$. The current regime only determines the parameters, that is, the intercept ω_{r_t}, the ARCH parameter α_{r_t} and the GARCH parameter β_{r_t}.

This specification, however, appears practically infeasible when estimating the model. This is due to the fact that $V_{t-1}\{\varepsilon_t|\tilde{r}_t\}$ in (3) depends on the entire regime path $\tilde{r}_t$, because it depends on r_t and $V_{t-2}\{\varepsilon_{t-1}|\tilde{r}_{t-1}\}$, which depends on r_{t-1} and $V_{t-3}\{\varepsilon_{t-2}|\tilde{r}_{t-2}\}$, which depends on r_{t-2} and $V_{t-4}\{\varepsilon_{t-3}|\tilde{r}_{t-3}\}$, and so on.

Since the number of possible regime paths grows exponentially with t, this leads to an enormous number of paths to t. The econometrician, who does not observe regimes, has to integrate out all possible paths when computing the sample likelihood. This renders estimation intractable. The remaining specifications of the conditional variance are ways to avoid this problem of path dependence.

The second specification is based on Cai (1994) and Hamilton and Susmel (1994). They essentially remove the GARCH term, which is the cause of the path dependence, and thus use only an ARCH term in (3). Since $V_{t-1}\{\varepsilon_t|\tilde{r}_t\}$ then only depends on the current regime r_t, there is no problem of path dependence. (More precisely, Cai (1994) and Hamilton and Susmel (1994) use slightly different models in which $V_{t-1}\{\varepsilon_t|\tilde{r}_t\}$ not only depends on the current but also on a few recent regimes. The essential point is that the conditional variance depends only on a small number of regimes, which can be integrated out in the likelihood quite easily.)

The third specification of the conditional variance comes from Gray (1996a). He argues that the problem of path dependence can be solved without giving up the potentially important persistence effects of a GARCH term, as has been done in the second specification. The basic idea of Gray is to integrate out the unobserved regime path $\tilde{r}_{t-1}$ directly in the source of the path dependence, $V_{t-2}\{\varepsilon_{t-1}|\tilde{r}_{t-1}\}$ in (3), instead of only in the likelihood. This makes $V_{t-1}\{\varepsilon_t|\tilde{r}_t\}$ only depend on the current regime r_t, not on the path $\tilde{r}_{t-1}$, as is clear from the explanation of the path dependency problem below (3). As Gray shows, this is very convenient from an estimation point of view, because the likelihood can then be computed in a first-order recursive way, which speeds up the estimation process considerably. Since Gray uses the information observable at time $t-2$ when integrating out, he actually assumes that

$$V_{t-1}\{\varepsilon_t|\tilde{r}_t\} = \omega_{r_t} + \alpha_{r_t}\varepsilon_{t-1}^2 + \beta_{r_t}E_{t-2}[V_{t-2}\{\varepsilon_{t-1}|\tilde{r}_{t-1}\}], \tag{4}$$

where the expectation on the right-hand-side is across the regime path $\tilde{r}_{t-1}$, conditional on information I_{t-2}. Note that this is equivalent to integrating out only the single regime r_{t-1}, as the lag of (4) implies that $V_{t-2}\{\varepsilon_{t-1}|\tilde{r}_{t-1}\}$ is independent of $\tilde{r}_{t-2}$.

The main benefit of specification (4) is that there is no path dependence problem any more, although GARCH effects are still allowed. There is, however, one important inconvenience, especially regarding our focus of volatility forecasting: generating multi-period-ahead variance forecasts such as $V_{t-1}\{s_{t+1}\}$ turns out to be very complicated. This motivates our search for another specification that makes multi-period-ahead forecasting more convenient while preserving the attractive features of Gray's model.

Our specification of $V_{t-1}\{\varepsilon_t|\tilde{r}_t\}$ differs from Gray's (1996a) model in two ways. First, as the expectation in (4) shows, Gray integrates out the regime r_{t-1} at time $t-2$. We postpone this till $t-1$, the time at which the conditional variance $V_{t-1}\{\varepsilon_t|\tilde{r}_t\}$ is really needed. This allows us to use more observable information when integrating out the previous regime. This extra data embodies information about previous regimes and is thus useful.

The second difference is that, when integrating out the regime r_{t-1}, Gray does not use the information that the regime at time t is in the conditioning information of $V_{t-1}\{\varepsilon_t|\tilde{r}_t\}$. Particularly if regimes are highly persistent, r_t gives much information about r_{t-1}. In contrast to Gray, we do use this information.

In formula, our regime-switching GARCH(1,1) model is described by

$$V_{t-1}\{\varepsilon_t|\tilde{r}_t\} = \omega_{r_t} + \alpha_{r_t}\varepsilon_{t-1}^2 + \beta_{r_t}E_{t-1}[V_{t-2}\{\varepsilon_{t-1}|\tilde{r}_{t-1}\} \mid r_t], \tag{5}$$

where the expectation on the right-hand-side is across the regime path $\tilde{r}_{t-1}$, conditional on information I_{t-1} and r_t. Note that this is equivalent to integrating out only the single regime r_{t-1}, as the lag of (5) implies that $V_{t-2}\{\varepsilon_{t-1}|\tilde{r}_{t-1}\}$ is independent of $\tilde{r}_{t-2}$. By construction, $V_{t-1}\{\varepsilon_t|\tilde{r}_t\}$ only depends on the current variance regime r_t, so that $V_{t-1}\{\varepsilon_t|\tilde{r}_t\} = V_{t-1}\{\varepsilon_t|r_t\}$. Hence, there is no problem of path dependence. To complete the specification of the conditional variance, we impose $\omega_{r_t} > 0$ and $\alpha_{r_t}, \beta_{r_t} \geq 0$ to ensure positivity of $V_{t-1}\{\varepsilon_t|\tilde{r}_t\}$ for all t, just as for single-regime GARCH.

The final element of the regime-switching GARCH model is the conditional distribution. We assume that, conditional on I_{t-1} and $\tilde{r}_t$, the innovation ε_t has a t-distribution with ν degrees of freedom, where ν is assumed to be independent of the conditioning information, and with mean zero and variance $V_{t-1}\{\varepsilon_t|r_t\}$:

$$\varepsilon_t \mid I_{t-1}, \tilde{r}_t \sim t(\nu, 0, V_{t-1}\{\varepsilon_t|r_t\}). \tag{6}$$

The use of a t-distribution instead of a normal one is quite popular in the standard, single-regime GARCH literature (see Bollerslev, Chou and Kroner (1992)). For regime-switching models, a t-distribution can be extra useful. After all, in case of normality, a large innovation in the low-volatility period will lead to a switch to the high-volatility regime earlier, even if it is a single outlier in an otherwise tranquil period. Allowing for a t-distribution will thus enhance the stability of the regimes. Note that the t-distribution includes the normal distribution as the limiting case where the degrees of freedom go to infinity.

In summary, equations (1), (2), (5) and (6) describe our regime-switching GARCH model. It contains the standard, one-regime GARCH(1,1) model as a special case, since that model results when all regime-specific parameters are equal across regimes.

2.2. Properties of the model

The model just described has several interesting properties. We first show the increased flexibility regarding the volatility persistence of shocks. After that we present the convenient procedure for multi-period-ahead volatility forecasting, which we need to examine the forecast quality of regime-switching GARCH compared with single-regime GARCH, the focus of the paper. Then the unconditional variance, the estimation procedure, and inference about the unobserved regime are discussed.

2.2.1. Flexibility regarding volatility persistence

As motivated in the introduction, the reason to generalize the single-regime GARCH model by introducing regimes is to enhance the flexibility of the model to capture the persistence of shocks in volatility. One example is that in regime-switching GARCH a shock can be followed by a volatile period not only because of GARCH effects, but also because of a switch to the high-volatility regime.

The flexibility with respect to volatility persistence is further improved by the allowance for different ARCH and GARCH parameters across regimes. For instance, if shocks are more persistent in periods of high than in periods of low volatility, this can be captured by the regime specific parameters in (5). This has consequences for capturing the "pressure relieving" effect of some large shocks, that is, some shocks are not persistent at all but are followed by a tranquil period. Any regime-switching model can capture this to some extent by a shift from the high-volatility to the low-volatility regime. However, our regime-switching model with different parameters across regimes has a second source of neglecting large recent shocks. After all, if the low-variance regime is also the low-persistence regime, the large shock will be out of the market very soon after the switch to the low-variance regime. In this respect, our model generalizes the models in Hamilton and Susmel (1994) and Cai (1994), as their regime variances only differ by a multiplicative or additive constant, respectively, not by differences in the ARCH parameters.

2.2.2. *Recursive volatility forecasting*

Suppose we need the variance of the exchange rate change over a horizon h, conditional on information available at time $t-1$. Let $s_{t,h}$ denote the h-period change, that is, $s_{t,1} = s_t$ and $s_{t,h} = s_t + \cdots + s_{t-1+h}$ for $h > 1$. The variance of interest is thus $V_{t-1}\{s_{t,h}\}$. Because of the absence of serial correlation in the one-period changes (see below (1)),

$$V_{t-1}\{s_{t,h}\} = \sum_{\tau=t}^{t-1+h} V_{t-1}\{s_\tau\}. \tag{7}$$

Each variance on the right-hand-side is equal to

$$V_{t-1}\{s_\tau\} = \sum_{r_\tau=1,2} p_{t-1}(r_\tau) \cdot V_{t-1}\{\varepsilon_\tau | r_\tau\}, \tag{8}$$

where $p_{t-1}(r_\tau)$ is the probability that the regime at time τ is r_τ conditional on I_{t-1}. Note that we use the same symbol p_{t-1} for several probabilities (for instance, see (2) and (8)). The specific meaning of p_{t-1} is uniquely determined by the symbols in its argument. This results in a concise notation.

An important implication of our way of modeling the conditional variance in (5) is that $V_{t-1}\{\varepsilon_\tau | r_\tau\}$ in (8) can be computed in a first-order recursive manner using a formula analogous to the one Engle and Bollerslev (1986) have derived for the standard, one-regime GARCH model. Starting from $V_{t-1}\{\varepsilon_t | r_t\}$, appendix A shows that one can compute $V_{t-1}\{\varepsilon_\tau | r_\tau\}$ for $\tau > t$ by iterating forward on

$$V_{t-1}\{\varepsilon_{t+i} | r_{t+i}\} = \omega_{r_{t+i}} + (\alpha_{r_{t+i}} + \beta_{r_{t+i}}) \cdot E_{t-1}[V_{t-1}\{\varepsilon_{t+i-1} | r_{t+i-1}\} \mid r_{t+i}] \tag{9}$$

for $i = 1, \ldots, \tau - t$. This simplifies the computation of $V_{t-1}\{s_{t,h}\}$ in (7) substantially and represents one of the main advantages of our regime-switching GARCH model over Gray's (1996a) model.

2.2.3. Unconditional variance

In Appendix B we derive the following results for the "unconditional" error variance $V\{\varepsilon_t|r_t\}$. First, if $V\{\varepsilon_t|r_t = i\}$ exists for both $i = 1,2$ and both ω_1, ω_2 and is independent of t, denoted by σ_i^2, then

$$\begin{bmatrix} \sigma_1^2 \\ \sigma_2^2 \end{bmatrix} = (I_2 - A)^{-1} \cdot \begin{bmatrix} \omega_1 \\ \omega_2 \end{bmatrix}, \tag{10}$$

where I_2 is the identity matrix of order two and the (i,j)-th element of A is $A_{ij} = P\{r_{t-1} = j \,|\, r_t = i\}(\alpha_i + \beta_i)$ (appendix B gives expressions for the probabilities in A_{ij}).

Second, necessary conditions for the existence of both variances are A_{11}, $A_{22} < 1$ and $\det(I_2 - A) > 0$. So, given the definition of A_{ii}, a probability times the sum of the regime-specific ARCH and GARCH coefficients must be less than one for both regimes. Moreover, there is some restriction on a combination of the ARCH and GARCH coefficients across regimes.

To get a better understanding of these results, let us look at standard GARCH(1,1). There the unconditional variance is $\sigma^2 = (1 - \alpha - \beta)^{-1}\omega$ and the necessary (and sufficient) condition for its existence is $\alpha + \beta < 1$. Hence, we again see a correspondence between single-regime GARCH and regime-switching GARCH.

2.2.4. Recursive estimation

The regime-switching GARCH model can be estimated by maximum likelihood (ML). The likelihood function is derived in appendix C, using similar techniques as Gray (1996a). As for Gray's model, this likelihood has a first-order recursive structure, similar to that of single-regime GARCH. This speeds up the estimation process.

2.2.5. Recursive regime inference

Although regimes are not observed, one can estimate the probability that the process is in a particular regime at a specific time. This is, for instance, useful if one wants to classify a series into periods of low and high volatility.

Following Gray (1996a), we use two types of regime probabilities, namely ex ante and smoothed probabilities. The ex ante probability of regime r_t at time t, $p_{t-1}(r_t)$, is the conditional probability that the process is in that regime at time t using only information available to the econometrician at time $t-1$, that is, I_{t-1}. The smoothed regime probability $p_T(r_t)$, on the other hand, uses the complete data set I_T, thereby smoothing the ex ante probabilities. Hence, it gives the most informative answer to the question which regime the process was likely in at time t. The ex ante probabilities are computed during estimation (see appendix C). The smoothed probabilities can be calculated in a recursive manner starting from the ex ante probabilities, as appendix D shows using an algorithm based on Gray (1996b).

3. Empirical results

So far, we have generalized single-regime GARCH to regime-switching GARCH to obtain more flexibility regarding the volatility persistence of shocks. In this section we estimate both models and examine whether that generalization pays off empirically in terms of improved volatility forecasts, the central issue of the paper.

3.1. Data

We consider three major U.S. dollar exchange rates, namely, the dollar price of the British pound, the German mark and the Japanese yen. We have 4,982 daily observations for the exchange rate change s_t from January 3, 1978 to July 23, 1997. All rates have been obtained from Datastream.

Panel A of figures 1, 2 and 3 gives an indication of the volatility clustering of the three exchange rates under consideration over the sample period. As usual, all three plots show substantial volatility clustering. This is confirmed by (not reported) Box-Pierce tests for serial correlation in the squared exchange rate changes, as these are significant at any reasonable significance level.

The plots also demonstrate that shocks sometimes have a long effect on subsequent volatility, but that shocks can also be followed by a period of low volatility. For instance, in figure 1A the large peak in the squared change plot for the British pound on March 27, 1985 was followed by about half a year of substantial volatility. On the other hand, the G-5 Plaza announcement on September 22, 1985 to bring about a dollar depreciation had a sharp effect on the dollar the next day, as the second largest peak in the figure makes clear, but was followed by a period of low instead of high volatility. Therefore, at first sight the extra flexibility regarding volatility persistence that is present in regime-switching GARCH seems worthwhile.

3.2. Estimation results

This subsection presents the estimation results for the regime-switching GARCH model. Let GARCH($P_1, Q_1; P_2, Q_2$) denote a regime-switching model with Q_1 (Q_2) ARCH and P_1 (P_2) GARCH terms in the first (second) regime. These are obvious variants of the GARCH(1,1;1,1) model developed in subsection 2.1. The models for the pound contain an AR(1) term in mean equation (1) to correct for the small first-order autocorrelation found in the data.

For comparison, we also estimate five other models. Two of them are single-regime models, namely the constant variance model and the popular GARCH(1,1) model. Two other models belong to the regime-switching ARCH class. The ARCH(0;0) model has zero ARCH terms, so constant variance, in both regimes, as in Dewachter (1997) and Scheicher (1999); this model is used to analyze the effect of introducing only regimes. The other ARCH-type model, ARCH(Q_1;4) with Q_1 determined below, is in the spirit of Cai (1994) and Hamilton and Susmel (1994). It is, however, somewhat more general in the sense that the regime-specific ARCH models are allowed to

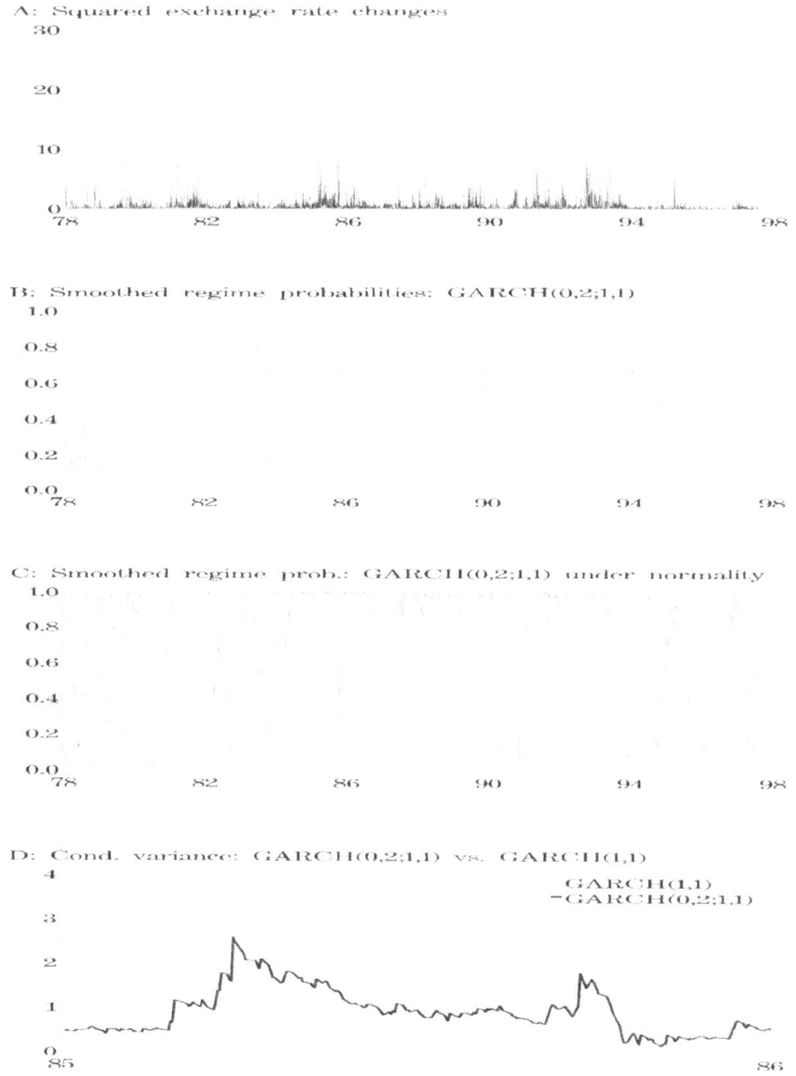

Fig. 1. British pound

vary across regimes in an unrestricted way, whereas in Cai (1994) and Hamilton and Susmel (1994) the difference between the low- and high-variance regime ARCH models is just an additive or multiplicative constant, respectively. The final model for comparison is Gray's (1996a) variant of regime-switching GARCH.

Table 1 presents the maximum likelihood estimation results. The inverse of

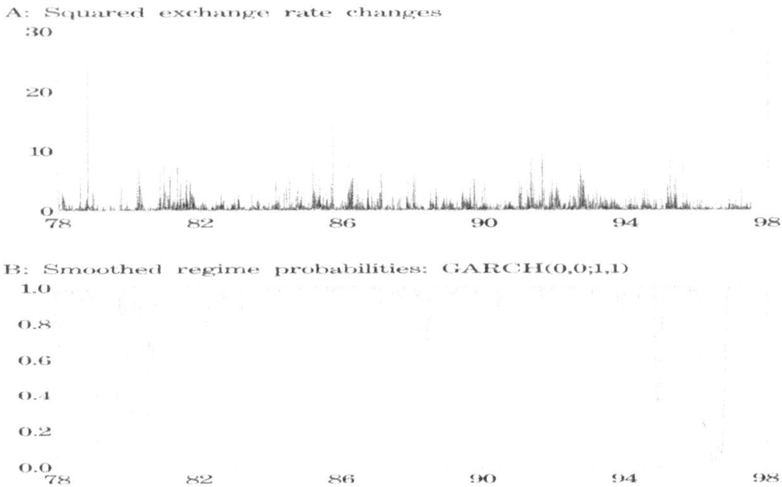

Fig. 2. German mark

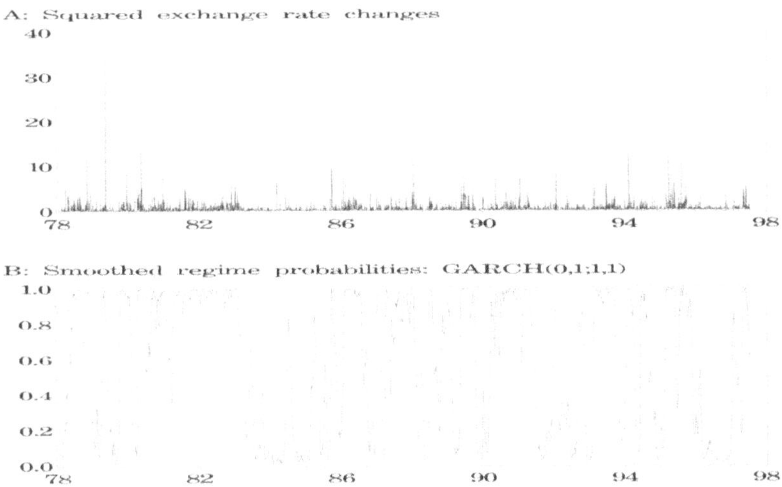

Fig. 3. Japanese yen

the degrees of freedom ν of the t-distribution (see (6)) is presented; testing for conditional normality then boils down to testing whether ν^{-1} differs significantly from zero. Moreover, for easier comparison of the models, we report the regime-specific unconditional variances σ_r^2 $(r = 1, 2)$ instead of the intercepts ω_r in the conditional variance formula (5); see (10) for the computation of σ_r^2. Finally, the last column of table 1 reports the log-likelihood using GARCH(1,1) as a reference, so that the values for the other models are dif-

Table 1. Estimation results

	μ	ν^{-1}	Low variance regime 1 σ_1^2	α_{11}	α_{21}	p_{11}	High variance regime 2 σ_2^2	α_{12}	α_{22}	α_{32}	α_{42}	β_2	p_{22}	logLik-G(1,1)
BRITISH POUND														
Const. variance	.01	.25					.46							−244.34
	(.01)	(.02)					(.02)							
GARCH(1,1)	.01	.19					.61	.06				.93		−4437.26
	(.01)	(.01)					(.18)	(.01)				(.01)		
ARCH(0;0)	.01	.17	.18			.984	.65						.987	−46.53
	(.01)	(.02)	(.01)			(.004)	(.04)						(.004)	
ARCH(2;4)	.01	.19	.16	.11	.11	.991	.58	.07	.04	.07	.07		.996	−19.56
	(.01)	(.02)	(.01)	(.04)	(.04)	(.003)	(.03)	(.02)	(.02)	(.03)	(.02)		(.002)	
GrayG(0,2;1,1)	.01	.19	.18	.21	.18	.999	.74	.06				.93	.999	+9.24
	(.01)	(.01)	(.03)	(.06)	(.06)	(.001)	(.23)	(.01)				(.01)	(.000)	
GARCH(0,2;1,1)	.01	.18	.15	.17	.10	.989	.58	.05				.93	.997	+19.34
	(.01)	(.02)	(.02)	(.07)	(.05)	(.007)	(.09)	(.01)				(.01)	(.002)	
GERMAN MARK														
Const. variance	−.00	.25					.50							−183.92
	(.01)	(.02)					(.02)							
GARCH(1,1)	−.01	.20					.70	.08				.91		−4778.34
	(.01)	(.01)					(.20)	(.01)				(.01)		
ARCH(0;0)	−.00	.15	.23			.984	.77						.982	−24.85
	(.01)	(.02)	(.02)			(.004)	(.04)						(.005)	
ARCH(0;4)	−.00	.16	.21			.983	.70	.06	.01	.07	.05		.987	−14.97
	(.01)	(.02)	(.02)			(.004)	(.05)	(.03)	(.02)	(.03)	(.02)		(.004)	
GrayG(0,0;1,1)	−.00	.20	.11			.998	.70	.08				.89	.999	−3.29
	(.01)	(.01)	(.01)			(.001)	(.11)	(.01)				(.01)	(.000)	
GARCH(0,0;1,1)	−.01	.19	.12			.981	.57	.07				.90	.998	+8.44
	(.01)	(.02)	(.01)			(.011)	(.07)	(.01)				(.02)	(.002)	

JAPANESE YEN													
Const. variance	−.01	.28				.50							−111.62
	(.01)	(.02)				(.03)							
GARCH(1,1)	−.01	.25				.61	.09				.87		−4682.58
	(.01)	(.02)				(.11)	(.02)				(.02)		
ARCH(0;0)	−.01	.20	.21		.975	.73						.975	+9.07
	(.01)	(.02)	(.02)		(.007)	(.04)						(.007)	
ARCH(1;4)	−.01	.20	.23	.08	.981	.71	.03	.04	.05	.00		.981	+16.28
	(.01)	(.02)	(.02)	(.04)	(.006)	(.05)	(.03)	(.03)	(.03)	(.02)		(.006)	
GrayG(0,1;1,1)	−.01	.21	.23	.10	.980	.80	.04				.48	.980	+12.59
	(.01)	(.02)	(.02)	(.04)	(.006)	(.07)	(.03)				(.17)	(.005)	
GARCH(0,1;1,1)	−.01	.21	.22	.09	.978	.68	.06				.78	.984	+16.52
	(.01)	(.02)	(.02)	(.04)	(.007)	(.05)	(.02)				(.10)	(.005)	

Standard errors in parentheses. "logLik-G(1,1)" denotes the log-likelihood of a model minus that of GARCH(1,1); for GARCH(1,1) it is the log-likelihood itself. The estimated models belong to the class of models described by equations (1), (2), (5) and (6), except for GrayG(0,Q_1;1,1) (Gray's (1996a) variant of GARCH(0,Q_1;1,1)), which uses (4) instead of (5). The parameter μ denotes the conditional mean, v^{-1} is the inverted degrees of freedom of the t-distribution for the innovation, σ_r^2 denotes the unconditional variance in regime r, α_{qr} and β_r are the regime specific ARCH and GARCH parameters, respectively, and the p_{rr} are the regime-staying probabilities. The estimated first-order autoregressive coefficient used for the pound only is 0.03 (0.01) for all models.

ferences with respect to GARCH(1,1). Note that one should be careful when interpreting differences in log-likelihoods in terms of likelihood ratio tests. First, not all models are nested. Second, testing the null of a single-regime against a regime-switching model involves unidentified parameters (the regime-staying probabilities) under the null, so that the asymptotic distribution of the likelihood ratio is not the usual χ^2-distribution (see Hansen (1992)). In this paper we do not formally test for the significance of the second regime, because the focus of the paper concerns forecasting quality, so that we concentrate on the effects of regimes on that.

3.2.1. *Single-regime GARCH*

As is typically found, the standard, one-regime GARCH(1,1) model provides a much better fit than the constant variance model. For instance, the increase in log-likelihood of the GARCH model over the constant variance model is 244.34 for the British pound, so that ARCH and GARCH effects are statistically very important. GARCH(1,1) is also the preferred model within the class of GARCH(P, Q) models, as the likelihood ratios of GARCH(1,1) versus GARCH(2,1) and GARCH(1,2) are 1.12 and 0.00, respectively, for the pound, 0.92 and 0.00 for the mark, and 1.90 and 0.00 for the yen, which are all insignificant. This is in accordance with Bollerslev et al. (1992), who state that in most applications $P = Q = 1$ is sufficient.

As usual, the estimated sum of the ARCH and GARCH parameters $(\alpha + \beta)$ is large for all three series, pointing at high volatility persistence of individual shocks. This may indicate parameter instability, as argued in the introduction. We estimate regime-switching models to analyze whether the high volatility persistence is indeed spurious.

3.2.2. *Regime-switching ARCH(0;0)*

Let us first consider the regime-switching ARCH(0;0) model, in which persistence of regimes is the only source of volatility clustering. Table 1 shows that for the three rates there is a distinction between a low- and a high-volatility regime, where the unconditional variance in the latter is three to four times as large.

The variance regimes are also persistent, since the staying probabilities p_{11} and p_{22} are all above 0.975. To get a better idea about the amount of persistence that such staying probabilities imply, we compute the expected duration of the high-variance regime. Conditional on being in this regime ($r_t = 2$), this is (see Hamilton (1989))

$$\sum_{h=1}^{\infty} h \cdot P\{r_t = 2, \ldots, r_{t+h-1} = 2, r_{t+h} = 1 \mid r_{t=2}\}$$

$$= \sum_{h=1}^{\infty} h \cdot (p_{22})^{h-1}(1 - p_{22}) = (1 - p_{22})^{-1}. \quad (11)$$

Table 2. Diagnostics for residual conditional heteroskedasticity

	BRITISH POUND		GERMAN MARK		JAPANESE YEN	
	ρ_1	Q_{10}	ρ_1	Q_{10}	ρ_1	Q_{10}
Const. variance	0.11*	533.26*	0.12*	371.09*	0.09*	164.25*
	(0.01)	[0.00]	(0.01)	[0.00]	(0.01)	[0.00]
GARCH(1,1)	0.01	5.29	0.00	8.02	0.02	13.00
	(0.01)	[0.87]	(0.01)	[0.63]	(0.01)	[0.22]
ARCH(0;0)	0.03*	44.69*	0.03*	25.29*	0.03*	16.15
	(0.01)	[0.00]	(0.01)	[0.00]	(0.01)	[0.10]
ARCH(Q_1;4)	−0.01	26.15*	0.00	25.59*	0.01	8.29
	(0.01)	[0.00]	(0.01)	[0.00]	(0.01)	[0.60]
GrayG(0,Q_1;1,1)	−0.00	6.30	0.01	27.08*	0.00	16.67
	(0.01)	[0.79]	(0.01)	[0.00]	(0.01)	[0.08]
GARCH(0,Q_1;1,1)	−0.00	6.47	0.00	9.33	0.01	8.87
	(0.01)	[0.77]	(0.01)	[0.50]	(0.01)	[0.54]

Standard errors in parentheses and p-values in square brackets; * is significant at the 5% level. The first-order autocorrelation, ρ_1, and the Box-Pierce statistic of order ten, Q_{10}, are computed from the squared normalized residuals. Note that the normalization of residuals under a regime-switching model entails integrating out the unobserved regime in the variance, as in (8).
The specifications of the models are given in the notes below table 1.

For a typical ARCH(0;0) staying probability of 0.98, this implies an expected duration of 50 (working) days, which is about 2.5 months.

The log-likelihood gives a first idea of whether the regime persistence is an important source of volatility clustering. For the pound and mark the log-likelihood is lower than for GARCH(1,1), but for the yen it is higher. Hence, regimes can be an important mechanism to capture volatility clustering.

This is confirmed by table 2, which gives tests for autocorrelation in the squared normalized residuals (see the notes below the table for the computation of the normalized residuals). The first-order autocorrelations ρ_1 and the Box-Pierce tests Q_{10} show that the conditional heteroskedasticity in the normalized residuals is greatly reduced when going from the constant variance model to the regime-switching model with constant regime-specific variances. However, the conditional heteroskedasticity tests also make clear that there is still heteroskedasticity left (we use a significance level of 5% throughout the paper). Apparently, there is also volatility clustering within a regime.

3.2.3. Regime-switching ARCH(Q_1;4)

To capture the remaining conditional heteroskedasticity, we first add only ARCH terms to the model, so no GARCH terms yet. To get some insight into the magnitude of volatility clustering across the regimes, we start with a model with several ARCH terms in both regimes. For parsimony, we restrict the number of ARCH terms to four in both regimes, that is, ARCH(4;4). We find that four ARCH terms is too much for the low-variance regime: for the pound two ARCH terms suffice (likelihood ratio of ARCH(2;4) versus ARCH(4;4) is 0.74, which is insignificant because the p-value is [0.69]), for the mark zero terms suffice (1.87 [0.76]) and for the yen one term (3.79 [0.29]). In contrast, the high-volatility regime keeps its four ARCH terms, as reducing that number to the number of ARCH terms in the first regime yields likelihood ratios of 23.71 [0.00] for the pound, 19.76 [0.00] for the mark, and 7.06 [0.07] for the yen. We thus obtain ARCH(2;4) for the pound, ARCH(0;4) for the mark, and ARCH(1;4) for the yen, thereby highlighting that there is more volatility clustering in the high- than in the low-variance regime for our data.

The latter result is supported by Chaudhuri and Klaassen (2000), who find for weekly data on East Asian stock index returns that there is more conditional heteroskedasticity in the high- than in the low-volatility regime. Our evidence, however, is in contrast with the models in Cai (1994) and Hamilton and Susmel (1994). Their regime-specific ARCH models only differ by an additive or multiplicative parameter, respectively, so that, for instance, the number of ARCH terms is the same across regimes. Since we find evidence of longer volatility persistence in the high-volatility regime, we prefer our asymmetric approach for the data in this paper.

The usefulness of the regime-switching ARCH approach appears from the tests in table 2. For the yen there is no remaining conditional heteroskedasticity after estimation of ARCH(1;4). For the other two exchange rates, however, the regime-switching ARCH models are insufficient. The remaining conditional heteroskedasticity can be attributed to the high-variance regime, as the likelihood ratios given above show that higher-order ARCH estimates are insignificant for the low-volatility regime.

3.2.4. Regime-switching GARCH

The residual conditional heteroskedasticity can be modeled by adding ARCH terms to the high-volatility part of ARCH(Q_1;4). However, that increases the number of parameters substantially. For reasons of parsimony it is better to use a GARCH term in the high-variance regime. This leads to regime-switching GARCH(0,Q_1;1,1).

Table 2 shows that the evidence of residual conditional heteroskedasticity that was present for regime-switching ARCH on the pound and mark has disappeared when using regime-switching GARCH. Moreover, table 1 demonstrates that the log-likelihood increases a lot after the introduction of GARCH terms, namely 38.90 for the pound and 23.41 for the mark. Remarkably, this increase is achieved by using fewer instead of more parameters. After all, the regime-switching GARCH models have two parameters less than regime-switching ARCH, and the difference becomes even larger when the regime-switching ARCH models are extended to capture the residual volatility clustering. For Japan, with no residual conditional heteroskedasticity after ARCH(1;4), it is not surprising the increase in the log-likelihood is negligible (0.24). However, also there GARCH(0,1;1,1) has fewer parameters than ARCH(1;4). We thus find that GARCH terms can be important to capture volatility persistence. Subsection 3.2.2 has shown that regimes are also important. The advantage of regime-switching GARCH models is that they allow for both.

The outperformance of regime-switching GARCH over regime-switching ARCH also holds for the fourth-order regime-switching ARCH variants in Cai (1994) and Hamilton and Susmel (1994). First, regime-switching GARCH removes the residual volatility clustering that is present for their models for the pound and mark. Second, the increments in the log-likelihood are

40.46 (pound), 24.93 (mark) and −0.34 (yen) for the Cai version, and 43.12 (pound), 23.14 (mark) and 1.10 (yen) for the Hamilton-Susmel model. Third, regime-switching GARCH is more parsimonious: for the pound, mark, and yen the number of parameters is 0, 2, and 1 lower, respectively, than for their models and the difference becomes larger when the Cai and Hamilton-Susmel models are extended to account for the residual volatility clustering.

Next, we relate our version (5) of regime-switching GARCH to Gray's (1996a) variant (4). As table 1 shows, the parameter estimates for Gray's specification are roughly the same as for our specification. However, the log-likelihood for Gray's specification is lower, namely 10.10, 11.73 and 3.93 for the three rates. This is because Gray's model makes less efficient use of the conditioning information when integrating out regimes (see below (4)). This is perhaps also the reason why there is some conditional heteroskedasticity left in the normalized residuals for Gray's model. Besides the theoretical advantages, as given in section 2, we thus also find empirical support for our model over Gray's variant.

Figures 1B, 2B, and 3B provide some additional insight into our regime-switching GARCH model. They plot the estimated smoothed probabilities of being in the high-volatility regime, as defined in subsection 2.2.5. The two European currencies have experienced fewer regime shifts than the Japanese yen. Apparently, sudden shifts in the variance are more important for the description of the yen than for the European currencies, where the conditional variance is governed more by smooth transitions (GARCH effects) from high-volatility periods to low ones. This supports the conclusion given above that both regimes and GARCH terms can be important.

An issue closely related to the persistence of regimes is the allowance for extra leptokurtosis by a *t*-distribution, as in (6). Without this, the persistence of the, for example, low-volatility regime would have been lower, since then a large sudden change in the exchange rate would have been considered earlier as a shift to the high-volatility regime. This is illustrated by figure 1C, which gives the smoothed regime probabilities of the regime-switching GARCH model for the British pound under the restriction of normality: more regime switches occur.

3.2.5. *Comparison of regime-switching with single-regime GARCH*

Though our regime-switching GARCH model outperforms regime-switching ARCH and Gray's regime-switching GARCH, the main reason to introduce the model was to improve on single-regime GARCH. Using the log-likelihoods in table 1, we indeed document an increased fit of 19.34 (UK), 8.44 (Germany) and 16.52 (Japan). Because the regime-switching GARCH methodology generalizes single-regime GARCH, this improvement is presumably not surprising, even though the GARCH($0,Q_1;1,1$) variants used here do not strictly encompass GARCH(1,1).

It is, however, interesting to find out where the improved fit originates from, so as to derive the key differences between the two models. We do this in two stages. First, we examine for which kinds of observations regime-switching GARCH outperforms GARCH. Then we show which model differences are responsible for that.

Since both models focus on volatility, any difference in fit is presumably related to the volatility. Therefore, to find out when regime-switching GARCH is better, we regress the log-likelihood contribution of an observation for regime-switching GARCH minus that for GARCH, dl_t, on a simple measure of past volatility, s_{t-1}^2, and its square. We correct the standard errors for autocorrelation and heteroskedasticity using the Newey and West (1987) asymptotic covariance matrix. (Following West and Cho (1995), we take Bartlett weights and use the same data-dependent automatic lag selection rule. This rule has certain asymptotic optimality properties and was introduced by Newey and West (1994).) The regression results (not reported) show that, although both slope estimates are positive for all three countries, they are all insignificant.

A potential reason for this insignificance is that both dl_t and s_{t-1}^2 are very volatile and may contain much noise. For instance, s_{t-1}^2 is sometimes low even in an otherwise volatile period. To reduce the effect of both sources of noise, we transform dl_t into the binary variable $1[dl_t > 0]$, which is one if regime-switching GARCH is better, and proxy past volatility by the logarithm of the average of, say, ten past squared changes $s_{t-1}^2, \ldots, s_{t-10}^2$. The regression model thus now tries to explain the probability of outperformance from past volatility. The estimates for past volatility and its square are again positive for all three countries, but now they are clearly significant (t-values between 6 and 9). A plot of the parabolic dependence of the estimated probability of outperformance on past volatility shows that regime-switching GARCH outperforms single-regime GARCH particularly in tranquil and volatile periods.

Next, we analyze the reasons for this. Because the main difference between the two models concerns the variance specification, a difference in the log-likelihood contributions is very likely caused by a difference in the variance estimates, $d\hat{V}_{t-1}\{s_t\}$. Indeed, a graph of $d\hat{V}_{t-1}\{s_t\}$ against past volatility demonstrates that regime-switching GARCH has lower variance estimates in tranquil as well as volatile periods. We thus conclude that the improved fit originates from lower variance estimates in both tranquil and volatile periods.

To explain this in terms of the model differences, we first consider the volatile periods. The regime-switching model is then mainly in the high-volatility regime 2, so that the difference with GARCH likely originates from the differences between the estimated second regime parameters and the estimated standard GARCH parameters. Indeed, if we reestimate the regime-switching GARCH model under the restriction $(\alpha_{12}, \beta_2) = (\hat{\alpha}, \hat{\beta})$ and then again regress $1[dl_t > 0]$ on past volatility and its square, the outperformance of regime-switching GARCH in volatile periods disappears. (This may be surprising, as the differences between $(\hat{\alpha}_{12}, \hat{\beta}_2)$ and $(\hat{\alpha}, \hat{\beta})$ in table 1 are small at first sight. Nevertheless, a likelihood ratio test rejects the restriction $(\hat{\alpha}_{12}, \hat{\beta}_2) = (\hat{\alpha}, \hat{\beta})$ for Germany and Japan (not for the UK). Hence, the small differences are relevant.) Since restricting both α_{12} and β_2 is also necessary to remove the outperformance, the difference between the estimates of (α_{12}, β_2) and (α, β) is the reason for the outperformance in volatile periods. From table 1 we see that according to the regime-switching model shocks have a smaller direct effect on the volatility estimates ($\hat{\alpha}_{12} < \hat{\alpha}$) and their subsequent impact is also lower ($\hat{\alpha}_{12} + \hat{\beta}_2 < \hat{\alpha} + \hat{\beta}$); see Lamoureux and Lastrapes (1990) for this interpretation of α and β. We thus conclude that the outperformance in volatile periods is due to the smaller effect of shocks on variance estimates.

Next, we explain the outperformance in tranquil periods, which is caused by the lower regime-switching variance estimates. To abstract from the outperformance in volatile periods, this paragraph uses the restricted regime-switching GARCH model introduced above, so $(\alpha_{12}, \beta_2) = (\hat{\alpha}, \hat{\beta})$. This model also outperforms standard GARCH in tranquil periods and yields lower variance estimates there. The main difference between regime-switching and single-regime GARCH in tranquil periods is that the former has a separate regime for such periods. This regime is relevant for the outperformance if the latter depends on the probability of being in that regime, $P_{t-1}\{r_t = 1\}$. Therefore, we add the estimated probability as a regressor to the model that explains $1[dl_t > 0]$ from past volatility and its square. The estimated effect of the probability is significantly positive for all three countries (t-values between 7 and 11). Moreover, the effect of past volatility has disappeared. Hence we conclude that the outperformance in tranquil periods is obtained by the use of the low-variance regime.

The low-variance regime is used in two ways. First, it can explain why volatility is low for a long time. Second, as explained in subsection 2.2.1, it helps describe that several shocks are "pressure relieving," that is, are followed by a tranquil instead of volatile period. Figure 1D clarifies this by visualizing the impact of two particular shocks. It contains the conditional variance estimates of both GARCH(1;1) and GARCH(0,2;1,1) for the British pound over 1985 only. The persistent effect of the first shock on subsequent volatility is captured by both models (though the regime-switching GARCH variances are less affected by the shock, in line with our argument above). On the other hand, the pressure relieving effect of the second shock, which is the sharp fall in the dollar one day after the G-5 Plaza announcement on September 22, 1985, is better described by the regime-switching model. The reason is a temporary switch to the low-volatility regime, which helps reduce the variance estimates rather quickly.

3.3. Forecasting performance

So far, we have developed a regime-switching GARCH model to obtain more flexibility in capturing the persistence of shocks in volatility. We have shown that this is worthwhile from an in-sample point of view. In this subsection we analyze whether regime-switching models can also improve on the out-of-sample performance of single-regime GARCH.

The volatility forecasts of interest are the forecasts at time $t-1$ of the variance of the exchange rate change over a h-day horizon, that is, $\hat{V}_{t-1}\{s_{t,h}\}$. They follow from subsection 2.2.2 after substitution of the estimation results of table 1. We analyze two forecast horizons, namely one day ($h = 1$) and ten days ($h = 10$).

To get some insight into the generality of the results, we need an extensive out-of-sample period. Therefore, we split the sample into two parts of both 2,491 days; the second half starts at October 20, 1987. As usual, we reestimate the models using the first half and, keeping the parameters fixed to save on estimation time, use the observations of the second half to generate the forecasts $\hat{V}_{t-1}\{s_{t,h}\}$. We also do the reverse, that is, estimate the parameters on the second half and use the first half for forecasting.

To investigate the quality of the volatility forecasts, we need some measure of "observed volatility." Since $V_{t-1}\{s_{t,h}\} = E_{t-1}\{(s_{t,h} - h \cdot \mu)^2\}$, an obvious candidate is the (mean adjusted) squared change $(s_{t,h} - h \cdot \mu)^2$. However, one can obtain a more accurate measure following an idea advocated by Merton (1980) and Schwert (1989) and formalized by Andersen and Bollerslev (1998). They argue that the single squared change, though unbiased, is a noisy indicator for the latent volatility in the period, because the idiosyncratic component of a single change is large. The noise is reduced by taking the sum of all squared intra-period changes, and the smaller the subperiods, the larger the noise reduction. Since the highest frequency available to us is daily data, this idea results in the sum of squared daily changes over the h days in the forecast period: $\sum_{\tau=t}^{t-1+h}(s_\tau - \mu)^2$. This measure is unbiased, just as the single squared change, but it is more accurate (for $h > 1$; for $h = 1$ both measures are equivalent). Therefore, we prefer this measure. Substituting the estimate $\hat{\mu}$ for μ, we thus define observed volatility $v_{t,h}$ over the h days $t, \ldots, t-1+h$ as

$$v_{t,h} = \sum_{\tau=t}^{t-1+h} (s_\tau - \hat{\mu})^2. \tag{12}$$

As stated in the introduction, the paper is motivated by the claim that single-regime GARCH forecasts are too high in volatile periods. This claim is based on the standard forecast efficiency regression

$$v_{t,h} = \gamma_0 + \gamma_1 \hat{V}_{t-1}\{s_{t,h}\} + \eta_\tau \tag{13}$$

(see also Pagan and Schwert (1990)). If the mean and variance forecasts are (conditionally) unbiased, that is, $\hat{\mu} = E_{t-1}\{s_t\}$ and $\hat{V}_{t-1}\{s_{t,h}\} = V_{t-1}\{s_{t,h}\}$, then regression (13) implies $\gamma_0 = 0$ and $\gamma_1 = 1$. To test both implications we estimate (13) by OLS and correct the standard errors for autocorrelation and heteroskedasticity following Newey and West (1987), as explained in subsection 3.2.5. We also correct the standard errors for the uncertainty originating from the fact that the parameters used to compute the forecasts are not known but are estimated. This correction is based on West and McCracken (1998). As we keep the parameters fixed over the forecasting period, we have what they call the "fixed sampling scheme". Because in our study the in-sample and out-of-sample periods have the same number of observations, West and McCracken show that we have to multiply the Newey-West standard errors by $\sqrt{2}$.

The results are in table 3. For each model and horizon we have two estimates for both γ_0 and γ_1; the left one is based on the usual procedure of estimating the parameters from the first half of the sample and obtaining forecasts from the second half, while the right one is computed from the reverse procedure. We see for the GARCH(1,1) model that in eight out of twelve cases both implications $\gamma_0 = 0$ and $\gamma_1 = 1$ are significantly rejected (an asterisk for the estimate of γ_1 means that it is significantly different from one, not zero). For all twelve cases the estimate of γ_0 is larger than zero and the estimate of γ_1 is smaller than one. This is in line with the results of West and Cho (1995), among others.

The finding of $\gamma_0 > 0$ and $\gamma_1 < 1$ suggests that low GARCH(1,1) forecasts underestimate the true volatility or that high forecasts overestimate volatility, or both. To distinguish between the two cases we reestimate (13), but now allowing for a break in the regression line at, say, the median forecast (allowing for more breaks does not alter the conclusion). That is, one pair (γ_0^-, γ_1^-) is relevant for forecasts below the median and another pair (γ_0^+, γ_1^+) for forecasts above the median. The results (not tabulated) show that the estimates of (γ_0^-, γ_1^-) are close to (0, 1) (average estimate is (−0.00, 1.02) for the one-day and (−0.38, 1.09) for the ten-day horizon) and that they are nowhere significantly different from (0, 1). The estimates of (γ_0^+, γ_1^+), however, differ substantially from (0, 1) (averages are (0.23, 0.55) and (2.96, 0.43)) and in nine out of twelve cases the difference is significant. Therefore, high GARCH forecasts generally overestimate the true variance, while low GARCH forecasts do not underestimate volatility. This is in line with the in-sample result that regime-switching GARCH improves on GARCH by reducing the high GARCH forecasts in volatile periods and by reducing instead of increasing the low GARCH forecasts in tranquil periods (see subsection 3.2.4). We thus conclude that single-regime GARCH volatility forecasts are too high in volatile periods.

To compare the regime-switching models to GARCH in this respect, we return to the standard forecast efficiency regression (13), so without the break. Table 3 shows that the regime-switching models do better than GARCH(1,1), as $\gamma_0 = 0$ and $\gamma_1 = 1$ are generally not rejected. Apparently, the excessive GARCH forecasts are sufficiently reduced by the regime-switching models. In subsection 3.2.5 we have shown that this is caused by the smaller persistence of shocks in volatility. Hence, allowing for more flexibility in volatility persistence by using regimes is worthwhile to improve the standard GARCH forecasts in the sense of regression (13).

Another way to compare the forecasts is by using the mean squared error (MSE) defined as the mean of $(v_{t,h} - \hat{V}_{t-1}\{s_{t,h}\})^2$ over the out-of-sample period. Table 3 gives the MSE for GARCH(1,1) and the difference in MSE with respect to GARCH(1,1) for the other models. The standard errors are the heteroskedasticity and autocorrelation consistent standard errors from a regression of $(v_{t,h} - \hat{V}_{t-1}\{s_{t,h}\})^2$ obtained from GARCH(1,1) (or the difference with respect to GARCH(1,1) for other models) on a constant; these standard errors need no further correction for estimation uncertainty (West (1996)).

Table 3 shows that in 11 out of 12 cases our regime-switching GARCH forecasts are better (lower MSE) than those from single-regime GARCH. Moreover, in 6 cases the outperformance is significant. Hence, also for the MSE criterion regime-switching GARCH improves on single-regime GARCH in terms of volatility forecasting. This does, of course, not mean that single-regime GARCH forecasts are bad. After all, Andersen and Bollerslev (1998) show that GARCH(1,1) yields good volatility forecast. We only conclude that regime-switching GARCH forecasts are better.

For the two variants of regime-switching ARCH we find an improvement over single-regime GARCH in 15 out of 24 cases (4 significant). These improvements are all for the mark and yen, as for the pound GARCH is the best in all 8 cases (1 significant). This is partly in line with our conclusion from the in-sample fit in subsection 3.2 that GARCH gives a better fit for the pound and regime-switching ARCH yields a better fit for the yen; for the mark the GARCH fit is better but the forecasts are worse. Hence, as in subsection 3.2.4, both regimes and GARCH effects can be important to model volatility, which is another argument for using regime-switching GARCH.

Table 3 also shows that there is some preference of our model over Gray's (1996a) variant of regime-switching GARCH for the one-day horizon, as the MSE for our model is lower in 5 out of 6 cases. For the ten-day horizon we

Table 3. Out-of-sample volatility forecasting statistics

	One-day forecast horizon								Ten-day forecast horizon							
	MSE-G(1,1)		γ_0		γ_1		$\tilde{R}^2$		MSE-G(1,1)		γ_0		γ_1		$\tilde{R}^2$	
BRITISH POUND																
Const. variance	.051*	.058*			.88	.98	0	0	4.00*	4.66			.89	.98	0	0
	(.017)	(.028)			(.10)	(.12)			(1.24)	(3.30)			(.11)	(.13)		
GARCH(1,1)	.697	.998	.05	.08	.84	.78	.062	.058	11.20	16.39	.55	1.03	.82	.72	.256	.226
	(.112)	(.262)	(.04)	(.06)	(.11)	(.16)			(2.55)	(4.44)	(.39)	(.59)	(.10)	(.16)		
ARCH(0;0)	.011	.024	−.04	−.02	1.06	1.04	.048	.030	0.84	2.10	−.77	−.02	1.14	1.00	.198	.121
	(.009)	(.024)	(.06)	(.07)	(.19)	(.24)			(0.70)	(2.54)	(.80)	(.90)	(.23)	(.29)		
ARCH(2;4)	.009*	.015	.00	−.02	.95	1.01	.050	.043	0.61	1.71	−1.00	−.52	1.18	1.09	.214	.139
	(.004)	(.015)	(.06)	(.08)	(.17)	(.22)			(0.62)	(2.14)	(.77)	(1.19)	(.23)	(.34)		
GrayG(0,2;1,1)	.002	−.002	.03	.05	.89	.85	.059	.059	–	–	–	–	–	–	–	–
	(.002)	(.007)	(.05)	(.06)	(.13)	(.15)										
GARCH(0,2;1,1)	.001	−.004	.02	.07	.90	.80	.060	.061	−0.03	−0.56	.22	.79	.90	.76	.259	.253
	(.002)	(.003)	(.05)	(.06)	(.14)	(.14)			(0.27)	(0.34)	(.43)	(.58)	(.12)	(.15)		
GERMAN MARK																
Const. variance	.036*	.033*			.89	.98	0	0	1.87	0.42			.89	.98	0	0
	(.017)	(.016)			(.09)	(.11)			(1.47)	(1.91)			(.10)	(.11)		
GARCH(1,1)	.817	1.208	.12*	.12*	.68*	.69*	.040	.029	14.51	22.18	1.39*	1.93*	.61*	.54*	.122	.031
	(.121)	(.323)	(.05)	(.05)	(.11)	(.12)			(2.60)	(6.08)	(.56)	(.90)	(.11)	(.15)		
ARCH(0;0)	.000	−.013	.03	−.12	.87	1.31	.039	.038	−1.23	−2.77	−.10	−.76	.96	1.20	.178	.143
	(.009)	(.011)	(.07)	(.08)	(.18)	(.24)			(0.92)	(1.58)	(.87)	(.89)	(.22)	(.23)		
ARCH(0;4)	−.002	−.016	.04	−.01	.86	1.05	.042	.040	−1.31	−2.80	−.43	−.80	1.02	1.20	.184	.143
	(.007)	(.012)	(.08)	(.06)	(.18)	(.15)			(0.90)	(1.57)	(.85)	(.86)	(.21)	(.21)		
GrayG(0,0;1,1)	−.004*	−.008	.09	.11	.73*	.76	.046	.034	–	–	–	–	–	–	–	–
	(.002)	(.005)	(.05)	(.06)	(.11)	(.15)										
GARCH(0,0;1,1)	−.009*	−.011*	.06	.08	.82	.81	.050	.036	−1.48*	−1.69*	.43	1.44	.83	.68	.199	.095
	(.003)	(.004)	(.06)	(.06)	(.13)	(.15)			(0.44)	(0.60)	(.67)	(.94)	(.14)	(.18)		

JAPANESE YEN																
Const. variance	.005	.002			.87	.96	0	0	−0.14	−2.27			.87	.96	0	0
	(.014)	(.011)			(.09)	(.09)			(0.88)	(1.69)			(.10)	(.09)		
GARCH(1,1)	.996	1.414	.16*	.19*	.55*	.56*	.009	.005	17.35	23.59	1.19*	3.17*	.57*	.30*	.052	−.096
	(.157)	(.481)	(.05)	(.08)	(.10)	(.14)			(2.45)	(7.61)	(.61)	(1.08)	(.10)	(.17)		
ARCH(0;0)	−.022*	−.021	−.07	.03	1.09	.90	.025	.018	−2.16*	−3.08	−1.87	1.41	1.34	.68	.102	.038
	(.011)	(.014)	(.08)	(.10)	(.23)	(.23)			(0.71)	(1.65)	(1.25)	(.98)	(.32)	(.20)		
ARCH(1;4)	−.021*	−.027	.06	.02	.82	.93	.024	.023	−2.29*	−3.12	−.40	1.30	1.00	.70	.113	.041
	(.009)	(.016)	(.06)	(.10)	(.16)	(.23)			(0.64)	(1.67)	(.91)	(.98)	(.23)	(.20)		
GrayG(1,0;1,1)	−.021*	−.022	.05	.05	.82	.86	.025	.019	–	–	–	–	–	–	–	–
	(.008)	(.017)	(.07)	(.12)	(.17)	(.27)										
GARCH(1,0;1,1)	−.024*	−.010	.04	.15*	.84	.65*	.028	.011	−2.32*	−1.44	−.46	2.72*	1.01	.40*	.117	.012
	(.008)	(.007)	(.07)	(.06)	(.17)	(.12)			(0.62)	(0.83)	(.90)	(.98)	(.22)	(.16)		

Standard errors in parentheses (details in section 3.3); * is significant at 5%.
"MSE-G(1,1)" is the mean squared forecast error of a model minus that of GARCH(1,1); for GARCH(1,1) it is the MSE itself; γ_0 and γ_1 are the intercept and slope in the forecast efficiency regression (13); $\tilde{R}^2$ is the restricted R^2 defined by (14).
There are two estimates for each statistic. This reflects the two different out-of-sample periods: the left (right) estimate is based on forecasts for the second (first) half of the sample, that is, 2,491 days, using the first (second) half for estimation.
The specifications of the models are given in the notes below table 1. For Gray's (1996a) variant of GARCH(0,Q_1;1,1) we are unable to compute multi-day-ahead forecasts.

cannot make such a comparison, since we are unable to forecast more than one day ahead with Gray's model.

A final means to compare the volatility forecasts is to analyze the coefficient of determination, R^2, of the forecast efficiency regression (13). The standard R^2 measures the explanatory quality of a linear combination, $\gamma_0 + \gamma_1 \hat{V}_{t-1} \cdot \{s_{t,h}\}$, of the forecast. However, one is interested in the quality of the forecast itself, not a linear combination of it. Therefore, we prefer the R^2 under the restriction $\gamma_0 = 0$ and $\gamma_1 = 1$,

$$\tilde{R}^2 = 1 - \frac{V\{v_{t,h} - \hat{V}_{t-1}\{s_{t,h}\}\}}{V\{v_{t,h}\}}. \tag{14}$$

This forecasting statistic is similar to the R^2-type measure used by Gray (1996a). It is generally smaller than the standard (unrestricted) R^2 and it can be negative.

The values of $\tilde{R}^2$ in table 3 confirm the conclusions obtained from the MSE above. In particular, our regime-switching GARCH forecasts are better (higher $\tilde{R}^2$) than those from single-regime GARCH in 11 out of 12 cases. The average improvements are 0.007 for the 1-day horizon and 0.057 for the 10-day horizon.

These improvements may seem low. However, the average $\tilde{R}^2$ are also low (0.034 for $h = 1$ and 0.099 for $h = 10$ for single-regime GARCH). This does not mean that the forecasts are bad, as Andersen and Bollerslev (1998) show. The primary reason for the low R^2 (and thus low $\tilde{R}^2$ and low improvements in $\tilde{R}^2$) is the noise in the observed volatility measure $v_{t,h}$. As discussed above (12), this noise can be reduced by taking the sum of squared changes over smaller subperiods. To give an indication of the magnitude of the effect of this noise reduction on R^2, Andersen and Bollerslev compute the R^2 for a GARCH(1,1) model on daily mark/dollar and yen/dollar exchange rates both using a single squared daily change and using the sum of 288 squared five-minute changes in a day. The R^2 increases from on average 0.036 to 0.436. They conclude that GARCH does provide good volatility forecasts despite the low R^2 that one typically obtains using a single squared change. (Note that their argument also explains why for our series $\tilde{R}^2$ is higher for the ten-day than for the one-day horizon, as we have reduced the noise in the ten-day observed volatility by using ten instead of one squared changes.)

To put the $\tilde{R}^2$ improvements given above into perspective, we divide them by the average $\tilde{R}^2$. We conclude that the relative outperformance of regime-switching GARCH over single-regime GARCH is 22% ($h = 1$) and 58% ($h = 10$), which is quite substantial.

4. Conclusion

This paper is based on the observation that forecasts from the widely-used GARCH model are significantly too high in volatile periods. We argue that this is due to the well-known high degree of persistence of individual shocks in volatility according to GARCH estimates. Therefore, we develop a model with more flexibility regarding volatility persistence, that is, not all shocks have to be highly persistent. The model generalizes GARCH by using two regimes with different levels of volatility and regime-specific GARCH formulas to describe the variance within the regimes. It is thus a regime-switching GARCH model.

Its specification shares the attractive features of Gray's (1996a) version of regime-switching GARCH, such as the recursiveness of the likelihood function. Our model, however, is preferable in other respects. For instance, multi-period-ahead volatility forecasting is a recursive procedure similar to standard GARCH and is much more convenient than with Gray's variant. Moreover, our model makes better use of the conditioning information to integrate out the unobserved regimes, which translates into a better fit.

In the empirical part of the paper we estimate the model using about twenty years of daily data on three U.S. dollar exchange rates (British pound, German mark and Japanese yen). The out-of-sample study shows that the problem of excessive single-regime GARCH forecasts in volatile periods disappears when using regime-switching GARCH. Moreover, regime-switching GARCH yields significantly better volatility forecasts than single-regime GARCH. We quantify the relative outperformance by 22% for the one-day and 58% for the ten-day horizon.

The other empirical results can be summarized as follows. First, including regimes is important, since even a regime-switching model with constant regime-specific variances sometimes outperforms standard GARCH. Second, there is conditional heteroskedasticity within regimes. Thus there is a need for ARCH or GARCH terms. Third, the heteroskedasticity differs across regimes, as more ARCH terms are needed in high-volatility regimes. This is in contrast with the regime-switching ARCH models of Cai (1994) and Hamilton and Susmel (1994). Fourth, GARCH terms, which are not allowed in regime-switching ARCH models, are important, because even single-regime GARCH is sometimes better than regime-switching models with several ARCH terms. Finally, a t-distribution instead of a normal one for the error term helps make the regimes more stable.

There are a number of other possible applications of the model. For example, the proposed technique of averaging out unobserved regimes to avoid path-dependence of the likelihood function may also be useful in models that combine switches in the mean with a GARCH variance specification (see Klaassen (1999)). Moreover, regime-switching GARCH volatility forecasts can be used to analyze the effect of volatility on stock returns and to price options, for which volatility assessments are crucial.

Our results also yield several methodological suggestions for future research. Regime-switching GARCH generalizes standard GARCH by making the volatility persistence of shocks more flexible. Of course, it does so in a specific way, which is presumably not the optimal one. Moreover, we have not tried to rationalize the timing of the estimated regime switches in our data from an economic point of view, for instance, in terms of financial market liberalization, changes in exchange rate policies, or oil shocks. The regimes are only used as a technical means to obtain more flexibility regarding volatility persistence, just as the standard GARCH model is only a technical means to model volatility persistence. This appears, nevertheless, worthwhile, as we do find that the regime-switching GARCH forecasts are better than the GARCH ones. Hence, the paper suggests that it is promising to study volatility persistence in more detail, including the economic mechanisms behind it, to improve volatility forecasts even further.

Appendices

A. Volatility forecasting

In this appendix we give an expression for $p_{t-1}(r_\tau)$ in the volatility forecasting formula (8) and prove the recursive formula (9).

For the future regime probability in (8) we have

$$p_{t-1}(r_\tau) = \sum_{r_{t-1}=1,2} p_{t-1}(r_{t-1}) \cdot p_{t-1}(r_\tau | r_{t-1}), \tag{15}$$

where $p_{t-1}(r_{t-1})$ is discussed in (31). For the multi-period-ahead probability on the right-hand-side of (15), we form the time-constant Markov transition matrix M:

$$M = \begin{bmatrix} p_{11} & 1 - p_{22} \\ 1 - p_{11} & p_{22} \end{bmatrix}. \tag{16}$$

Using the $(\tau - (t-1))$-th power of M, the theory of Markov processes states that

$$p_{t-1}(r_\tau | r_{t-1}) = (M^{\tau-(t-1)})_{r_\tau r_{t-1}}, \tag{17}$$

so that (15) can be computed.

In the remaining part of this appendix we prove (9). More precisely, we derive the special case $i = \tau - t$ of (9),

$$V_{t-1}\{\varepsilon_\tau | r_\tau\} = \omega_{r_\tau} + (\alpha_{r_\tau} + \beta_{r_\tau}) E_{t-1}\{V_{t-1}\{\varepsilon_{\tau-1} | r_{\tau-1}\} \mid r_\tau\}, \tag{18}$$

as for the other i the derivation is analogous. The formula can be proved by repeatedly using the law of iterated expectations. Using definition (5), we get

$$\begin{aligned} V_{t-1}\{\varepsilon_\tau | r_\tau\} &= E_{t-1}[V_{\tau-1}\{\varepsilon_\tau | r_\tau\} \mid r_\tau] \\ &= E_{t-1}[\omega_{r_\tau} + \alpha_{r_\tau}\varepsilon_{\tau-1}^2 + \beta_{r_\tau} E_{\tau-1}\{V_{\tau-2}\{\varepsilon_{\tau-1} | r_{\tau-1}\} \mid r_\tau\} \mid r_\tau]. \end{aligned} \tag{19}$$

For the ARCH part

$$\begin{aligned} E_{t-1}[\varepsilon_{\tau-1}^2 | r_\tau] &= E\{\varepsilon_{\tau-1}^2 | r_\tau, I_{t-1}\} \\ &= E[E\{\varepsilon_{\tau-1}^2 | r_{\tau-1}, r_\tau, I_{t-1}\} \mid r_\tau, I_{t-1}] \\ &= E_{t-1}[E_{t-1}\{\varepsilon_{\tau-1}^2 | r_{\tau-1}\} \mid r_\tau], \end{aligned} \tag{20}$$

where the last equality uses that the error distribution given the contemporaneous variance regime does not depend on the future variance regime.

For the GARCH part in (19) we use similar techniques to obtain

$$
\begin{aligned}
&E_{t-1}[E_{\tau-1}(V_{\tau-2}\{\varepsilon_{\tau-1}|r_{\tau-1}\}\,|\,r_\tau)\,|\,r_\tau]\\
&\quad = E[E(V\{\varepsilon_{\tau-1}|r_{\tau-1},I_{\tau-2}\}\,|\,r_\tau,I_{\tau-1})\,|\,r_\tau,I_{t-1}]\\
&\quad = E(V\{\varepsilon_{\tau-1}|r_{\tau-1},I_{\tau-2}\}\,|\,r_\tau,I_{t-1})\\
&\quad = E[E(V\{\varepsilon_{\tau-1}|r_{\tau-1},I_{\tau-2}\}\,|\,r_\tau,r_{\tau-1},I_{t-1})\,|\,r_\tau,I_{t-1}]\\
&\quad = E[V\{\varepsilon_{\tau-1}|r_{\tau-1},I_{t-1}\}\,|\,r_\tau,I_{t-1}]\\
&\quad = E_{t-1}[V_{t-1}\{\varepsilon_{\tau-1}|r_{\tau-1}\}\,|\,r_\tau].
\end{aligned}
\tag{21}
$$

The penultimate equality uses that $I_{\tau-2}$ given $r_\tau, r_{\tau-1}, I_{t-1}$ is independent of r_τ, since the Markov structure implies that the distribution of variance regimes $(r_{\tau-2}, r_{\tau-3}, \ldots)$ conditional on $r_{\tau-1}$ and r_τ is independent of r_τ; this makes the changes $(s_{\tau-2}, s_{\tau-3}, \ldots)$ also independent of r_τ once $r_{\tau-1}$ is given.

Substituting the results for the ARCH and GARCH parts in (19) gives formula (18). The required probability in (18) is

$$
p_{t-1}(r_{\tau-1}|r_\tau) = \frac{p_{t-1}(r_\tau|r_{\tau-1})\cdot p_{t-1}(r_{\tau-1})}{p_{t-1}(r_\tau)}, \tag{22}
$$

where the switching probability follows from (2) and the regime probability $p_{t-1}(r_{\tau-1})$ follows in a similar way as $p_{t-1}(r_\tau)$ in (15); the denominator is given by (15).

B. Unconditional error variance

Here we derive expression (10) for the "unconditional" error variance $V\{\varepsilon_t|r_t\}$ and the three necessary conditions for its existence.

Suppose $V\{\varepsilon_t|r_t\}$ exists for both $r_t = 1, 2$ and for all ω_1, ω_2. Using the variance definition (5), repeated use of the law of iterated expectations yields

$$
\begin{aligned}
V\{\varepsilon_t|r_t\} &= \omega_{r_t} + \alpha_{r_t} E\{\varepsilon_{t-1}^2|r_t\} + \beta_{r_t} E\{V_{t-2}\{\varepsilon_{t-1}|r_{t-1}\}\,|\,r_t\}\\
&= \omega_{r_t} + \alpha_{r_t} E\{E\{\varepsilon_{t-1}^2|r_{t-1},r_t\}\,|\,r_t\}\\
&\quad + \beta_{r_t} E\{E\{V_{t-2}\{\varepsilon_{t-1}|r_{t-1}\}\,|\,r_{t-1},r_t\}\,|\,r_t\}\\
&= \omega_{r_t} + \alpha_{r_t} E\{V\{\varepsilon_{t-1}|r_{t-1}\}\,|\,r_t\} + \beta_{r_t} E\{V\{\varepsilon_{t-1}|r_{t-1}\}\,|\,r_t\}\\
&= \omega_{r_t} + (\alpha_{r_t} + \beta_{r_t})\cdot E\{V\{\varepsilon_{t-1}|r_{t-1}\}\,|\,r_t\},
\end{aligned}
\tag{23}
$$

where the penultimate equality uses that the distribution of the error given the contemporaneous variance regime does not depend on the future variance regime.

Next, assume that $V\{\varepsilon_t|r_t = 1\}$ and $V\{\varepsilon_t|r_t = 2\}$ do not depend on t and denote them by σ_1^2 and σ_2^2, respectively. Then

$$\begin{bmatrix} \sigma_1^2 \\ \sigma_2^2 \end{bmatrix} = \begin{bmatrix} \omega_1 \\ \omega_2 \end{bmatrix} + \begin{bmatrix} A_{11} & A_{12} \\ A_{21} & A_{22} \end{bmatrix} \cdot \begin{bmatrix} \sigma_1^2 \\ \sigma_2^2 \end{bmatrix}, \tag{24}$$

where $A_{ij} = P\{r_{t-1} = j \mid r_t = i\}(\alpha_i + \beta_i)$; expressions for the probabilities involved are at the end of this appendix.

Let A be the matrix with elements A_{ij}. Since we have assumed that both unconditional variances exist for all ω_1, ω_2, the matrix $I_2 - A$ is invertible, so that the unconditional variances are indeed given by (10).

Necessary conditions for the existence of both variances can be derived as follows. Because $\alpha_{r_t}, \beta_{r_t} \geq 0$ implies that the variances are strictly positive for all ω_1, ω_2 (> 0) the four elements of $(I_2 - A)^{-1}$ in (10) must be nonnegative and $(I_2 - A)^{-1}$ may not have a zero row. The four elements follow from

$$(I_2 - A)^{-1} = \frac{1}{\det(I_2 - A)} \begin{bmatrix} 1 - A_{22} & \alpha_1 + \beta_1 - A_{11} \\ \alpha_2 + \beta_2 - A_{22} & 1 - A_{11} \end{bmatrix}, \tag{25}$$

where we have used $A_{12} = \alpha_1 + \beta_1 - A_{11}$ and $A_{21} = \alpha_2 + \beta_2 - A_{22}$. Since $\alpha_i + \beta_i - A_{ii} \geq 0$ for both regimes $i = 1, 2$, the nonnegativity of $(I_2 - A)^{-1}$ implies through (25) that $\det(I_2 - A) > 0$, so that $1 - A_{11} \geq 0$ and $1 - A_{22} \geq 0$. However, neither A_{11} nor A_{22} may be unity; otherwise $\det(I_2 - A) = -(\alpha_1 + \beta_1 - A_{11})(\alpha_2 + \beta_2 - A_{22})$, so that $\alpha_i + \beta_i - A_{ii} \geq 0$ for both regimes would imply that $\det(I_2 - A) \leq 0$, which is not the case. Hence, the three necessary conditions are $A_{11}, A_{22} < 1$ and $\det(I_2 - A) > 0$.

To compute the unconditional error variance in (24), we need the probability $p(r_{t-1}|r_t)$ that the previous regime was r_{t-1} given that the current regime is r_t. Using Bayes' rule, we have

$$p(r_{t-1}|r_t) = \frac{p(r_t|r_{t-1}) \cdot p(r_{t-1})}{\sum_{r_{t-1}=1,2} p(r_t|r_{t-1}) \cdot p(r_{t-1})}, \tag{26}$$

where $p(r_t|r_{t-1})$ is constant (see (2)) and the theory of Markov processes gives the unconditional probabilities (see Hamilton (1989)):

$$\begin{aligned} p(r_{t-1} = 1) &= \frac{1 - p_{22}}{2 - p_{11} - p_{22}} \\ p(r_{t-1} = 2) &= \frac{1 - p_{11}}{2 - p_{11} - p_{22}}. \end{aligned} \tag{27}$$

C. Estimation

In this appendix we derive the likelihood function of the regime-switching GARCH model and show that it has a first-order recursive structure, as claimed in subsection 2.2.4.

To obtain the likelihood function, we first need the density of the exchange rate change at time t conditional on only observable information. Let $p_{t-1}(s_t)$ denote this density evaluated at an exchange rate change equal to s_t. It can be split up as

$$p_{t-1}(s_t) = \sum_{r_t=1,2} p_{t-1}(s_t|r_t) \cdot p_{t-1}(r_t). \tag{28}$$

The first term on the right-hand-side, $p_{t-1}(s_t|r_t)$, denotes the density of the exchange rate change at time t evaluated at the value s_t conditional on I_{t-1} and on the regime having value r_t. This t-density follows from formulas (1), (5) and (6). It is, however, not straightforward how to compute the conditional variance in (5), as this requires integrating out the regime path $\tilde{r}_{t-1}$ in $E_{t-1}[V_{t-2}\{\varepsilon_{t-1}|\tilde{r}_{t-1}\} \,|\, r_t]$. Because $V_{t-2}\{\varepsilon_{t-1}|\tilde{r}_{t-1}\}$ depends only on r_{t-1}, we just need $p_{t-1}(r_{t-1}|r_t)$, the probability that the previous regime was r_{t-1} given that the current regime is r_t and given the information I_{t-1}:

$$p_{t-1}(r_{t-1}|r_t) = \frac{p_{t-1}(r_{t-1}) \cdot p_{t-1}(r_t|r_{t-1})}{p_{t-1}(r_t)}, \tag{29}$$

where

$$p_{t-1}(r_t) = \sum_{r_{t-1}=1,2} p_{t-1}(r_{t-1}) \cdot p_{t-1}(r_t|r_{t-1}). \tag{30}$$

The constant switching probability $p_{t-1}(r_t|r_{t-1})$ follows from (2).

The remaining term in (29) and (30) is $p_{t-1}(r_{t-1})$. This probability is crucial, since all regime probabilities in the paper can be derived from it. Using similar techniques as in Gray (1996a), the following formula shows that this probability has a first-order recursive structure, which simplifies its computation substantially:

$$\begin{aligned} p_{t-1}(r_{t-1}) &= p_{t-2}(r_{t-1}|s_{t-1}) \\ &= \frac{p_{t-2}(s_{t-1}|r_{t-1}) \cdot p_{t-2}(r_{t-1})}{p_{t-2}(s_{t-1})} \\ &= \frac{p_{t-2}(s_{t-1}|r_{t-1}) \cdot \sum_{r_{t-2}=1,2} p_{t-2}(r_{t-2}) \cdot p_{t-2}(r_{t-1}|r_{t-2})}{p_{t-2}(s_{t-1})}. \end{aligned} \tag{31}$$

Hence, the variables to compute $p_{t-1}(r_{t-1})$ are its previous values $p_{t-2}(r_{t-2})$ and the constant $p_{t-2}(r_{t-1}|r_{t-2})$ for $r_{t-2} = 1,2$ and the previous densities $p_{t-2}(s_{t-1}|r_{t-1})$ and $p_{t-2}(s_{t-1})$. This makes the computation of $p_{t-1}(r_{t-1})$ a first-order recursive process.

The second term on the right-hand-side of (28), $p_{t-1}(r_t)$, is the conditional probability that the current regime is r_t. It is given by (30).

Having discussed both terms on the right-hand-side of (28), we can now compute the density of interest, $p_{t-1}(s_t)$, being a mixture of two t-densities. This density can then be used to build the sample log-likelihood $\sum_{t=1}^{T} \log(p_{t-1}(s_t))$ with which all parameters in the regime-switching GARCH model can be estimated.

From a practical point of view, it is important to realize that the log-likelihood has a first-order recursive structure, similar to that of a standard, one-regime GARCH(1,1) model. After all, for (29) and (30) one needs the constant $p_{t-1}(r_t|r_{t-1})$ and the first-order recursive probability $p_{t-1}(r_{t-1})$ in (31) for all four combinations of (r_t, r_{t-1}); density (28) can then be computed from (30), the previous change s_{t-1}, (29) and the previous variances $V_{t-2}\{\varepsilon_{t-1}|r_{t-1}\}$ for $r_{t-1} = 1, 2$. This first-order recursiveness of $p_{t-1}(s_t)$ speeds up the calculation of the sample log-likelihood substantially. To start up the recursive process, we set the required variables equal to their expectation without conditioning on the information set, that is, the "unconditional" variance $\sigma^2_{r_t}$ in (10).

D. Regime inference

As stated in subsection 2.2.5, the smoothed probability that the regime was r_t at time t, $p_T(r_t)$, can be computed recursively. More generally, any ex post regime probability $p_\tau(r_t)$, for a given future time $\tau \in \{t, t+1, \ldots, T\}$, can be computed in a recursive manner, starting from the ex ante probability $p_{t-1}(r_t)$. In this appendix, we verify that claim.

One can write $p_\tau(r_t)$ for both regimes $r_t = 1, 2$ as

$$p_\tau(r_t) = p_{\tau-1}(r_t|s_\tau)$$

$$= \frac{p_{\tau-1}(s_\tau|r_t) \cdot p_{\tau-1}(r_t)}{\sum_{r_t=1,2} p_{\tau-1}(s_\tau|r_t) \cdot p_{\tau-1}(r_t)}. \tag{32}$$

Suppose first that $\tau = t$. Then $p_\tau(r_t)$ follows directly, as $p_{\tau-1}(r_t)$ and $p_{\tau-1}(s_\tau|r_t)$ in (32) are known from the estimation process (see appendix C).

Hence, let us suppose from now on that $\tau > t$. The computation of (32) requires two inputs. The first is the previous ex post probability $p_{\tau-1}(r_t)$, which is known from the previous recursion for both r_t. The second ingredient of (32) is the density $p_{\tau-1}(s_\tau|r_t)$ for both regime outcomes. Its computation requires a number of steps. We first write it as

$$p_{\tau-1}(s_\tau|r_t) = \sum_{r_\tau=1,2} p_{\tau-1}(s_\tau|r_\tau) \cdot p_{\tau-1}(r_\tau|r_t), \tag{33}$$

where we use that the conditional distribution of s_τ given r_τ does not depend on the earlier regime r_t. This formula itself has two ingredients. The first one is the density $p_{\tau-1}(s_\tau|r_\tau)$ for both regime combinations, which is known from the estimation process.

The second term needed in (33) is the $(\tau - t)$-period-ahead regime-switching probability $p_{\tau-1}(r_\tau|r_t)$ for all regime outcomes. Once it has been computed, it should be saved, since it will be needed in the next recursive step. Making use of the Markov structure of the regime process, it can be written in terms of $(\tau - 1 - t)$-period-ahead switching probabilities

$$p_{\tau-1}(r_\tau|r_t) = \sum_{r_{\tau-1}=1,2} p_{\tau-1}(r_\tau|r_{\tau-1}) \cdot p_{\tau-1}(r_{\tau-1}|r_t). \tag{34}$$

Again there are two ingredients. First, we need $p_{\tau-1}(r_\tau|r_{\tau-1})$ for all regime combinations. These are constant and follow from (2).

The second ingredient of (34) is $p_{\tau-1}(r_{\tau-1}|r_t)$ for all regime combinations. We have

$$p_{\tau-1}(r_{\tau-1}|r_t) = p_{\tau-2}(r_{\tau-1}|r_t, s_{\tau-1})$$

$$= \frac{p_{\tau-2}(s_{\tau-1}|r_{\tau-1}) \cdot p_{\tau-2}(r_{\tau-1}|r_t)}{\sum_{r_{\tau-1}=1,2} p_{\tau-2}(s_{\tau-1}|r_{\tau-1}) \cdot p_{\tau-2}(r_{\tau-1}|r_t)}, \tag{35}$$

where we use that the conditional density of $s_{\tau-1}$ is independent of the earlier regime r_t once $r_{\tau-1}$ is given. We have two ingredients. First, the conditional density $p_{\tau-2}(s_{\tau-1}|r_{\tau-1})$ for both regime outcomes. It is known from the estimation process. Secondly, we need the $(\tau - 1 - t)$-period-ahead switching probability $p_{\tau-2}(r_{\tau-1}|r_t)$ for all regime combinations. This one was saved during the previous recursion, if $\tau > t + 1$. If $\tau = t + 1$, it equals one.

This completes the algorithm to compute (33), which is the second ingredient of (32). For each recursion one has to compute (35), use the result to compute (34) and use this to compute (33). Using this in (32) yields the ex post probability $p_\tau(r_t)$ from $p_{\tau-1}(r_t)$. Therefore, starting from the ex ante probability $p_{t-1}(r_t)$ one can recursively compute the ex post probability $p_\tau(r_t)$.

References

Andersen TG, Bollerslev T (1998) Answering the skeptics: Yes, standard volatility models do provide accurate forecasts. International Economic Review 39:885–905

Ang A, Bekaert G (1998) Regime switches in interest rates. NBER Working Paper No. 6508

Bollerslev T (1986) Generalized autoregressive conditional heteroskedasticity. Journal of Econometrics 31:307–327

Bollerslev T, Chou RY, Kroner KF (1992) ARCH modeling in finance. Journal of Econometrics 52:5–59

Cai J (1994) A Markov model of unconditional variance in ARCH. Journal of Business and Economic Statistics 12:309–316

Chaudhuri K, Klaassen F (2000) Have east Asian stock markets calmed down? Evidence from a regime switching model. Mimeo University of Amsterdam

Dewachter H (1997) Sign predictions of exchange rate changes: Charts as proxies for Bayesian inferences. Weltwirtschaftliches Archiv 133:39–55

Engle RF (1982) Autoregressive conditional heteroskedasticity with estimates of the variance of U.K. inflation. Econometrica 50:987–1008

Engle RF, Bollerslev T (1986) Modeling the persistence of conditional variances. Econometric Reviews 5:1–50

Fong WM (1998) The dynamics of DM/£ exchange rate volatility: A SWARCH analysis. International Journal of Finance and Economics 3:59–71

Gray SF (1996a) Modeling the conditional distribution of interest rates as a regime-switching process. Journal of Financial Economics 42:27–62

Gray SF (1996b) An analysis of conditional regime-switching models. Working paper Fuqua School of Business Duke University

Hamilton JD (1989) A new approach to the economic analysis of nonstationary time series and the business cycle. Econometrica 57:357–384

Hamilton JD, Susmel R (1994) Autoregressive conditional heteroskedasticity and changes in regime. Journal of Econometrics 64:307–333

Hansen BE (1992) The likelihood ratio test under nonstandard conditions: Testing the Markov switching model of GNP. Journal of Applied Econometrics 7:S61–S82

Kaufmann S, Scheicher M (1996) Markov-regime switching in economic variables: Part I. modelling, estimating and testing. – part II. a selective survey. Institute for Advanced Studies University of Vienna Economics Series No. 38

Klaassen FJGM (1999) Long swings in exchange rates: Are they really in the data?. CentER for Economic Research Tilburg University Discussion Paper No. 9908

Lamoureux CG, Lastrapes WD (1990) Persistence in variance, structural change, and the GARCH model. Journal of Business and Economic Statistics 8:225–234

MacDonald R, Taylor MP (1992) Exchange rate economics: A survey. IMF Staff Papers 39:1–57

Meese RA, Rogoff K (1983) Empirical exchange rate models of the seventies: Do they fit out of sample?. Journal of International Economics 14:3–24

Merton RC (1980) On estimating the expected return on the market: An exploratory investigation. Journal of Financial Economics 8:323–361

Newey WK, West KD (1987) A simple, positive semi-definite, heteroskedasticity and autocorrelation consistent covariance matrix. Econometrica 55:703–708

Newey WK, West KD (1994) Automatic lag selection in covariance matrix estimation. Review of Economic Studies 61:631–653

Pagan AR, Schwert GW (1990) Alternative models for conditional stock volatility. Journal of Econometrics 45:267–290

Perron P (1989) The great crash, the oil price shock, and the unit root hypothesis. Econometrica 57:1361–1401

Scheicher M (1999) Nonlinear dynamics: Evidence for a small stock exchange. Empirical Economics 24:45–59

Schwert GW (1989) Why does stock market volatility change over time?. Journal of Finance 44:1115–1153

Timmermann A (2000) Moments of Markov switching models. Journal of Econometrics 96:75–111

West KD (1996) Asymptotic inference about predictive ability. Econometrica 64:1067–1084

West KD, Cho D (1995) The predictive ability of several models of exchange rate volatility. Journal of Econometrics 69:367–391

West KD, McCracken MW (1998) Regression-based tests of predictive ability. International Economic Review 39:817–840

V Methodological Contribution

Power issues when testing the Markov switching model with the sup likelihood ratio test using U.S. output

Patrick J. Coe*

Department of Economics, University of Calgary, 2500 University Drive N.W., Calgary, AB Canada T2N 1N4

First Version Received: March 2000/Final Version Received: March 2001

Abstract. The likelihood ratio (LR) test statistic for the test of a linear AR(1) model against the alternative of a Markov switching model does not possess the standard χ^2 distribution. Garcia (1998) derives the asymptotic distribution of the Sup LR test statistic under these non-standard conditions allowing the researcher to easily compare the two models. This paper examines the power properties of this test statistic using Monte Carlo experiments calibrated to U.S. output growth data. The results suggest a test of reasonable power. When the experiments are calibrated to annual data, power is 82% at 200 observations. When the experiments are calibrated to quarterly data power is 57% for the same sample size.

Key words: Markov switching model, power of sup LR test

JEL classification: C15, C22

1. Introduction

The most common approach to studying the business cycle has been to consider fluctuations around a single long-run trend. However, recently models in which the trend rate of growth itself is subject to stochastic shifts have been used to model real output; see, for example, Hamilton (1989), Lam (1990), Durland and McCurdy (1994) or Potter (1995). One interpretation of this latter approach is that the economy moves between states of high and low growth.

---

* I would like to thank, without implicating, Jim Nason and two anonymous referees for their insightful comments and suggestions. Financial support from Economic and Social Research Council research grant R000235524 is gratefully acknowledged.

** For publication in EE – Special Issue "Advances in Markov-Switching Econometrics", co-edited by James Hamilton and Baldev Raj.

The use of these models is not confined to modelling the business cycle. For example, Cechetti, Lam and Mark (1990) use Hamilton's Markov switching model to look at real dividends and consumption, while Ruge-Murcia (1995) uses it to model inflation and government spending, and Turner, Startz and Nelson (1989) use it to model excess stock returns.

While estimation of these models is relatively straightforward, testing between, for example, a model with a single state and one with two states is problematic for two reasons. First, the parameters which define the transition between the two states are not defined under the null hypothesis of only one state. In a two state Markov Switching model the probabilities which describe the transition between the two states are undefined under the single state null. As a result, the likelihood ratio (LR) test statistic does not possess the standard χ^2 distribution. The presence of these nuisance parameters is typically referred to as Davies' problem.

A second problem occurs because the null hypothesis yields a local maximum in the likelihood function. In this case the scores with respect to the transition probabilities and any parameters describing the second state are identically zero under the null hypothesis. As a result these scores will not have positive variances. Again, this means that the LR test statistic does not possess the standard distribution.

Recently two approaches to dealing with these problems have been proposed. Hansen (1992, 1996) uses empirical process theory to bound the asymptotic distribution of the LR test statistic. This involves setting a grid over different values of the transition probabilities and the parameters which describe the second state. The constrained likelihood is then optimized with respect to the nuisance parameters at each point of the grid. Clearly, this becomes computationally burdensome as the gridsearch becomes more extensive or the model becomes more complex. A second drawback is that it gives a bound for the likelihood ratio test statistic and not a critical value.

Garcia (1998) offers an alternative approach. He treats the transition probabilities as nuisance parameters and derives the asymptotic distribution of the Sup LR test in terms of the remaining parameters of the model using the distributional theory of Davies (1987) and Andrews and Ploberger (1994).[1] While this does not tackle the zero scores problem described above, Garcia uses Monte Carlo experiments to show that these asymptotic distributions are very good approximations to their empirical counterparts. This is consistent with the finding of Lee and Chesher (1986), that the usual asymptotic distribution of the LR statistic is still valid in the presence of zero scores. This method has two advantages over that proposed by Hansen; it provides a critical value for the likelihood ratio test statistic rather than a bound and is computationally much less demanding.[2]

Garcia explores the power of this Sup LR test with respect to three applications in the literature, Cecchetti et al's model for consumption growth, Turner et al's model for excess stock returns and Hamilton's (1989) original model for GNP growth. He finds that at nominal size of 5% the power of the Sup LR statistic is 49.5%, 60.9% and close to 80% respectively.

---

[1] This asymptotic distribution is the supremum of a χ^2 functional. These χ^2 processes have covariance matrices which are functions of the two nusiance parameters, p and q.

[2] Garcia provides asymptotic critical values for three models and proposes a simulation method for the Sup LR test for other models.

Hamilton's original application of the Markov switching model is to quarterly post-war U.S. real GNP. When applying their approach to this model and data neither Garcia or Hansen reject the linear autoregressive model in favor of the Markov switching alternative. These and other results have led to the suggestion that there is now less evidence for non-linearity in U.S. output than there was 10 years ago. See, for example, Potter (1999).

However, it is well known fact that low power can be a concern for many tests of non-linearity when the number of observations is low. See for example, Ganger and Teräsvirta (1993). This paper further investigates the power properties of the Sup LR test of a linear AR(1) model against a simple Markov switching alternative using Monte Carlo experiments calibrated to U.S. per capita real GDP growth data.

It asks how power varies with number of observations available to the researcher. Data is generated under the assumption that the true DGP is a simple 2 state Markov switching model with one autoregressive parameter in which the mean of the series can vary with the underlying regime. It is then asked whether the Sup LR statistic is able to recognize that the true DGP is the Markov switching alternative.

When the data generating process (DGP) is calibrated to U.S. annual per-capita real GDP data the power of the Sup LR test reaches approximately 95% by a sample size of 300 for a test with size of 5%. When the DGP is based on quarterly U.S. per-capita real GDP data it reaches approximately 90% when the sample size reaches 400. This is clearly greater than what is currently available to the empirical macroeconomist. For sample sizes in the neighborhood of those currently available this paper suggests the Sup likelihood ratio test is a test of reasonable power. For a sample size of 200 power is approximately 82% for annual data and 57% for quarterly data. For a sample size of 100 these figures fall to 48% and 31% respectively.

The remainder of the paper proceeds as follows. Section two describes a simple version of Hamilton's Markov switching model with two states and one autoregressive parameter and estimates this model and a linear model using quarterly and annual U.S. per-capita real GDP data. Section three generates data using the parameter estimates for the Markov switching model and the power properties of the Sup LR test statistic are explored across different sample sizes.

2. A simple Markov switching model

This section briefly describes a simple, two state version of Hamilton's Markov switching model with one autoregressive parameter, MSAR(1), and the restrictions that imply a linear AR(1) model. It also presents estimates of the two models using U.S. data for the growth rate of real, per-capita GDP.

In the two state model, a single time series, $\{y_t\}$, has the following stochastic process:

$$y_t - \mu(S_t) = \rho(y_{t-1} - \mu(S_{t-1})) + u_t, \tag{1}$$

where $u_t \sim i.i.d.\ N(0, \sigma_u^2)$ and $|\rho| < 1$. This model varies from an AR(1) model as it allows for discrete shifts in the mean of the series, $\mu(S_t)$, with the underlying regime, S_t. There are two regimes, identified by $S_t = 0$ and $S_t = 1$. The mean of the series differs across these regimes and is given by:

$$\mu(S_t) = \alpha + \gamma S_t. \tag{2}$$

The regime is modelled as the outcome of an unobserved first order Markov process. Each period there is a fixed probability of switching between the two states. These transition probabilities are:

$$\begin{aligned} &P(S_t = 1 \mid S_{t-1} = 1) = p, \quad P(S_t = 0 \mid S_{t-1} = 1) = 1 - p, \\ &P(S_t = 1 \mid S_{t-1} = 0) = 1 - q, \quad P(S_t = 0 \mid S_{t-1} = 0) = q. \end{aligned} \tag{3}$$

The current and past regimes, remain unobserved. Inference about these regimes, based on the observed time series $\{y_t\}$, is made using a non-linear filter similar to that described by Hamilton (1989).

Under the null hypothesis of $\gamma = 0$ this model reduces to a linear AR(1) model. However, the parameters p and q which describe the transition between the two states, are not defined under this null hypothesis. This is the so-called Davies' problem referred to earlier. The presence of these nuisance parameters means that the LR test statistic has a non-standard distribution. The second problem occurs because under the null hypothesis the scores with respect to p, q and γ are identically zero. Again this means that the LR test statistic does not have the standard χ^2 distribution. As mentioned earlier, Garcia derives the asymptotic distribution of the Sup LR test when the first of these problems exists and shows that this distribution is very close to the empirical distribution despite the presence of the second problem.

Table 1 contains estimates of this model and a linear AR(1) model using annual and quarterly U.S. data for the growth rate of per-capita real GDP.

Table 1. Parameter estimates for AR(1) & MSAR(1) models

	Annual data (1900–1994)		Quarterly Data (61:1–97:4)	
	AR(1)	MSAR(1)	AR(1)	MSAR(1)
p		0.364		0.365
		(0.228)		(0.291)
q		0.958		0.967
		(0.027)		(0.019)
α	1.7123	2.665	1.968	2.362
	(0.858)	(0.698)	(0.373)	(0.360)
γ		−15.018		−8.010
		(2.515)		(1.618)
ρ	0.310	0.287	0.330	0.328
	(0.098)	(0.125)	(0.078)	(0.110)
σ	5.710	4.542	3.014	2.532
	(0.419)	(0.403)	(0.176)	(0.172)
log-likelihood	−293.98	−288.37	−368.26	−362.35

Standard errors are in parentheses

The annual data are taken from table D-1a of Maddison (1995). The quarterly data is from the Federal Reserve Economic Database.[3] Each model is estimated twice, once using annual data from 1900 to 1994 and once using quarterly data from 1961Q1 to 1997Q4. Twice the difference in the log-likelihoods is 11.22 for the estimates based on annual data and 11.82 for the estimates based on quarterly data. The estimate of ρ for the single state model is 0.310 when annual data is used to estimate the model and 0.330 when quarterly data is used. Both of these values exceed Garcia's 95% asymptotic critical value for $\rho = 0.337$ of 8.68. However, they do not exceed his 99% asymptotic critical value of 12.00. This suggests the null of an AR(1) model should be rejected in favor of the Markov switching model at the 5% significance level but not the 1% significance level.

3. Monte Carlo experiments

This section generates artificial data under the alternative hypotheses of the MSAR(1) model. This data is then used to estimate the AR(1) and MSAR(1) model and calculate the power of the Sup LR test.

The state at time t is generated as follows. If $S_{t-1} = 1$ then a random variable which takes on the value one with probability $\hat{p}$ and the value zero with probability $1 - \hat{p}$ is drawn. If $S_{t-1} = 0$ then a random variable which takes on the value one with probability $1 - \hat{q}$ and the value zero with probability $\hat{q}$ is drawn. The initial value of the state at time $t = 1$ is one with probability $\pi = (1 - q)/(2 - p - q)$ and zero with probability $1 - \pi$.

In the Markov switching model the unobserved state is one of many factors that determine the dynamic process of a time series. As a result, it is possible that one could observe a relatively high growth rate for output even when the economy is in the low growth state. To allow for this y_t is generated conditional on S_{t-1} and y_{t-1} as follows. If $S_{t-1} = 1$ then, with probability $\hat{p}$, y_t is:

$$\hat{\alpha} + \hat{\gamma} + \hat{\rho}(y_{t-1} - \hat{\alpha} - \hat{\gamma}) + w_t \tag{4}$$

and, with probability $1 - \hat{p}$, it is:

$$\hat{\alpha} + \hat{\rho}(y_{t-1} - \hat{\alpha} - \hat{\gamma}) + w_t \tag{5}$$

where $\hat{\alpha}$, $\hat{\gamma}$ and $\hat{\rho}$ are the relevant parameter estimates for the DGP of interest, and w_t is drawn from a mean-zero normal distribution with standard deviation $\hat{\sigma}_u$. Similarly, if $s_{t-1} = 0$ then, with probability $\hat{q}$, y_t is:

$$\hat{\alpha} + \hat{\rho}(y_{t-1} - \hat{\alpha}) + w_t \tag{6}$$

and, with probability $1 - \hat{q}$, it is:

$$\hat{\alpha} + \hat{\gamma} + \hat{\rho}(y_{t-1} - \hat{\alpha}) + w_t. \tag{7}$$

---

[3] This data is available from the website of the Federal Reserve Bank at St Louis, http://www.stls.frb.org/fred/. Quarterly real GDP and monthly population data are used to construct a quarterly GDP per capita series. The quarterly series (GDP92) is divided by the population (POP) figure for the middle month of the quarter.

Table 2. Power of the Sup LR test

Frequency of the Dataset the Experiment in Calibrated to	Sample Size			
	$T = 100$	$T = 200$	$T = 300$	$T = 400$
Annual	0.4820	0.8150	0.9495	0.9880
Quarterly	0.3075	0.5720	0.7805	0.8865

These size adjusted power figures are based on 2000 replications of Monte Carlo experiment described in section 3 of the text. These figures are calculated with respect to Garcia's 95% asymptotic critical value for $\rho = 0.337$ which is 8.68.

The initial value, y_1, is $\hat{\alpha} + \hat{\gamma} + w_1$ with probability π and $\hat{\alpha} + w_1$ with probability $1 - \pi$.

The values of the six parameters given by the estimates of the MSAR(1) model in table 1 are treated as true values and $T + 200$ observations for y_t are generated. The first 200 are discarded to minimize the influence of starting values and the remainder are used to estimate the one and two state models, and to calculate the Sup LR test statistic. The power of this test statistic is given in table 2 for sample sizes of 100, 200, 300 and 400.

Consider first the Monte Carlo experiments calibrated to annual U.S. real, per-capita GDP data. At the present time, the longest annual time series available to the empirical macroeconomist is typically between 100 and 200 observations. For a sample size of 100 annual observations the power of the Sup LR test with actual size set at 5% is 48%. When the sample size rises to 200 observations, this figure rises to 82%. Currently, most quarterly macroeconomic time series typically consist of somewhere between 100 and 200 observations. When the DGP is based on quarterly U.S. data the false null hypothesis is rejected in favor of the true alternative in only 31% of the simulations for a sample size of 100. When the number of observations rises to 200 this figure rises to 57%. These figures suggest that, while not 95%, the power of this test is quite reasonable in samples of the size an empirical macroeconomist might expect to work with.

For an actual size of 5%, the power of the Sup LR test statistic reaches 95% at 300 annual observations and almost 90% at 400 quarterly observations. Both of these sample sizes exceed those that are typically currently available. Finally, the fact that, for the same number of observations, power is higher when the experiment is calibrated to annual data than when it is calibrated to quarterly data suggests that not just the number of observations matter, but also the span of the data.

4. Conclusions

This paper examines the power properties of the Sup LR test statistic when the null hypothesis is that the data is generated by a linear AR(1) model and the alternative is the MSAR(1) model in which the mean of the series changes with regime. Monte Carlo studies calibrated to annual and quarterly U.S. per capita GDP data suggest that this test has reasonable power in sample sizes that are typically available to the empirical macroeconomist. Potentially interesting avenues for future research are how the power of this test statistic varies as the model is extended beyond the simple MSAR(1) model with homoskedastic errors and whether power can be improved upon by moving away from the univariate framework to look at vector autoregressive models that incorporate Markov switching.

References

Andews DW, Ploberger W (1994) Optimal tests when a nuisance parameter is present only under the alternative. Econometrica 62:1383–1414

Cecchetti SG, Lam P-S, Mark NC (1990) Mean reversion in equilibrium asset prices. American Economic Review 80:398–418

Davies RB (1987) Hypothesis testing when a nuisance parameter is present only under the alternative. Biometrika 64:33–43

Durland JM, McCurdy TH (1994) Duration-dependent transitions in a markov switching model of U.S. GNP growth. Journal of Business and Economic Statistics 12:279–288

Garcia R (1998) Asymptotic null distribution of the likelihood ratio test in Markov switching models. International Economic Review 39:763–788

Granger C, Teräsvirta T (1993) Modelling Nonlinear Economic Relationships. Oxford University Press, Oxford

Hamilton JD (1989) A new approach to the economic analysis of nonstationary time series and the business cycle. Econometrica 57:357–384

Hansen BE (1992) The likelihood ratio test under non-standard conditions: Testing the Markov switching model of GNP. Journal of Applied Econometrics pp. S61–S82

Hansen BE (1996) Erratum: The likelihood ratio test under non-standard conditions: Testing the Markov switching model of GNP. Journal of Appled Econometrics 11:195–198

Lam P-S (1990) The Hamilton model with a general autoregressive component. Journal of Monetary Economics 26:409–432

Lee L-F, Chesher A (1986) Specification testing when score test statistics are indentically zero. Journal of Econometrics 31:121–149

Maddison A (1995) Monitoring the World Economy 1820–1992, OECD, Paris

Potter SM (1995) A non-linear approach to US GNP. Journal of Applied Econometrics 10:109–125

Potter SM (1999) Nonlinear time series modelling: An introduction. Technical Report 87, Federal Reserve Bank of New York, Staff Report

Ruge-Murcia FJ (1995) Credibility and changes in policy regime. Journal of Political Economy pp. 176–208

Turner, Christopher M, RS, Nelson CR (1989) A Markov model of heteroskedasticity, risk, and learning in the stock market. Journal of Financial Economics 25:3–22

List of Referees

Donald W.K. Andrews
Yale University, USA

Monica Billio
Università Ca' Foscari, Venice, Italy

Nicolas P.B. Bollen
University of Utah, USA

Simon M. Burgess
University of Bristol, UK

Jun Cai
City University of Hong Kong, Hong Kong

Marcelle Chauvet
University of California, Riverside, USA

Siddhartha Chib
Washington University, USA

Sylvia Frühwirth-Schnatter
Vienna University, Austria

Lawrence R. Glosten
Columbia University, USA

Bruce E. Hansen
University of Wisconsin, USA

Andrew Harvey
University of Cambridge, UK

Chang-Jin Kim
University of Washington, USA

Hans-Martin Krolzig
University of Oxford, UK

Rob Luginbuhl
Vrije Universiteit Amsterdam, The Netherlands

Ian Marsh
University of California, San Diego, USA

Maria Soledad Martinez Peria
World Bank, Washington, DC, USA

Robert E. McCulloch
University of Chicago, USA

Grant McQueen
Brigham Young University, USA

Grayham E. Mizon
University of Southampton, UK

Bruce Mizrach
Rutgers State University, USA

José G. Montalvo
Universitat Pompeu Fabra, Barcelona, Spain

Alberto Musso
European University Institute, Florence, Italy

Charles R. Nelson
University of Washington, USA

Ragnar Nymoen
University of Oslo, Norway

Venkatesh Panchapagesan
Washington University, USA

Richard Paap
Erasmus University Rotterdam, The Netherlands

Gabriel Perez Quiros
European Central Bank, Frankfort, Germany

Robert W. Rich
Federal Reserve Bank of New York, USA

Andrew K. Rose
University of California, Berkeley, USA

Francisco J. Ruge-Murcia
University of Montreal, Canada

Tobias Rydén
Lund University, Sweden

Huntley Schaller
Carleton University, Canada

Dan Sichel
Federal Reserve Board, Washington, USA

Martin Sola
University of London, UK

Raul Susmel
University of Houston, USA

Jonathan Temple
University of Bristol, UK

Ping Wang
Loughborough University, UK

Zhiwei Zhang
University of California, San Diego, USA

GPSR Compliance
The European Union's (EU) General Product Safety Regulation (GPSR) is a set of rules that requires consumer products to be safe and our obligations to ensure this.

If you have any concerns about our products, you can contact us on

ProductSafety@springernature.com

In case Publisher is established outside the EU, the EU authorized representative is:

Springer Nature Customer Service Center GmbH
Europaplatz 3
69115 Heidelberg, Germany

www.ingramcontent.com/pod-product-compliance
Ingram Content Group UK Ltd.
Pitfield, Milton Keynes, MK11 3LW, UK
UKHW020846100925
462761UK00008B/43
9783642511844